Kyriakos Tsantsanoglou
Studies in Sappho and Alcaeus

Trends in Classics – Supplementary Volumes

Edited by
Franco Montanari and Antonios Rengakos

Associate Editors
Stavros Frangoulidis · Fausto Montana · Lara Pagani
Serena Perrone · Evina Sistakou · Christos Tsagalis

Scientific Committee
Alberto Bernabé · Margarethe Billerbeck
Claude Calame · Jonas Grethlein · Philip R. Hardie
Stephen J. Harrison · Richard Hunter · Christina Kraus
Giuseppe Mastromarco · Gregory Nagy
Theodore D. Papanghelis · Giusto Picone
Tim Whitmarsh · Bernhard Zimmermann

Volume 79

Kyriakos Tsantsanoglou

Studies in Sappho and Alcaeus

—

DE GRUYTER

ISBN 978-3-11-076339-3
e-ISBN (PDF) 978-3-11-063039-8
e-ISBN (EPUB) 978-3-11-063086-2
ISSN 1868-4785

Library of Congress Control Number: 2019947137

Bibliographic information published by the Deutsche Nationalbibliothek
The Deutsche Nationalbibliothek lists this publication in the Deutsche Nationalbibliografie; detailed bibliographic data are available on the Internet at http://dnb.dnb.de.

© 2021 Walter de Gruyter GmbH, Berlin/Boston
This volume is text- and page-identical with the hardback published in 2019.
Editorial Office: Alessia Ferreccio and Katerina Zianna
Logo: Christopher Schneider, Laufen
Printing and binding: CPI books GmbH, Leck

www.degruyter.com

Preface

The recent discovery and publication of large papyri containing poems by Sappho, sparked off a large-scale interest, which gave birth to an extensive production of scholarly treatises on the poetry of the archaic poets of Lesbos. To this wider dialogue I have also contributed with a number of articles, fourteen of which are included in the present volume. Some of them have already been published in classical journals, others not.

I have to admit that, in spite of their appealing object, my articles do not refrain from my usual positivistic policy. It has been my conscious effort to avoid wide-ranging ventures and to restrict myself to concrete observations which help in constructing a stable text. When this necessary stability is established, the field is then open to broader interpretations. Especially in the case of papyri, the blind acceptance of the editio princeps, a common practice in our scholarship, proves hazardous. I attempted, at the expense of time and leisure, never to start a papyrus investigation taking the original reading for granted. On the other hand, I realize that, by discussing in detail exiguous observations such as the shape of particular letters, I often end up in making the approach to the articles a laborious and boring enterprise. I only hope to be forgiven by the reader. Yet, I know that too often a slight trace that establishes even a single letter, may unexpectedly lead to a great profit in the sense of the text examined.

Some articles appear moving in much the same spheres: the first three around the old age of Sappho in connection with the topic of the poetic survival, the last three around the worship of the so-called 'Lesbian Triad'. The articles in each group are products of a research sequence in progress with successively proposed solutions, and so both some contradictions and some repetitions were inevitable. No doubt, it might be possible for two or three articles to be merged in one, at the cost, however, of the fascination of continuous creation.

Another deficiency is related to the subjective circumstances in composing some of the articles. Age and the accompanying health conditions may have occasionally impeded me to peruse and examine at length the relevant bibliography. In addition, the economic environment, in a time of financial collapse of my country, brought about a sudden suspension of every acquisition whether of books or periodicals in our libraries, even of access to the scholarly digital libraries. It was thanks to my younger colleagues, who resorted to inventive techniques for gaining access to alternative sources, that I managed to somehow replace these deficiencies.

I close the account of my shortcomings with a natural grievance. The latest boom in Sapphic and Alcaic research made its appearance during my advanced years and frail health. So, I have been unable to confirm some of my findings with a visit to Lesbos and was forced to depend on indirect sources for the contentious spots I am describing. Still greater is, however, my complaint for not being able to convince younger scholars to take on the task. I only hope that, whenever the necessary investigation will be carried out, my proposals won't be recorded as mere illusions.

The list of acknowledgments is short. Apart from the persons gratefully mentioned in each article, my colleagues Gregory Sifakis and Michalis Tiverios offered me unstintingly their friendly help. Jürgen Hammerstaedt's deft criticism was of great assistance for several articles. Sotiris Tselikas, a consummate but low-profile scholar, was a steadfast cooperator who saved me from numerous blunders. Antonios Rengakos not only proposed the publication of the book in the Trends in Classics Supplementary Volumes of De Gruyter GmbH, but was also a constant and tenacious source of encouragement.

Thessaloniki, May 2019

Contents

Preface —— V
List of Figures —— IX

1 Sappho Illustrated —— 1

2 Sappho on her Funeral Day: P.Colon. 21351.1–8 —— 28

3 Kleïs as Promoter of Sappho's Poetry (Fr. 59 V.) —— 38

4 Sappho's (?) Orpheus Song —— 42

5 P. Sapph. Obbink: the *Kypris Poem* —— 72

6 Sappho's Epithalamians —— 86

7 Sappho *Tithonus Poem* —— 114

8 Sappho 1.18–19 V. —— 118

9 The Banquet of the Gods and the Picnic of the Girls —— 121

10 The Danaans in Lesbos —— 147

11 Sappho 27 V., Alcaeus 308 Lib., and the Homeric *Hymn to Hermes* —— 162

12 Alcaeus on the Lesbian Triad Festival —— 169

13 The Location of the Lesbian Triad Temenos —— 192

14 Who was Onymacles the Athenian? —— 204

Bibliography —— 213

List of Figures

Ch. 1, Fig. 1: National Museum of Athens hydria-calpis inv. no. 1260 —— 1
Ch. 1, Fig. 2: Drawing of the above vase-painting by Jules Chaplain —— 2
Ch. 1, Fig. 3: Detail of the above showing the written roll in Sappho's hands —— 9
Ch. 7, Fig. 1: Supralinear correction on v. 7 of the *Tithonus Poem* (P. Colon. 21351 l. 3) —— 115
Ch. 8, Fig. 1: Detail from cod. P of Dion. Halicarn. *De comp. verb.* 23 —— 119
Ch. 9, Fig. 1: The Florence ostrakon containing Sappho's fr. 2 —— 142
Ch. 13, Fig. 1: Coin of Sicilian Acragas —— 195
Ch. 13, Fig. 2: Map of the Gulf of Kalloni with the places mentioned in the article —— 197
Ch. 13, Fig. 3: The Γιαλοβούνι promontory as seen from the hill of Pyrrha —— 198
Ch. 13, Fig. 4: Γιαλοβούνι in the Google Earth Images —— 198
Ch. 13, Fig. 5: Enlargement of the Google image showing particular spot of the octastyle temple —— 199

1 Sappho Illustrated

The Epithanatians

Fig. 1: National Museum of Athens inv. no. 1260, ARV² 1060, *Paralipomena* 445.

Figure 1 shows one of the best-known vase-paintings presented on an Attic red-figured hydria-calpis found in Vari.[1] It is attributed to a painter of the Polygnotus

---

I am grateful to Gregory Sifakis, Michalis Tiverios, and Stavros Tsitsiridis for their assistance. Special thanks to Jürgen Hammerstaedt for his fruitful advice and good-natured endurance.

1 A south-east district of Athens identified with the ancient deme of Anagyrous.

Fig. 2: Drawing by Jules Chaplain. From Albert Dumont and Jules Chaplain, *Les Céramiques de la Grèce propre. Vases peints et terres cuites*, Paris 1881, pl. VI.

Group and is dated in 440–430 BC. The main female figure appears seated on a comfortable klismos holding a half-opened papyrus roll, the typical book form in antiquity. She is absorbed in her reading, while three standing girls watch her attentively. The girl on the left, bearing the inscription ΝΙΚΟΠΟΛΙΣ, is stretching her right arm above the seated woman. Two girls are standing on the right. The first, inscribed ΚΑΛΛΙΣ,[2] holds out a chelys-type lyre, i.e., one with a tortoise shell resonator, toward the seated woman, while the second uninscribed girl, rests her hand on the shoulder of Kallis. The seated woman can be recognized thanks to the inscription ΣΑΠΠΩΣ (sic) written above her hands that hold the papyrus. It should be noted that the name inscriptions, having been added by the painter after firing the vase, are today invisible. They were, however, still visible in the 19th century, when the vase was excavated and published. The

---

[2] Both names are well recorded. Καλλίς is apparently a hypocoristic of the numerous names with first component Καλλι-.

painting was then interpreted as depicting an everyday scene at the circle of the poetess of Lesbos, with herself reading her poems and her pupil-friends listening.

The Book Roll. Former Attempts

Apart from the general interpretations of the painting,[3] to which I shall shortly add my own, already since the end of the 19th century there have been attempts to read the text that could be seen in the half-opened roll. These letters belong to the initial painting, before the vase was fired, and so are fairly well discerned. The first attempt seems to have been made by Maxime Collignon, who published the catalogue of the painted vases of the National Archaeological Museum of Athens.[4] His reading was: Θεοί ἠερίων ἐπέων [ἄ]ρχομαι ἄγγ[ελος] ν[έων] ὕ[μ]ν[ων]. Later, H. Heydemann published his own proposal,[5] reading on the rolled up ends of the papyrus ΠΤΕΡΟΕΤΙ ΕΠΕΑ, which he corrected to πτερόε<ν>τ(α) ἔπεα, and on its inside area Θεοί· περ(ὶ) τῶν ἐπέων ἄρχομαι ᾄ[δειν. Still later, Domenico Comparetti, assisted by the archaeologist Federico Halbherr,[6] read Θεοί· ἠερίων ἐπέων ἄρχομαι ἄλλων, just like P. Kretschmer,[7] who also read ἄρχομαι ἄλλ[ων], though with the ending ων supplemented.[8]

In 1922, J.M. Edmonds, making use of enlarged photographs and the assistance of the archaeologists B. Leonardos and A.J.B. Wace, proposed a somewhat different reading.[9] He first noticed that the flanking words, written on the rolled up ends and therefore on the outer side of the roll, must be the title of the book. The title should read not ΠΤΕΡΟΕΤΑ ΕΠΕΑ, as it seems at first look, but reversely ΕΠΕΑ ΠΤΕΡΟΕΤΑ, as it would become apparent if the roll was spread face downwards. He also noticed that "the rolled-up part of the book held by the right hand [of Sappho] is intended to be bulkier than the part held by the left. The latter indeed may be regarded as the first curl beginning the left-hand 'roll-up', a

---

3 I refer only to three recent approaches to the topic: Snyder (1997), 108–119; Yatromanolakis (2007), 146–164; Ferrari (2010), 101–102.
4 *Catalogue des vases peints du Musée national d'Athènes*, Paris 1878, Catal. No. 517; a copy of the book roll on pl. V, 28 and 29.
5 Heydemann (1881), 465–472 [469–470].
6 Comparetti (1886), 41–80.
7 Kretschmer (1894), 93.
8 The mainstream view about the inscription was expressed by W. Aly in RE s.v. Sappho (1920), 2384: "Sapphisch klingen die Worte gerade nicht". In the supplementary article by M. Treu in RE-Supplementband XI (1968) there is no mention whatsoever of the words of the book roll.
9 Edmonds (1922), 1–14. His views were first announced, in January 1921, to the Cambridge Philological Society.

curl which will not be completed till the reader proceeds to the next column". Thus, the text seen on the interior side of the roll must represent the first column, therefore the opening, of the book. The first word read on this first column is ΘΕΟΙ, which Edmonds takes either as an invocation of the poetess at the opening of her book, similarly to the formula found at the opening of numerous official decrees, or as the heading of the first part of Sappho's book, which might start with hymns to the gods, as was the case with Alcaeus' Alexandrian edition. He finally inclines to the view that the presence of the invocation ΘΕΟΙ "is due simply to the artist". What follows, according to Edmonds, are the letters, written in 11 very narrow lines (or 12 with the inclusion of the first line ΘΕΟΙ), which he read as: ΗΕΡΙ | ΩΝ | ΕΠΕ | ΩΝ | ΑΡΧ | ΟΜ | ΑΙΑ | ΛΛΟ | ΝΑ | ΤΩ | Ν. This leads to his final reading:

Ἔπεα πτερόεντα
Θεοί.
ἠερίων ἐπέων ἄρχομαι ἀλλ' ὀνάτων.

The text following θεοί was considered by Edmonds a verse of Sappho, actually the first verse of an introductory poem to the pre-Alexandrian edition of Sappho prepared by the poetess herself. As for the metrical form of the verse, Edmonds found some similarities with several Sapphic and Alcaic fragments, but none exactly similar. Finally, he translated: 'The words I begin are words of air, but for all that good to hear,' 'beneficial'.

In the same year (1922), Edmonds published Sappho's fragments in the first volume of his *Lyra Graeca*. There (180–181), he prefixed to her known fragments, as fr. 1a, the verse he read on the vase-painting. He only changed the initial of the first word from η to α (ἀερίων) for adapting the Ionic ἠερίων to the dialect of Lesbos.[10] Another proposal, which, however, went unnoticed by the scholarly community, was C.R. Haines's in *Sappho. The Poems and Fragments*, London 1926. His drawing of the book roll (p. 53) seems to be the most faithful of all previous transcriptions, but the reconstruction he proposes is rather odd: θεοι, ηεριων επεων αρχομαι, αλλ' <α>ναιτι<ω>ν. In any case, Edmonds's views, whether of a first verse or of a pre-Alexandrian Sappho edition collected and arranged by the

---

10 Od. Elytis, the Greek 1979 Nobel laureate in Literature, opened his Sappho translation (1984) with Ἀρχινῶ τὸ τραγούδι μου μ' αἰθέρια λόγια | μὰ γι' αὐτὸ κι ἁπαλὰ στὸ ἄκουσμα, 'I start my song with aethereal words, but on that account soft to hear'. He followed Edmonds's *Lyra Graeca* in placing the verse at the beginning of the Sappho fragments and in translating ἀερίων = 'aethereal', and ὀνάτων = 'soft to hear', but mistranslated Edmonds's 'for all that' as 'on that account', instead of 'in spite of that'.

poetess, did not convince the dominant trend in classical scholarship. There is no mention whatsoever of the Attic hydria verse in E. Lobel, Σαπφοῦς Μέλη (1925), in E. Lobel/D.L. Page, *Poetarum Lesbiorum fragmenta* (1955), in E.-M. Voigt, *Sappho et Alcaeus* (1971), and in D.A. Campbell, *Greek Lyric* (1982). Without mentioning even the possibility that the text may come from Sappho, D.L. Page, *Poetae Melici Graeci* (1962), includes it in the *fragmenta adespota*, 938 d, where the text is published as

θεοί· ἠερίων ἐπέων ἄρχομαι ....,

and the app. cr. as θεοι|ηερι|ων|επε|ων|αρχ|ομ|α.α|τ..|τ.|v. He obviously followed J.D. Beazley, who had noted in 1928, *Greek Vases in Poland*, Oxford, 9 n. 2 (end, continued in p. 10): "the vase shows (besides επεα and πτεροετα) θεοι ηεριων επεων αρχομα.ατ..ν.τ.ν, where my dots represent misshapen and uncertain letters. The last part, where the roll narrows, is evidently meaningless". Due to an oversight, Page omitted the third last line that contained N. from Beazley's reading. It was also Beazley's remark about the meaningless last part of the text that accounts for the numerous dots of Page's text. Campbell, *Greek Lyric* (1993), fr. 938 (d), followed Page (with the oversight) both in the text and the apparatus, only omitting θεοί, which he mentions in a note. He translates: "Airy words I begin" and notes "Lofty? Early?". Henry Immerwahr in his Online Corpus of Attic Vase Inscriptions includes under no. 764 the Athens hydria. He agrees with the prevalent reading down to ἄρχομαι α-, but his last lines are IΝΛ | ΝΤ | ΤΙ | Ν. He proposes that all this is miswritten for ἀείδειν. The latest treatment of the vase-painting text known to me was by D. Yatromanolakis,[11] who also agrees with the prevalent reading down to ἄρχομαι α-, but continues with ΙΝ. | ΝΤ | Τ. | Ν. He translates the readable words as "gods, with airy words I begin ...". Later he considers 'lofty' as the sense implied by 'airy'. At the same time, other scholars wholly discredit the evidence of the book roll text. Fr. Ferrari (2010), 102 remarks: "It is worth noting that the two recognizable sequences of letters on the roll, ἔπεα πτερόεντα, refer to a frequent epic formula and hence do not allude to a text that the poet has composed or is in the act of composing. Instead, they refer to an epic episode that has come to her memory and whose exact diction she has decided to verify."

---

[11] In an extended and inspired discussion (see note 3 above). See also his ingenious, 'Visualizing Poetry: An Early Representation of Sappho', *CPh* 96 (2001), 159–168, on the Bochum kalyx-krater with Sappho dancing on one side of the krater and a shy young girl fleeing from her (?) on the other.

The Painting and the Book Roll

My approach intends to present the close relationship between the specific scene depicted on the vase-painting and the inscribed text of the book roll in association with an important portion of Sappho's poetry. I start from the last. In a paper inscribed 'Sappho on her Funeral Day', *ZPE* 170 (2009), 1–7, I attempted some different readings and supplements in, as well as a general interpretation of, the first and less complete of the three poems contained in PColon. 21351+21376. Below is the text I reconstructed then, with one or two necessary improvements, together with a translation. I only note in advance that the extended supplements of the last four verses were made *exempli gratia*, for indicating, that is, not the words missing but the sense expected.

```
1                                              ]γδα
2                                              ]ξαι
3                                              ]ξον
4                    ] ου [
5       ×–⏑⏑–⏑⏑] εὔχομ' [⏑–⏑– –
6       ×–⏑⏑–⏑⏑ ὤ]ς νῦν θαλ[ί]αν γέ[νεσθαι
7       ×–⏑⏑–⏑⏑–] · νέρθε δὲ γᾶς πέρ[αισσ]αι
8       τὰν πᾶκτιν ἔμον λοῖσθον ἔχοισαν γέρας ὡς [ἔ]οικεν·
9       καὶ πάρ με φίλαι παί]ζοῖεν ὡς νῦν ἐπὶ γᾶς ἔοισαν."
10      πάραυτά μ' Ἄβανθις] λιγύραν [δ]ῶκεν ἔλοισα πᾶκτιν·
11      "ἀλλ'," εἶπον, "ἔγωγ', ἀλεμ]άτα, τὰν καλάμοισ' ἀείδω."     ⊗
```

"[...] I pray [...] that a festivity tak[es place] like now [...]; and that I pass under the earth having [the paktis] suitably as [my la]st gift of honour. [And may my beloved girls pl]ay (dance, have fun) [at my side (at my house)] as now that I am upon earth." [Straightaway Abanthis] took the clear-voiced paktis and gave it [to me]. ["But", said I, "you waste your lab]our; for my part, what I am singing is reed songs."

It is clear that Sappho, at least in the part put in quotes, is addressing her pupil-friends. To whom the whole narration is addressed we do not know. She is speaking about her imminent death and is, in a way, staging her final hours. ὡς νῦν, repeated twice, shows that the girls are having a party with music (πᾶκτιν) and dance (παί]ζοῖεν), and are expecting Sappho to sing for them (ἀείδω). She prays that she may pass to the underworld[12] during a similar party having the paktis as

---

[12] I had a different supplement in my original paper. περάω is a verb often describing in poetry the passing to the hereafter: *Il.* 5.646 πύλας Ἀΐδαο περήσει, Alc. 38a.8 Ἀχέροντ' ἐπέραισε, Thgn. 906 εἰς Ἀΐδαο περᾶν. The form is aorist infinitive from εὔχομαι. The -σσ- also in *Od.* 5.409 ἐπέρασσα vulg.; editors either prefer the variant ἐτέλεσσα or normalize writing ἐπέρησα. Cf.

a last gift of honour. One of the girls misunderstanding offers her the paktis, which she declines saying that what she is singing now are reed songs, mournful, that is, appropriate for a funeral; cf., among numerous parallels, Soph. fr. 849 R. ἔναυλα κωκυτοῖσιν, οὐ λύρα, φίλα. 'For my part', ἔγωγ(ε), goes with ἀείδω, with γε in its usual restrictive force: 'you may well play the paktis, not *I* '. Finally, the vocative ἀλεμάτα refers to the girl handing the paktis to Sappho: 'oh time-wasting girl' = 'you are wasting your labour'.

The words of Sappho's song evidently conjure up the painting on the Athens hydria. The scene is undoubtedly of an indoors party, as is obvious from the seated Sappho and the wreaths hung on the wall. If, as evidenced by the old archaeologists, the girl at the left, Nikopolis, stretched out her arm in order to crown Sappho with another wreath, invisible now, this is also a testimony to the fact that the scene was from a girls' party. References to the wreaths used in adorning one another in Sappho's circle see in Sa. fr. 81, 92.10, 94.12–17, 98a, 103.9, 125. The position of the third unnamed girl is somewhat peculiar. Her gaze is not directed at Sappho but at Kallis, and by placing her hand on Kallis' shoulder she seems as if trying to prevent her from handing the instrument to Sappho. Kallis offers Sappho a lyre and not a paktis, as in the poem. We are not certain about the shape and size of the paktis, but, if it is identified, as done by many scholars, with a large harp-like instrument, the change in the painting may be due to artistic reasons, because the big size of the instrument would fill the whole space between Sappho and Kallis, thus ruining the symmetry of the painting. Still, the poem next to the present one in the PColon. 21351+21376, the Tithonus poem, speaks of the φιλάοιδον λιγύραν χελύνναν (line 2; fr. 58.12 V.) in conjunction with the girls of Sappho's circle (line 1 παῖδες). χελύννα or χέλυς is the lyre with a resonator of a tortoise shell, that is to say, the instrument that is offered to Sappho in the painting. The name of the girl is not Abanthis, as I proposed, but my proposal was made *exempli gratia*. Kallis fits in perfectly: παραύτικα Κάλλις] λιγύραν [δ]ῶκεν ἔλοισα πᾶκτιν.

But most important is the posture of Sappho in the painting. She is seated on the comfortable klismos reading from her book roll. She is neither singing nor dancing nor playing an instrument nor even standing erect, as she is represented in all other vase-paintings. She does not participate in the party that is going on

---

also ἐάω, where forms with -ασσ- are found as variants in Hom. and Parm. 8.7. See Schwyzer, *GG* I 752, 784, and especially for the Aeolic dialects, Blümel (1982), 190 § 207. As regards the papyrus, I believe that the tongue that contains the]αι should be slightly bent to the left, for gaining both an alignment of the vertical fibres and one letter space less.

beside her, she does not even communicate with the girls around her whose attention is wholly focused on her. She is not in the process of writing the poem that is visible on the book roll she is holding. She is rather pondering over what is already written on it.[13] The painting doesn't help us understand whether she is ill or not. But the image recalls a picture familiar to the Athenians of the mid-5th century and later, when the Vari hydria was painted. It is identical with numerous funerary reliefs, Hegeso's, Ampharete's, Mnesarete's, Mynnia's perhaps being most alike, especially the first two which are almost contemporary with the vase-painting, and where the woman depicted is seated on a klismos and not a diphros. Not only is the stance identical, but mostly the appearance of the female figure, who is preoccupiedly deep in thought as if carried away bodily, while the persons around try to communicate with her.

A seated woman reading from a book roll is a fairly common theme in the Attic 5th and 4th cent. BC vase paintings. H. Immerwahr[14] lists thirty-two vase paintings of seated women reading from or simply holding a book roll. Nineteen of them are or can be identified with Muses, but the rest show common women in domestic contexts. None of them can be readily described as showing a funerary scene, with the exception of a white lekythos with a woman reading to another woman by the Painter of Athens, ca. 460 BC.[15] In all probability, it is this common theme that our painter recast as an illustration for a Sappho poem enriched with the theme of the funerary stelae, in response to an order placed by a learned person. He gave the painter the model with the text of the verse, and, after the vase was fired, asked him to add the names of the characters. Also, though scenes of seated women being adorned are very usual, some of them in pre-marriage scenes, I was impressed by the hydria-kalpis RISD 22.114 (ARV² 1049.47, Beazley no. 213616), to a certain extent a 'sister' vase of the Vari hydria, no doubt a product of the same workshop. It cannot be accidental that marriage is a principal poetic theme of Sappho.

If, however, the message of the painting is plaintive and funereal, can Sappho be reading an innocent verse like the one restored by Edmonds (ἠερίων ἐπέων ἄρχομαι ἀλλ' ὀνάτων) declaring that her poems are 'beneficial to hear'? No doubt, this is the meaning of ὀνητός - ὄνατος, 'beneficial, useful, profitable'.

---

13 Schefold (1943), 56, was perhaps the first to comment on the substantially different representation of Sappho here. He speaks of her faraway mood, burdened with an inner vision. He also draws attention to the loving protectiveness combined with admiration shown by the surrounding friends. Snyder (1997), 115, also notes the painting's downcast atmosphere: Sappho is a "much more subdued figure" [ ] "slumped in her chair, passively reading from the book-roll".
14 Immerwahr (1964), 17–48, and (1973) 143–47. Also, Cole (1981), 219–221, 223.
15 Privately owned, Immerwahr (1973), 146–147, pl. 33–34.

Yet, I would certainly expect poets like Hesiod or the late Hellenistic didactic poets to be boastfully declaring that their verses are useful and profitable, but could hardly imagine Sappho saying so. Further, though its formation is absolutely legitimate, the verbal adjective is only lexicographically recorded, its meaning resulting either from the stem of ὀνίνημι or from the much commoner negative ἀνόνητος.

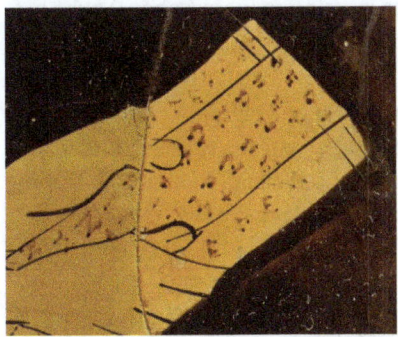

Fig. 3: Detail showing the written roll in Sappho's hands.

An admirably clear photograph published by the Athens National Archaeological Museum in the Web on the occasion of the International Women's Day 2016 (see a coloured photo at http://www.pemptousia.gr/2016/03/h-imera-tis-ginekas-sto-ethniko-archeologiko-mousio/) helped me read the text of the roll Sappho is holding. My reading does not differ much from the text that most scholars established. On the back of the roll, ΠΤΕΡΟΕΤΑ (sic) and ΕΠΕΑ are conspicuous, constituting the title of the book Ἔπεα πτερόε<ν>τα, as it would be read if the roll was opened on its backside. On the inside portion of the roll, I read |^{1}ΘΕΟΙ |^{2}ΗΕΡΙ |^{3}ΩΝ |^{4}ΕΠΕ |^{5}ΩΝ |^{6}ΑΡΧ |^{7}ΟΜ |^{8}ΑΙΑ |^{9}ΓΝΩ |^{10}ΝΣ |^{11}ΤΕ |^{12}Ν[. The readings are different from those already proposed only toward the end of the text, in lines 9, 10, 11; i.e.,

Comparetti	|^{9}ΑΛΩ |^{10}Ν ...,
Edmonds	|^{9}ΑΛΟ |^{10}ΝΑ |^{11}ΤΩ|,
Cairns	|^{9}ΑΛ . |^{10}ΝΑ . |^{11}ΤΙ|,
Beazley	|^{9}Τ .. |^{10}Ν . |^{11}Τ .|,
Immerwahr	|^{9}ΙΝΑ |^{10}ΝΤ |^{11}ΤΙ|,
Yatromanolakis	|^{9}ΙΝ . | . |^{10}ΝΤ|^{11}Τ .|,
Tsantsanoglou	|^{9}ΓΝΩ |^{10}ΝΣ |^{11}ΤΕ|.

In line 9 the first character is a clear Γ with its short horizontal somewhat raised in obtuse angle, a characteristic of the early Euboean script, but found also in Boeotia and in Corinth. However, here I would not ascribe it to the typical features of any local script, but would consider it a rough and hurried product of the painter's brush within the norm of the Ionic alphabet.[16] The letter is certainly not lambda, whose form in the names of the girls (νικοπολις, καλΛις) is the usual isosceles lambda of the second half of the 5th c. The only scholar who recognized a Γ here was Collignon, the first editor of the inscription (note 4 above), who proceeded, however, to a fanciful ἄγγ[ελος] ν[έων] ὕ[μ]ν[ων]. The next letter is N, as recognized by Immerwahr and Yatromanolakis. The third letter is drawn slightly off-line to avoid Sappho's right-hand thumb hiding it, but a curve is clearly visible with a thick low end, identical to the omegas of lines 3 and 5, thus indicating an Ω and not an O, which obviously has no end. In line 10, following an unquestionable N, the portion of the letter that is not hidden under Sappho's thumb belongs clearly to Σ, as Edmonds himself admitted: "the second [letter] I can best describe as the upper half of the angular-shaped Σ". The erroneous proposal for an obliquely written Α, unlike all other alphas, was A.J.B. Wace's. In line 11, after a certain T, a vertical stroke mostly hidden under Sappho's palm can be an iota or any other letter with a left-hand vertical, certainly a vowel for averting an impossible cluster of five consecutive consonants. I, H, and E, are possible. With ΑΓΝΩΝ, since neither ΣΤΙΝ- nor ΣΤΗΝ- make any sense, I choose ΣΤΕΝ-, though E seems to miss a microscopic portion of its upper horizontal; it keeps it, however, in E's low horizontal. These observations concerning E are based on the quintuply magnified photograph I am using. The absence or preservation of tiny parts of the horizontals are absolutely invisible in the actual size of the vase.

The text then established from the image of the roll is:

Ἔπεα πτερόε<ν>τα
Θεοί
ἠερίων ἐπέων ἄρχομαι αγνῶν στεν[

It is likely that the verse should end with [ἀχουσα / [ἀχοισα, i.e., στεν[ἀχουσα or the dialectal στεν[ἀχοισα, or even [αχόντων, i.e., στεν[αχόντων, with the verses personified as usual in poetry, both ancient and modern, in the meaning = στονοέντων. In either case, the hidden end under Sappho's hand would be easily restorable as to its sense by the viewers of the painting. To avoid confusing the

---

16 Several similar obtuse angled gammas, not characterized as exceptional, are found in Lang (1976), in sherds later than the mid-5th cent. BC.

readers with alternative though equivalent supplements, I shall henceforward use the supplement στενάχουσα, which better specifies who is actually speaking and also prevents four consecutive plural genitives. Though the vase is Attic and its date is 440–430 BC, a few decades before the official introduction of the Ionic alphabet in Athens (403/2), the alphabet used in the painting is the Ionic. Athenian inscriptions, especially private ones, show that the Ionic alphabet was often used long before its standardization. If we assume that this is the case here, especially since the model used by the painter was apparently written in Ionic script by an Athenian, we can read ΑΡΧΟΜΑΙ as subjunctive ἄρχωμαι. We shall promptly refer to the function of the hortatory subjunctive in similar cases. Finally, with the regular, both in the epic and in the Lesbian poetry, elision of the final -αι of middle and passive endings before an initial vowel, we restore a typical dactylic hexameter:[17]

ἠερίων ἐπέων ἄρχωμ' ἁγνῶν στεν[άχουσα.

An alphabet that uses (in Threatte's notation system) Η for [ε·], Ω for [ɔ·], omits Η=[h], still uses also Ο for [ɔ·], suggests an Athenian who is trying to write a verse in Ionic dialect and in Ionic script. Threatte, II 259–60, with regard to the ΣΑΠΠΩΣ of the present vase inscription, wonders whether Ω stands for [o·] (what is going to become the 'spurious' diphthong ου), as in other Attic dipinti mainly of the first half of the 5th century (I 48–49). This cannot be excluded, but the variation of Ω = [ɔ·] and [o·], Ο = [ɔ] and [ɔ·], all in the same short inscription, seems too much, though Threatte indicates a great diversity in the mixture of the old Attic and the Ionic alphabet in the pre-Eucleidian decades. αγνων would suit also a Lesbian verse, but ἠερίων rules this out. (For the occasional omission of the rough spirit [h] in pre-Eucleidian inscriptions, cf. *IG* I³ 36, 424/3 BC, 3–4 Αγνόδεμος, but 4–5 τἔι hιερέαι, in the part of the inscription that was written in the old Attic alphabet.) On the other hand, changing ἠερίων to ἀερίων, as Edmonds did, is inadvisable, since ἀερίων is not only the Lesbian form (or ἀὐερίων?) but also the Attic one. And if our painter wanted to write something familiar to himself, he would not need to change α- into η-. Is then the verse deliberately written in the epic dialect? The limited facts established point toward this target. Therefore, following the convention of noting the rough breathing in

---

[17] The Ο for Ω, in spite of the fact that the omega is used in the inscription, may have been caused by influence of the old Attic alphabet, but it may well be ascribed to the possibility that the painter did not realize the metrical identity of the verse.

our texts even when the alphabet omits it, I publish ἀγνῶν, not ἀγνῶν or ἄγνων. And this preference drags along also στεν[άχουσα, not στεν[άχοισα.

The issue of the proemial verses is broader and deserves a more comprehensive examination, which of course cannot be made here. The best known hexametric proems are the so-called 'Homeric Hymns' (Thuc. 3.104), which, with their typical close ἄρχε δ' ἀοιδῆς or σεῦ δ' ἐγὼ ἀρξάμενος μεταβήσομαι ἄλλον ἐς ὕμνον or αὐτὰρ ἐγὼν ὑμέων τε καὶ ἄλλης μνήσομ' ἀοιδῆς, show plainly that what they introduce is melic songs. And melic songs imply, apart from the lost melos, also lyric metres and dialectal texts, at least what we conventionally call 'Doric' dialect of the lyric poetry. With regard to the archaic lyric poetry it has been proposed that Alcm. *PMG* 26 (the *kerylos* poem) is such a proem, while in the Lesbian poetry we have the testimony of [Plut.] *Mus.* 4.1132D (cf. *ib.* 6.1133C) that Terpander composed προοίμια κιθαρῳδικὰ ἐν ἔπεσιν, i.e. in dactylic hexameters and presumably in epic dialect. In Sappho, two hexametric proems can be observed: the vase-painting proem discussed here and one that shall be referred to below (Sa. 103.1). They both present a developed state of the proem, as they introduce not a song but a collection of songs, i.e., a melic book of Sappho each. In any case, I believe that such proems are typically composed not only in dactylic hexameters but also in the epic dialect.[18]

It is expected that a short hexametric poem proemial to a lyric song, say a love song, would share to a certain extent both the theme and the style of the song. However, when it introduces a collection of poems, it is natural that it would be confined to the general mood of the poems or to an epigrammatic mention of the theme or the themes. Further, it is obvious that a hexametric proemial line should have a formal style different than that of the songs of a melic poet who could spread his personal subject matter spaciously to several verses.

It is clear now that the meaning of the verse is no longer 'The words I begin are words of air, but for all that good to hear', 'beneficial', or any of the other versions proposed. Nevertheless, the new meaning still eludes us. 'Let me begin in lament', even though the participle is truncated, is satisfactory. But what is the meaning of ἠέρια ἔπεα and ἀγνὰ ἔπεα? Also what is the meaning of ἔπεα πτερόεντα here?

---

18 Accordingly, if Alcm. 26 is really such a proem, it must be cleared of the numerous scholarly interventions in the source of the fragment (Antigon. Caryst. *Mir.* 23, p. 8 Keller) that aimed at reconciling the text transmitted with Alcman's Laconic dialect: παρσενικαί for the transmitted παρθ-, ἰαρόφωνοι for ἱεροφ-, φέρην for φέρειν, ποτήται for ποτᾶται; ἰαρός for εἴαρος is a different case. Only μελιγάρυες is transmitted with inherited ᾱ, more a poetic than a dialectal element.

To start with, is this verse Sappho's? We cannot be sure, but this is what the vase painter claims. Not simply because he presented Sappho reading the roll, but mainly because he wrote, not above the seated woman but above the book roll, obliquely and parallel to its upper edge, ΣΑΠΠΩΣ, i.e., Σαπφῶς, genitive of Σαπφώ, according to the ancient grammarians, equally legitimate with Σαπφοῦς.[19] Then, the genitive can mean only one thing: 'Book, odes, verses of Sappho'.

The lamenting in the verse goes well with the moribund Sappho of the painting and of her funeral day poem. It may then introduce, not the edition of Sappho's poems, but one of the books of this edition, a book of plaintive odes, where Sappho would lament her own approaching death. Can Ἔπεα πτερόεντα be the title of this book, as the painter also seems to claim by placing the words on the outside of the roll? The usual interpretation of the most common epic formula ἔπεα πτερόεντα (προσηύδα) or ἔπεα πτερόεντ' (ἀγόρευε), 'winged words', implies, according to the ancient commentators, the swift speech, words uttered rapidly, the parallel usually adduced being Od. 7.36 τῶν νέες ὠκεῖαι ὡς εἰ πτερὸν ἠὲ νόημα. A secondary metaphor, from πτερόεις ἰός, 'flying arrow', was claimed to lead to 'words spoken accurately on target'. In any case, there must be a difference between the words spoken by epic characters occasionally addressing one another (e.g., Achilles addressing Athena in Il. 1.201) and the words composed by a poet crystallized in a title.

On the other hand, πτερόεις or ποτανός was used in post-Homeric poetry for 'lofty, exalted, elevated, inspired', the meaning that Yatromanolakis, p. 162, assumed for ἠερίων ἐπέων; e.g., Pind. I. 5.63 πτερόεντα ... ὕμνον, P. 5.114 ἔν τε Μοίσαισι ποτανός (sc. Arcesilas), Pai. 7B.13 πο]τανὸν ἅρμα Μοισᾶ[ν; and numerous playful instances in Ar. Av. 1372–1409, the Kinesias scene. Possibly, it is in this way that we should approach the title Ἔπεα πτερόεντα (= Lofty Poems).

However, if this is the title of the specific book, this would mean that Sappho does not consider her other poems elevated and inspired, but demeaningly places them on a lower level. Be that as it may, when a poet entitles a book of verses while he mourns his own approaching death, it is unthinkable that he would ever omit the crucial issue of posthumous fame. Will his work be forever interred with his body? It is the concept put forward by Cicero, Tusc. Disp. 1.34 *poëtae nonne post mortem nobilitari volunt?* Therefore, I would opt for a further meaning of ἔπεα πτερόεντα given especially by the moribund poetess. She views her ἔπεα no longer as items of her immediate pursuit, since she will not be able to sing them by herself, but as objects of universal promulgation, 'winged verses' that will fly

---

19 *PMG* 979 (adesp. 61) from Herodian. π. κλίσ. ὀνομ. fr., II 755 adn. Lentz. The ending is dialectally normal (Schwyzer *GG* 1, 478–479). See also Threatte's opinion mentioned above.

alive in an infinite future or in eternity when she will be corporally absent. We shall discuss later the Ennius verses that Cicero quotes to that effect and which repeat Sappho's words almost verbatim.

At any rate, the labelling, whether 'Lofty verses' or 'Verses flying in eternity', matches better the whole Sappho edition than a single book. Then the book roll Sappho is holding in the vase painting must represent her entire poetic work. Edmonds's remark that the rolled-up part of the book held by Sappho's left hand may be regarded as the first curl beginning the left-hand 'roll-up', i.e., the first column of the book roll, is not correct, because the right-hand curl is only slightly bulkier than the left-hand curl, as the elementary conventions of perspective drawing demand. The painter is interested in showing that Sappho reads the specific poem from her own roll (hence ΣΑΠΠΩΣ), not in indicating the column where the poem was found. If my interpretation of fr. 58 (POxy. 1787) 1–10 is correct (see below), Sappho must have planned the edition of her corpus, if not completed it, when she realized that she was approaching death's door. Why not the title of the edition too?

ἠέρια ἔπεα in the opening of the verse seem at first sight to harmonize with this sense of winged words, 'words of air, airy verses'. However, the word expected for the area of this infinite flight would be either αἰθήρ or, more generally, οὐρανός. 'Air', in the sense familiar to us, was designated as ἀήρ first by Anaximenes and Empedocles, who referred to it as a primary natural element, a notion most inappropriate for Sappho's image. In both Homer and Hesiod, ἀήρ/ἠήρ means 'mist, haze'. I cannot resist the idea that this is how the adjective is used here: 'verses of mist, of gloom, dark words'. In Eur. *Phoen.* 1534–5, Antigone is addressing her blinded father: ἀέριον σκότον ὄμμασι σοῖσι βαλών, 'gloomy darkness'.[20] The only testimony I have been able to find of ἠέριος or ἀέριος used of songs, verses, words, and the like was in Aristophanes *Av.* 1389 ἀέρια καὶ σκοτεινὰ καὶ κυαναυγέα, sc. ἔπη, for his contemporary dithyrambs. Yet, the metaphor works differently; not 'dark' = plaintive and mournful verses, but 'dark' = obscure and not perspicuous ones, in contrast to λαμπρά.[21]

---

[20] Yatromanolakis (2001), 161 n. 376, notes that the *Phoenissae* phrase is obelized in Diggle's edition (in Murray's too), but the reason has nothing to do with the sense of ἀέριον. Also, he is right in pointing out that ἠέριος occurs in the meaning 'misty, dimly seen' only in the Hellenistic period, but the meaning 'mist, haze' of ἀήρ/ἠήρ already in Homer and Hesiod cannot be neglected.

[21] *Il.* 18.505 κηρύκων ... ἠεροφώνων, usually translated μεγαλοφώνων, πληρούντων φωνῆς τὸν ἀέρα (so Hesychius), sounds discordant, if the heralds were supposed to shout through the mist. Photius *Lex.* ι 65, *Suda* ι 197 ἰεροφώνων· μεγαλοφώνων, very likely referring to the Ho-

Finally, I hope that ἁγνὰ ἔπεα will not open a new dispute on the use of the epithet for Sappho (Alc. 384 Ἰόπλοκ' ἄγνα μελλιχόμειδε Σάπφοι or -μειδες ἄπφοι), but here it is definitely used for ἔπεα, words or verses. The closest parallel in the Lesbians is Sa. 44.26 ἄειδον μέλος ἄγνον for the song sung by the πάρθενοι in the wedding of Hector and Andromache.[22] An emphasis has been given, perhaps in excess, to the religious even arcane character of that μέλος ἄγνον, in a way as extension of the image of Sappho herself who, connected with the description of the Alcaeus verse, has been presented as a venerable person endowed with sacral solemnity in the manner of a priestess of Aphrodite.[23] I do not believe that anything similar is involved in the present case. Since ἁγνῶν here implies poetic characteristics differing from her former poetry, Sappho is likely to invert the pervading tone of that poetry. No longer poems suggestive of erotic desire, but pure, chaste in thought, socially decent.[24]

The Sappho Book

A whole book consisting of plaintive poems? We know that some of Sappho's books were distinguished according to the metre, but a thematic division was known only for Ἐπιθαλάμια, the wedding songs, which are mentioned as a separate book with a specific title: Serv. georg. 1.31 *Sappho ... in libro qui inscribitur Ἐπιθαλάμια ait ...*; D.H. *Rh.* 4.1 καὶ παρὰ Σαπφοῖ τῆς ἰδέας ταύτης παραδείγματα, ἐπιθαλάμιοι οὕτως ἐπιγραφόμεναι ᾠδαί; POxy. 2294]φέρονται ἐπιγεγρα[- ἐπιθα]λάμια. The POxy. reference was especially treated by Denys Page[25] who identified Ἐπιθαλάμια with Sappho's Book 9 and the ten incipits cited in the same papyrus, i.e. fr. 103 V., with Book 8. I do not fully agree with Page's

---

meric usage, is more reasonable, since it designates the voice of the heralds, i.e., their profession, as filled with divine power. However, in the 2nd c. AD Oppian *Hal.* 1.621 (and in other late poets), ἠερόφωνοι, used for the flock of cranes flying back from warmer lands, is understandable as 'sounding through the air'. I cannot rule out that Oppian devised his ἠερόφωνοι by conflating a misinterpretation of Alcman's *PMG* 26.1, ἱερόφωνοι, also describing the chorus-girls who sing like a flock of halcyons, certainly not in the air, with the Homeric, already corrupt, ἠεροφώνων.

22 Right after the maidens sang a μέλος ἄγνον, there follows in the text ἴκανε δ' ἐς αἴθερα ἄχω θεσπεσία. The sentence does not make the μέλος 'airy', but rather 'divinely sounding in the sky'.
23 Gentili (1966), 42–44 = *Poesia e pubblico nella Grecia antica* (Milano 2006), 322–324.
24 Possibly, this is the meaning of μέλος ἄγνον in fr. 44 too; the maidens' song is 'pure, chaste' and not bawdy and ribald, as was the habit for the male companions of the groom to sing during marriage celebrations.
25 (1995), 116–119. Cf. now Puglia (2008), 1–8, with further bibliography.

reconstruction, and since it is only natural that a book of funereal poems must be placed last, I would place it after the Ἐπιθαλάμια; and if the books of Sappho's lyric poems are nine,[26] this plaintive book must be Book 9.

Accordingly, the dactylic hexameter of the hydria roll must be the first verse of a poem introductory to Sappho's book of funereal odes. θεοί, the first word on the roll, may be, as Edmonds observes, the usual invocation we find before the opening of public decrees. It is also occasionally introducing (also in the singular θεός or θεὸς τύχα or θεὸς τύχα ἀγαθά) oracular questions, like those found at Dodona.[27] However, though invocations of gods at the opening of poetic texts, in the type of Μῆνιν ἄειδε, θεά, are frequent, we never find the concise invocation θεοί, and what is more *extra metrum*. Therefore, we may suppose, that the word was placed there by the painter as a signal that what the viewer reads is not just any Sappho verse, but the opening of the particular book. Is the title Ἔπεα πτερόεντα of the same character as θεοί, a paratext or prelims devised by the painter? What we discussed above about the meaning of ἔπεα πτερόεντα makes this supposition extremely unlikely.

We can guess which surviving fragments belonged to this book.

Initially, the opening of the proemial dactylic poem of the painting:

⊗   ἠερίων ἐπέων ἄρχωμ' ἀγνῶν στεν[άχουσα.

We do not know how long this proem was, but I guess that it must have been distinctly shorter than the other poems of the book. Sappho seems to have used the same metre in the proem of at least one more book. The first incipit in the bibliographical fragment 103 V. is dactylic, unlike the rest nine incipits that are hipp^{2c}. Below, in '6. Sappho's Epithalamians', I am dealing with fr. 103 V. and the order of the last books of Sappho's edition. I only state in advance that the first incipit does not read]˰εν τὸ γὰρ ἐννεπε[.]η προβ[, as published, but – ∞] μὲν τότ' ἄρ', ἔννεπ', ἔον προβ[εβηκότ- ⏑ – –. It is not only the initial order of the verse that testifies to its being proemial, but primarily the emblematic word ἔννεπ(ε), addressed, as it seems, to the Muse or some other god or goddess. As for the hortatory subjunctive in the book roll verse, it is a typical, also emblematic, first-person opening, singular or plural, of proems, always involving divine beings invoked whether out of reverence or for offering inspiration or, more simply, for specifying the subject of the poem: Hes. *Th.* 1 Μουσάων Ἑλικωνιάδων ἀρχώμεθ' ἀείδειν, 36 (second proem) τύνη, Μουσάων ἀρχώμεθα, *h. Hom.* 25 (*In*

---

26 Tullius Laurea, *AG* 7.17, ἐμῇ ... παρ' ἐννεάδι; Su. σ 107 ἔγραψε δὲ μελῶν λυρικῶν βιβλία θ'.
27 Dakaris, Vokotopoulou, and Christidis (2013), 286.

Musas et Apollinem) 1 Μουσάων ἄρχωμαι Ἀπόλλωνός τε Διός τε, *Epigoni* fr. 1 Νῦν αὖθ᾽ ὁπλοτέρων ἀνδρῶν ἀρχώμεθα, Μοῦσαι, Aratus *Phaen.* 1 Ἐκ Διὸς ἀρχώμεσθα, Theocr. *Id.* 17.1 Ἐκ Διὸς ἀρχώμεσθα καὶ ἐς Δία λήγετε, Μοῖσαι.[28] This involvement of gods in poetic proems prefacing longer songs, irrespective of the verb mood, is more than a typical feature; it is almost mandatory. Possibly, it was the absence of gods in Sappho's proem that prompted the painter or rather the learned person who placed the order of the painting to add the *extra metrum* θεοί, at the same time warning that the verse was initial of a book. (For a further suggestion on the meaning of θεοί here, admittedly a bold one, see below at the end of '6. Sappho's Epithalamians'.)

Fr. 150 V. from Maximus Tyrius 18.9 p. 232 Hob. must certainly be placed in the same book. It is usually published in various forms and metres. It is here restored in a form, as I believe, metrically apter and much closer to the text of Maximus than in previous editions:[29]

οὐ γάρ θέμις ἐν μοισοπόλων θρηνέμεν· οὔ κ<εν> ἄμμι
πρέποι τάδε.

1 μοισο- Blomf., μουσο- Max. | οἰκίᾳ post μουσοπόλων Max., <δόμῳ> Hartung, nihil (ellipsis) Ts. | θρῆνον εἶναι Max., θρ. ἔμμεναι Blomf., θρ. ἔμμεν Wil., θρηνέμεν (vel θρηνέμεν'; epic. e θρήνημι) Ts. | οὐκ Max., οὔ κ᾽ Lobel, οὔ κ<εν> Ts. **2** τάδε πρέποι Lobel

The attempt to restore gl²ᶜ verses dictated the beginning from the middle of the verse, the addition of the unnecessary δόμῳ, a lacuna of 5 syllables following Wilamowitz's θρῆνον ἔμμεν, and a transposition of the words πρέπει τάδε for avoiding the lengthening of the previous syllable or the acceptance of *correptio attica* in Sappho. The metre restored here is ˌhipp²ᶜ.

V. Di Benedetto very sagaciously compared fr. 150 with the first period of the famous Ennius distich (*var.* 17–18 Vahl.)

nemo me dacrumis decoret, nec funera fletu
faxit. quor? volito vivu' per ora virum.[30]

The first period of the distich is really identical with the Sappho fragment. But the second part from *quor* to *virum* recalls fr. 58 (POxy. 1787) 10,[31] the final verse of

---

[28] The Theocritus opening critically repeats Aratus' incipit; Tsantsanoglou (2009b), esp. 62 ff.
[29] See below, '2. Sappho on her Funeral Day'.
[30] Di Benedetto (2005).
[31] Line 9 Hunt, 10 Lobel. Yatromanolakis follows Hunt, who starts the text with] ˌδἀ[: (2008), esp. 239, n. 11. However, the low tip of a vertical that intersects the longum sign above the alpha

the fragmentary poem previous to the Tithonus poem. Primarily, however, *volito* not only recalls the title of Sappho's book roll, but also shows the meaning she aimed to convey to the familiar phrase ἔπεα πτερόεντα (= *verba volitantia*).

```
1                                    ] φ[
2                                    ] . δᾶ[
3                                    ]
4                                    ]ηα
5                                    φ]ύγοισα[   ]
6                    ].[. .]. .[     ] ἐδάχθην
7    ×–⏑⏑– πάγ]χυ θ[έ]οι[ς], ἀλλ[ὰ παράγαγ' α]ὔταν
8    ×–⏑⏑–⏑⏑] ἄχθος· [ζ]ὰ τί λ[ῆμα τ]εῖσαι
9    χρῆ μ', ὤστε πάις κεκλο]μένα τὰν [πολυώ]νυμόν σε
10   τῶ κύδεος ἄνδρων ἔ]νι θῆται στ[ύ]μα[σι] πρόκοψιν;         ⊗
```

1 lineam verticalem praeterit Hunt; disp. Lobel   **6** ΔΆΧ, i.e. δήχθην Voigt,]ἐδ- Ts.,]ιδ- Hunt al.   **7** Θ[.́]ΟΙ[, vel θέοις vel θέοισ', Ts. | ἀλλ[ὰ παράγαγ' α]ὔταν; verbum e.g. e Sa. 16.11 suppl. Ts.   **8** ἄχθος dub. Voigt | 'ĂTÍ, mox Κ[, Λ[, Ν[, simm.' (Lobel-Page); inclinatio lineae Λ[indicat |]ΕΙCΑ, I sup. A disp. Ts. | suppl. Ts.   **9** init. e.g. suppl. Ts. | ÉNĀ, κεκλο]μένα Di Benedetto | [πολυώ]νυμον Voigt   **10** init. e.g. suppl. Ts. | ΘĤ | στ[ύ]μα[σι] Hunt (pro στυμάτεσσι; de dat. pl. breviore in Lesbiis vid. A.M. Bowie, *The Poetic Dialect of Sappho and Alcaeus*, Salem N.H., 1981, 119–122), στ[ύ]μα[τι] Stiebitz | PÓK

"] having fled [...] I was irritated [... fu]lly (to) the gods, but the heavy grief [... misled] her. What of[fence should I] pay for, [so that my daughter, call]ing [for aid] upon you the [multi]nominal goddess, may bring about furtherance [of my fame i]n the mouths [of men]?"

It seems likely that frs. 58 and 150 refer to the same incident. As Maximus Tyrius narrates, Sappho is inflamed with anger at her daughter's lament for her impending death, because it is improper to wail in a poet's house. Obviously, what is implied is that the poetic gift ensures immortality for the Muses-attendant. The addressee is Aphrodite, to whom Sappho must have recounted her anger (5 ἐδάχθην, 'I was irritated') at her daughter's plaintive reaction and, apparently, tried to find excuses for her misbehaviour: 'it was the load of grief that misled her' (6–7 ἀ[λλὰ παράγαγ' α]ὔταν [...] ἄχθος). The ode closes with Sappho asking Aphrodite what should she do, so that after her demise, Kleïs, her daughter, could achieve a posthumous furtherance (θῆται ... πρόκοψιν) of her fame in the mouths of men (ἄνδρων ἔ]νι ... στ[ύ]μα[σι] = Ennius' *per ora virum*). The tilt of the stroke following τί suggests Λ. Then, τί λ[ῆμα ... | χρῆ με is possible. Normally, what is

---

of] . δᾶ[(read by Hunt as an angular *spiritus lenis*) must belong to the previous line, most likely a φ.

expected to stand in between is an infinitive. However, the letters read after a five-letter gap are]εισα, which definitely oppose that suggestion. Yet, as far as I know, it was not observed that an iota is written above the final alpha, as it seems by the first hand. I do not know why the iota of the diphthong at the end of the verse and the distich was written above the alpha, though there is plenty of space to the right, but the fact is that it was. Thus,]εισαι can belong to a small group of infinitives ending in -εῖσαι (ἀεῖσαι, δανεῖσαι, δεῖσαι, ἐρεῖσαι, πεῖσαι, σεῖσαι, τεῖσαι; a few more do not scan). τί λ[ῆμα τ]εῖσαι seems to be fitting, if Sappho is offering to pay for a possible offence of her daughter toward the gods (7 πάγ]χυ θ[έ]οι[c]), for which she presented excuses in the previous verses.

As I have obviously placed the contents of POxy. 1787 (and, accordingly, those of PColon. 21351+21376) in Sappho's Ninth and last Book, it is necessary to state my grounds for doing so. POxy. 1787, a large papyrus with some long and many short fragments (58–86 V.), was assigned to the Fourth Book by A.S. Hunt, its first editor, *Ox. Pap.* XV (1922). His arguments, presented on p. 26, can be summarized as follows. The Second and Third Books are each metrically homogeneous and arranged in two-line strophes whereas the Fifth Book was probably metrically diverse and arranged in three-line strophes; it is then reasonable that POxy. 1787, which consists of metrically homogeneous fragments arranged in two-line strophes, must be assigned to the Fourth Book. However, Hephaestion (*Poëm.* 1.2, p. 63 C.) describes the two-line strophes, actually couplets of metrically identical verses, referring to Sappho's Second and Third Books, not the Fourth. Yet, the argument on the vicinity of metrically homogeneous books persisted, and the assignment of POxy. 1787 to the Fourth Book was consolidated, though Lobel-Page published ΣΑΠΦΟΥΣ ΜΕΛΩΝ $\overline{\Delta}$? (their query) and Page, *Sappho and Alcaeus*, p. 114, noted that "The evidence for Book IV is not quite so satisfactory." In any case, Hephaestion's reference is not restrictive. We can confidently argue that the two-line strophes did not show up in the whole of the Fourth Book (otherwise Hephaestion would not speak of δεύτερον καὶ τρίτον Σαπφοῦς but would add καὶ τέταρτον Σαπφοῦς), but not that it was absent from any other Sappho Book. Further, the homogeneity of Sappho's Second and Third Books is categorically stated by Hephaestion on the basis of their metres: 7.7, p. 23 C. καλεῖται Σαπφικὸν τεσσαρεσκαιδεκασύλλαβον, ᾧ τὸ δεύτερον ὅλον Σαπφοῦς γέγραπται; 10.6 p. 34 C. καλεῖται Σαπφικὸν ἑκκαιδεκασύλλαβον, ᾧ τὸ τρίτον ὅλον Σαπφοῦς γέγραπται. Even the homogeneity of the First Book is referred to in the same manner: *Schol. metr.* Pind. P. 1, 2.5 Drachm., possibly from Hephaestion's unabridged treatise, ἑνδεκασύλλαβον (sic codd.) Σαπφικόν, ᾧ τὸ πρῶτον ὅλον Σαπφοῦς γεγραμμένον. However, in describing $_\wedge$hipp^{2c}, the metre of POxy. 1787, Hephaestion 11.5, p. 36 C., states καλεῖται δὲ Αἰολικόν, ὅτι Σαπφὼ πολλῷ αὐτῷ ἐχρήσατο, which must refer to more than one books. Of course, I cannot prove that the Fourth Book did not contain also a number of poems in ˏhipp²ᶜ, but I believe it is absolutely reasonable, from the contents point of view, that the mournful poems of POxy. 1787, what I call Epithanatians, must be assigned to Sappho's Ninth and final Book. Since, however, some fragments of the same papyrus do not seem to have plaintive themes, it is possible that the papyrus contained also the Eighth Book, an extremely small book, which also shared the ˏhipp²ᶜ metre. The question deserves special investigation, but provisionally I can state that fr. 81 V. which is partly overlapped by POxy. 1787 fr. 33 is very likely to come from the vicinity of fr. 103.12 (9), i.e. from Sappho's Eighth Book.[32]

POxy. 1787 continues with what has been dubbed 'the Tithonus poem'. The very fragmentary text of POxy. 1787 was considerably supplemented by PColon. 21351, i.11–ii.8. The Cologne papyrus not only was the oldest surviving Sappho papyrus (first half of the third century BC), but was also an extremely tidy and meticulously calligraphed copy. However, the Cologne papyrus has a different poem before the Tithonus one. It is the poem on the funeral day of Sappho, which we mentioned above in connection with the vase-painting. It is better to repeat it for completeness, without commenting on it:

Fr. ? (PColon. 21351, i.1–11)

```
1                                           ]γδα
2                                           ]ξαι
3                                           ]ξον
4              ] . ου . [
5      ×–⏑⏑––⏑⏑–] εὔχομ' [⏑–⏑––
6      ×–⏑⏑––⏑⏑ ὠ]ς νῦν θαλ[ί]αν γέ[νεσθαι
7      ×–⏑⏑––⏑⏑–] · νέρθε δὲ γᾶς πέρ[αισσ]αι
8      τὰν πᾶκτιν ἔμον λοῖ]σθον ἔχοισαν γέρας ὡς [ἔ]οικεν·
9      καὶ πάρ με φίλαι παί]ζοῖεν ὡς νῦν ἐπὶ γᾶς ἔοισαν."
10     παραύτικα Κάλλις] λιγύραν [δ]ῶκεν ἔλοισα πᾶκτιν·
11     "ἀλλ'," εἶπον, "ἔγωγ', ἀλεμ]άτᾳ, τὰν καλάμοισ' ἀείδω."      ⊗
```

I believe that now we can restore in 10 παραύτικα Κάλλις], transferring the name of the painting to the poem, without being blamed for begging the question.

The 'Tithonus poem' of POxy. 1787 as supplemented by PColon. 21351 and by scholarly intervention comes next. The supplements of 1–2 are mine, though I have been aided by several other proposals. Supplementing 13–14 is a desperate task.

---

[32] See Hammerstaedt (2011); Lidov (2011). Also, B. Acosta-Hughes (2010).

Fr. 58.11–26+59 V.

⊗ Μοίσαν ἐπιδείξασθ' ἰ]οκ[ό]λπων κάλα δῶρα, παῖδ₍ε₎ς,
2 καὶ παίξατε κὰτ τὰ]ν φιλάοιδον λιγύραν χέλυνναν.
  ἔμοι δ' ἄπαλον πρίν] ποτ' [ἔ]οντα χρόα γῆρας ἤδη
4 ἐπέλλαβε, λεῦκαι δ' ἐγ]ένοντο τρίχες ἐκ μελαίναν,
  βάρυς δέ μ' ὁ [θ]ῦμος πεπόηται, γόνα δ' οὐ φέροισι,
6 τὰ δή ποτα λαίψηρ' ἔον ὄρχησθ' ἴσα νεβρίοισιν.
  τά <γ' ὀν>στεναχίσδω θαμέως, ἀλλὰ τί κεν ποείην;
8 ἀγήραον ἄνθρωπον ἔοντ' οὐ δύνατον γένεσθαι.
  καὶ γάρ π[ο]τα Τίθωνον ἔφαντο βροδόπαχυν Αὔων
10 Ἔρωι διελάθεισαν βάμεν' εἰς ἔσχατα γᾶς φέροισα[ν
  ἔοντα [κ]άλον καὶ νέον, ἀλλ' αὖτον ὔμως ἔμαρψε
12 χρόνωι πόλιον γῆρας, ἔχ[ο]ντ' ἀθανάταν ἄκοιτιν.
                φθ]ιμέναν νομίσδει,
14   ]αις ὀπάσδοι.
  ₍ἔγω δὲ φίλημμ' ἀβροσύναν,₎ [ἴστε δὲ] ₍τοῦτο, καί μοι₎
16 τὸ λά₍μ₎προν ἔρως ἀελίω καὶ τὸ κά₍λον λέ₎₍λ₎ογχε.   ⊗ ?
  ἐπῖν[   ].[. . .]γό.[
18 φίλει ₍[
  καιν[

1 × − ‿ ‿ Μοίσαν βαθυκόλ]πων Stiebitz, ὔμμες πεδὰ Μοίσαν ἰ]οκ. West, ὔμμιν φίλα Μοίσαν ἰ]οκ. olim Di Benedetto, γεραίρετε Μοίσαν ἰ]οκ. Di Benedetto, φέρω τάδε Μοίσαν ἰ]οκ. Gronewald-Daniel, αἰ στέργετε Μοίσαν ἰ]οκ. fort. Ferrari, Μοίσαν (vel Θέαν) ἐπιδείξασθ' ἰ]οκ. Ts.   2 λάβοισα/ἔλοισα πάλιν τ]ὰν Gronewald-Daniel, χορεύσατε κὰτ τ]ὰν olim Di Benedetto, ἐλίσσετε κὰτ τὰ]ν Ferrari, σπουδάσδετε καὶ τὰ]ν West, πρέπει δὲ λάβην τὰ]ν Di Benedetto, καὶ παίξατε κὰτ τὰ]ν Ts.   3 ἔμοι μὲν ἔκαρψεν] Snell, κέκαρφ' ἄπαλόν μοι] Gronewald-Daniel, ἔμοι δ' ἄπαλον (hoc iam Gronewald-Daniel) πρίν] Di Benedetto   4 ἐπέλλαβε· West, διώλεσε· Di Benedetto | λεῦκαι et ἐγένοντο Hunt, δ' Lobel   7 ΓΑΝ s.l. disp. Ts. et corr. in γ' ὀν   10 ἔρωι δέπας εἰσανβάμεν Gronewald-Daniel, ἔρωι φ..αθεισαν βάμεν' West, ἔρωι λα[λ]άγεισαν βάμεν' Janko, ἔρωι <ἰ>φι δάμεισαν βάμεν' Ferrari, Ἔρωι δ₍ι₎ελάθεισαν βάμεν' olim Ferrari, disp. Ts.   13-14 alii alia suppl.   15-16 Clearch. Sol. fr. 41 Wehrli (= Ath. 15.687b)   15 [ἴστε δὲ] Di Benedetto   17 incertum an novi carm. initium

I translate only the verses that include suggestions of my own: 1–2 "Display the fair gifts of the violet-bosomed Muses (or 'goddesses'), girls, and dance to the melodious clear-sounding lyre"; 7 "These things I often bemoan, but what could I do?"; 10 "pierced through by Eros (or 'by desire')". 13–14 are left unsupplemented, except for the obvious φθ]ιμέναν. 15–16 "But I feel affection for daintiness, you know this well, and for me the love for the sun (i.e., love of life) comprises both the brightness (sc. of the sun) and the beauty."

I only wish to stress the pivotal role of the distich 15–16, two of the finest verses in Greek poetry. Elucidating these verses has been a protracted activity of the classical community based on the interpretations of ἁβροσύνη and ἁβρότης found in LSJ, 'splendour, luxury'. This activity[33] is focused on the socially positive or negative reception of the notions of splendour and luxury in moral and political respect. The research was limited in the context of only these two verses without examining the general tenor of the poem, but also disdaining the interpretation of Clearchus of Soli, the only complete, or nearly so, source of the distich. Furthermore, the wholesale socio-moral interpretation of ἁβροσύνη, without considering if it is employed for males or females, for teenage girls or young women is entirely faulty. An ἁβρός man may be a dandy or an effeminate person. Yet, the young Sappho, as depicted on the Bochum kalyx-krater, is no doubt ἁβρά, i.e. elegant and stylish. The shy girl on the reverse side of the same krater is also ἁβρά, i.e., charming and delicate. The purport of the distich cannot be apprehended if the idea of the old age and the imminent death of the poetess is not reckoned. The question is not simply of staying alive, something Zeus could offer Sappho, as he did to Tithonus. As her pupil-friends know well, what she feels affection for is ἁβροσύνη, loveliness, daintiness or charming elegance, and for her a life is worth living only if the love for the sun (i.e., the desire of staying alive) comprises not only the brightness of the sunlight but also the beauty, τὸ καλόν. It is this καλόν that she, just like Tithonus, does not possess any longer. At least, as long as she is still alive, let her enjoy the καλὰ δῶρα of the Muses as they are displayed by her pupil-friends.

The text in PColon. is interrupted at line 12. For the rest we resort again to POxy. 1787. Lines 17–19 may or may not belong to the same poem. A paragraphos is visible between 16 and 17, which would normally connect the verses with the 'Tithonus Poem'. If, however, what looks like a paragraphos is no more than the middle stroke of a coronis, we should assume a new poem starting with ἐπῑν[, as Lobel-Page and Voigt did (59 V.).[34]

It is better now to return to POxy. 1787 and see whether the fragments following the Tithonus poem in it can belong to this book of moribund Sappho. The fact that they come from the same papyrus and share the same metre ($\_{\wedge}$hipp^{2c}) speaks strongly for this surmise. They are frr. 60–87 V., some of them consisting of more than one small pieces. However, because of their small size and their fragmented state, it is unreliable to draw any general conclusions about their subject. On the other hand, as I explained above, it is also difficult to say whether all of them come from the same book or some can belong to the previous one. I distinguish

---

[33] Well reflected in Yatromanolakis (2007), 127 ff., especially in his lengthy footnote 264.
[34] Lundon (2007). See here below '3. Kleïs as Promoter of Sappho's Poetry'.

the fragments 62–65, which, in spite of their desperate condition, evoke both themes: of the dying Sappho and her posthumous survival.

The sense of the poem leaves no doubt that fr. 62 comes from this specific book. Together with fr. 63, they cover most part of a single column of POxy. 1787. It is a short poem of twelve verses or six distichs. I have tried to get a clear sense of the text, a hard task because of the heavily mutilated verses.

Fr. 62 V.

```
     ⊗   Ἐπτάξατε̣[
2        δάφνας ὄτα̣[
         πὰν δ' ἄδιον[
4        ἦ κῆνον ἐλο[
         καὶ ταῖσι μὲν ἀ̣[
6        ὀδοίπορος ἄν[....]..[
         μύγις δέ ποτ' εἰσάιον· ἐκλ̣[
8        ψύχα δ' ἀγαπάτα συν[´
         τέαυτ'· ἃ δὲ νῦν ἔμμ[
10       ἴκεσθ' ἀγάνα[ι
         ἔφθατε· κάλαν[
12       τά τ' ἔμματα κα̣[          ⊗
```

1 ΠΤΆ῾Ε̣ **2** ΌΤ **3** ΠᾸ῾ΝΔᾸ῾Δ **4** ῾ΗΚΗ͂Ν | ΕΛΌ[; fort. ἔλο[ντ- **5** ΤΑΙ͂C | fort. ἄ[λλαισι **6** ὈΔΌΙ | Ᾱ῾Ν; fort. ἄν[υσσ- **7** ΜΎΓ | ΠΟΤ' | ΟΝ· **8** ΨΫ́ | ΠᾹ́Τ **9** ΤΈΑΥΤ[.]Ν leg. Hunt et corr. τέαυτα; malim τέαυτ['] ἀ̣ legere, cum spir. len. angul. (cf. hic infra spir. len. sup. ἔμμ[et praesertim fr. 63.2 Υ῾Π); τέαυτ'· ἃ δὲ Ts. | ΝΥ͂Ν | Ε῾Μ; ἔμμ[ατα Diehl **10** Ϊ́ΚΕCΘ' | ἀγάνα[ι vel alio casu **11** x marg. sin. | ΈΦ | ΤΕ· **12** ΤΑΤ' | κα̣[ὶ Diehl

Sappho's addressees are more than one: 1 ἐπτάξατε, 10 ἴκεσθ(ε), 11 ἔφθατε. The poetess is elsewhere using the plural when she is addressing her pupil-friends. Now, as time has gone by, they must have grown up. Sappho seems to scold them for showing exceeding faintheartedness ('you cowered'). The reference to bay laurel clears up the cause of their fear. They avoided calling on her fearing that they would find her on the deathbed, and bay laurel was supposed to have apotropaic qualities in ominous circumstances like that. Thphr. *Char.* 16.1.1 ἀμέλει ἡ δεισιδαιμονία δόξειεν <ἂν> εἶναι δειλία πρὸς τὸ δαιμόνιον, ὁ δὲ δεισιδαίμων τοιοῦτός τις, οἶος ἐπιτυχὼν ἐκφορᾷ [...] δάφνην εἰς τὸ στόμα λαβὼν οὕτω τὴν ἡμέραν περιπατεῖν. It is obvious that Sappho is resentfully mocking them. 3–4 'Everything is more enjoyable than meeting that one (masc.)' seems to be said in irony about the girls' attitude toward Θάνατος or θάνατος. E.g., ἦ κῆνον ἔλο[ντ' εἰς Ἀχέροντ-, 'him having taken (me) to Acheron'? In 5–6 Sappho distinguishes her pupil-friends from some other females (ταῖσι μὲν ἄ[λλαισι?), probably unconcerned townswomen in Lesbos. 'For them I was no more than a wayfarer who finished his journey' (6 ὀδοίπορος ἄν[υσσα/ε κέλευθον?), but from you I expected some words of sympathy. 7 'Yet, I hardly heard any'. ἐκλ[may belong to ἐκλ[ιμπάνετ' or ἐκλ[είπετε, 'you desert (me)'. What was left for her to go through with was her one and only life (8 ψύχα δ' ἀγαπάτα συν[').[35] All this rebuke appears to end abruptly with a single word: 9 τέαυτ(α), 'This is what I had to say!'. Cf. expressions like Aesch. *Pr.* 500 τοιαῦτα μὲν δὴ ταῦτα or Soph. *El.* 696 καὶ ταῦτα μὲν τοιαῦτα, though ταῦτα is more usual in similar situations: LSJ s.v. οὗτος C.VII.[36] Be that as it may, the girls have come now in a mild and gentle disposition (ἀγάναι dative sing. or nominative pl.), bringing Sappho some garments (ἔμματα) and something else (12 τά τ' ἔμματα κα[ὶ ?) for soothing her. The poetess is still bitterly ironic. ἔφθατε: 'You came in time (before my death). Your presents will be put to good use', apparently said ironically. The mood is entirely different than in the 'Tithonus poem' or the 'Funeral day poem' or the hydria painting, where her personal agony is impregnated with the loss of the companionship. This is the only outspoken complaint of Sappho about her pupil-friends. Does it mark a temporal evolution of her psychology? Or is it just a fit of temper?

If fr. 62, especially its tragic line 8, suggested a feeling of utter loneliness before death, it is natural that in fr. 63 Sappho would turn to the god of loneliness, Oneiros, the god of dreams, a most personal god who would not desert her as long as she was alive. It is also a short poem consisting of ten lines or five distichs in all. Though the beginnings of the verses survive, the lacunae till their ends are quite large.

Fr. 63 V.

⊗ Ὄνοιρε μελαινα[
2   φ[ο]ίταις, ὄτα τ' ὔπνος [
     γλύκυς θέος, ἦ δεῖν' ὀνία σμ[
4   ζὰ χῶρις ἔχην τὰν δύναμ[αι
     ἔλπις δέ μ' ἔχει μὴ πεδέχην[ν
6   μηδ' ἐν μακάρων ἔλ[πιδα νάσοισ' ὑπέθηκα ναίην.
     οὐ γάρ κ' ἔον οὔτω[,'

---

[35] It cannot be excluded that ψύχα ἀγαπάτα might be said about Kleïs, Sappho's only daughter (cf. fr. 132.2), but the unfamiliar use of ψύχα combined with the whole context weakens the possibility.

[36] This reading becomes necessary after deciphering the traces following ΤΕΑΥΤ: not [.]ΝΔΕ, as was read by Hunt and naturally corrected by him to τέαυτα δέ, but as ΤΕΑΥΤ[']ΑΔΕ with the angular soft breathing written as in ΕΜ (same line) or, even more similarly, as in fr. 63.2 Υ'Π.

8   ἀθύρματα κα.[
    γένοιτο δέ μοι[
10 τοὶς πάντα[⊗

1 -α[ις πτερύγεσσιν Hunt, -α[ν κατὰ νύκτ' ὃς … Snell   **2** Φ[́]Ι | ΌΤΑΤ' : 'potius ὅτε τ(ε) homericum quam ὅτε τ(οι)' Voigt |Υ ̋Π | [κατέχηι με Latte   **3** ΛΎ | ']ΟC· Voigt, ΈΟC· Hunt, malim ΈΟC; 'γλ. θ. et ad ὕπν. (tum ̋Υ. scribend.) et ad ὄν. (sic Treu) referri potest' Voigt | ἭΔΕΙΝ' | ΝΊᾹ | ὀνίας μ[edd., ὀνίας μ[νάματα Diehl, ὀνία σμ[ῦξεν ἄσα τ' ἔμ'· οὐ γὰρ Ts.   **4** ΖΆΧΏΡΙCΈΧ | τᾶν edd., τᾶν Ts. | δύναμ[ιν Diehl, δύναμ[αι Ts.   **5** ΔΈΜ' | ΔΈΧ   **6** μηδὲν edd., μηδ' ἐν Ts. | ἐλ[π- Diehl, ἔλ[πομ' ἔγων Schadew., ἔλ[πιδα νάσοισ' ὑπέθηκα ναίην Ts.   **7** ΓΆΡ | ΚΈΟΝ | ΌΥ | οὕτω[ς ἄπορος, e.g. Ts.   **8** ΘΫ́Ρ | Λ[, Ν[, Κ[, simm. | κάλ[λιστα Ts.   **10** fort. τοὶς πάντα[ς

Whether Hunt's or Snell's e.g. supplement is adopted in line 1 or whether γλύκυς θέος refers to Sleep or to Dream, the tenor of Sappho's invocation is clear. She seems to have been disheartened from her futile entreaties to the other gods, and so she turns to the only god who can offer her, even fleetingly, some hope.[37] Lines 3–4 describe her distresses. With the negation closing line 3, she explains that she cannot stand alone away from them: οὐ γὰρ | χωρὶς αὐτῶν δύναμαι διέχειν. Intransitive διέχην (ζὰ … ἔχην in tmesis) is augmented with χῶρις + τᾶν, feminine demonstrative genitive plural, referring to the distresses of the previous line. However, ὀνίας is gen. sing. To account for the plural τᾶν one should join ὀνία with a second feminine subject. Sa. 1.3 μή μ' ἄσαισι μηδ' ὀνίαισι shows the way. Possibly, ὀνία σμ[ῦξεν ἄσα τ' ἔμ'· οὐ γὰρ | … . 'For I cannot stand apart, alone, separate from them'. σμύχω and κατασμύχω, 'burn in a slow fire, burn up', are predominantly used metaphorically of grief, love or other strong feelings. In 5 she is probably expressing the hope to avoid taking part in the tribulations of Hades (κάκων, πόνων, δείνων). In contrast (possibly, 5 ending with αὐτάρ), at 6 she declares that she did not cherish hopes for dwelling in the Islands of the Blessed. Read not μηδέν but μηδ' ἐν, which combined with μακάρων leads unavoidably to ἐν μακάρων … νάσοισι. μηδ(έ) is not connected with 5 μὴ πεδέχην, but is adverbially introducing a contrasting independent sentence: 'neither did I cherish hopes'. For ἔλπιδα … ὑπέθηκα, see LSJ s.v. ὑποτίθημι II 1. The legend about eternal life accompanied by felicity in the Islands of the Blessed is stressed in the Attic skolion *PMG* 894: φίλταθ' Ἁρμόδι', οὔ τί που τέθνηκας, | νήσοις δ' ἐν μακάρων σέ φασιν εἶναι, | ἵνα περ ποδώκης Ἀχιλεὺς | Τυδείδην παρ' ἐσθλὸν Διομήδεα. Sappho, though communicating with a supernatural being, feels obliged to declare how down-to-earth she is. In line 7 she explains the declaration

---

[37] Fränkel (²1962), 210, misapprehending the cause of Sappho's distress, gets a completely wrong idea about the poem.

of the previous line: 'For (if I cherished such hopes), I would not be so anguished, so hopeless'; e.g., οὕτω[ς ἄπορος. Given that Sappho's main concern in this particular situation is the posthumous survival and promulgation of her poetry, it is not surprising that she is using for her poems an informal term, in line with the familiar atmosphere created: ἀθύρματα κάλ[λιστα. The 'most beautiful playthings' were later used in poetry for 'songs'; Pi. *Pyth.* 5.23 Ἀπολλώνιον ἄθυρμα. Bacchylides, though speaking of an athlete, takes up the whole idea: *Epin.* 9.85–87 σὺν δ' ἀλαθείᾳ βροτῶν | κάλλιστον, εἴπ[ερ καὶ θάνῃ τις,] | λε[ί]πεται Μουσ[ᾶν βαθυζώνων ἄθ]υρμα (suppl. Blass). Also, in the epigram attributed to the same poet: *Epigr.* 1.3 ἐν ἀθύρμασι Μουσᾶν. In 9 γένοιτο δέ μοι[, she must demand a special offer, of which the only surviving relic is 10 τοὶς πάντα[, rather τοὶς πάντα[ς, 'everybody, the whole world', which recalls the verses 8–9 of fr. 65 ὅ]σσοις φαέθων [ἀέλιος ... | πάνται κλέος, and 10 of fr. 58 τῶ κύδεος ἄνδρων ἔ]νι θῆται στ[ύ]μα[σι] πρόκοψιν.

Fr. 65 V.

```
       .....]π̣ι̣τα[
2      .. Ἀνδ]ρόμε[δα
       ... ἀ]λ̣' ἔλας[ον
4      π]ροτ', ἤν, νέμε[ταί σοι
       Ψάπφοι, σὲ φίλ[εισ(α)
6      Κύπρω{ι} β[α]σίλ[ηα

       καί τοι μέγα δ[ῶρον
8      ὅ]σσοις φαέθων [
       πάνται κλέος [

10     καί σ' ἐνν Ἀχέρ[οντ
       .. [......]υπ[
```

Paragraphi post 6 (incerta) et 9 (certa) fort. divisionem in tristicha indicant; cf. fr. 88.
1] . ϹΙΤΑ Hunt,]ΠΥΦΑ, simm. Lobel,]ΠΙΤΑ Ts.   **2** Ἀνδρομέ[δα Hunt   **3**]Δ,]Λ | Θ[, Β[Lobel-Page, C[Ts.; ... ἀλ]λ' ἔλασ[ον dub. Ts.   **4** ΗΝ | π]ροτ', ἤν, νέμε[ταί σοι (tmesis); ἤν interjectio, Ts., 'ΗΝ, non intellegitur' Voigt   **5** σὲ φίλ[ημμ' Diehl, σὲ φίλ[εισ(α) Ts.   **6** ΚΥΠ | fort. Κύπρω scribend. esse cens. Lobel | ϹΙΛ | β[α]σίλ[ηα edd.   **7** ΚΑΙ | καίτοι edd., καί τοι Η. Fränkel | δ[ῶρον Η. Fränkel   **8** Φαέθων Hunt, Wil., φαέθων [ἀέλιος Fränkel   **9** ΠΑΝΤΑΙ, 'deb. ΠΑΝ (quod leg. Hunt dubit.)' Voigt   **10** ΚΑΙ

I confine myself only to the points that seem to connect the fragment with the book that concerns us here. Firstly, I greatly doubt that Aphrodite is the speaker here, as suggested by Diehl, H. Fränkel, and Wilamowitz. I do not believe that Sappho would represent the goddess speaking *nominatim* about Andromeda, the antagonist of the poetess in Lesbos (line 2), or referring to herself as Κύπρω{ι} βασίλ[ηα (line 6). Instead, I would suggest that the speaker announces Cypris's decisions to Sappho. I have a strong feeling that Oneiros, the γλύκυς θέος whom Sappho addressed in 63, now serves as a representative of the goddess. After advising the poetess to drive away (line 3 ἀλ]λ' ἔλασ[ον) her anxieties, he reveals that Cypris grants her (4 προτ', ἤν, νέμε[ταί σοι, 'look, she grants you'; προσνέμω, -ομαι), as a patent testimony of her love (5 σὲ φίλ[εισα), a great gift (7 καί τοι μέγα δ[ῶρον; suppl. Fränkel), what we saw Sappho was desperately begging the gods to grant her; namely, the diffusion of her glory all over the world (8–9), to whoever the sun looks down upon (8 φαέθων [ἀέλιος, sc. κατόρει, sim., Fränkel, coll. Sol. 14.2, Eur. *Hipp.* 849–50). Even in Acheron (line 10) she will not be forgotten; cf. frr. 55, 147.

Still, though it may sound truistic, I believe that the investigation into the last books of Sappho needs to be continued. The evidence given by POxy. 2294 (Sa. 103 V.) and the last poem of PColon. 21351+21376 can, in my view, prove worthwhile and productive.

2 Sappho on her Funeral Day: P.Colon. 21351.1–8

The first of the three poems contained in P.Colon. 21351+21376, this one almost exclusively in 21351, has been less discussed, because of its extreme fragmentariness.¹ Apart from the first edition by M. Gronewald and R.W. Daniel (2004) (referred to below as *edd. pr.*), I have made use of the articles of West (2005), Di Benedetto (2005), Hardie (2005), Livrea (2007), Bettarini (2008), Gronewald and Daniel (2007).² Naturally, I also used the digital image of the papyrus in the Web.

```
 1                                      ] . δα
 2                                      ]ξαι
 3                                      ]ξον
 4               ] . ουμ[
 5    × – ⏑ ⏑ – – ⏑ ⏑ –] εὔχομ' [ ⏑ – ⏑ – –
 6    × – ⏑ ⏑ – – ⏑ ⏑ –]ς νῦν θαλ[ί]αν γε[
 7    × – ⏑ ⏑ – – ⏑ ⏑ –] . · νέρθε δὲ γᾶς πεδ[ὰ ἴσχ]ην
 8    × – ⏑ ⏑ – –]σθον ἔχοισαν γέρας ὡς [ἔ]οικεν
 9    × – ⏑ ⏑ – –]ζοιεν ὡς νῦν ἐπὶ γᾶς ἔοισαν
10    × – ⏑ ⏑ – –] λιγύραν [δ]ῶκεν ἔλοισα πᾶκτιν
11    × – ⏑ ⏑ – – ⏑]άτα τὰν καλάμοισ' ἀείδω.          ⊗
```

1.] . . . *edd. pr.*; right-hand end of top horizontal prior to δα; μί]γδα?
2.] αι *edd. pr.*
3.] . ν *edd. pr.*
4.] . ο . [*edd. pr.*;].ου . [West rightly.
5.] υχ . [*edd. pr.*;] εὔχομ' [Di Benedetto rightly.
6.] . νῦν *edd. pr.*;]ς is palaeographically possible (a high trace which may belong to the top end of c) and sense-wise likely *coll.* 9 ὡς νῦν.
   θαλ[ί]α γέ[νοιτο or γε[νέσθω, proposed by *edd. pr.*, are very likely, but I would rather prefer θαλ[ί]αν γ ἐ[νεσθαι depending on 5 εὔχομ(αι); πα[West, who supplements πα[ρέστω (or πά[ρεστι or πὰ[ρ ἄμμι).

---

1 I have time and again pestered Prof. J. Hammerstaedt with my suspicions for solving the numerous puzzles of this intriguing poem. He has saved me from many blunders, and if I have not always followed his advice, the fault is mine. My indebtedness to him is immense.
2 With the line-numbering increased by 3, since the ends of three verses visible in col. I of P.Colon. 21376 are now added in the beginning. I follow the new numbering, still referring to the editors as *edd. pr.*

7. γε̣.[...].. ('γ oder π') *edd. pr.*; π̣ε̣.[West rightly, supplementing περ[ίσχ]οι ('may ... surround me'). The traces before the lacuna are described by *edd. pr.* as "vertikale, im unteren Bereich durchkreuzte Haste". The description, which was kindly reaffirmed for my sake by Dr. R.W. Daniel, does not suggest any Greek letter. After many futile attempts, I have ended up with δ, somewhat larger than the delta of 11 αειΔω, but similar or even smaller than the delta of 'Tithonus poem' 1 Δωρα. Its greatest part survives, though the low left-hand part of the triangle is faded but visible, possibly wiped away, because it was written very close to the preceding ε. The scribe then rewrote the delta somewhat more to the right, with the bottom left-hand angle of the second delta clearly surviving. However, the scribe did not wipe away the tip of the original triangle as he did with its lower part. Perhaps the papyrus was at this point dangerously thin and he was afraid he might damage it. Also, a tiny strip along the edge of the papyrus seems unwritten. It is, however, common in papyri that letters are often worn away at the edges or the cuts, something observed at several places in this papyrus too. Finally, a further inverted triangle, which appears under the bottom horizontal of what I read as δ, is no more than a stain or blot, as Prof. Hammerstaedt rightly noticed. After the lacuna, the line closes with traces of two letters: two uprights, the first straight and the second bent outward at its ends, the typical way the scribe writes the η (e.g., 'Tithonus poem' line 8 αγΗρα[); then, traces of two more verticals, from the top of the first of which a descending oblique starts; as it seems, a ν. Obviously, an infinitive in -ην also depending on 5 εὔχομ(αι) just like 6 γέ[νεσθαι. West is right that the papyrus has π̣ε̣.[, not γε̣.[, but περ[ίσχ]οι is unlikely, since, apart from the ρ and the οι, which do not agree with the traces, it is also too short to cover the lacuna. I propose πεδ[ὰ ἴσχ]ην, i.e. πεδ' ἴσχην, 'to keep, to hold with me'. The *scriptio plena* is used for indicating the adverbial sense of πεδά and avert reading πεδίσχην. The supplement fills the gap exactly. [I now read πέρ[αισσ]αι. See above '1. Sappho Illustrated.]

8.]..ν ("runder, danach schmaler Buchstabe") *edd. pr.*; e.g. Μοίσει]ον West, ἔσ]λον Di Benedetto. At the beginning, a high curve suggests c. Following θ, with its somewhat bent ellipse, the scribe must have written initially ιν, possibly misled by the common λοίσθιον. He corrected his error straightaway by wiping off the iota, yet using its upper part as the left-hand side of the omicron, which was now, naturally, both smaller and closer to the following ny than usual. This is why the final product looks like a clumsy rho.

9.]. *edd. pr.*;]ζ West rightly, supplementing θαυμά]ζοιεν.

10. [α]ἴ κεν *edd. pr.* The tiny trace read as iota is too short for ι. It may well belong to a bottom tip of any short letter. I suggest the second curve of omega, because [δ]ῶκεν is naturally suggested by ἔλοισα. [θ]ῆκεν is less likely.

11.] . . . α . κάλα, Μοῖσ᾿, ἀείδω *edd. pr.*, who read in the beginning *fort.* χε]λύνναν. The *edd. pr.* discuss but dismiss καλάμοισ᾿; χε]λύνναν θαλάμοισ᾿ West.]λύνναν is impossible ('dissonante con la descrizione delle tracce' Di Benedetto). Following the first α, a long horizontal compatible with either π or τ, but with no vertical visible. A rightward bending oblique: α or λ. A horizontal at the same height as the previous one, perhaps a bit shorter. Following the third α, traces of a vertical with some uncertain ink marks at its top right-hand side; γ is possible. After them, traces of a long vertical; *edd. pr.*'s κ is possible. I read with some reservations]ατα τὰγ καλάμοισ᾿.

I would then propose the following text:

```
1                                ] . δα
2                                ]ξαι
3                                ]ξον
4                   ] . ουμ[
5    × – ⏑ ⏑ – – ⏑ ⏑ –] εὔχομ᾿ [⏑ – ⏑ – –
6    × – ⏑ ⏑ – ⏑ ⏑ ὠ]ς νῦν θαλ[ί]αν γέ[νεσθαι
7    × – ⏑ ⏑ – ⏑ ⏑ –]· νέρθε δὲ γᾶς πεδ[᾿ ἴσχ]ην
8    τὰν πᾶκτιν ἔμον λοῖ]σθον ἔχοισαν γέρας ὡς [ἔ]οικεν·
9    καὶ πάρ με φίλαι παί]ζοῖεν ὡς νῦν ἐπὶ γᾶς ἔοισαν."
10   πάραυτά μ᾿ Ἀβανθις] λιγύραν [δ]ῶκεν ἔλοισα πᾶκτιν·
11   εἶπον δ᾿· "ἔχε τάν· ἀλεμ]άτα τὰγ καλάμοισ᾿ ἀείδω."        ⊗
```

[...] I wish [...] that a festivity tak[es place] like now [...]; and, under the earth, that I [kee]p with me [the paktis] to have it suitably as [my la]st gift of honour. [And let my beloved girls pl]ay (dance, have fun) [at my side (at my house)] as now that I am upon earth." [Straightway Abanthis] took the clear-voiced paktis and gave it [to me]. [But I said "Keep it; slug]gish as I am, what I sing is reed songs."

The poem has so far been interpreted – and accordingly supplemented – as a reference to the honour bestowed on Sappho after death. Following West, who entitled the relevant part of his article 'Posthumous honour for Sappho', Di Benedetto, Hardie, Livrea, and Bettarini kept to the same path, each, however, with significant differences as to the extent of this posthumous repute: future generations, the afterworld, both future generations and the afterworld. Di Benedetto and Hardie, besides the references to Sappho's fragments that deal with the survival of the poetic honour, make also the most of Horace 2.13, where the Roman poet describes how, in a state of unconsciousness after a nasty accident, he found himself in Hades and saw there Sappho singing on the lyre her love songs, along with Alcaeus who sang his political faction songs, both to an audience of admiring shadows. More down-to-earth, Bettarini limits Sappho's interest to the present world, because, after death, even if honoured properly, she would not possess the admiration she now enjoys. None of these interpretations can be excluded, but, though I share Bettarini's manner of approach, I believe that the few different readings I claim to have made allow a different interpretation, perhaps more appropriate to the situation implied.

The singer speaks as if being at death's door, in a poem that is followed in the Cologne papyrus by another speaking of the tribulations of old age ('Tithonus poem', fr. 58.11–22), while the latter is followed in P.Oxy. 1787 by some verses (fr. 58.23–26) speaking possibly also of death (23 ?φθ]ιμέναν νομίσδει) and of the desire of being alive (26 ἔρως ἀελίω).[3] The verses preceding the Tithonus poem in P.Oxy. 1787 (fr. 58.1–10) are too damaged to associate with anyone of the topics belonging to this Sapphic cycle. However, Di Benedetto treating the theme of the poetic immortality mentions the famous Ennius distich repeatedly referred to by Cicero:

nemo me dacrumis decoret, nec funera fletu
faxit. quor? volito vivu' per ora virum.

He rightly connects the first part down to *faxit* with Sappho fr. 150, from Maximus Tyrius 18.9:

οὐ γὰρ θέμις ἐν μοισοπόλων <δόμωι>
θρῆνον ἔμμεν' <.......> οὔ κ' ἄμμι πρέποι τάδε.

"**1** μοισο- Blomf. : μουσοπόλων | δόμῳ Hartung (obl. Page 132) : οἰκίᾳ **2** ἔμμεν Wil., SS 20 (ἔμμεναι Blomf.) : εἶναι | L(obel) : οὐκ | πρέποι Steph., codd. ap. Heins. (Max. Tyr., Lugd. Bat. 1614) : πρέπει Ursin. (e cod. ?), rec. Ahr., Bgk., al.; τάδε πρέποι L., ut evitaretur correptio" Voigt

No doubt, 6 θαλίαν γένεσθαι in our poem, must also be associated, since what Sappho wishes is to have a festivity, not mourning, in her funeral. Di Benedetto finds no connection with Sappho in the second part of Ennius' distich, from *quor* to *virum*. But this part seems to be somehow related to fr. 58.9–10, the final verses of the poem preceding the Tithonus poem in P.Oxy. 1787. The verses are published as

---

3 See Appendix, below.

]μένα ταν[....ώ]νυμόν σε
]νι θῆται στ[ύ]μα[τι] πρόκοψιν.

With Di Benedetto's and Voigt's sound supplements (κεκλο]μένα τὰν [πολυώ]νυμόν σε ... θῆται), we have Sappho addressing as usually Aphrodite (for πολυώνυμον cf. Eur. *Hipp.* 1, Theoc. 15.109) and mentioning another female person who will call upon the goddess for aid, in order to promote or advance something (θῆται ... πρόκοψιν). Why should Sappho announce to Aphrodite that another female will call upon her requesting something? Apparently, because Sappho will not be able to make the request herself, therefore after her death. στ[ύ]μα[τι] was proposed by F. Stiebitz and accepted by Lobel and subsequent editors, who took the phrase to mean "in order to give success to her own mouth, i.e. her (whose?) poetry and singing". Another possibility would be to follow Hunt, who had published στ[ύ]μα[σι] in the plural. By supplementing then ἀνδρῶν ἔ]νι θῆται στ[ύ]μα[σι] πρόκοψιν, we have a close parallel to Ennius' verse: "(in order that), having called upon you, o goddess of many names, she promotes *x* in the mouths of men" = *per ora virum*. What she will promote is uncertain, but I believe that '(my) fame, (my) repute, (my) name' would be welcome, evidently in a genitive depending on πρόκοψιν. A word like κλεηδόνος would both scan in the beginning of a verse and give a reasonable sense. If πρόκοψιν ought to be qualified, e.g. ἀΐνναον, 'everlasting', the adjective should stand at the opening of the verse and κλεηδόνος with the necessary conjunction (ὡς?) should be removed to the opening of the previous verse. *Exempli gratia*, of course, I would propose:

κλεηδόνος ὡς, κεκλο]μένα τὰν [πολυώ]νυμόν σε,
ἀΐνναον ἀνδρῶν ἔ]νι θῆται στ[ύ]μα[σι] πρόκοψιν.

However, fr. 150, which patently shows the same topic of the moribund singer, has or rather is published in a different metre: tl^c | ̣ia gl in Lobel–Page, gl^{2c}? in Voigt. I believe that the following formulation in hag^{2c} is simpler and closer to the original text:

οὐ γὰρ θέμις ἐν μοισοπόλων θρηνέμεν· οὔ κεν ἄμμι
πρέποι τάδε.

'For it is not proper to lament in the house of Muse-attendants; these things would be unbecoming for us.' For the idiomatic ellipsis ἐν μοισοπόλων we read in Maximus ἐν μουσοπόλων οἰκίᾳ, with a word avoided in poetry (needlessly changed to δόμῳ by Hartung). A dactyl is needed for replacing Maximus' θρῆνον εἶναι. An infinitive like θρηνέμεν' might do, though the -μεναι infinitive, attested in the epic, occurs only in athematic verbs in Lesbian (ἔμμεναι, βάμεναι). One would normally expect θρήνην, but a legitimate epic form should not be banished from Lesbian poetry. οὐκ, already emended to οὐ κ' by Lobel, must expand to οὔ κεν. We cannot know whether the alterations were made in the process of the text's transmission in Maximus Tyrius or were deliberately made by the author. Not only is hag[2c] restored without supplements or gaps, but, very importantly, πρέποι τάδε, by being placed at the opening of the second verse, does not lengthen the previous syllable and need not have the words transposed as editors were formerly obliged to do (τάδε πρέποι Lobel, al.).

The fragment in Maximus Tyrius 18.9 is connected with Sappho's daughter: ἀναίθεται (sc. Σωκράτης) τῇ Ξανθίππῃ ὀδυρομένῃ ὅτι ἀπέθνησκεν, ἡ δὲ (sc. Σαπφώ) τῇ θυγατρί. Thus, with Kleïs, Sappho's daughter, appearing on the scene, we may speculate about the subject of 58.9–10, the female person who will promote, with Aphrodite's aid, Sappho's repute in the mouths of men after her death. It is not allowed to mourn in the house of a poet. So Kleïs is not supposed to grieve over her mother's loss, but must have another, more intellectual, duty, that of propagating Sappho's poetry and music. I cannot exclude that fr. 150 stood near the first lines of the poem of 58.1–10, but, in any case, it is most likely that it belongs to the hag[2c] cycle of poems in Sappho's Book 4 that speak of the poetess's old age and imminent death.[4]

To return to the P.Colon. poem, Di Benedetto's plausible reading of 5] εὔχομ' [shows that we are dealing with the expression of a wish by the singer, and that we should expect one or more infinitives specifying the object of her wish. 6 γέ[νεσθαι and 7 πεδ[' ἴσχ]ην [now πέρ[αισσ]αι; see above] are both possible. ὠ]ς νῦν θαλ[ί]αν γέ[νεσθαι would also specify the setting in which the poem's story evolves: a singing party, apparently of Sappho's young girls, in the presence of the old and ailing poetess, most likely at her home. For the singular θαλίαν, apart from Xenophanes *IEG* 1.12 referred to by *edd. pr.*, cf. also Archil. 11.2 καὶ θαλίαν ἐφέπων ("θαλίας Plut. : θάλειαν Tzetz. codd., unde θαλίαν Boissonade" West), where the subject is very similar. But ὠ]ς νῦν, combined with 7 νέρθε δὲ γᾶς, shows that Sappho is speaking of her funeral day, during which she wishes a festivity to take place 'just as now'. πεδ[' ἴσχ]ην, if correct, must denote either something material attached to herself in the grave or, figuratively, something abstract that she was supposed to maintain after her death. [νέρθε δὲ γᾶς πέρ[αισσ]αι, 'to pass to the underworld', is both palaeographically and sense-wise likelier.] However, the second wish was rather unlikely to be granted

---

[4] I believe that it is proper to start using the term 'cycle', employed in the Roman lyric poetry scholarship, also for Sappho's poetry.

by the people close to her as the first one, but had to be fulfilled by the gods. Also, the reference to a last gift of honour in line 8 (cf. [Theocr.] 23.20 f. δῶρα ... λοίσθια, Nonn. Dion. 11.239–241 δῶρον ... λοίσθιον, IG 14.1721 λοισθοτάτας χάριτας) and the mention of a musical instrument in line 10 make the possibility of a material object, namely the musical instrument itself, very likely. The name of the musical instrument should be found in the beginning of the verse. πᾶκτις, was already found twice in Sappho's fragments. 156.1 is only a reference to the melodious sound of the instrument. But 22.10–11 comes from an internal scene at Sappho's milieu: the poetess bids Ἄβανθις to take the paktis and sing of her beloved Gongyla, who had departed from the group (in the brilliant restoration of M.L. West, *Maia* 22, 1970, 319). It seems, however, that the paktis was not just another instrument among those named by Sappho. The harp-like instrument, whose origin was connected by many sources with Lydia (West, *Ancient Greek Music*, 71 n. 101), is elsewhere connected personally with her: fr. 247 V. from Ath. 14.635b Μέναιχμος δ' ἐν τοῖς περὶ Τεχνιτῶν (fr. 5 Müll.) τὴν πηκτίδα, ἣν τὴν αὐτὴν εἶναι τῇ μαγάδιδι, Σαπφώ φησιν εὑρεῖν ..., 635e καὶ τὴν Σαπφὼ δέ φησιν οὗτος, ἥτις ἐστὶν Ἀνακρέοντος πρεσβυτέρα, πρώτην χρήσασθαι τῇ πηκτίδι. It is aimless to speculate whether Sappho was the inventor or the introducer or the innovator of the instrument, but a personal, possibly emotional, relation with it cannot be doubted. Menaechmus' source must have been none other than Sappho's poems. If so, the paktis would be the most suitable object (ὡς ἔοικεν) to accompany Sappho in her grave as a last gift of honour (ἔμον λοῖ]σθον ... γέρας); and not just any paktis, but her own paktis, so justifying the definite article before it. Musical instruments are a common find in ancient tombs, the latter sometimes dubbed 'the poet's tomb' or 'the musician's tomb'.

Within this context, it would be hazardous to theorize about Sappho's desire to continue to sing in Hades in front of the blessed shadows, though the placing of the instrument in the tomb certainly implies such an unexpressed aspiration. We still are inside Sappho's close environment, and the poetess speaks of the θαλία she wants to have on the day of her funeral. παίζω, apart from the general sense 'have fun', is also used both of dancing (*Od.* 8.251, Dipylon oinochoe graffito, *al.*) and of playing on a musical instrument (*h. Ap.* 206, Ar. *Ra.* 230, *al.*); K. Dover, *Aristophanes Frogs*, pp. 57–59. This is exactly what Sappho wants, with the optative of wish, from the girls to do by her side, just as they used to do before. Of course, πάρ με φίλαι παί]ζοῖεν ὡς νῦν ἐπὶ γᾶς ἔοισαν implies, just like 3 ὡ]ς νῦν θαλ[ί]αγ γέ[νεσθαι, that the girls' party is now on. On hearing these words, a girl took the paktis and gave it to Sappho to accompany their singing and dancing. We do not know who she is, but a proper name is here indispensable. She might well be Κλεΐς, Sappho's daughter, given the fragment 150. πάραυτά μ(οι)

Ἄβανθις] is published entirely *exempli gratia*, the specific girl's name being used first because it scans in the gap, second because it recurs in 22.10–11 combined with the paktis, and third because it also recurs at inc. auct. 35.8 (].ιν ὄρχησθ[˙ ἐρό]εσσ᾽ Ἄβανθι), which not only is obviously Sappho's but is also, in all likelihood, written in hag[2c].

There can be scores of possible supplements for the terminal verse, but the gist must be that the poetess rejects the offer, stating that what she can sing belongs to the domain of wind instruments. The direct words of the poetess are actually the 'pointe' of the song: "Keep it; sluggish as I am, what I sing is pipe songs". Pragmatically, the difference between paktis- and pipe-playing is, of course, that the first is normally played by the singer herself, whereas the second needs to be played by a piper who accompanies the singer. And Sappho, infirm as she is, cannot play the paktis. The construction is τὰ ἐν καλάμοισιν ἀειδόμενα ἀείδω. For ἐν + dative of instrument + 'sing', cf., e.g., Telestes *PMG* 810 πρῶτοι ... ἐν αὐλοῖς ... Φρύγιον ἄεισαν νόμον; it is remarkable that the Selinuntian poet of dithyrambs juxtaposes Phrygian auletic music with Lydian hymns sung accompanied on the paktis; cf. also Pi. *Ol.* 5.19 Λυδίοις ἀπύων ἐν αὐλοῖς; *I.* 5.27 κλέονται δ᾽ ἔν τε φορμίγγεσσιν ἐν αὐλῶν τε παμφώνοις ὁμοκλαῖς. But the essence of the closing words is that her song cannot be but sorrowful, unsuited for a stringed instrument like the paktis. The references in tragedy to threnodic music as ἄλυρος, ἀφόρμικτος, ἀκίθαρις, meaning auletic, are numerous. τυμβαύλης was the piper employed in funerals for accompanying the dirges. Soph. fr. 849 R. is striking: ἔναυλα κωκυτοῖσιν, οὐ λύρα, φίλα. Obviously, Sophocles' ἔναυλα = Sappho's τὰ ἐν καλάμοισι. The story goes back to Echembrotus, the Arcadian aulode, who in 586 B.C., when Sappho was probably still alive, was expelled from the Pythian contest, both himself and his sort of music, because the sound of aulody was deemed to be inauspicious. In the words of Pausanias, 10.7.5, ἡ γὰρ αὐλῳδία μέλη τε ἦν αὐλῶν τὰ σκυθρωπότατα καὶ ἐλεγεῖα {θρῆνοι} προσᾳδόμενα τοῖς αὐλοῖς. It is this mood created by καλάμοισ᾽ that suggests ἀλεμ]άτα, in a gap where many different supplements might be considered (ἐράτα, ἀθανάτα, or superlatives: e.g. κεδνοτάτα *et sim.*). Be that as it may,] ἀλεμάτ[is used by Sappho, 26.5, though it is uncertain if it is used of herself or of her adversaries, and in what sense. At Alc. 70.4 it is used of the poet's enemies, Pittacus' buddies, who are described as ἀλέματοι, the word being usually translated as 'foolish' or 'idle', a rendering that depends on the connection with ἠλεός, 'insane', + μάταιος, 'vain', recorded in the Etymologica and other lexica. The meaning 'idle' is good enough, but the closest sense seems to be 'inert, sluggish, weak, frail'. Theocr. 15.4 ὦ τᾶς ἀλεμάτω ψυχᾶς is translated 'What a helpless thing I am!' (Gow), but the scholia *ad loc.* translate ἐπίπονος, apparently in the sense 'sensitive to fatigue, easily exhausted' found in Theophr. *Sens.* 11. For the form in -άτα cf. Synes. *Hymn.* 1.636 ἀλεμάτας (γᾶς), perhaps = 'inert, lacking (spiritual) vigour'. Synesius was well versed in Aeolic poetry; *Eikasmos* 19 (2008) 47 f.

The poem ends with ἀείδω, without expounding whether Sappho did eventually sing to the sound of pipes or not. A pragmatist might claim that pipes and pipers were not available in Sappho's house at the time; and a rationalist that a lamentation would conflict with her interdict against wailings in a poet's house so forcefully expressed in fr. 150. Strictly, the prohibition is against wailings in a dead poet's house, and Sappho is still alive. But literally speaking, she is breaching the prohibition herself, since she is right now singing the song we are dealing with, and the song is sorrowful and lugubrious, as is the whole cycle it belongs to. Insofar as we do not know Sappho's music, we cannot know whether the song would be accompanied by pipes or not. What matters most is that τὰν καλάμοισ᾽ ἀείδω is no more than a figurative way for a lyric poet to say "I am at death's door".

Appendix: The ἀβροσύνα verses

The Tithonus poem is followed in P.Oxy. 1787 by some verses believed to be speaking also of death (23 φθ]ιμέναν νομίσδει, as supplemented already by Hunt) and of the desire of being alive (ἔρως ἀελίω, as interpreted by the Peripatetic Clearchus, fr. 41 Wehrli from Ath. 15.687b). It has been adequately discussed (with different supplements and interpretations proposed), whether these verses, possibly also with the addition of the three relics of verses in fr. 59 V., constitute the opening of a new poem – perhaps even a complete tetrastichal poem – or the conclusion of the Tithonus poem, which was, for some unknown reason, omitted in the Cologne papyrus.[5] The surviving evidence is, to my mind, inconclusive. Intuitively – if such an approach could be relied upon – I would side with the end-of-poem interpretation. It is difficult to believe that Sappho ended referring to her personal case with "but what could I possibly do?" The mythical exemplum should normally provide a counterpart for her own situation. The Tithonus story teaches that it would be unwise to ask for immortality, much less for everlasting youth. The most she may expect from her beloved goddess is health and a postponement of the fated end. *Exempli gratia,*

---

[5] For references to the discussion and the several proposals, see Livrea (2007).

pap. 23 καὶ Κύπρις ἔοικός με σάων μὴ φθ]ιμέναν νομίσδει,   13 Tith.
24 αἴθ' ὡς ὑγιείαν ἐράταν ἀγλαΐσ]αισ' ὀπάσδοι.   14
25 ₍ἔγω δὲ …   15

σάων: inf. of σάωμι = σαόω, 'keep safe, preserve'; *Il.* 21.238 ζωοὺς σάω | αἴθ' ὡς … ὀπάσδοι: cf. *Il.* 7.157, al. εἴθ' ὡς ἡβώοιμι | ἀγλαΐσ]αισ': 'honouring me'.

"And if the Cyprian goddess deems it proper to retain me not dead, let her honour me by granting the beloved health. But I etc." The wish for personal health does not impair her love of ἀβροσύνα, which must be the point emphasized in the poem. The subjects underlying ἀβροσύνα are the παῖδες of the opening verses, who are actually forgotten after ten verses that described Sappho's sufferings and the Tithonus myth. They are endowed with Μοίσαν ἰ]οκ[ό]λπων κάλα δῶρα and are possibly singing and playing the φιλάοιδον λιγύραν χελύνναν. To them must Sappho return in ring composition and declare that, in her eyes, her love of staying alive is tantamount to her love of ἀβροσύνα, a property embodying beauty and splendour as attributes not only of the girls, but also of their pursuits, i.e. singing and dancing. "If I wish to stay alive, it is only for enjoying your loveliness." And the parenthetic (hence omitted by Clearchus) clause of 25, must be Di Benedetto's ἴστε δὲ τοῦτο, addressed directly to the παῖδες of the first verse.[6]

pap. 25 ₍ἔγω δὲ φίλημμ' ἀβροσύναν,₎ [ἴστε δὲ] τοῦτο, καί μοι   15 Tith.
26 τὸ λά₍μ₎προν ἔρως ἀελίω καὶ τὸ κά₍λ₎ον λέ₍λ₎ογχε.   16

Whether the three mutilated verses of fr. 59 V. open a new poem or continue the Tithonus poem, I cannot say. The paragraphos above its second verse (the first verse belongs to the opening of fr. 58.26) is exactly similar to the paragraphoi that divide distichs of the same poem, and does not seem to be a remnant of the coronis that separates different poems in the same papyrus. Yet, the visible evidence is too meagre to lead to certain conclusions.

---

[6] Cf. similar parenthetic clauses in Sappho, 26.11–12 ἔγω δ' ἔμ' ₍αὔται | τοῦτο σύ₎νοιδα; 27.8–9 εὖ δ' ἐ[πίστε₍αι | κα]ὶ σὺ τοῦτ'; 60.9 σὺ δ' εὖ γὰρ οἶσθα, 88.13 (Steinrück) τοῦ[τ- ‿‿—‿‿—] συνίη₍σθα καὔτα.

3 Kleïs as Promoter of Sappho's Poetry (Fr. 59 V.)

(Fr. 58 V.)

⟨φθ⟩ιμέναν νομίσδει
14   ]αις ὀπάσδοι.
⌊ἔγω δὲ φίλημμ' ἀβροσύναν,⌋ [ἴστε δὲ] ⌊τοῦτο, καί μοι⌋
16   τὸ λά⌊μπρον ἔρως ἀελίω καὶ τὸ κά⌋λον λέ⌊λ⌋ογχε.   ⊗?

Fr. 59 V.

ἐπῖν[   ].[. . .]γό.[
2 (18) φίλει.[
καιν[

The end of the Tithonus Poem is interrupted in PColon. 21351 at line 12. For the rest we resort to POxy. 1787. The distich 13–14 is mutilated, but it is clear that, after the mythological exemplum of the love between the immortally youthful Dawn (since she is born every new day) and the everlastingly aging Tithonus, Sappho must be adapting the exemplum to her own case.

νομίσδει ... ὀπάσδοι seem to belong to a conditional sentence (protasis in present indicative, apodosis in optative). Both parts of the sentence must share the same subject, and since ὀπάσδοι usually expresses granting by the gods of something requested, the one who is called on to offer something can well be a god/goddess: 'let him/her grant'. The preceding]αις may be the ending of a participle, i.e. -σ]αις or -σ]αισ', connected with the god/goddess in question, but can also be an elided fem. pl. dative, -αισ(ι). I would imagine something like: 'If the god regards me as due to die, let him/her grant me the gratification of dying in your company.' The poem starts with young girls singing and dancing, while Sappho declares that she is unable to join, as she would like to, because of her age problems. It is reasonable then that the poem's cycle would close accordingly. Lines 15–16 convey exactly this sense: 'For me life is worth only when it is linked with beauty (τὸ καλόν)'. The distich seems really to close the poem. The idea that Sappho prays to die while being in company with her beloved girls is manifest in the poem that is written before the Tithonus poem in PColon. 21351, i.1–11: 7] ˌ · νέρθε δὲ γᾶς πέρ[αισσ]αι̣ | (8 ...) | 9 καὶ πάρ με φίλαι παί]ζοῖεν ὡς νῦν ἐπὶ γᾶς ἔοισαν (suppl. Ts.).[1]

The sequence in POxy. 1787 is separated from the distich by the end of a stroke which is similar to the usual paragraphos that divides the distichs, though slightly longer, if compared with the next stroke under φίλει[, which is undoubtedly a paragraphos. The end of the protruding middle horizontal stroke of a coronis cannot be excluded.[2] If a paragraphos, we would have sequence of the same poem, if a coronis, the beginning of a new poem. What is really going on can be shown only by the sense of the relics of text and primarily by the first line of what Lobel-Page and Voigt separate as fr. 59. Are we dealing with the opening of a new poem or with lines 17–19 of the Tithonus poem?

However, ἐπῖν[remained undeciphered. The only options seemed to be either the verbal imperfect forms ἐπῖν[ομεν, -ετε, the Lesbian of which is, however, ἐπώνομεν, -ετε, or completely irrelevant phrases like ἐπ᾽ Ἴναχον or ἐπ᾽ ἰνίον.[3] There was, however, another choice, which was closely linked to the themes of Sappho's book of 'epithanatians'. I propose

ἔπ᾽ ἰν[ις ἐμοί,

= ἔπεστί μοι θυγάτηρ. The sense conveyed by ἔπι is quite different than ἔστι in, e.g., Sa. 132 ἔστι μοι κάλα πάις. There, ἔστι μοι = 'I have, I own', projects a feeling of pride and pleasure; here, ἔπεστί μοι, almost = 'what remains for me is' (LSJ s.v. ἔπειμι (A) II of Time, *to be hereafter, remain*), a glimmer of hope within utter loneliness.[4] The latter is the feeling generally projected in the book of 'epithanatians'. But the introduction of Sappho's daughter, Kleïs, is more significant, because she is a person emblematic of another theme that torments Sappho in the same book: her posthumous fame as a poet. Sappho, as it seems, assigns the task of promoting her fame to her daughter. The idea can be corroborated if the next verse starts with

φίλεισ[ά με.

---

1 Above, in '2. Sappho on her Funeral Day', I read and supplemented the infinitive πέραισσαι differently.
2 Lundon (2007).
3 ἐπ᾽ Ἰνδ-, apart from being irrelevant, would not need the longum sign in the papyrus.
4 Cf. *Od.* 2.58–9 (= 17.537–8) οὐ γὰρ ἔπ᾽ ἀνήρ, | οἷος Ὀδυσσεὺς ἔσκεν, ἀρὴν ἀπὸ οἴκου ἀμῦναι.

The indeterminate low tip following φίλει may well belong to the low angle of a straight-lined C, as is usually written by the scribe of POxy. 1787; e.g., Sa. 62.7 μύγιC, 63.4 χῶριC, al.

In fr. 150 V., Kleïs is involved in her mother's poetic legacy:

οὐ γάρ θέμις ἐν μοισοπόλων θρηνέμεν· οὔ κ⟨εν⟩ ἄμμι
πρέποι τάδε.

Maximus Tyrius, 18.9 p. 232 Hob., the source of the fragment, relates that Sappho is infuriated at her daughter's mourning for her impending death, because it is improper to lament in a poet's house. Obviously, what is implied is that the poetic gift ensures immortality for the Muses-attendant. Fr. 58.1–10 V. certainly comes from the same book, possibly even from the same poem.

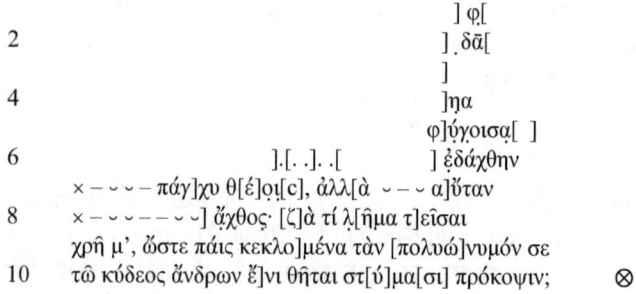

The addressee is Aphrodite, to whom Sappho, after recovering from a serious illness (5 ? ἐκ θανάτω φ]ύγοισα), must have recounted her anger (6 ἐδάχθην, 'I was irritated') at her daughter's plaintive reaction and, apparently, tried to find excuses for her misbehaviour: 'it was the load of grief that misled her' (7–8, e.g., ἀ[λλὰ παράγαγ' α]ὔταν [...] ἄχθος). The ode closes with Sappho asking Aphrodite what she should do, so that, after her demise, her daughter could achieve a posthumous advancement (10 θῆται ... πρόκοψιν) of her fame in the mouths of men (10 ἀνδρῶν ἔ]νι ... στ[ύ]μα[σι] = Ennius *var*. 18 Vahl. *per ora virum*).[5]

Fr. 62 V., is a poem of unusual mood, in fact a rebuke against her former pupils who lived in Lesbos, but avoided visiting her during her illness. When they eventually pay her a visit, she scolds them angrily and ironically for their fearful reaction toward approaching death. She says that she feels deserted but for a single person:

---

5 See above '1. Sappho Illustrated'.

μύγις δέ ποτ' εἰσάιον· ἐκλ[ιμπάνετε (*vel* ἐκλείπετε)
8   ψύχα δ' ἀγαπάτα συν[' (*fort.* συν[έπασχ(ε))

'I hardly ever heard your sound; you des(erted me) [...], but my only-begotten soul comm(iserated with me)'. ψύχα functions as an endearing term for 'beloved child'; cf. Eur. *Andr.* 419 πᾶσι δ' ἀνθρώποις ἄρ' ἦν ψυχὴ τέκν(α); Hel. *Aeth.* 1.8.4 ὦ φιλτάτη καὶ ψυχὴ ἐμὴ Χαρίκλεια.[6]

In any case, the two themes of moribund Sappho, that of the affection she craved for youthful beauty and that of the role she entrusted to Kleïs for the posthumous propagation of her poetry, could not cohabit in the same poem. I confidently believe that fr. 59 V. opened a new poem.

If ἔπ' ἴν[ις ἐμοί is, as I believe, the opening of a new poem, does the initial E affect the theory that P.Oxy. 1787 adheres to the principle of alphabetic arrangement of the poems? We miss the opening of the Tithonus poem, which is the preceding poem, but thanks to the Cologne papyrus we can possibly reconstruct it. I have proposed Μοίσαν ἐπιδείξασθ' ἰ]οκ[ό]λπων κάλα δῶρα παῖδες, an opening that would disprove the theory, if M was prior to E in the poems' order.[7] However, the possibility that the first word was an imperative starting with a letter from A to E and the second word Μοίσαν cannot be excluded (e.g., ἐκδείξατε Μοίσαν ἰ]οκ[ό]λπων κάλα δῶρα παῖδες). In any case, I strongly doubt that P.Oxy. 1787 adheres to the alphabetic principle, since, in the only manifest instance of two consecutive poems that have their first verses intact, the initials are ε (fr. 62 ἐπτάξατε) and ο (fr. 63 Ὄνοιρε), and it is hard to believe that in a whole book of Sappho no poem started with a letter between ε and ο.[8]

---

6 I had explained the phrase differently in the past, but I was wrong; see above '1. Sappho Illustrated'.
7 '1. Sappho Illustrated'.
8 Dale (2015), esp. 19 n. 29, notes the same argument, though he claims that 'this point shouldn't be pressed too far'. In support of his view, he strangely presents the case of Pindar's epinicians, which, if arranged alphabetically, would have eleven (twelve in my counting) poems intervening between ε and ο.

4 Sappho's (?) Orpheus Song

P.Colon. 21351+21376.21–33 (MP⁹ 1449.01, *LDAB* 10253)

Papyrus, Script, Date

Two extremely mutilated ends of verses, that followed the Tithonus poem in P.Colon. 21351, were partly supplemented with 21376, which provided the first part of the verses, but also the left-hand half of the text following, in a length of eleven more lines – a new poem whose surviving part extended to thirteen papyrus lines. The new poem, written in a different hand, was separated from the Tithonus poem by a slightly larger interlinear space, a paragraphos, longer than the usual ones that divided the distichs of the previous poem, and an unusual sign in the left-hand margin of the first verse, described as standing for a coronis that marked the beginning of a new poem. Since, as far as I can see, I follow a completely different approach to the poem than all the articles I have consulted,[1] I hope to be forgiven for avoiding to discuss former proposals on the subject, though I do not neglect to mention the different readings and supplements of the scholars in the commentary.

Below, I print my diplomatic transcription of the text, somewhat different than the original edition by M. Gronewald and R.W. Daniel in *ZPE* 154 (2005), 7–12, and *Kölner Papyri*, Band 11 (*Papyrologica Coloniensia* vol. VII/11) 2007, no. 429, pp. 1–11.

```
         ψιθυροπλοκεδολιεμυθωναυτουργ[
                  οι γε
2        επιβουλεπαι[[βογολ[...]ετ[....]ακ[..]η[
         εταιρεαφερπω:δ[
4        [[προςμακρον]]: τ[
         [.]χαν:απνουςπρο[
6        [.]αοιςα[[c]]τερωντε[
         [.]ςπυριφεγγεοςαελ[
8        [.]επαςακουω:θρα[
         [.]ρουκορονορφεακ[
10       [..]πεταπαντακ[
```

---

[1] Gronewald/Daniel (2004); idd. (2005); Del Corso (2004), 48–49, n. 61; Esposito (2005); Magnani (2005); Rawles (2006); Lundon (2007); Gronewald/Daniel (2007); Yatromanolakis (2008); Puglia (2008); Bierl (2009); Hammerstaedt (2011); Clayman (2011). If I have missed some articles about the Orpheus poem, I apologize for the omissions.

12 [.]ϲτανερατανλα[
    [..]φθογγονλυραν.ι[
    [..]νεργονεχοιϲαπαν[

The first thing that immediately strikes the eye is the writing of the text. Unlike that of the two former poems, which was highly proficient, this one is a product, if not exactly of a cacographer, at least of an untidy and disorderly hand. Judging from the fact that the first scribe uses old epigraphic character forms (square zeta, dotted theta), or old forms among modern ones (often square epsilons among curvilinear ones; once a Timotheus type omega [col. i 9 Ωϲνυν], once an in-between form [col. ii 3 θαμεΩϲ], regularly a curvilinear one), but only lunar sigma, one may deduce that he is rather aged, professional, and certainly practised. On the contrary, the second scribe is unable to keep a steady layout. Though continuing the same column with the first scribe (col. ii), he does not align the text with the former portion of the column, his surviving left-hand margin extends outward, his line-height is larger,[2] the size of his letters is unsteady. The elegance of the first scribe's handwriting is utterly opposed to the second one's clumsiness. J. Hammerstaedt, who gave a thorough account on the two scribes and their handwriting with fully elucidating figures, rightly compares the second of them with the scribe of *GMAW* 30, whose hand is similarly described by E.G. Turner: "Varying alignment, stance, and size of letters show the scribe's relative lack of skill." Still, I believe that the appraisal of our scribe's performance is much too lenient. Both he and the scribe of *GMAW* 30 are low on expertise, say young schoolboys, but young schoolboys can be good or poor; and our student is clearly poor. Even the shapes of his letters are often unlike each other. I have counted c. 7 different epsilons and c. 5 different sigmas. If to these traits we add his extraordinary carelessness, as is evident from his repeated deletions of text written erroneously, and his neglect, as we shall see, of the metrical presentation of the greatest part of the poem, we may definitely assess his competence at a very low level. In spite of the differences in the script, I would follow most of the scholars who date the writing of both texts in the Cologne papyrus to the first half of the third century BC.[3] As for the level of the scribe's erudition, the assessment depends on whether the errors I claim to have detected will be accepted or not. The same acceptance will also dictate whether the text can be regarded as the autograph of a

---

2 Puglia (2008a), 16–17, reckons that the space of the 13 lines of the second scribe, can accommodate 15 lines of the first.

3 As proposed by Yatromanolakis (2008), 248 ff., who made a meticulous description of the two hands. My only reservations would pertain to his highlighted '*perhaps*', 247, as regards the second scribe's carelessness.

poet or a provisional version of a poem noted down by the poet himself on a blank space left in a Sappho roll.⁴

Only for making my subsequent technical arguments understood, I preprint the final text I am proposing, without commenting in advance on my proposals.

1 «μυθοπλόκε, ψιθύρων δολίων αὐτούργ', |² ἐπίβουλε
2 παῖ βροτολ̣οιγέ' τ' ["Ερω, κ]ακ[ότ]η̣[τος] |³ ἑταῖρε, ἀφέρπω.»
3 δ[
3a |⁴ [[πρὸς μακρὸν]]
4 τ[|⁵ ἀ]χὰν
5 ἄπνους ⌊πρὸ[ς μακρὸν⌋ Διὸς αἰθέρα]
6 |⁶ [λ]αοις ἀ[[c]]τέρων τε [φωτῶν,]
7 |⁷ [ἐ]ς πυριφεγγέος ἀελ.[ίου σέλας]
8 [ἄστρων |⁸ τ'] ἐπαεῖς' ἀκούω
9 Θρά[ϊκος Οἰά|⁹γ]ρου κόρον Ὀρφέα
10 κ[αὶ Καλλιόπας λιγείας.]
11 |¹⁰ [ἑρ]πετὰ πάντα κ[λαῖε κακὸν μόρον,]
12 |¹¹ [ἅ]ς τὰν ἐρατὰν λα[βοῖς' ἅλς]
13 |¹² [εὔ]φθογγόν <τε> λύραν κι[θάριζ' ἔτι]
14 |¹³ [cυ]νεργὸν ἔχοιcα πάν[ται]
    [Θραϊκίαν ἄνεμον]

Metre

Something else that must be specified is no doubt the metre. The width of the column in the papyrus was predetermined by the previous scribe, whose texts consisted of long verses (ₐhipp²ᶜ = 16 syllables) each occupying a single line. In my judgement, the scribe of the present poem started with two dactylic hexameters, roughly equal to the former verses (16 syllables in the first verse, 17 in the second). His writing was, however, disordered and quite spacious, and so he must have left wide spaces at the missing ends of the first two lines (as they are known to us from the previous poem), for fear that he would be unable to accommodate complete words there. So, he was forced to break the hexameters and write the last word of the first in his second line and the last two of the second in his third line. This disorder affected also the writing of the purely lyrical part of the poem, which, again in my judgement, consisted of stanzas of two cola, one long, but shorter than a hexameter, and one short. The condition worsened because of the serious lack of attention by the scribe, who deleted some words in

---

4 Puglia (2008a), 16, and Clayman (2011), n. 59, depending on a conjecture of Lundon (2007), 159–60, n. 49.

lines 2 and 4, deletions that necessitated, at least in the case of 4, rewriting the correct text. So, the scribe, whose assignment was, as it seems, to write each colon, long or short, in distinct lines and separate the distichs by a paragraphos, was forced to write the text as if καταλογάδην and to resort to dicola for indicating the end of the distichs. I strongly believe that this was the function of dicolon in the present papyrus, and has nothing to do with changes of speakers or singers.[5] This was mainly done down to line 4. From 5 on, even if the line is not occupied wholly by one verse, there is, at least, an attempt to end the lines with a complete verse, as in lines 5 and 9 which start with a remainder of the previous verses. But, whenever the layout allowed, the scribe wrote the whole verses in separate lines, as in 6, 10, 11, 12, 13. Granted that my supplements are correct, the most copious of the countable lines must have been lines 5 and 7 with 30 characters, the least copious line 6 with 19 characters. The 30 characters of lines 5 and 7 are not an impossible number, if compared with the 35 characters of line 2 of the hexameters or the 40 of line 10 of the Tithonus poem, written in the same column, but in a slightly smaller size of letters. This means that not all lines were flush with the missing right-hand margin. The long verse usually occupies the whole line till its end, the short one a little more than its half. Still, sometimes, because of the scribe's negligence, the καταλογάδην format returned, as in the end of 7 and 8. Naturally, this disorder will affect also our line numbering, which, in the poetic edition, is different from the one of the diplomatic transcription. I have tried to refer to the lines of the diplomatic transcription as 'lines', to those of the poetic edition as 'verses'.

As I mentioned above, the poem, in my restoration proposal, starts with two dactylic hexameters. Their transmission problems will be discussed later. The hexametric distich is separated from the lyric part by dicolon. The strictly lyric part from verse 3 on is strophic, each stanza consisting of two cola: an acatalectic dactylic tetrameter (–⏗–⏗–⏑⏑–⏑⏑ : 4 da) and, separated by word-end, an acephalous hipponactean or, in West's terminology, hagesichorean (×–⏑⏑–⏑–– : ˎhipp = hag). The contractions noted in the dactylic part are those visible or reconstructed in the few extant verses (5, 9, 11, 13). The dactylic tetrameter is combined, in spite of the word-end, by synapheia with the acephalous hipponactean. Both cola are separately common in the archaic lyric poetry. E.g., both occur in Alcman, the

---

5 As proposed by Rawles (2006). Lundon (2007), 156 n. 32, regardless of his different approach, is close to this view; cf. 161 f. The *Fragmentum Grenfellianum*, also written καταλογάδην, may present a similar attempt of its scribe to offer a text κεκωλιϲμένον, though the dicola and the paragraphoi do not always agree with our concept of metrical units; Esposito (2005) 11–12, 28–29.

dactylic tetrameter in Archilochus epodes, the acephalous hipponactean is found κατὰ μέτρον in Sa. 168B, the δέδυκε μὲν ἀ cελάννα poem, and is a common constituent of Sapphic metres. However, I was not able to find other occurrences of their combined presence. The fact that the dactylic part admits contraction, whereas the Aeolic part (acephalous hipponactean) does not, is a usual feature of epodic metres. The scribe apparently considers the combined cola of a stanza single metrical units, since, just as he does at the end of the hexametric distich (ἀφέρπω:), he places a dicolon after the acephalous hipponactean (4 ἀ]χάν:, 8 ἀκούω:), but not after the dactylic tetrameter (9 Ὀρφέα).

The device of joining, in a metrically unusual manner, in a sort of rhythmical syncopation, a dactylic tetrameter with a colon that starts with a non-princeps, especially short Aeolic cola (penthemimers), is usually connected with drama and, specifically, with Sophocles (West, *GM* 129–30). The earliest occurrence seems, however, to be the verses attributed to Terpander (*PMG* 697; cf. Ar. fr. 591.55 K.–A.):

ἀμφί μοι αὖτις (*vel* αὖτε) ἄναχθ' ἑκατηβόλον | ἀειδέτω φρήν

(–⏑⏑–⏑⏑–⏑⏑–⏑⏑|⏑–⏑––: 4 da | pe). The combined cola, obviously constituting the proem of a song, are referred to as example of the Terpandrian citharodic ὄρθιος νόμος (Su. α 1701 al.). The latter is also related with the κατὰ δάκτυλον εἶδος (Glaucus Rheg., *FHG* 2, fr. 3). Another dactylic tetrameter was attributed by Aristarchus to Terpander (*SLG* 6 Page, Ar. fr. 590.19 K.–A.):

κύκνος ὑπὸ πτερύγων τοιόνδε τι (–⏑⏑–⏑⏑–⏖–⏑⏑|),

obviously followed by some form of ἀείδω ('*sc. cantat*' K.–A.). I would propose, e.g., μ' ἄειδεν ἄρτι (μ' = μοι), though a longer colon cannot be excluded. The poet is supposedly reproducing the swan song; cf. Ar. *Av.* 769 ff. Both tetrameters are the openings of songs and seem to have served, unaltered or varied, as proems to odes or antodes in comic parabases. The melody of the ὄρθιος νόμος must have been strained to a high pitch or volume, as shown both by its name (cf. Aesch. *Ag.* 1153) and by description (ἀνατεταμένως: Timachidas quoted in Sch. Ar. *Ran.* 1282).

This is not the place to discuss whether the verses attributed to Terpander are authentic or not, but the similarity with the papyrus poem is striking. The only difference is the colon attached to the dactylic tetrameter, which is not a penthemimer but an acephalous hipponactean. To put it down in a different metrical notation, the stanza is not 4 da | pe, but 4 da | pe^d, with the usual in Lesbian poetry dactylic expansion. The salient feature of the rhythmical syncopation is retained. However, the commonest combination of 4 da, especially in late lyric poetry, is with another expansion of the penthemimer, the ithyphallic, which starts, however, with a princeps: $-\cup-\cup--$, ith or, put differently, $-$pe.

Be that as it may, the metre of the Orpheus poem can be considered cognate also with that of the other two poems of the Cologne papyrus. These poems are written κατὰ μέτρον in expanded acephalous hipponacteans ($_{\smile}$hipp^{2c}), whereas the Orpheus poem is strophic, with the simple acephalous hipponactean ($_{\smile}$hipp) as one of its two constituents. The double choriambic expansion serves, apart from other rhythmic criteria, also the enlargement of the narrative space. The same goal is achieved, though with different rhythmic effects, through the dactylic tetrameter of the Orpheus poem. Though the distinction between strophic and κατὰ μέτρον poems is evident, it is significant that the latter are presented in the papyri as couplets – greater musical units? – separated with paragraphoi; Hephaestion *Poëm*. 1.2, p. 63 C.

The expanded acephalous hipponacteans of the first two poems of the Cologne papyrus ('Sappho's funeral day', 'Tithonus poem') are manifestly written in Sappho's advanced age. So is also the poem that precedes the Tithonus poem in P.Oxy. 1787 (Sa. 58.1–10) as well as fr. 150, which patently shows the same topic of the moribund singer.[6] These poems were placed first by Hunt and then by the subsequent editors in Sappho's fourth book. I strongly doubt this placement, which is based on extremely fragile evidence. The only argument for it is the supposition that all the books that were metrically homogeneous must be placed together. So, since each of the first three books is metrically homogeneous and the fifth heterogeneous, it follows that POxy. 1787, which seems to contain poems of the same metre, must be placed in the fourth book. Moreover, according to Hephaestion's testimony (*Poëm*. 1.2, p. 63 C.), the metre of Books Two and Three is a two-line stanza consisting of a repetition of the same verse (gl^{2d} for Book II and gl^{2c} for III). Hunt argues that since POxy. 1787 consists of similar two-line stanzas of the same verse ($_{\smile}$hipp^{2c}), it follows that the poems of the papyrus must belong to the Book immediately adjacent to II and III, therefore IV. However, Hephaestion, speaking about the two-line stanzas, does not refer to Book IV and supplements his description of $_{\smile}$hipp^{2c} with the statement (*Ench*. 11.5, p. 36 C.) καλεῖται δὲ Αἰολικόν, ὅτι Σαπφὼ πολλῷ αὐτῷ ἐχρήσατο. I am elsewhere attempting to show that the seventh book consists of metrically heterogeneous epithalamians and thus is entitled Ἐπιθαλάμια, the eighth book consists of a small number of metrically homogeneous epithalamians of a different character than those of the

---

6 See above '2. Sappho on her funeral Day', for the interpretation of 58.1–10 and the metrical restoration of fr. 150, and '1. Sappho Illustrated', for the advanced age poetry of Sappho.

seventh book; finally, the ninth book consists of the old-age or rather moribund poems mostly metrically homogeneous. POxy. 1787 must contain poems of the last two books, and the Cologne papyrus only of the last.[7]

Provisional Text

Before proceeding with the text, one or two things related with the poem's transmission should be made clear. The two previous poems on the papyrus show signs of a scholarly mindfulness not only in the editorial technique but also in the classification of the poems by theme and metre, and, in consequence, by book. Given the antiquity of the Cologne papyrus, one could claim that it was written before the establishment of a standard text of the lyric poets in a scholarly Alexandrian edition.[8] That the Cologne papyrus and POxy. 1787, irrespective of the c. 5 centuries lapse of time between them, represent two different editions is evident from the fact that in each of them the Tithonus poem is preceded by a different poem. A combination of metre and theme must be the factor determining the division into books, and this may well predate the Alexandrian edition. But what about the arrangement of the poems within each book? If the second editor felt the need to rearrange the poems, the reason must have been the decision to present the poems of the book in alphabetical order. Which means that in the pre-Alexandrian edition the order was not alphabetical. What it was we do not know, but a reasonable surmise might be a close thematic order, i.e., groups of poems constituting thematic cycles. For instance, I believe that Sa. 63 is answered by Sa. 65 in POxy. 1787, with Sappho in the first addressing Oneiros and stating her requests for posthumous poetic fame, while Oneiros in the second announces to her the acceptance of her requests by Cypris.[9] It is clear that the Alexandrian grammarians did not start from scratch. They must have utilized one or more older editions, whose division in books they respected. However, their edition, apart from introducing the alphabetical classification must have also systematized the dialectal traits and their typical orthography. Earlier, all sorts of variations must have appeared in the text transmitted, something expected in every poetic genre, but mostly in the melic dialectal poetry, especially when this poetry

---

7 More detailed approach below, in '6. Sappho's Epithalamians. The Last Three Books'.
8 Cf. Yatromanolakis (2008), 239 ff.
9 Fr. 3 (containing Sa. 61–63) and 4 (containing Sa. 65) in POxy. 1787 are placed beside each other in the Oxyrhynchus glass frame. However, I am unable to examine the fibres for checking whether they could follow each other in the roll.

happened to be still alive and popular, yet among people unfamiliar with the particular dialect, for whom some forms would be distasteful or unintelligible. A typical example is the dialectal change from Aeolic and Doric into Attic in some *scolia* (e.g., *PMG* 891, 904).[10] It is natural that the changes mostly tend to regularize, i.e. to 'epicize' or 'Atticize', the most peculiar dialectal features. For instance, in a Lesbian poem, one would expect the -ω genitive to be regularized to -ου, but the inherited ᾱ would not need to change to η. When, however, the 'regularization' of such a peculiarity affects the metre, it is expected that the changes might be more drastic. In the previous poems of the Cologne papyrus that were written by a skilfull scribe, the ending -ίϲδω was normalized to -ίζω, ϲελάθειϲαν to διελάθειϲαν, ὀνϲτεναχίϲδω to ἀνϲτεναχίζω, while consonant assimilation was used extensively (ἐγ μελαίναν, κεμ ποείην, πολιὸγ γῆραϲ), traits that would be cleared away in the Alexandrian edition.[11] The curious thing about these two papyri so distant between themselves is that, at least as I claim, PCol., the old one, is arranged alphabetically, whereas POxy., the new one, thematically. Still, I doubt that PCol. represents a dialectally accurate edition. Rather than resort to the old principle *recentiores non deteriores*, I would suggest that different versions, pre- and post-Alexandrian, must have been circulating in parallel throughout antiquity.

Below is presented my reconstruction of the poem with its metrical analysis but without an adjustment to the Lesbian dialect, followed by a translation of the reconstructed text and a commentary. No apparatus criticus is added for the obvious reason that practically all textual interventions are mine. I must warn the reader that the reconstruction is made *exempli gratia*, with no presumption, that is, that I am always attaining the target of restoring the particular word or phrase that is missing, but of piecing together the details of the story narrated by the poet.

```
          «μυθοπλόκε, ψιθύρων δολίων αὐτούργ᾿, |² ἐπίβουλε                6 da ‖
   2      παῖ βροτολ῾οιγέ᾿ τ᾿ [῎Ερω, κ]ακ[ότ]η[τοϲ] |³ ἑταῖρε, ἀφέρπω.»
                                                                         6 da ‖
          δ[                                      [-⏑⏑-⏑⏑-⏑⏑-⏑⏑]   4 da |
   3a     |⁴ [πρὸϲ μακρὸν]
   4      τ[              |⁵ ἀ]χὰν                 [×-⏑⏑--]-  hipp ‖
          ἄπνουϲ ˪ πρὸ[ϲ μακρὸν˩ Διὸϲ αἰθέρα]     -◡-[◡-⏑⏑-⏑⏑  4 da |
   6      |⁶ [λ]αοιϲ ἀ[[ϲ]]τέρων τε [φωτῶν,]      ×-⏑⏑-⏑[- -  hipp ‖
          |⁷ [ἐ]ϲ πυριφεγγέοϲ ἀελ[ίου ϲέλαϲ]      -⏑⏑-⏑⏑-⏑[⏑-⏑⏑  4 da |
```

---

10 See Yatromanolakis (2008), 245–247.
11 Tsantsanoglou (2009c).

8	[ἄϲτρων |⁸ τ'] ἐπαεῖϲ' ἀκούω	x−]⌣⌣−⌣−− ˌhipp ‖
	Θρά[ΐκοϲ Οἰά|⁹γ]ρου κόρον Ὀρφέα	−[⌣⌣−◡◡]−⌣⌣−⌣⌣ 4 da |
10	κ[αὶ Καλλιόπαϲ λιγείαϲ.]	[x−⌣⌣−⌣−−] ˌhipp ‖
	|¹⁰ [ἕρ]πετὰ πάντα κ[λαῖε κακὸν μόρον,]	−⌣⌣−◡◡[−⌣⌣−⌣⌣ 4 da |
12	|¹¹ [ἇ]ϲ τὰν ἐρατὰν λα[βοῖϲ' ἄλϲ]	x−⌣⌣−⌣[−− ˌhipp ‖
	|¹² [εὔ]φθογγόν <τε> λύραν κι[θάριζ' ἔτι]	−◡◡−⌣⌣−⌣[⌣−⌣⌣ 4 da |
14	|¹³ [ϲυ]νεργὸν ἔχοιϲα πάν[ται]	x−⌣⌣−⌣−[− ˌhipp ‖
	[Θραϊκίαν ἄνεμον]	

"Fable-weaver, self-fabricator of fraudulent slanders, Er[os], treacherous and pestilent boy, companion of wick[edness], I am going away." [...] s[uch ... w]ail toward the high [Zeus's aether] and the other [human] folks, to the fire-blazing [brightness] of the sun [and the stars], breathless do I hear that Orpheus, son of Thra[cian Oeag]rus a[nd sweet-voiced Calliope], sang out. All beasts la[mented the wicked death, ti]ll [the sea] took the beloved and melodious lyre [and continued] pla[ying it], being assisted in every way [by the Thracian wind, ...]

Dialect

A few general observations may be useful before approaching the text in a proper and detailed line by line commentary. To begin with, we must distinguish the initial hexameters, which were originally conceived as epic-Ionic. But, concerning the lyric part of the poem, I cannot speak at first sight for a specific dialect of the transmitted text, much less for a specific authorship or date—of course, prior to the first half of the third century BC. 4 ἄ]χαν, 6 α⟦ϲ⟧τέρων, 7 ἀελ[, 9 Θρά[ΐκοϲ, 12 τὰν ἐραταν, 14 ἔχοιϲα may belong to several dialects, especially to the conventional 'Doric' of lyric poetry, from Alcman to the Hellenistic poets, but also to Lesbian. However, this precariousness is deceptive. (*a*) In 4–6 ἄ]χαν ... πρὸ[ϲ ... [λ]αοιϲ, depending on a verb of addressing not yet cleared up, the preposition is bound to go with an accusative noun (LSJ s.v. πρόϲ C. I 5). This means that 6 [λ]αοιϲ can only be the Lesbian λάοιϲ, acc. pl. of λᾶοϲ, by no means the dat. pl. [λ]αοῖϲ or [λ]αοῖϲ' or [λ]άοιϲ'. (*b*) The prepositional phrase is joined with the gen. pl. α⟦ϲ⟧τέρων. We shall discuss later about the deletion of sigma by the scribe or rather a corrector. Dictionaries present ατεροϲ as the Doric (aspirate) and Aeolic (non-aspirate) form of the Attic-Ionic ἕτεροϲ. This is true, but the fact is that in poetry it is only in the Lesbians and the Aeolizing idylls of Theocritus that the form occurs.[12] Thus, it is clear that πρὸϲ ... λάοιϲ ἀτέρων is necessarily a segment of a Lesbian poem. (*c*) A third case, more complicated, is 8]επαϲ ἀκούω, which

---

[12] The old form survived also in the Attic ἅτεροϲ, θάτερον etc., but only in crasis, which produces a long alpha; Schwyzer, *GG* i.401.

the edd. articulate] ̠πᾶc ἀκούω and translate 'Ich bin ganz Ohr' or 'I am all ears'. I believe it renders ἐπᾷc(αι) ἀκούω, the Atticized version of ἔπαεις' ἀκούω. The omission of the iota adscriptum can be charged to the careless scribe, though its omission, when it is mute, is quite usual as early as the beginning of the fourth century.[13] What concerns us here is not so much the obvious Atticization of ἐπαεῖc(αι) as the fact that the elision of the diphthong αι in active infinitives, as ἐπαεῖc', ἐπάεις', or ἐπᾷc', is possible only in Lesbian lyric and in comedy—and it is plain that we are not dealing with comedy. Hamm 40 § 81 calls the phenomenon 'besonders auffällig'.

Even in cases where Lesbian is excluded, as 9 Οἰάγ]ρου, one should hasten to add 'unless they are regularized', i.e., they underwent the expected process during the transmission of dialectal texts. Soft examples of this 'regularization' have already been illustrated in the previous scribe's texts. The remaining criteria depend on subjective judgement and are limited to the metre and the style. The vocabulary, characterized by the *edd. pr.*, 13, 'z.T. geradezu "modern"', with reference to words like αὐτουργός, ἐπίβουλος, ἀφέρπω, πυριφεγγής, cυνεργός, is, to my mind, absolutely fitted for enriching the diction of the surviving archaic lyric poetry. No rule has been discovered so far that permits Homer to use εὐεργός and κακοεργός, but forbids a Lesbian poet to use αὐτουργός. cυνεργός is used by Pindar (*Ol.* 8.32), ἐπίβουλος and αὐτουργία by Aeschylus in choral songs (*Su.* 587, *Eum.* 336). It is very insecure to date words that occur in classical lyric poetry or in choral parts of the dramatic poetry, because they often belong to the traditional legacy of the archaic lyric production that has mostly vanished. Compound adjectives built on the pattern of πυριφεγγής are too common to document from the epic onward; Schwyzer *GG* i.513 f. Nor can I understand why are βαίνω / ἀποβαίνω, ἔρχομαι / ἀπέρχομαι, εἶμι / ἄπειμι, cτείχω / ἀποcτείχω, ὁρμάομαι / ἀφορμάομαι legitimately archaic, but not their synonymous ἕρπω / ἀφέρπω. The scarcity or the abundance of the vocabulary, poetic or prose, in any era is not irrelevant to the number of texts that survived from this era.

The specific strophic metre, used in a full-sized poem, combined with a moderately high-flown yet straightforward and non-extravagant style with unsophisticated phrase- and verse-structure, rules out a Hellenistic date and suggests an archaic one. It is also completely alien to the rhetorical and prosaic everyday diction of the *Fragmentum Grenfellianum*, with which it has been compared. Now, when a melic poem with a theme about love (and Eros), approaching death, as

---

13 Schwyzer, *GG* i.201 ('um 400 vielfach'; *IG* 12,2:645). Threatte, i.358 f., offers isolated examples of ᾱ for ᾱι from the 4th century on. Blümel (1982), 87 § 99 dates the phenomenon already in the 5th century (*IG* 12,2:1).

well as about music (especially stringed) and poetry, and their introduction to Lesbos, is placed in a papyrus after two more melic poems with a theme about love (and Eros), approaching death, music (especially stringed) and poetry, their story being located in Lesbos, and the latter are demonstrably Sappho's, one is inevitably tempted to ascribe also the unattributed one to her. And it is all the more so, if the poem contains three Lesbian dialectal peculiarities and opens with a compound epithet, even if conjecturally restored, an *hapax legomenon* in the entire ancient Greek literature, that qualifies the same god (Eros) as in its unique occurrence which is explicitly identified as Sappho's; see the commentary on 1–2.

What remains is 5 ἄπνουc which is also a case of Atticization. The question is particularly complicated, and will be discussed *ad loc.*, in the line by line commentary. As mentioned above, 9 Οἰάγ]ρου > Οἰάγ]ρω is a case of necessary adjustment, which falls under the category of extreme dialectal traits that are likely to undergo regularization, the particular form running also the risk of being mistaken for a dative. All other cases are unnoticeable in this papyrus, which has no accents or breathing-marks: psilotic ἀτέρων, recession of the accent in several words. The rest occur in supplements, like ἀελ[ίου] ~ ἀελ[ίω], [λιγείας] ~ [λιγήας], [ἑρ]πετά ~ [ὄρ]πετα.

In any case, the papyrus text is published and supplemented above as a non-Lesbian poem. For the sake of scholarly rigour, it would be better to keep some reservations, since the possibility that a poet might make his poem known together with the Sapphic poems in a thematic anthology cannot be ex ante excluded. Actually, the suggestion for a thematic anthology in the Cologne papyrus has been made repeatedly, but the truth is fully indeterminate. The two Sapphic poems are no doubt completely connected palaeographically, thematically, and metrically. But the third poem is written by a different hand, in a somewhat different layout, and is composed in a different metre. Thematically, it is connected with Sappho's poems, but there may be scores of reasons why somebody adds a poem with a cognate subject to formerly written ones. As I mentioned above, if I am right in detecting certain scribal errors of understanding (1 ψιθυροπλοκε δόλιε μύθων, 6 αςτέρων), the possibility of dealing with the preliminary draft of a poem composed by the owner of the papyrus is ruled out. In any case, retaining the arguments from the metre and the archaic style, but also considering the localist pride of the inhabitants of Lesbos for their musical and poetic superiority, no Lesbian poet can be excluded, not even Terpander, who apart from the privilege of seniority that might justify a claim to the Orphic legacy, shares also the kindred metre, and needs not to be thoroughly adapted into the dialect of Lesbos.

Commentary

1–2. Both initial hexameters are problematically transmitted, harshly impairing the approach to the whole poem, therefore calling for drastic intervention. If my critical suggestions seem sometimes to be exaggerated, this has nothing to do with any propensity for hypercorrection, a characteristic that I do not possess. My admittedly bold proposal is dictated by the obvious negligence and unreliability of the scribe. As regards the hexameters, it is understandable that if they belong to a Lesbian poem, they must enjoy the freedoms observed in the other hexametric poems of the Lesbians (Page, *Sappho and Alcaeus* 65 ff., West *GM* 33 f. and n. 7).

ψιθυροπλόκε δόλιε μύθων αὐτουργέ does not scan in any credible lyric metre. A fully resolved + an all-drag dochmiac (⏑⏑⏑⏑⏑⏑ −−−−−) have been proposed, mainly on the analogy of the *Fragmentum Grenfellianum*, where, however, not a single fully resolved dochmiac occurs. But the difference between the two pieces, both metrically and stylistically, is colossal. Further, I do not know how the final open syllable of the second dochmiac could come to terms with the same vowel that opens the next word (-γε ἐπι-). Moreover, dochmiacs cannot be accommodated in the rest of the poem. It seems that the scribe, negligent and ignorant of metrics, possibly writing from memory, mixed up the cognate words, ψιθυροπλόκε μύθων for μυθοπλόκε ψιθύρων, dragging also δολίων into the train of vocatives that follow. Such large-scale text errors are usually attributed to the physical corruption of the exemplar copied,[14] but there is no such evidence here. Were it not for the other errors, I might attribute this one to a mischievously teasing schoolchild, but their abundance leads us inevitably to his sheer carelessness.

μυθοπλόκε: Sa. 188 V. from Max. Tyr. 18.9 (p. 232 Hobein) τὸν Ἔρωτα Cωκράτης coφιcτὴν λέγει, Σαπφὼ μυθοπλόκον (the entire quotation from Maximus in fr. 219 V.). The *hapax* word not only is attested in Sappho, but is also connected with the same subject, Eros.[15] This Sappho fragment, together with Sa. 1.2 παῖ Δίος δολόπλοκε, has been paralleled with the transmitted ψιθυροπλόκε by almost every scholar, but none of them took the risk of restoring the adjective attested as Sappho's. Actually, Magnani, 42 n. 6, conjectures that the combined occurrence of Sa. 188 μυθόπλοκος and Sa. 1.2 δολόπλοκος 'suggerisce la possibile safficità di ψιθυρόπλοκος'; cf. Lundon, 164–165. The second syllable of

---

14 West (1973), 19.
15 The next time the word turns up is in the second half of the 10th century: Theodosius Diaconus *De Creta capta* 952, where the adjective describes Homer.

μυθοπλόκε is short as is normal in the epic, but also in Sappho's hexametric 105a.2 μαλοδρόπηες.

ψιθύρων δολίων αὐτουργέ: Though ψιθυρίζω means literally 'to whisper', ψίθυρος is attested substantively only as *nomen agentis*, 'whisperer, slanderer' (Pind. *P.* 2.75, al.), and adjectivally in the sense 'whispering, slandering' (Soph. *Aj.* 148 τοιούςδε λόγους ψιθύρους πλάccων, al.). I am reluctant to take it here as substantive, the whole phrase ψιθύρων δολίων αὐτουργέ then meaning 'creator, begetter of fraudulent whisperers'. No doubt, an adjectival ψιθύρων, 'slanderous', substantivized neuter for ψιθύρων λόγων, with δολίων qualifying it, i.e. 'self-fabricator of fraudulent slanders', is more suitable here. Possibly, it is this unattested use that is implied by those who adopt ψιθυροπλόκε as a genuine reading: 'slander-weaver' and not 'slanderer-weaver'. In Modern Greek, ψίθυρος means only 'the whisper'. Yet, this sense is not attested in ancient Greek, the deverbative ψιθύριςμα being used for the nominal sense.– *AP* 3.3.5 (*IMT* Kyz. Kapu Dağ 1720) (anon.) δολίοις ψιθυρίςμαcιν for slanders concerning an illegal erotic affair. Harp. 310.7 (s.v. ψιθυριςτὴς Ἑρμῆς) ἐτιμᾶτο δ' Ἀθήνηςι καὶ ψίθυρος Ἀφροδίτη καὶ Ἔρως ψίθυρος.

ἐπίβουλε παῖ; cf. Pl. *Symp.* 203d κατὰ δὲ αὖ τὸν πατέρα (sc. Πόρος) ἐπίβουλός ἐςτι (sc. Ἔρως) τοῖς καλοῖς καὶ τοῖς ἀγαθοῖς, ... ἀεί τινας πλέκων μηχανάς; also, 205d ὁ μέγιςτός τε καὶ δολερὸς ἔρως; antithetically, 197d. In Modern Greek Renaissance poetry, *Erotokritos* B 628, Γ 352 τὸ πίβουλο κοπέλλι (= 'treacherous boy') for Eros.

βογολ̣[pap.^ac (βοτον̣[*edd. pr.* ['vielleicht']), but a large P is inserted between B and O, almost effaced now but leaving a part of its vertical and its whitish trace for the rest clearly visible. βογολ̣[is struck out with horizontal lines which are broken up by the lacuna, so that we cannot say where they reached. One of these horizontals coincides with the horizontal of Γ giving, perhaps intentionally, the impression of Τ. The letters that follow in the same line after the gap, though faded, do not show any striking out and so do the letters surviving after the second gap, ΑΚ and Η̣. It is unclear what the supra lineam \I and ΓΕ are correcting as well as why ΒΟΓΟΛ was struck out, since it had been corrected. Rather the sequence of actions is opposite, and the scribe, after drawing the first deleting strokes on the erroneously written word, changed his mind and decided to correct it with supralinear corrections. Can the first supralinear letters be ΟΙ? The right-hand side of omicron, here at the edge of the gap, is sometimes written as a straight-line backslash, as in the two former omicrons of βΟγΟ-. The iota is clear enough. The second supralinear correction is ΓΕ. In the regular height of the line, a faded Ε is visible. It is obvious that βροτολοιγέ is intended, though it is uncertain why the supralinears ΟΙ and ΓΕ are somewhat distanced from each other.

Perhaps the erroneous readings contained one or two more letters, and so the supralinear corrections were written above them.– According to Rawles, βοτο [, related with oxen, suggests Hermes, just as ψιθυροπλόκος, δόλιος, and ἐπίβουλος. As for the supralinear corrections, he proposes βο]υαγέ also referring to Hermes. Puglia discerned the vertical between B and O, but read β'ι'οτον. Bierl: 'Oder wollte der Schreiber etwas wie βροτο im Sinne von ἐν βροτοῖςι zu Papyrus bringen?'

The faded E is followed by the left-hand tip of a top horizontal compatible with Z, Ξ, Π, and T. The first two are obviously excluded for metrical reasons. If the trace belongs to T, I would supplement βροτολ'οιγέ τ' [Ἔρος κ]ακ[ότ]η[τος]. The supplement is one letter longer than the space provided, if the scribe's accuracy can be trusted. Yet, I would venture a different proposal. Can Ἔρω be an alternative vocative of Ἔρως/ος? The form is unrecorded, the only vocatives I could spot occurring in Hellenistic epigrams (e.g., Posidipp. 138 AB [AP 12.120] cὺ δ᾽, Ἔρως). However, the parallel ἥρως has a voc. ἥρω: PMG carm. pop. 871 ἐλθεῖν, ἥρω Διόνυςε, which Page characterized as 'inauditum' suggesting older emendations. Still, voc. ἥρω reappears in late funerary inscriptions: SEG 31:1018 (from Saittai, Lydia) Ἄνθηρε ἥρω, χαῖρε; IG IX,2 1192 (from Thessalic Demetrias) ἥρω χρηςτ[έ] χαῖρε; several more from Pelasgiotis (IG IX,2 905, 954, 946a), sometimes with the missing sigma supplemented by the edd. The voc. ἥρω is accepted as legitimate by Schwyzer, GG i.837 (addenda to p. 480), thus confirming the general remark that 'the vocative of masculines and feminines is usually the pure stem' (Smyth § 248: πόλι, βοῦ, Ἄρτεμι, παῖ, νεᾶνι). Further, Schwyzer's observations on the inflection of ἔρως, γέλως (i.514), as well as (i.480) of ἥρως (gen. ἥρω, acc. ἥρω) and ἅλως (gen. ἅλω), make the vocative ἔρω quite likely.

βροτολοιγός, the usual epithet of Ares, is occasionally used for Eros in Hellenistic epigrams (AP 12.37 Dioscorides; 5.180 Meleager; 9.221 Marcus Argentarius), whose poets may well derive it from older literature.

κ]ακ[ότ]η[τος] ἑταῖρε: Both ἑταῖρος and ἑταίρα are sometimes connected with abstract notions: Il. 9.2 φύζα φόβου κρυόεντος ἑταίρη, Od. 17.270–71 φόρμιγξ ..., ἣν ἄρα δαιτὶ θεοὶ ποίηςαν ἑταίρην, h. Merc. 290 μελαίνης νυκτὸς ἑταῖρε, Pl. R. 439d ἐπιθυμητικόν, πληρώςεων τινων καὶ ἡδονῶν ἑταῖρον, Phdr. 253e ἀληθινῆς δόξης ἑταῖρος ... ὕβρεως καὶ ἀλαζονείας ἑταῖρος, Plu. 2.622b γέλωτα μὴ μώμου μηδ᾽ ὕβρεων ἀλλὰ χάριτος καὶ φιλοφροςύνης ἑταῖρον. Here, κακότης (the top of a right-hand vertical as of H or N is visible; A is impossible), as companion of Eros, may refer either to the god's own wickedness or to the misery and distress suffered by his victims. In the second case, however, misery's companion was the victim himself. If so, Alc. 10.1 ἔμε παίςαν κακοτάτων πεδέχοιcαν is a close parallel. But in that case, we should have to write κακότητοc ἑταῖροc in the nominative; a conjecture that would be welcome, since it would heal the hiatus of the end of the hexameter. It is in the same sense, 'misery, distress', that the word is used also in Alc. 117 b.31 α]ῖcχοc κα[ὶ κα]κό[τα]τ' ὠλομέν[αν, for the feelings experienced by a prostitute, as well as in Alc. 132.3–4 βαρύνθην | κὰκ κ]εφάλαν κακότατα πόλλα[v. Sa. 3.12] ῃc κακότατο[c is uncertain, though many words in the context seem to point in the same direction (λύπηc, ὄνειδοc, ἄcαιο). If 'misery' is the prevailing sense in the Lesbians, the conjecture ἑταῖροc ἀφέρπω should be taken very seriously. And Orpheus, who after losing his wife experienced a slanderous offensive that led to his ferocious murder, can well describe himself as companion of misery. The scribe who, as it seems, believed that the whole distich contained nouns in vocative, and so turned δολίων to δόλιε, may have well also turned ἑταῖροc to ἑταῖρε.– κ]ακ[έ Bierl.

ἀφέρπω: 'I am going away'. The sense 'I am dying' is also possible; see Pempelus 142.8 Thesleff (*The Pythagorean texts of the Hellenistic period*, Åbo 1965) ἀφέρποντεc (sc. προγενέτορεc) αἰζηοῖc νέοιc cφόδρα ποθεινοί. However, if, as the story goes, Orpheus' words, i.e. the hexametric distich, were miraculously vociferated after his decapitation, the verb should also mean 'I am going away'. Orpheus' story, as we shall soon discuss, does not end simply with a death. It is, at the same time, a departure, a relocation, a removal of his attributes, music and poetry, to a new homeland; ἀφέρπω, that is, in its ambivalent sense. Thus, the meaning of κακότητοc ἑταῖροc ἀφέρπω would be complemented: 'I am departing in company with my misery'. – The *edd. pr.* note the similarity of the opening of the poem with the opening of Sappho 1. Bierl: 'Ich gehe weg, d.h. in den Tod (elliptisch εἰc Ἄιδου οἶκον)'.

Still, with regard to metre, this hexametric distich has some evident exceptional features at the end of its second verse. First, a breach of Hermann's bridge, and second, a harsh hiatus between ἑταῖρε and ἀφέρπω, if the scribe's reading is accepted. When we spoke above about the freedoms enjoyed by the Sapphic hexameters, we meant freedoms in relation to the Lesbian melic prosody, not in relation to the epic rules. We do not know whether the hexameters used by Sappho[16] differ and in what terms from the epic hexameters. No more than 10 full hexameters of Sappho survived, some needing to be emended, (104 a, 105 a, b, 106, 142, 143 V.) plus four half hexameters (107, 108, 109, 149 V.). We can add two more (111 V.) by recognizing their melic character and making a necessary emendation.

---

[16] No dactylic hexameters by Alcaeus have reached us.

If my observations are correct, they add four more to the sum.[17] To my mind, no violation of the epic rules is visible in these lines. It is only at the close of the second hexameter of the poem under discussion that we find these peculiarities. And, if we might claim that the hiatus can be eliminated by writing ἑταῖροc, the breach of Hermann's bridge remains.

Be that as it may, being perhaps intuitively convinced that we are dealing with a consummate poet, I cannot resist the hypothesis that through whatever anomaly a deliberate effect may be intended. ἀφέρπω, 'I am passing away', is both the last word of the dying poet and the high point of the poem, just as τὰν καλάμοιc᾽ ἀείδω, 'the songs I am singing are deathly', were the last words of the poetess and the high point of the first poem that survived in the Cologne papyrus. By dislocating the typical joints of the verse at its crucial spot, the poet may be actually imitating the spasmodically faltering wail of the agonizing poet, at the same time highlighting the purport of the verse.

The initial dactylic distich is referred to in verse 4 as ἀ]χάν, and Orpheus' action in verse 8 as ἐπαεῖc(αι). These hexameters constitute a literal quotation of Orpheus' lament. Instead of composing a commonplace 'Orpheus accused Eros as fable-weaver etc.' or even 'Orpheus sang: "Fable-weaver, Eros etc."', the poet opens the poem with the lament itself, 'Fable-weaver, Eros etc.', and continues with 'Thus sang out Orpheus'. This makes the opening more passionate and dramatic, with the grievance of the dying Orpheus turning into a heading of the poem. However, Orpheus' mythical personality imposes the employment of both the epic metre and the epic dialect. Whatever verisimilitude was intended in a literal quotation of the 'inventor' of the dactylic hexameter (Critias 88 B 3 D.-K.) would be ruined if the verses were metrically and dialectally other than epic. Therefore, I do not believe that, even in the case that the rest of the poem is in Lesbian, ἀπέρπω, κακότατοc and recession of the accent should be restored in the hexameters. Can the fact that the distich is supposed to be loudly performed to a lyre accompaniment have any association with the high pitch and volume of the ὄρθιοc νόμοc and the ἀνατεταμένωc (forte) mode of delivery of the Terpandrian citharodic melody in the melic metre that will follow? It is also reasonable to conjecture that the distich was performed in a sort of παρακαταλογή,[18]

---

[17] In addition to the verses read in the Orpheus song, also 103.1 V. (below, '6. Sappho's Epithalamians. The Last Three Books'), as well as the verse read in the painting of the Attic hydria NMA 1260 (above, '1. Sappho Illustrated').

[18] Pseudo-Aristotle Problemata 918a 12: διὰ τί ἡ παρακαταλογὴ ἐν ταῖc ᾠδαῖc τραγικόν; ἢ διὰ τὴν ἀνωμαλίαν; παθητικὸν γὰρ τὸ ἀνωμαλὲc καὶ ἐν μεγέθει τύχηc ἢ λύπηc. τὸ δὲ ὁμαλὲc ἔλαττον γοῶδεc.

somehow *parlando* in recitative style, fully discreet from the melody of the lyric part of the poem. Can this style be more tolerant of strict rules, possibly allowing the breach of Hermann's bridge? If some melic hexameters in tragedies can be considered parallel, we find such breaches in the hexameters of Aesch. *Eum.* 352 and the corresponding, rather unorthodox, 365, which belong to a passage (347–53 ~ 360–66) that can hardly be considered melic, as it expresses in spoken yet elevated style the grievances of the Erinyes against the immortals. They are not simply recited verses, but they may well be declaimed in recitative.

3–4. The entire verse 3, apart from the initial δ[, falls in the papyrus gap. Instead of the acephalous hipponactean that should have followed the tetrameter of the second part of line 3, of which only δ[survived, the scribe started writing inattentively the next tetrameter. Believing that he was writing the acephalous hipponactean, he closed the words with the dicolon that normally closes the metrical unit 4 da + ˌhipp, at least when the text is written καταλογάδην as in this verse. The *edd. pr.* consider the dicolon 'möglich', and publish it queried. Actually, its high dot, almost touching the horizontal of τ, is plainly visible, and the low dot, though slightly effaced, is clear enough. The scribe found out his error straightway and struck out with ink the erroneous text. Of the dicolon he sponged off partly the low dot, but he left the high dot undeleted to avoid any damage to the horizontal of τ. Reading the struck out text (πρὸς μακρὸν) was tough. The non-deleted τ[seems to start the correct acephalous hipponactean. That it is τ and not π is evident not only from the quite long horizontal to the left of the vertical, but also from the rightward tilting foot of the vertical (cf. 6 τε [). The acephalous hipponactean starts with τ[and ends with ἀ]χάν in line 5, followed by the regular dicolon.] ˌν: (?) *edd. pr.* The right-hand obtuse angle of χ is clearly visible after the gap (the fork of κ is distinctly acute), followed by the upper part of a triangular letter, which, being between χ and ν, can only be α. After the ν, according to the *edd. pr.*, 'Hochpunkt oder Dikolon'. However, the dicolon is the only lectional sign used by the scribe. The low dot is under the right-hand tail of N, forming a greater tilt than usual, but quite allowable for our scribe's standard. Speaking of the high dot, Rawles claims that '[it] might ... be the top of a high letter (by any reading, some ink has been lost in the vicinity) ... If dicolon is to be read here, it seems to be followed either by asyndeton or by a delayed particle, which might make it seem a little less likely'. However, no ink seems to have been lost in the vicinity and no letter could intervene between]χαν and απνουc. If it is a dicolon, it must have a metrical value, and no syntactical effects should be expected from it.

As regards the reference to an internal quotation, the verse possibly recalls Terpander *SLG* 6, as interpreted and supplemented *exempli gratia* before: κύκνοc ὑπὸ πτερύγων τοιόνδε τι, 'sc. cantat' K.–A. or <μ' ἄειδεν ἄρτι> (e.g. Ts.). ἀχά, meaning 'cry of sorrow, wail', is restored in its 'Doric' form at Eur. *Med.* 149 (Χο.) ἄιες, ὦ Ζεῦ καὶ Γᾶ καὶ φῶς, | ἀχὰν οἵαν ἁ δύστανος | μέλπει νύμφα;, 205 (Χο.) ἀχὰν ἄιον πολύστονον γόων, | λιγυρὰ δ' ἄχεα μογερὰ βοᾷ | τὸν ἐν λέχει προδόταν κακόνυμφον· | θεοκλυτεῖ δ' ἄδικα παθοῦσα, *Hipp.* 584, *IT* 180, where the codd. present always ἰαχάν (at *Hipp.* 584 both Barrett and Diggle print ἰάν following Weil and P.Oxy. 2224). Thematically, the passages from *Medea* are considerably close to the papyrus poem, since what is described is a wail (ἀχά) that is sung (ἐπαεῖcαι ~ μέλπει) to the gods in heaven (πρὸc μακρὸν Διὸc αἰθέρα ~ ὦ Ζεῦ - θεοκλυτεῖ), to the mortals on the earth (πρὸc ... λαοιc ἀτέρων τε φωτῶν ~ καὶ Γᾶ), and the natural light (ἐc πυριφεγγέοc ἀελίου cέλαc ἄcτρων τ' ~ καὶ φῶc). Cf. *Il.* 13.837 ἠχὴ δ' ἀμφοτέρων ἵκετ' αἰθέρα καὶ Διὸc αὐγάc. Similarly to *Medea*'s 149 ἀχὰν οἵαν and 205 ἀχὰν ἄιον πολύcτονον, we can fill the lacuna with an adjective qualifying the wail: e.g., τ[οίαν cτονόεccαν |⁵ ἀ]χάν.

5. ἄπνουc, whether masculine or feminine, if it is to be connected with the subject of ἐπαεῖcαι, sc. Ὀρφέα, or with its object, sc. ἀχάν, should have been ἄπνουν. However, ἄπνουc can refer to the speaking person (ἄπνουc ... ἀκούω), in the sense 'breathless with awe, with excitement' = 'voiceless, speechless'. It is true that ἄπνουc does not occur in this emotional sense, but the physical symptom of breath shortness because of strong emotion was undoubtedly known, and is in fact vividly described by Sappho in fr. 31 V.: 7 ff. ὡc γὰρ ἔc c' ἴδω βρόχε' ὤc με φώνη|c' οὐδὲν ἔτ' εἴκει, | ἀλλὰ κὰμ μὲν γλῶccα †ἔαγε† κτλ. The important thing is, however, that ἄπνουc refers to the 'I' of the poem, here the poet, who appears to empathize with the dying Orpheus and to identify with his feelings. Be that as it may, by writing ἄπνουν in the sense 'lifeless' we would be more consistent with the Orpheus myth. In Ovid's description of Orpheus' death, *Met.* 11.52 f. *flebile lingua murmurat exanimis*, it is clear that *exanimis* renders our ἄπνουc in the sense 'lifeless', since the whole scene is placed after Orpheus' decapitation and is characterized a miracle (51 *mirum*).

In any case ἄπνουc or ἄπνουν are contracted in the Attic-Ionian manner. The uncontracted ἄπνοοc does not scan. A contraction of οο does exist in the Lesbian dialect (Hamm 33 § 64 e), but it produces ω not ου. Did our scribe 'regularize' an originally contracted ἄπνωc by turning it to ἄπνουc? Given his capabilities, I greatly doubt that he would be able to distinguish a contracted ἄπνοοc > ἄπνωc from a contracted adverb ἀπνόωc > ἄπνωc. Both ἀπνόωc and ἄπνωc are unattested, but contracted parallels are provided mainly by Pollux: 1.16.6 ὥcπερ καὶ τὰ ἐπιρρήματα ... ἐπίπνωc; 2.230.3 τὰ δ' ἐπιρρήματα εὔνωc, ..., κακόνωc, ... ἀγχίνωc, πολύνωc, δύcνωc; 4.23.6 τὰ δ' ἐπιρρήματα ... εὔρωc; add Xen. *Cyr.* 6.4.15 ὁμόνωc. These contracted forms need not be considered late formations, since the phonological phenomenon is old. If ἄπνωc (= ἄπνουc) was accepted as the original reading, the sense would naturally not change, but if it was misunderstood as an adverb, its function might be extended to Orpheus as well. Though a definitive answer to our queries is impossible, I believe that the poet would prefer, even if he was Lesbian, to employ the contracted nominative ἄπνουc than perplex his listeners as to who is short of breath or breathless. The same practice is followed exceptionally in the epic and some Ionian poets, where, though such o-stem nouns are normally uncontracted, we encounter occasionally contracted forms of νόοc and χειμάρροοc (Chantraine, *Grammaire homérique*, 1, p. 30 § 14, pp. 196–197 § 82; West, *Studies in Greek Elegy and Iambus*, 84 f.).– G.B. D'Alessio (ap. Rawles 11) prefers to associate ἄπνουc with the dead tortoise, whose shell was used by Hermes for constructing the lyre.

πρὸ[c μακρόν is retrieved from the deleted text of line 4. For the rest, Ὄλυμπον suggests itself, but I cannot accommodate it metrically. Eventually, I supplement πρὸc μακρὸν Διὸc αἰθέρα. For Διὸc αἰθήρ cf. Eur. *Ion* 1079, frs. 839, 985, Hdt. 7.8.38, *SH* (adesp. papyr.) 928 col. 1.1. Cf. also *Orac. Sibyll.* 3.313, Quint. 7.242.– πρ . [('unbestimmte Spur') and προ[λείπω *vel* προ[λίποιμι (sc. τὸ φάοc) edd. pr.; πρῶ[τοc Rawles for Hermes, who was the first to produce melody ἄπνουc, that is, without blowing the aulos.

6. *Edd. pr.* read φ]άοc, connecting it with ἀcτέρων. Only the left-hand half of the omicron has survived at the edge of a gap. If completed, the space between it and the sigma would be quite large requiring a narrow letter to be filled. Actually, the high tip of the iota is clearly visible. I propose [λ]αοιc. If it was dative plural, it would be syntactically incongruous after πρὸc + accusative. The question has been discussed extensively above. Lesbian acc. plural λάοιc would be perfect.

ἀ[c]τέρων: The scribe may have been misled by ΦΩΤΩΝ (i.e. φωτῶν), taken as if from φῶτα, by 7 [ἐ]c πυριφεγγέοc ἀελ[ίου cέλαc/φάοc], and verse 8 [ἄcτρων], naturally, if they are correctly supplemented. 'And to the assemblies of the other (i.e. than the Thracian maenads) human beings'. See Denniston *GP* 517 for the mild postponement of τε.– φ]άοc ἀcτέρων τε [καὶ cελάναc ... καὶ *edd. pr.*; ὀμνύω τὸ]| φ]άοc κτλ. Puglia (*fortasse*).

I acknowledge that all sorts of discolorations are expected to occur in the surface of a papyrus, especially one retrieved from cartonnage like the present piece, but my impression from an enlarged photograph is that a man-made roundish spot or stain is visible upon and around the c of αcτερων, as if someone tried in the past to sponge it off. Also, a large X-shaped crossing out can be seen upon C. It is uncertain who made the sponging off (the scribe himself or a corrector?), but the large X must have been made by a corrector (a teacher or the owner?). This deletion is perhaps the most striking proof that we are not dealing with the autograph draft of a late poet's poem, because no poet would ever mix up 'stars' with 'other'.

7.] ̣ *edd. pr.*, who supplement [τ]ὸ̣ c ([ἐ]c) is likelier. The curve, which is too large for O, seems to approach a full circle, but the circle remains open. The low curve of c (and ε) sometimes turns high: line 6 ἀ⟦C⟧τέρων, 8 ἐπᾶC', 13 ἔχοιCα. However, it is uncertain whether the spot that approaches the upper curve is ink or a fibre which extends its downward course much beyond the boundaries of sigma. The preposition πρός with acc. denotes a direct address to specific targets like gods or people, whereas ἐc with acc. an address to an indistinct and indeterminate target like light.

πυριφεγγέοc: πυριφεγγέc pap.[ac] One more variant of our scribe's epsilon, with a wide upper curve that covers the entire letter, but an angular low part, can be seen in -φE- The scribe or the corrector found out the error of πυριφεγγεc, and made some confusing attempts to restore πυριφεγγέοc. A small C (or E?) was added under the horizontal of the second gamma as if hanging from it, and an awkward Ç was written in place of the second E. πυριφεγγής was recorded from late literature sometimes qualifying the sun (*edd. pr.* mention Orph. *Arg.* 214 πυριφεγγέοc Ἡελίοιο), but εὐφεγγής, χρυcοφεγγής occur in Aeschylus, καλλιφεγγής in Euripides. ἀελ[ίου or, if Lesbian, ἀελ[ίω.

cέλαc] or φάοc]: Cf. ἁλίου cέλαc Aesch. *Eu.* 926, Soph. *El.* 17, Ar. *Av.* 1711; φάοc ἁλίω Sa. 56.1 ('ἅλιοc apud nostros insolitum' Voigt), φάοc ἠελίοιο *Il.* 1.605 *al.* Another possibility is φλόγα] followed in the next verse by e.g. [μῆναc]: cf. Simon. *PMG* 581.3 ἀελίου τε φλογὶ χρυcέαc τε cελάναc. I prefer the neuter supplements, which explain the emergence of the erroneous πυριφεγγέc.

8. First, there is a problem with the writing of line 8. It contains the end of verse 8 and the beginning of verse 9, filling the whole line till its end, as is shown by the fact that the scribe is obliged to cut Οἰά-γρου in two. The number of letters in line 8 is 20 (or 21, if the dicolon after ἀκούω is included). This is a small number compared with the 28 (or 29 with *scriptio plena*) and 34 letters of the first two lines. Naturally, I don't take into account the lines that consist of a full metrical verse each (6, 10, 11, 12, 13), since their contents were determined by the verse's size. If the scribe did not decide to divide Οἰά-γρου in midline for some unknown reason, the likeliest thing is that something intervened between Θράϊκοc and Οἰα-, possibly an erroneous word or phrase, which he later deleted, as he did in lines 2 and 4.

τ'] ἐπᾶc': 'Am Anfang eher ν als c' *edd. pr.* However, what looks like the upper part of the letter is not ink. What is visible is the mid horizontal and the bottom curve of an E. We discussed above the case of the contracted ἐπᾶc' and claimed that it must be an 'Atticization' of an original ἐπαεῖϲ' or ἐπάειϲ', and that the elision of the diphthongal ending of an active infinitive points to the Lesbians.– [.]. πᾶϲ vel πᾶϲ' ἀκούω edd. pr., usually translated 'Ich bin ganz Ohr' or 'I am all ears', whether masculine or feminine. ψόγουϲ (vel simm.) ἀναίτι]|ο]ϲ πᾶϲ' ἀκούω Puglia.

ἐπαείδειν-ἐπάδειν and ἐπαοιδή-ἐπῳδή are terms especially connected with Orpheus, not so much in the sense of singing loudly as of singing a charm or an incantation. At any rate, the hexametric distich does not constitute a simple cry. It needs Orpheus' miraculous ability to sing, after his murder, a lament that is being heard by all mortals and immortals, the sun and the stars. Cf. Pl. Chrm. 157c ἐπᾷϲαι ταῖϲ τοῦ Θρᾳκὸϲ ἐπῳδαῖϲ.

9. Contracted Θρά[ικιον or Θρή[ικιον, not Θραΐκιον or Θρηΐκιον, was proposed by edd. pr. (the form with H is palaeographically unlikely). Alc. 45.3 Θραικ[(ΘΡΑΙ pap.; ¯ m.²) is supplemented contracted Θραικ[ίαν (sc. θάλαϲϲαν) Lobel (olim), Θραικ[ίαϲ (sc. ζὰ γαίαϲ) Diehl, or uncontracted Θραΐκ[ων (sc. ζὰ γαίαϲ) Lobel (postea). The longum sign, added by m.² in the Alcaeus papyrus, obviously suggests the uncontracted form. Here, Θρᾴ[ϊκοϲ qualifying Οἰά|γ]ρου is simpler.– θρή[νοιϲα μιμοῦμαι Puglia.

Οἰά|[γ]ρου: The three longs are necessary. If Lesbian, Οἰάγρω.

10. The period can well end after Ὀρφέα. If, however, the construction follows the metrical pattern, a further characterization of Orpheus should complete the couplet, even though the next period (11 ff.) would then start asyndetically. Given that the poem deals with Orpheus' singing excellence, it would be strange, if only the name of his father were mentioned in his parentage. Οἴαγροϲ, 'lonely in the wilderness', implied Orpheus' relationship with wildlife, but his connection with singing was suggested by the name of his mother, the Muse Καλλιόπα, meaning 'beautiful-voiced'. λιγείαϲ (Lesb. λιγήαϲ) is proposed exempli gratia from Stesich. PMG 63.1 Καλλιόπεια λίγεια.– Κ[αλλιόπαϲ τε (τόν) edd. pr. ('vielleicht').

11. [ἑρ]πετὰ πάντα κ[λαῖε; if Lesbian, ὄρπετα. Obviously, what is meant by ἑρπετά is 'animals', not 'reptiles'. The lament of the wildlife is described by the epigrammatist Damagetus, AP 7.10.7–8 ἐπωδύραντο δὲ πέτραι | καὶ δρύεϲ, ἃϲ ἐρατῆι τὸ πρὶν ἔθελγε λύρηι; also, Ovid, Met. 11.44–49.– [ἑρ]πετὰ πάντα κ[ηλοῦντα or κ[ηλήϲαντα (ἀοιδᾶι) edd. pr.

κ[λαῖε κακὸν μόρον,] exempli gratia. κακὸν μόρον Il. 6.357, 21.133, Od. 1.166, 11.618; κλαίουϲα κακὸν μόρον AP 7.627.5 (Diodorus).

12. [ἇ̑]ϲ: The 'punktförmige Spur oben' (edd. pr.) is a wide top curve that does not continue on the right-hand side, therefore necessarily a sigma. The space before it suffices for only one letter. I supplement [ἇ̑]ϲ, Doric for ἕωϲ (ἇϲ Lesbian), construed with a past tense indicative verb, the reconstructed in verse 13 κι[θάριζ᾽ ἔτι: 'All animals lamented the wicked death, till the sea took the lyre and continued playing it'.

τὰν ἐρατάν appears as epithet of musical instruments: in Damagetus' epigram mentioned above, referred to already by the *edd. pr.*, Orpheus' lyre is described as ἐρατῆι ... λύρηι; also, *h. Hom. Merc.* 153 χέλυν ἐρατήν. In the case of Orpheus, perhaps not a typical epithet, but one describing the special relationship of the wildlife with Orpheus' enchanting music. Actually, ἑρπετὰ ... κλαῖε ... ἆc ... ἃλc ... κιθάριζ᾽ ἔτι is describing the relief felt by the wildlife for the rescue of their beloved lyre. There was no other place for supplementing the necessary subject of λα[βοῖcα, ἔχοιcα, and κι[θάριζε], i.e. the sea, and so I resorted to the monosyllable ἅλc, though no certain nominative singular seems to have been attested. Emp. B 56, mentioned in LSJ as an exceptional nominative occurrence for 'sea', rather combines 'salt' and 'sea': ἅλc ἐπάγη ῥιπῆcιν ἑωcμένοc ἠελίοιο (note the masculine). On the contrary, Moschus fr. 1.3 ἁ μεγάλα μ᾽ ἅλc, though a product of emendation (Edmonds), is distinctly possible. The note of LSJ, s.v. ἅλc (B), 'generally of shallow water near shore', is fitting here, since the sea must have received the lyre near the shore. – Puglia associates the adj. ἐρατάν with the deceased Eurydice.

13. Obviously, a reference to the legend that, after Orpheus' dismemberment, his lyre was thrown into the sea, where it continued ringing. Phanocles, fr. 1.16–17 (Powell) ἠχὴ δ᾽ ὣc λιγυρῆc πόντον ἐπέcχε λύρηc, | νήcουc τ᾽ αἰγιαλούc θ᾽ ἁλιμυρέαc, 'and thus the sound of the clear-ringing lyre extended over the sea and the islands and the sea-washed shores'. There is no space available to add Orpheus' severed head too, as in Phanocles, 11–14.

[εὔ]φθογγόν <τε> λύραν: cf. Aristonous, *Paean in Apoll.* 15 (Powell) εὐφθόγγου τε λύραc. The necessary τε that connects the two epithets of λύρα also fills the missing metrical position.

κι[θάριζ᾽ ἔτι]: '12 [verse 13] Gegen Ende ist Dikolon möglich' *edd. pr.* But the supposed dicolon would have a tilt opposite not only to the other dicola but also to the rest of the written text. What looks like a dicolon can be a kappa, especially if, as I discern, the supposed low dot is actually a stroke in an angle that agrees only with the low prong of the fork of kappa. Its tall upright is almost completely abraded, leaving, however, intact its top end and some faint traces in the rest. The upper prong of the fork of kappa, which falls in a tiny part of the papyrus surface that was scraped away, is not visible. The iota that follows, though mixed up with a vertical fibre, is certain.

κιθάριζ(ε): Cf. *h. Merc.* 423 λύρῃ δ᾽ ἐρατὸν κιθαρίζων; Clin. test. 1 (Ath. 14.624a) ἀναλαμβάνων τὴν λύραν ἐκιθάριζεν.

14 f. Certainly παν[('vielleicht πᾶν oder πάν[τα' *edd. pr.*). Πᾶν[α would be possible. However, I was unable to find any connection of Pan with the legend of Orpheus, though the alliance of a god and a mortal who both had close association with wildlife and music would seem natural. On the other hand, I do not see in what way Pan might assist the sea in making the lyre continue ringing. Possibly, πάν[τα singular masculine connected with e.g. ἄνεμον. Κάλαϊc, Orpheus' alleged lover, was a winged son of Thracian Boreas. His name is derived in Schol. Pind. *Pyth.* 4.182 from καλῶc ἄημι or ἄω. In Ovid, *Met.* 11.43, Orpheus' soul *in ventos ... recessit*. But the assistance implied by cυνεργόν is manifest in Lucian's account of the myth: *Ind.* 11.8 τὴν λύραν δὲ αὐτὴν ὑπηχεῖν τῶν ἀνέμων ἐμπιπτόντων ταῖc χορδαῖc, 'the lyre echoed as the winds fell upon the strings'. However, since the floating lyre had a specific route from Thrace to Lesbos, not every wind was needed for assisting the sea; just the North wind, which in the area is called Θραϊκίαc or Θραικίαc.[19] Therefore, it might be preferable to choose πάν[ται, e.g. [cυ]νεργὸν ἔχοιcα πάν[ται] | [Θρᾱϊκίαν ἄνεμον], 'being assisted in every way by the Thracian wind'. 'In every way' would include both the musical assistance by blowing upon the lyre strings and the conveyance of the lyre to Lesbos.– According to Puglia (with Franco Ferrari), [cυ]νεργὸν ἔχοιcα πάν[των πόνων ἐμῶν, with the 'abbandonata' declaring that the lyre was assistant in her pains.

Authorship

To sum up, though the questions about the nature of the poem are more or less answered, the authorship issue is still pending.[20]

What speaks against a Sapphic authorship? (*a*) The dialect, which seems to follow the conventional 'Doric' of lyric poetry, though the surviving text does not present any prohibitive discrepancies between Lesbian and 'Doric'. The usual tendency to epicize or Atticize dialectal texts may justify the non-Lesbian forms: ἄπνουc, Οἰάγ]ρου and ἐπᾶc(αι), the first of which may be original, the second and the third impose necessary emendation. However, three cases of exclusively Lesbian features strongly debilitate the argument. (*b*) The vocabulary contains

---

[19] It is still called Θρακιάc in Modern Greek.
[20] From the sum of my readings on the subject, it is fair to single out Clayman (2011). I believe she approached the truth about the theme and the object of the poem, but by accepting the views expressed on its metre, dialect, and vocabulary as indisputable facts, and by avoiding to deal with the text, she regretfully falls into the trap of the supposed autograph in a Hellenistic anthology.

some words that first appear in later literature. Yet, none of the words described as 'modern' must obligatorily be excluded from an archaic poem. (c) The heterometric structure of the ode's opening, with its initial hexametric quotation dramatically connected with the lyric part, is, to the best of my knowledge, all but unique. However, the phenomenon is unique in the whole of Greek poetry, not only in Sappho. (d) The anisosyllabic character of the dactylic constituent in the lyrical part of the poem, with contraction allowed, though it is common in the other epodic poetry, is not witnessed in Aeolic poetry. However, it is not impossible. See Terpander SLG 6 Page, Ar. fr. 590.19 K.–A., κύκνος ὑπὸ πτερύγων τοιόνδε τι, where the third biceps is contracted. Obviously, Terpander is paralleled not as a dialectal Lesbian paradigm, which he is not, but as a metrical precedent. (e) The metre of the lyrical part is different from that of the preceding or neighboring poems whether in the Cologne papyrus or in POxy. 1787. But no testimony exists that the specific book of Sappho (which I claim that it was the Ninth) had exclusively one and the same metre. (f) The myth of Orpheus with the characteristics mentioned in the poem is first attested in Simonides PMG fr. 567. But nothing can preclude an unknown earlier attestation.

What speaks for a Sapphic authorship? (a) Primarily the inclusion of the poem in a papyrus roll containing Sappho poems. The change of scribe in this poem certainly weakens the argument, but the change is combined with the breaking off at the end of the previous poem, which suggests an extraordinary situation in the copying procedure; see below. (b) If the poem is thematically cognate with the other two of the papyrus, one wonders why the roll should contain a thematic anthology and not a Sapphic cycle. (c) As mentioned above, some scribal errors of understanding (1 ψιθυροπλόκε δόλιε μύθων for μυθοπλόκε ψιθύρων δολίων, 6 ἀςτέρων for ἀτέρων), entirely rule out the idea that the text is the preliminary draft of a poem composed by the owner of the papyrus. (d) μυθοπλόκος, the opening word, which is unique in the Greek literature, not only is attested as Sappho's but is also qualifying the same god, Eros. Yet, the word is not transmitted accurately so, but is restored, at the same time, however, contributing in restoring a perfect metre. (e) All three poems in the papyrus refer to stringed instruments. (f) The theme also fits well the other two poems in the papyrus, since all three speak not merely of a person's love and death, but also deal with the topic of love and death interwoven with the poetic status of the moribund person. As mentioned above, the last words of the poetess's quotation in the first poem of the Cologne papyrus and the last word of the poet in the present poem are equivalent, since both declare the deathly end of the poetic identity. (g) Personal erotic behaviour may also be a common feature, since homoerotic love that leads by means of calumny to social scandal is in the center of the third poem and is poetically justified in the second – of the first and of the poem prior to the Tithonus poem in P.Oxy. 1787 only the final parts survive. (*h*) All three poems are located in Lesbos having to do with the practice of poetry/music in the island, the first two in real life, the third – at least in its surviving portion – in the mythical world, but probably as a mythical exemplum for real life.

A further argument, perhaps more decisive, may be added here. The alphabetic arrangement of Sappho's poems by their first verse had been noticed by Hunt already in 1914, and was hesitantly supported by Lobel in his *Caπφοῦc Μέλη* in 1925, p. xv–xvi. Lobel's inklings were verified with the publication of P.GC inv. 105 by Fish - Burris - Obbink[21] and of P. Sapph. Obbink, which belongs to the same roll.[22] However, all these observations were limited to Sappho Book 1. Only Lobel had suggested that in P.Oxy. 1787 (which, as he believed, belonged to Book 4) four poems with an incipit of ε were represented (Sa. 59, 62, 82, LP 87 (1) [om. Voigt]).[23] In P.Colon. 21351+21376, the only poem with a visible incipit is the poem under discussion: ψιθυροπλοκε or, if my proposal is accepted, μυθοπλοκε. Yet, the incipit of the previous poem (Tithonus poem) can be easily restored. What is transmitted in the first verse of the poem in the Cologne papyrus, combined with P.Oxy. 1787, is:

×–⏑⏑–– ἰ]οκ[ό]λπων κάλα δῶρα, παῖδ.ε.c,
×–⏑⏑––]μ φιλάοιδον, λιγύραν χέλυνναν.

It was proposed already in 1926 by Stiebitz that the substantive qualified by ἰοκόλπων is Μοίcαν, but the name could fill either the two syllables preceding ἰοκόλπων or the two initial ones of the verse. Every restoration proposal so far follows the first option. I believe that, stylistically, the second option is preferable, with a verbal form in-between on which κάλα δῶρα would depend. *Exempli gratia*,

---

21 Burris, Fish and Obbink (2014).
22 See West (2014), esp. 1, 3, and Obbink (2015), 4 and esp. 11 (n. 15). Dale (2015).
23 I now agree that Sa. 59 is most likely a new poem and not the end of Sa. 58 ('Tithonus poem'); see above '3. Kleïs as Promoter of Sappho's Poetry (fr. 59 V.)'. Sa. 62 starts with ε (ἑπτάξατε), but this does not support the alphabetic argument, since the next poem in the same column starts with ο (Ὄνοιρε); see below. Sa. 82, from Heph. *Ench.* 11.5, p. 36 C., εὐμορφοτέρα Μναcιδίκα τὰc ἁπάλαc Γυρίννωc, is, in my view, a distinctly atypical Sapphic incipit. It is considered a first verse, because of Hephaestion's habit to cite the first verse of a poem as an example of a metre. Here, however, Hephaestion cites two verses, one with a long initial anceps (Sa. 82) and another with a short one, fr. 92 ἀcαροτέραc οὐδάμα πω, Ἴρανα, cέθεν τύχοιcαν, which nobody ever thought of as an incipit; POxy. 1787 fr. 34.5 εὐ]μορφο[τέρα proves nothing. LP 87 (1) starts with ε (ἐπ[) after a coronis.

Μοίϲαν ἐπιδείξαϲθ' ἰ]οκ[ό]λπων κάλα δῶρα, παῖδιεͺc,
καὶ παίξατε κὰτ τὰ]ν²⁴ φιλάοιδον, λιγύραν χέλυνναν.

Μοίϲαν is a most convenient incipit right before μυθόπλοκε in an alphabetic arrangement of the poems, especially in a low-frequency initial letter of the Greek language such as μ. However, Ἐκδείξατε Μοίϲαν ἰ]οκ[ό]λπων κτλ. is equally possible. The suggestion that fr. 59, which follows contiguously fr. 58 (the Tithonus poem) in P.Oxy. 1787, presents an incipit with ε (ἐπῖν[), does not invalidate the argument, since the case comes from a different papyrus.²⁵ In any case, I doubt that P.Oxy. 1787, which gives a different poem than the Cologne papyrus before the Tithonus poem (fr. 58.1–10), adheres to the alphabetic principle. In the only manifest instance of two consecutive poems that have their first verses intact, the initials are ε (fr. 62 ἐπτάξατε[) and ο (fr. 63 Ὄνοιρε), and it is hard to believe that in a whole book of Sappho no poem started with a letter between ε and ο.²⁶

As for the end of Sappho's Tithonus poem we may conclude that it has been omitted in P.Colon. 21351+21376, since the verses of Sa. 58.23–26 are missing. In my view, Di Benedetto's proposal, that the last four verses of Sa. 58 + the three of 59 open a new poem, the ἀβροϲύνα poem, a proposal accepted by many scholars, cannot stand. It presupposes that the Tithonus poem closed with the end of the mythical exemplum, in other words, that Sappho used an exemplum but did not exploit it. A mythical exemplum in lyrical poetry is typically followed by a reference to the lyrical 'I', thus linking the message of the myth with the real situation described in the poem. Sappho is complaining about the effects of old age on herself. The Tithonus myth teaches that not even immortality can eliminate these effects, it actually aggravates them, especially when the old person lives in close relationship with a young person (Eos, Tithonus' immortal wife, eternally young since she is born every new morning). This is exactly how Sappho associates the myth with her personal situation. We do not know what was said in 23–24, though it is likely that a god is mentioned (Κρονίδαιc?) who can grant either death or

---

24 Di Benedetto χορεύϲατε κὰτ τὰ]ν. Cf. Pind. *Paian.* 52g.11 γλυκὺν κατ' αὐλόν.
25 Luppe (2004); Tsantsanoglou (2009a), esp. 6–7. Yatromanolakis (2008), 240 ff. connects fr. 59 with 58, but proposes two different sympotic versions. Di Benedetto (2004) and (2006) believed that the four verses open a separate poem. Lundon (2007) finds that sometimes remnants of a coronis can give the misleading impression of paragraphoi. See n. 23 above.
26 Dale (2015), 19 n. 29, notes the same argument, though he claims that 'this point shouldn't be pressed too far'. In support of his view, he strangely presents the case of Pindar's epinicians, which, if arranged alphabetically, would have eleven (twelve in my counting) poems intervening between ε and ο.

health (?). What she feels affection for is ἀβροcύνα, gracious elegance, a decorous synonym of female beauty, and life for her is not worth loving (ἔρωc ἀελίω) if it is limited to the sun's brightness and is not coupled with beauty, τὸ καλόν. It is this καλόν she lacks now personally, though living in close bond with it, i.e. with the παῖδεc, who in the opening of the poem are dancing while she is unable to join in. These παῖδεc of the first line, an essential component of the comparison, by no means could be forgotten after the mythical exemplum.

However, apart from these arguments, which may be regarded as subjective, there exists objective and factual evidence, that was not given due attention. The 'undeutliches Zeichen' at the poem's beginning was described by most scholars as standing for a coronis. But the basic function of the coronis is that of separating two poems or large verse units. And this function is fully reflected on its shape which is divided in two, with the upper half covering the margin at the end of the previous unit and the lower half the one at the opening of the next unit. In the middle, a horizontal stroke indicates the point of the division. Even the dullest of scribes should know this function of the coronis and would try to draw it in a comparable manner. Here, the sign is entirely different. A very detailed description of the sign is given by Lundon (2015), 154 f. However, I am completely unable to see the 'segno vagamente zoomorfico che richiama il volatile del papiro di Timoteo – pare infatti di poter distinguere testa, becco, collo, corpo', which Lundon believes to stand for a coronis. I also fail to understand how 'la sua (sc. del segno) posizione, la sua funzione, la sua forma e il suo orientamento a sinistra' (n. 26) relate to the sign of P.Colon., which, as I see, has a different position, opposite the first verse of the second poem only, a completely different form, and an orientation clearly to the right. As for its function, it is a matter of interpretation. The two poems are divided by a paragraphos, longer than the usual paragraphos that divides the distichs of the Tithonus poem. I may be wrong, but I have the impression that a normal distich paragraphos has been extended to show the division of the poems. The sign in question is drawn on the left of the new poem's first verse. The thickness and the tone of the ink suggest the scribe of the Tithonus poem. It looks like a slash with an arrow-point projection at its bottom. At its top, two short rightward horizontal strokes appear. The slash is also crossed by two longer horizontal strokes. The long horizontal strokes must be *obeli* (–), the usual critical signs that mark spurious verses. However, as I do not find double *obeli* in literary papyri, it seems that the upper *obelus* was noted first, for marking that something was wrong at the end of the Tithonus poem, no doubt the omission of a number of verses, whereas the lower one must have been placed right opposite the first verse of the Orpheus poem, where we conjectured an extended corruption. The main sign is, however, the critical sign known as *ancora inferior*. It appears in the shape of ⩔, sometimes also with a pointed end or in other versions. The *ancora* usually indicates omissions made good elsewhere, the place where the correction was to be found being designated with the words ἄνω or κάτω, i.e. the upper or the lower margin. The shape of the sign here (downward arrow) indicates the upper margin.[27] I do not know what the function of the two short horizontal strokes is. Given the great antiquity of the Cologne papyrus, I cannot exclude the possibility that the design with the two horizontal strokes was the original form of the *ancora*. Still, the space between the two parallels may well indicate the exact position of the omission, here being under the last verse of the Tithonus poem and before the beginning of the Orpheus poem. It is this exact position that is also highlighted with the upper *obelus*. Though much of the upper margin and a considerable part of the lower one in this area has survived, no trace of the omitted verses is visible. On the other hand, the omission was so large that I doubt if the margins offered sufficient space for making it good. Another possibility that could be considered is that here the *ancora* indicates not omission but erroneous text put right elsewhere. Actually, the definition of the *ancora inferior* in the *Anecdotum Parisinum* is *ad humilius vel inconvenientius quid enuntiatum*, '(placed) at some defective or unsuitable reading'.[28] If so, the *ancora* would indicate where the correction of the corrupt opening of the Orpheus poem was to be found. Yet, I find this possibility less likely, being content with the low *obelus* as marking the erroneous opening.

This means that the scribe of the Cologne papyrus omitted 4 verses from the end of the Tithonus poem; thus the whole poem consisted of 8 distichs. Naturally, it is impossible to reconstruct the circumstances of the writing of the papyrus. Yet, it is obvious that something extraordinary must have happened, since the first scribe ended his writing of the Tithonus poem leaving it unfinished, but marked the omission in a marginal sign, before passing the baton to an inexperienced scribe who started with another poem. Above, in enumerating the arguments that speak for a Sapphic authorship, I referred to '(g) Personal erotic behaviour may also be a common feature, since homoerotic love that leads by means of calumny to social scandal is in the center of the third poem and is poetically justified in the second'. Is it coincidental that these two cases were the omitted parts in the Cologne papyrus? The final verses of the Tithonus poem, where

---

27 McNamee (1992), 13, remarks that the sign's '"business end"– the directional pointer – was normally the open part of its central shaft'.
28 Gudeman, *RE*, art. 'Kritische Zeichen', col. 1926; Turner (²1987), 16, pl. 12, 34, 41; McNamee (1992), 11–13, and *passim*.

Sappho declares her personal love of ἀβροcύνα, i.e., female beauty, were completely omitted, while another scribe was commissioned to write the Orpheus poem, which seems to consist of a dramatic apology for the unorthodox situation. A bowdlerizing Greek scribe in third century BC Egypt would be a most exceptional occasion. It cannot be ruled out, though some more convincing explanation would be preferable.

If the poem is written in the archaic times, it must be the oldest reference to Orpheus and the first account of his death. Could it be that the legend about the lyre was inspired by the present poet? Be that as it may, whoever may have invented or exploited it, the reference, which can be associated with the localistic pride about the musical prominence of the Lesbians (Sa. 106 πέρροχοc, ὠc ὄ τ᾽[29] ἄοιδοc ὀ Λέcβιοc ἀλλοδάποιcιν), seems to be a subtly expressed Dichterweihe. If, further, Antissa in Lesbos, where the lyre was said to have been washed ashore, was mentioned, along with her most famous son, Terpander,[30] some Terpandrian traits we encounter in the poem, e.g., the particular lyric metre, can be possibly justified as honorific reminders.

But the poetological interconnection provides only the frame for unfolding the erotic subject. Because, as mentioned before, the poem is about love that leads by means of calumny to social scandal and to personal disaster, at the same time, however, to poetic prominence and immortality. Orpheus was a poet and musician, actually the paragon of poetry and music, who was slandered as having fallen in love with young Kalaïs, the son of Boreas, thus introducing male homosexual love into Thrace: Phanocles 1.5–6

ἀλλ᾽ αἰεί μιν ἄγρυπνοι ὑπὸ ψυχῇ μεληδῶναι
ἔτρυχον θαλερὸν δερκομένου Κάλαϊν.

Therefore, the Thracian women or maenads killed and dismembered him, in the words of Phanocles, 1.9–10,

---

[29] Not ὅτ(α) but ὅ τ(οι), in the usual employment of the particle 'with a proverb or general reflection': Denniston *GP* 542 f.
[30] E.g., Nicomachus of Gerasa, *Exc.* 1: ἀναιρεθέντοc δὲ τοῦ Ὀρφέωc ὑπὸ τῶν Θρᾳκικῶν γυναικῶν τὴν λύραν αὐτοῦ βληθῆναι εἰc τὴν θάλαccαν, ἐκβληθῆναι δὲ εἰc Ἄντιccαν πόλιν τῆc Λέcβου. εὑρόνταc δὲ ἀλιέαc ἐνεγκεῖν τὴν λύραν πρὸc Τέρπανδρον. It is noteworthy that, as in the papyrus song of Orpheus, no mention is made of the head of Orpheus. Ovid, *Met.* 11.55, mentions the shore of Methymna (*Methymnaeae ... litore Lesbi*). Sappho's hometown was Eresos. All three towns are close to each other, in the north and west side of Lesbos.

οὕνεκα πρῶτος ἔδειξεν ἐνὶ Θρήκεccιν ἔρωταc
ἄρρεναc, οὐδὲ πόθουc ᾔνεcε θηλυτέρων,

or, as Ovid puts it, *Met.* 10.83-85,

ille etiam Thracum populis fuit auctor amorem
in teneros transferre mares, citraque juventam
aetatis breve ver et primos carpere flores.

Now, Sappho, was a poetess and musician, heir of Orpheus, born and grown in the island where his singing lyre was washed ashore, envied for her poetic and musical skill, who, as the analogy demands, was slandered as having fallen in love with young girls in her circle, thus advocating female homosexual love in Lesbos. No evidence has survived that during her lifetime she had fallen victim to this accusation. All testimonies to the opposite are relatively late and come from tackling ambivalent passages in her poems. We miss the end of the poem. So, we do not know whether the analogy was expressly referred to or was left to the listeners to assume. The latter seems more likely. But neither is anything explicit said about Orpheus whether in the distich of his death cry or in the narration that follows. However, what most concerns us here, whoever the poet may be, is that he/she associates physical death with poetic immortality, and being himself/herself a poet, his/her own physical death with poetic immortality. The death cry of Orpheus passes to the present poet's mouth, summing up all the concerns of Sappho's last book, beauty and love, love and poetry, poetry and death, death and lasting poetic renown.

It is time now to see how the poem would appear if it were written by Sappho:

```
        «μυθοπλόκε, ψιθύρων δολίων αὐτούργ᾽, ἐπίβουλε
 2      παῖ βροτολοιγέ τ᾽ [Ἔρω, κ]ακ[ότ]η[τοc] ἑταῖρε, (vel -ροc) ἀφέρπω.»
        δ[
 4      τ[            ἄ]χαν
        ἄπνουc ⌊πρὸ[c μάκρον⌋ Δίοc αἴθερα]
 6      [λ]άοιc ἀ⟦c⟧τέρων τε [φώτων,]
        [ἐ]c πυριφέγγεοc ἀελ[ίω cέλαc]
 8      [ἄcτρων τ᾽] ἐπάειc᾽ ἀκούω
        Θρᾴ[ϊκοc Οἰάγ]ρω κόρον Ὀρφέα
10      κ[αὶ Καλλιόπαc λιγῆαc.]
        [ὄρ]πετα πάντα κ[λαῖε κάκον μόρον,]
12      [ἆ]c τὰν ἐράταν λά[βοιc᾽ ἄλc]
        [εὔ]φθογγόν <τε> λύραν κι[θάριcδ᾽ ἔτι]
14      [cύ]νεργον ἔχοιcα πάν[ται]
        [Θραϊκίαν ἄνεμον]
```

5 P. Sapph. Obbink: the '*Kypris Poem*'

Of the two poems[1] that survived in *P. Sapph. Obbink*,[2] the second one, tagged by the editor as "Kypris Poem" (*KP*), is a most interesting piece, a perfect counterpoint to fr. 1 Ποικιλόθρον' ἀθανάτ'Ἀφρόδιτα. The poetess, who in that poem supplicates her patron goddess to help her in attracting the object of her love, seems here to complain about exactly the opposite: about not allowing her to be freed from the bonds of love. Our reading and restoration proposals followed by a translation and some short comments are presented below:

⊗ πῶc κε δή τιc οὐ θαμέωc ἄcαιτο,
    Κύπρι δέcπο̣ι̣ν̣', ὄττινα [δ]ὴ φιλ̣[ήcαι,
    κωὒ] θέλοι μάλιcτα πάθε̣'_ἐκδά[μ]αc̣[cαι;
        μή μ'] ὀνέχηcθα·
    πᾶι 'μάλοιcί μ' ἀλεμάτωc δαΐcδ[ηc;   5
    εἰ μ' Ἔρω λῦ{ι}c'· ἀντὶ γόνω με cίν[ν̣ε̣αι.
    πόλλ' ἀπά[μ]μαι μ'. οὐ πρό[παρ οἶ] πέρηcα̣[ν
        ὄττ' ὀνεέρξαι
    — ⏑ — × —] cε· θέλω [δὲ — —
    — ⏑ — × —]το πάθη[⏑ — —   10
    — ⏑ — × —] ̣αν· ἔγω δ' ἔμ' ̣αὔται
        τοῦτο cύ̣νοιδα
    ]β̣[ρ]ότοιc̣[. . .] ̣[
    — ⏑ — × —]ε̣ναμ[— ⏑ — ×
        ] ̣[̣] ̣[15

PSO = *P. Sapph. Obbink*, *P. Oxy.* = *P. Oxy.* 1231 fr. 16, Ts. = Tsantsanoglou-Tselikas[3]

2 δέcπο̣ι̣ν̣' leg. Benelli |]ττινα̣[*P. Oxy.*, ὄττιν[. .]η *PSO* | [δ]ὴ Burris (ap. Obbink) : [μ]ὴ Ferrari | φιλ̣[είη Obbink : φιλ̣[ήcαι Ts. : φίλ̣[ηcθα West, Obbink, Ferrari | ὄττινι μὴ φίλ̣[ηται olim Ts. inepte ‖ **3** κωὒ] E.E. Prodi : καὶ] Obbink : ὠc] Ferrari : κὠc vel κὤν vel τῶν West |

---

1 The article was written jointly by the author and Sotiris Tselikas. We are very grateful to J. Hammerstaedt for his deft and beneficial criticism to some former versions of this paper. Wherever we differed from his advices, we are to blame.
2 D. Obbink (2014). The opening of the second stanza has been integrated by Burris (2017) with fr. 4 of *P. GC* inv. 105, the papyrus to which *PSO* also belonged. So, we name this fragment also *PSO*. After this happy join, we thought it was proper not to discuss or mention in the app. cr. the proposals (ours included) that were made for this portion of the text before Burris's publication.
3 Our app. crit. is not exhaustive. For a more comprehensive one we refer the reader to Neri (2017).

πάθε᾿ ἐκδά[μ]ας[και; Ts. (ΠΑΘ PSO) : πάλιν κάλ[εςςαι Obbink : πάθος καλ[ύπτην West : πάθος κάλ[υψαι Ferrari ‖ 4 μή μ᾿] ὀνέχ. Ts. : ποῖ]ον ἔχ. (/ νῶν) Obbink : πῶς] ὀνέχ. Holford-Strevens (ap. Obbink) : οὐκ] ὀνέχ. West : μηδ᾿] ὀνέχ. Ferrari ‖ 5 παῖ 'μάλοιςι (sc. ἀμάλ.) Ts. : παῖ βάλοιςα Burris : (cὺν) ςάλοιςί Ferrari ‖ δαΐςδ[ης West : δαΐςδ[ην Obbink ‖ 6 εἰ μ᾿ Ἔρω Ts. : εἰμέρω Burris (iam ἰμέ]ρω<ι> Obbink, qui etiam de genetivo]ρω cogitat, Ferrari) ‖ λῦ{ι}ς᾿· ἀντὶ Ts. : λύςςαντι West, Burris : λύ{ι}ςαντι Obbink, Ferrari ‖ ΑΝΤΙ·ΓΟΝΩ PSO, P. Oxy. ‖ (ἀντὶ) γόνω Ts. : γόνωμ᾿ (= γουνοῦμαι) West : γόν᾿ ὤ<ι>μ᾿ Ferrari : λύ{ι}ςαντι γόν᾿ olim Tsantsanoglou ‖ με cίν[νεαι (an cίν[νη;?) Ts. : ἔγα[ιρε West : ἔγ[ω δὲ Ferrari ‖ 7 ΠΟΛΛΑΠΑΜΠΑΝΜ PSO (leg. Burris) : ΠΟΛΛΑΠΑ⟦Μ⟧ΜΑΙΜ PSO :]ΟΜ᾿ P.Oxy. (Hunt) :] ΙΜ (recte Lobel) ‖ πόλλα πάμπαν μ᾿ Burris : πόλλ᾿ ἀπά⟦μ⟧μα⟦ς⟧ μ᾿ olim Ts.; nunc πόλλ᾿ ἀπά⟦μ⟧μαι μ᾿ Neri, Ts. ‖]ΠΡΟ[et]ΤΕΡΗC[PSO (leg. Obbink) : ΠΡΕ[(leg. Ts. olim inepte) et]ΠΕΡΗC[(leg. West, Ferrari),]ΠΕΡΗCΑ[(leg. Ts.) ‖ πρότερ᾿ ἦς [᪴ – – vel ἦς[θα – – West : προ[τόνοις] περής[ην Ferrari (περής[ην olim West) : προτέρ᾿ ἦς[θα – × Burris : πρό[παρ οἴ] πέρηςα[ν Ts. (πρέ[πον ἦς] πέρηςα[ί μ᾿ olim inepte) ‖ 8 ΟΥΤ PSO (leg. Burris) : ΟΤΤ (leg. Ts.) ‖ οὔτ᾿ Burris : ὄττ᾿ Ts. ‖ ΟΝΕΕΡ Ι PSO :]ΑΙ P. Oxy. ‖ ὀνέερχ[θ]αι Burris (ςυν]εέρχ[θ]αι iam Obbink : αἴ κε]ν ἔερχ[θ]αι Ferrari) : ὀνεέρξαι Ts. ‖ 9 CE· P. Oxy. ‖ 10 ΠΑΘΗ[P. Oxy. ‖ πάθη[ν vel πάθη[μα ‖ 11s. Hunt ex Ap. Dysc. GG II/1 51.1 ss. et 80.10 ss. ‖ 13 β[ρ]ότοις Lobel : an ἀμ]β[ρ]ότοις?

"How could one not be often distressed, Lady Kypris, whomever one might fall in love with, and wouldn't wish above all to subdue utterly the sufferings? Don't hold me back. Why do you tear me to pieces with tender ones in vain? Come now! Set me free from Eros. You are hurting me in order to please your son. You lacerate me a lot. In the past, those who overcame the obstacles didn't (face you as enemy). I wish to ... And I can bear witness about this ... (im)mortals ...".

2. In *PSO* the area between ΤΙΝ and ΗΦΙ is completely abraded. In *P. Oxy.*, led astray by an old black and white photograph, we thought we could read] οττινι μ[. We were wrong. Obbink's δή (proposed by Burris) is, we believe, right. Beside ὄττινα, it stresses the indefinite notion, while the conditional relative clause is completed with an optative: φιλείη, as proposed by Obbink, or rather φιλήςαι, in agreement with the aorist ἄςαιτο of the apodosis. Subject τις: 'no matter whom one might fall in love with'. Is the phrase a smart way for concealing the gender of the object of love? The indefinite and generic references will turn to personal in line 4: μ(ε).

3. κωὒ] θέλοι, the second prong of the question, copulatively connected, comes as a natural consequence of the first, i.e. καὶ (πῶς κε δή τις) οὐ θέλοι ...; see Smyth, *GG* § 2874 (with § 2288).

Obbink's reading at the end of line 3 is far from certain. First, πάλιν is impossible and πάθος proposed by West[4] is much likelier. θ is the best reading, with its curves somewhat abraded, so that their remnants seem to be thinner than usual.

---

[4] West (2014).

However, following θ, a small curve cannot belong to ο; it can belong to the low part of an ε. Of the next letter only a low somewhat curved tip survives. It can belong to the low end of c or ε. α has also sometimes its right-hand tail extended, but not with an upward turn as here. Next, Obbink's reading κάλ[εccαι or κάλ[ηcθαι, 'to call back', 'to call again', or West's καλ[ύπτην and Ferrari's κάλ[υψαι, 'to conceal', 'to hide', cannot be verified. The question is what follows κ, which has unanimously been identified as α. It is a triangular letter, which unlike Λ has its low stroke horizontal. This would be readily read Δ, had this bottom horizontal not met the left-hand oblique somewhat higher than its low end. However, two more identical *deltas* can be found in *PSO: BP* 9 τὰ Δ' ἄλλα, 11 εὔΔιαι. The next letter, also triangular, with its free top right-hand oblique and the tip of a low left-hand oblique can be only α or λ, but, given that the cluster κδλ is impossible in Greek, we must settle for κδα. Now, we can also exclude reading ΠΆΘΕϹΚΔΑ[, which forms another un-Greek consonant cluster. The lacuna after ΠΆΘΕΕΚΔΑ[can accommodate either two middle-sized letters or one large (μ, π, ω). After the lacuna, the right-hand curved oblique of an α is visible. It is followed by an obvious c. Then, we can read πάθε'‿ἐκδά[μ]αc[cαι with the double ε in synecphonesis. The infinitive with ἐκ should mean 'defeat utterly', 'subdue utterly'. ἐκδάμνημι or ἐκδαμάω/-άζω is not recorded in LSJ[9], though it occurs in several late authors (*Aesop.* I 2 H.-H., *Fab. Synt. phil.* 5,3 [p. 156] ἐκδαμάcαcθαι, [Io. Chr.] *El. proph. PG* LVI 585,37 ἐκδαμαcθέντα, Theod. Cyrr. *Interpr. in Dan. PG* LXXXI 1420,16 ἐκδαμάζει, ἐκδαμάcει, Diosc. Aphr. fr. 6,21 Heitsch ἐξεδάμαccεν). Still, it occurs in Theogn. 1350 ἐξεδάμην καλοῦ παιδὸς ἔρωτι δαμείc, where the hyperbolical expression was not understood ('I am devastated having been subdued by the love for a handsome boy'), and being considered as a stylistically annoying repetition (ἐξεδάμην … δαμείc) was changed by Baiter to the insipid ἐξεφάνην κτλ.

1–3. We do not discuss the various past approaches (ours included) that depend on readings different than 2 ὄττινα̣ [δ]ὴ and 3 πάθε'‿ἐκδά[μ]αc[cαι, on which we now confidently base our analysis. To put the meaning of the first three verses in forthright everyday speech, one would rephrase it as follows: "When a woman's feelings are repeatedly hurt by someone she loves, no matter whom, Lady Kypris, isn't it natural that she would ardently wish to overwhelm the sufferings she is going through?". This does not sound like a supplication, much less like a commonplace conversation. It rather looks like an excuse of someone who has been disciplined for not acting in accord with the wishes and the rules imposed by the goddess. Being vexed at the object of desire and fighting against it seem to be breaches of Kypris' canons. In other words, what we should expect in the verses following must be complaining remarks about the punishments Sappho was submitted to. As for the generic formulation of the address (τιc, ὄττινα), this is a common pattern of praying: "What can one do, my God, when he suffers?" clearly implies "I am suffering".

4. After the generic reference to her problem, Sappho starts stating her personal requests. ὀνέχω must be used in the sense 'hold back', 'check' (see *LSJ*^{9} s.v. ἀνέχω A.II): *Il.* 23.426 ἄνεχ' ἵππουc, Theogn. 26 οὔθ' ὕων ... οὔτ' ἀνέχων, Ar. fr. 632 K.–A. οὐκ ἀνεῖχεc cαυτόν. "Don't hold me back (in the effort to overwhelm my sufferings)". Conjunctive in -ηcθα occurs in Aeolic; see Schwyzer, *GG* I 662.

5. After the new join, Burris reads παῖ βάλοιcά μ' and translates "To what end, having shot me". The trace before the second alpha in *PSO* is described as "small trace between midline and line of writing, slightly concave to left, suggestive of lower lobe of β". However, it is very conspicuously concave to right, ending upon the left-hand foot of the loop of alpha, and clearly belongs to the end of a leftward bending oblique, like Α, Δ, Κ, Λ, Μ, Χ. C would also be possible, had its upper curve been visible, and it is not. Even these options can be reduced if we consider the tilt of the stroke. The peeled off ink of the stroke has left a quite visible whitish trace. Thus, the whole tilt seems to exclude δ, κ, and χ. With only λ and μ left (α is excluded for obvious reasons), the most likely letter seems to be μ. The large lower lobe of β is completely dissimilar, with a strong concave to left, and obviously with no end. Cf. the *BP*, where line 19, just 6 verses before the present one, starts with καὶ μάλ'. In comparison with the ΜΑλ of the *BP*, the tilt is here slightly larger. It is, however, equal to the tilt of, *e.g.*, *BP* 20 λύθειΜεν, *KP* 3 ΜΑλιcτα, 5 αλεΜΑτωc. It is then easy to read, for the time being, παιμαλοιc μ'.

Burris ascribes some reading problems to a repaired tear that runs vertically through *PSO* causing a dislocation, both vertically and horizontally, between the two sides in the area of lines 5–8 of the *Kypris Poem*. However, we believe that the argument is pressed too far. The dislocation is visible, especially the vertical one. In the two previous lines 3 and 4 the vertical dislocation between θελοι and μαλιcτα and between ονεχ and ηcθα is conspicuous, but the horizontal dislocation is minimal or nonexistent, since practically nothing is missing between the two sides. The amount of overlap in the papyrus at this point cannot be different than what it is in the two previous lines. From what we can see, we fully agree with Obbink's original description as "dot on the line close to c and narrow, as of ι" (p. 13). There is no space available for an alpha, however small and "slightly intruding into the space of preceding c", since the preceding c is almost completely visible. If the low dot that survives in the right side of the tear was the right-hand tip of alpha, then we would have to posit an unexplainable sudden widening of the tear especially in this line. Obviously, the same thing applies also for the next lines (6 λυιc and not λυcc, 7 a M cut vertically in two). After αλεματ Obbink (p. 39) discerns a "round letter as o followed by short upright". Yet, he does not exclude the left lobe of ω, after which he sees "scattered traces, perhaps more suitable to remains of a round letter than a square one". As for the "scattered traces" we cannot discern any remains of a round letter. Nevertheless, given that only two options are possible, i.e., -των and -τως, the space before δ- does not suffice for a *ny*. Thus, we cannot but agree with the unanimously accepted ἀλεμάτως, though μ' ἀλέματον cannot be excluded.

Returning now to παιμαλοιcιμ', we propose πᾶι 'μάλοιcι, i.e. πᾶι ἀμάλοιcι, with prodelision or *synaloiphe* because of the same vowel (Hamm, 38f. § 80a, h). ἀμάλοιcι, dat. pl. of masc./neut. ἀμαλός/-όν (Lesb. ἄμ-), 'soft, young', describing young animals in Homer (ἄρν' ἀμαλήν, ἀμαλῇcι cκυλάκεccι); here, substantivized neuter, it refers to young, tender, and delicate persons, who can be connected with Eros and love, the theme of the song. Genderwise, Sappho keeps both strings to her bow. "To what end do you tear me to pieces with tender ones in vain?" Expectedly, the neuter ἄμαλα can conceal a not so hidden implication to the personal referent of Sappho's complaints. Her unsuccessful target of which she seeks to be set free was no doubt an ἀμάλα πάιc. The expression is used by Callimachus: fr. 502 Pf. παῖc ἀμαλή and possibly fr. 1.11 Pf. ἀμαλὴ παῖc, from the opening of *Aetia*.[5] The expedients used by Kypris for holding Sappho back in her initial erotic state were to no avail, since the repeated (θαμέως) attempts of the poetess to entice the object of her love had failed. Neither was the girl dissuaded nor was Sappho relieved of her sufferings. On the contrary, her tribulations worsened (μ(ε) ... δαίcδῃc).

6. The erotic expedients implied are under the jurisdiction not only of Kypris, but also of the male gods of Kypris' retinue, Eros, Himeros, Pothos. One of the first two is likely to appear in the opening of this verse, and they had already been alternatively proposed before Burris' join: ἔ]ρω<ι> or Ἔ]ρω<ι>, preferred by West, ἱμέ]ρω<ι> or Ἰμέ]ρω<ι> preferred by Obbink, ἱμέ]ρω<ι> λύ{ι}cαντι Obbink, Ferrari, μή μ' ἔ]ρω<ι> (*vel* Ἔ]ρω<ι>) λύccαντι West, the latter in accordance with his proposal κνώδαλ(α) in line 5, rendered 'mordacious pests'. The prevalent view is that ἵμεροc is involved here, whether in dative or in genitive. Yet, even though μ is one of the widest letters of the scribe, still ιμε was short for filling the initial gap. As regards the grammatical case of the substantive, Obbink (*ad l.*) asserts, "a genitive in]ρω might be expected, since the scribe does not otherwise omit iota adscript wherever we can tell, either in this papyrus or in P.GC. inv. 105". The new join seemed to solve the problem of space by writing

---

5 Tsantsanoglou (2007).

εἰμέρω<ι>, according to Burris. This is, however, an impossible spelling: ει for ῑ is widespread in the Roman period in prose texts and documents, but it never intruded into lyrical (and dialectal) texts. The supposed Εἴ[λιον in POxy. 2289 (Sappho fr. 17,6 V., as proposed by Burris, Fish, and Obbink[6]) reads actually Ἡ[, which is integrated as Ἥ[ραον.[7] As for εἰ, it is an exhorting interjection, possibly related with εἶ, the imperative of εἶμι, 'come on!', 'come now!', similar to ἴθι, manifest also in other exhorting interjections (εἶα, εἶέν). See LSJ[9] s.v. εἰ A: "interjectionally, in Hom., *come now!* c. imper.". Schwyzer also identifies it (*GG* I 639, 643, 798, primarily 804) with the Homeric exhorting expressions εἰ δέ and εἰ δ' ἄγε. Its etymological connection with the conditional εἰ (Aeol. αἰ) is disputable.

As for the superfluous *iota* of λυιc-, see *Et. Gen.* B (= *Et. M.* 254.16) about δεκάφυια,[8] τὸ γὰρ φύω Αἰολικῶς φυίω φαcὶ καὶ τὸ ἁλύω ἁλυίω. Cf. also θύω (LSJ[9] s.v. 2 = 'rage', 'seethe') ~ θυίω and ὀπύω ~ ὀπυίω. The etymologists see a suffix *-ye/o-* in φυίω (cf. Lat. *fio*, al.). It has been proposed that the form might be restored in Alc. fr. 10.5 V. φύει. The phenomenon has been traced in non-Aeolic environment: δίφυιοc occurring in Aesch. *Ag.* 1469 and the Hellenistic epigrammatist Antagoras (fr. 1.7 Pow.), and ζίφυιον found in inscriptions in Elis. This is the first evidence for λύω. Still, the *iota* of λυίω being a suffix should be normally dropped in the aorist. If so, whatever λυιc- stands for, it can only be explained as a hyperdialectism, and the form must be printed in the text, as Obbink does, λυ{ι}c-.

Further, the reading λυ{ι}cαντι need not impose changing the genitive of the noun to dative (Ἔρω<ι>), if a different articulation is adopted: εἰ μ' Ἔρω λῦ{ι}c', with the verb in middle imperative (λῦcαι); LSJ[9] s.v. λύω I.2.b "c. gen. rei [...] Med., prop. *get* one *loosed* or *set free*, λύcαcθαί τινα δυcφροcυνάων Hes. *Th.* 528; ὅcπερ Ἰὼ πημονᾶc ἐλύcατο Aesch. *Supp.* 1065 (lyr.)". Translate: "Come now! Set me free from Eros".

Then, λύcαντι γόν', which Tsantsanoglou has privately suggested in the past, is no longer applicable. Instead, it would be better to punctuate after λῦ{ι}c' and start a new sentence with ἀντὶ γόνω. It is noteworthy that both papyri, *P. Oxy.* and *PSO*, use a high dot for *diastole* between αντι and γόνω,[9] in order to avert reading Ἀντιγόνω. Here, ἀντὶ γόνω = 'in your offspring's interest, for his advantage, to please him'; cf. Soph. *El.* 537f. (Clytemnestra about Agamemnon's brother) ἀντ' ἀδελφοῦ δῆτα Μενέλεω κτανὼν / τἄμ', *OC* 1326f. (Polynices about

---

6 (2014), esp. 21.
7 See below '10. The Danaans in Lesbos (Sappho fr. 17 V.)'.
8 Cf. Call. fr. 516 Pf., with Pfeiffer's note *ad l.*
9 See Turner, *GMAW*[2] 11 n. 47.

Oedipus' daughters) ἀντὶ παίδων τῶνδε καὶ ψυχῆς, πάτερ, / ἱκετεύομέν cε.[10] It is interesting that all three parallels of this use of ἀντί concern cases of kinship. The introduction of the son here is normal, since Sappho explains the partial attitude of the goddess on mythological grounds. In the present case, Sappho and Eros act competitively, but the latter has expectedly the upper hand, as he enjoys his mother's favour.

Sappho, as is natural, mentions Eros plenty of times; once (fr. 159 V.) as Aphrodite's attendant, another time (fr. 198a V., from *schol*. Ap. Rh. 3.26b) with his origin traced back to Gaia and Ouranos, and another (fr. 198b V., from *schol*. Theocr. 13.1–2c) as son of Aphrodite and Ouranos; in fr. 164 V. someone calling τὸν ϝὸν παῖδα has been identified by Diehl with Aphrodite, while Paus. 9.27.3 (fr. 198c V.) noted that Sappho's references to Eros are contradictory. Eros is introduced here, as an intensive continuation of her entreaty: μή μ'] ὀνέχηcθα· ... εἰ μ' Ἔρω λῦ{ι}c(αι). The genitive Ἔρω is not recorded, but this must be coincidental. At least the grammarians clearly know it (together with the genitive Ἔρου), irrespective if sometimes they consider it an Attic declension genitive or an apocope of ἔρωτος: see Hdn. *GG* III/2 511.29 and 714.31; fr. 23.1 V. is published]ἔρωτος ἠλπ[, yet the form need not be compulsory. Even this unique occurrence may not be unquestionable, since different articulations, *e.g.*,] ἔρω τ' ὃc (*vel* ὅc') ἠλπ[ετ' or φ]έρω τ' ὅc' ἠλπ[are not impossible.

In any case, Eros, even if along with different maternal origins, is still the only son of Aphrodite mentioned by Sappho, and is also Aphrodite's son *par excellence* in later literature. On the other hand, Himeros does not appear in Sappho as a deity, and specifically as son of Kypris. None of them is mentioned in Homer, but in Hesiod Eros appears among the primeval powers (*Th.* 120), while Himeros resides on Olympus together with the Charites close to the abodes of the Muses (*Th.* 64). Both are present at the birth of Aphrodite as her companions (*Th.* 201f. τῆι δ' Ἔρος ὡμάρτηcε καὶ Ἵμερος ἕσπετο καλὸς / γεινομένηι τὰ πρῶτα). Scholars, attempting to reconcile Hesiod's reference with the conventional genealogy, in which Eros is known as Aphrodite's son, presume that when Aphrodite was born she was already pregnant with Eros and Himeros, and gave birth to them at her own birth. At Ov. *Fast.* 4.1 Venus is *geminorum mater Amorum*, but scholars disagree as to whether the twin brother of Eros implied is Himeros or Anteros. The

---

10 *OC* 1326 is often interpreted as 'in the name of', equated with 1333 πρόc νύν cε κρηνῶν, πρὸc θεῶν ὁμογνίων. However, here ἀντί, unlike πρόc, signifies 'in the interest of (for the benefit or the advantage of, as an equivalent for) your daughters and yourself', i.e. 'come on our side in return for the well-being of yourself and your daughters'. The true meaning is clarified near the end of Polyneikes' speech at 1342f. About this use of ἀντί, see Schwyzer, *GG* II 443,2.

pair of them appear more frequently in art usually undistinguishable and often loosely designated as Erotes. On the other hand, Pausanias (1.43.6) mentions Scopas' group of the triad of Eros, Himeros, and Pothos in Aphrodite's temple at Megara with the remark εἰ δὴ διάφορά ἐcτι κατὰ ταὐτὸ τοῖc ὀνόμαcι καὶ τὰ ἔργα cφίcι. At any rate, εἰ μ' Ἔρω λῦ{ι}c(αι) seems certain to us.

In *PSO* we read αντι·γονωμεcιν[. After με, the upper half of CI is clearly visible, followed by an uncertain letter of which only one upright tip has survived. Reading ν is not impossible. According to Hamm (166f. § 250a), the second person middle present indicative ending is the contracted -ηι, as the book fragments attest. The only papyrus fragment (*P. Oxy.* 1788 fr. 4), Alc. fr. 117b.32 V. ψευδη, is extremely uncertain. Lobel (*Ἀλκαίου μέλη* F 4) notes "nescio an etiam ΤΕΥΧΗ possis", as Hunt assisted by Lobel had read in *P. Oxy.* 1788 (1922): τευ ηδε[. As a matter of fact, it is possible to avoid either ψευδη or τευχη by reading and supplementing the passage of Alcaeus with two imperatives: τεῦχ' ἠδὲ [. . . . .]cαι.[11] Further, fr. 55.1 V., a book fragment, is frequently published κείcηι, in spite of the unanimous, though belonging to different sources, reading κείcεαι. The conjecture was made by anon. (K) *censor Darmst.* 1841 (= T. Bergk) in order to avoid a three-element synecphonesis (κείcεαι οὐ-). On synecphonesis with three elements see West, *GM* 13. Also, fr. 94.10 V.]λ̣[ά]θεαι, though difficult to read, is very likely (contrariwise, Hamm, *l.c.*: "bedenklich"), all the more so since the uncontracted syllables may perhaps cover two separate metrical positions. Here, the syllables must stand in synizesis. It might be easy to restore ἀντὶ γόνω μ' ἐcίν[εο, but the sense rather requires a present tense. In any case, the uncontracted ending must be admissible.

The *iota* of cίνομαι is always long. The only exception was considered to be the form found in Sapph. fr. 26.4 V. It was at Wilamowitz's suggestion that Hunt inserted Sappho's quotation from the *Etymologica*, ὄττιναc γὰρ εὖ θέω κεῖνοί με

---

[11] The passage of Alcaeus, addressed to a woman and intending to prevent her from becoming a prostitute, seems to close the description of the negative sides of the profession with the words: τεῦχ' ἠδὲ [cυνέργα]cαι, / κ]αὶ [π]λείαν [προ]κάκων ἐc χάτ[ιν ἐξί]ηι, "make (the aforementioned) and [work in a bro]thel, and you'll surely cast out into poverty full of utmost ills". In spite of the editors' five dots in l. 32, the seven letters of the supplement fit the gap accurately. The single -c- aorist of cυνέργα]cαι is normal (see Chantraine (1961), 177 § 201,II; Hamm (1957), 120 § 201b); cυνεργάζομαι is used for prostitutes working together in a brothel, cf. the title *Cυνεργαζόμεναι*, of a lost Herondas *Mimiamb*, compared with other *Mimiamb* titles (*Προκυκλὶc ἢ Μαcτροπόc* and *Πορνοβοcκόc*), as well as with its unique surviving verse which has an obvious erotic sense; ἐξί]ηι is second pers. sing. pres. ind. of ἐξίεμαι in passive sense. Finally, if the proposal is right, the problem whether χάτιc or χᾶτιc shows the correct quantity is definitely resolved.

μάλιcτα cίνονται (in the MSS orthography), at that time fr. 12 Bergk⁴, into the first lines of *P. Oxy*. cίνονται, however, could find no metrical position but at the end of the adonean, so the *iota* was considered short. It was because of this supposed cῐν- that Hamm (1957, 36 § 73b,3, 132 § 217a) was reluctant to associate the form with the Aeolic gemination of δίνν-, ὀρίνν-, κλίνν-, κρίνν-, ὀτρύνν-. The new position of the fragment requires reading cίννοντ(αι), which verifies Choerob. *An. Ox*. II 259.7 Cr., cίνονται· διὰ τοῦ ῑ· οἱ γὰρ Αἰολεῖc cίννονται λέγουcι, καὶ οὐχὶ cέννονται. The grammarian is averting the orthography with ει (see Hesych. c 334 H.; the typical way of rendering long *iota* in the Hellenistic/Roman period), which would be accounted for only if the Aeolians employed cένν-, but they didn't. It is then advisable to publish here cίγ[νεαι, though cίγ[νηι (or cίγ[νεο) cannot, of course, be excluded.

7. Burris reads πο.. απαμ.. νμ and publishes πόλλα πάμπαν, μ'. It is no doubt a difficult to read passage, especially since, as it seems, there are signs of scribal corrections in it. Following πολλαπα, the curved left-hand stroke of μ is certain, but another curved stroke runs upon it obviously for striking it off. After a gap, a leftward bending and conspicuously curved oblique is visible, no doubt the last stroke of a μ. The size of the gap fits exactly a double M, the largest letter of the scribe, of which only the left-hand portion of the first and the right-hand one of the second survived. There follows a clear α, and after it an uncertain ι, possibly struck off. Our initial reading was ἀπά⟦μ⟧μα⟦c⟧, imperfect second person singular of ἀπαμάω (*Od*. 21.300, *al*.; more usual is ἐξαμάω), 'mow down, lacerate', used here metaphorically like δαΐcδω and more figuratively than cίννομαι. In Lesbian, the verb is ἀπάμαμι. With the initial reading of the imperfect, the subject of ἀπά⟦μ⟧μαc is Kypris, after the correction ἀπά⟦μ⟧μα it would be Eros. However, POxy. 1231 reads at this place, as Lobel discerned,] .ιμ'ουπρ[. So, we accepted Camillo Neri's more reasonable proposal of a second person present tense of the middle ἀπάμαμαι (possibly Aeol. ἀπάμμαμαι), like πότη⟨ι⟩ or rather πότα⟨ι⟩ of πόταμαι in Sapph. 130.4 V., misspelled as πότε in a great part of Hephaestion's tradition.

After the first edition of *PSO*, where the final *omicron* of οὐ προ[was considered certain, with supplements such as πρότερ' (West), προ[τόνοιc] (Ferrari), προτέρ' (Burris), we were led astray by a coloured photograph published subsequently, and believed we saw a clear *epsilon*, thus attempting supplements with οὐ πρε[π followed by a short vowel. We were wrong.

7f. An oblong detached piece follows in an indeterminate distance after προ[. According to Obbink's calculations the gap extends to 0–3 letters, but it may well be larger. The first letter of the detached piece is no doubt π. The surviving upright is directed to the right, as is always the case with the second upright of π, unlike τ whose upright is leftward tilted. The last letter must be α, as is clearly visible, better in the black and white photograph than in the coloured one published by Obbink. With]περηcα[more or less certain, it is preferable, we believe, to postpone its restoration after discussing the adonean.

Here, Burris reads]ουτ. υ. ερ.[..] and publishes οὔτ' ὀνέερχ[θ]αι. It is the first four letters that appear in the new piece. Burris notes "8]ου, diagonal upper left stroke intersects with main stroke near midline, confirms υ rather than τ". However, no diagonal upper left stroke is visible. Only a horizontal almost connected with the horizontal of the following τ. A microscopic thickening at the point of junction with the vertical does not change the horizontal to diagonal. What we are dealing with is a clear double τ. Double τ is written by the P. GC. inv. 105 scribe almost like a wide π. It is exactly similar in fr. 2 c. ii 20 (Sapph. fr. 17.12 V.) καττο.[(κὰτ τὸ π[), which is clearly visible, or in fr. 3 c. ii 12 (fr. 5.3 V.) κωττιϝ...[(κὤττι ϝῶι), which is less clearly visible, also in the KP 2 οττιν.. As for υτ, a usual combination, it is written very differently, with the prongs of the upsilon's fork clearly distinct: e.g. fr. 1.6 (fr. 9.8 V.) ουτος (οὖτος), fr. 2 c. i 9 (fr. 16.11 V.) αυταν (αὖταν), al.

It is a basic grammar rule that the conjunction ὅτι is not elided and that the cases of ὅτ' found in Homer belong to ὅτε. West (GM 10) is more cautious. He mentions that ὅτι is elided "apparently in epic" and notes (n. 11): "at any rate there are cases where we must either say that ὅτι is elided or that ὅτε can be used in the sense of ὅτι before a vowel". Similar is the situation with the relative ὅ τι and ὅττι. At Od. 15.317 the tradition unanimously transmits ὅττ' ἐθέλοιεν, but Aristarchus corrects to ἅcc' ἐθέλοιεν, a correction accepted by modern editors. ὅττι θέλοιεν might be simpler, but θέλω is never found in Homer or Hesiod. If, here in Sappho, we read ὄττ' ὀνεερ.., we should have to do with a second instance of elided ὅττι. The verb that follows has been variously restored before the new join (]νε' ἐρα[ίc]αι vel – ⏑]ν ἔερχ[θ]αι West : cυν]έερχ[θ]αι Obbink : αἴ κε]ν ἔερχ[θ]αι Ferrari), now ὀνέερχ[θ]αι Burris. Be that as it may, by measuring the size of the gap between νεερ and the final ι as meticulously as possible, in order to decide whether three full-sized letters (the last one obligatorily α) could be accommodated in it, we concluded that some letter-clusters are immediately excluded as too long, e.g., αιcα (West), χθα (Obbink, West, Ferrari, Burris). Now, POxy. 1231 clearly reads]αι at the end of the verse. So, we propose ξαι, i.e., ὀνεέρξαι, which neatly fills the gap.

We propose οὐ πρό[παρ οἳ] πέρηcα[ν | ὄττ' ὀνεέρξαι, "In the past, those who overcame the obstacles didn't ...". πέρηcαν is 3rd pers. pl. impf. of the Lesb. πέρεμμι (= περίειμι), in the sense 'to be superior to another, surpass, excel', constructed with gen. pers., but also with acc. rei. Here, ὄττ' ὀνεέρξαι, 'whatever would hinder' = 'any obstacle', with the verb in optative because of the secondary tense of the relative clause οἳ πέρηcαν. The adonean of line 8 has no sign of punctuation at its end in both papyri. Therefore, the missing principal verb that is connected with the initial οὐ must be found in the opening of the next stanza in line 9, with the sentence ending with punctuation after cέ, obviously the object of the principal verb. The sense possibly demands something like '(didn't) face you as enemy'.

Thus, the indeterminately sized gap between προ and the detached piece extends to 4½ letters, and not 0–3 as formerly calculated – as is observed also by Ferrari who supplemented 5½ letters. The verse created is long, but is still shorter than several verses of the previous homometrical poem in the papyrus. As Obbink explains, the puzzling traces above]περηcα[do not belong to the previous line but are the remains of offsets left after the detached piece, originally folded, was unfolded during conservation. Though it is difficult to verify from the photographs, there is a strong impression that the two tiny top leftmost traces, which have the right line spacing from the π of]περηcα[, are not offsets but original ink, belonging to the feet of *alpha* and *iota*. If the oblong detached piece is shifted 4½ letters to the right, this αι falls exactly at the bottom of the end of 6 cίννεαι that we proposed alternatively to cίννηι.

It is very likely that the sentence ends at cέ, after which a high dot is noted in *POxy.*, although it is not certain whether it stands for a punctuation or for a mark cancelling the strange acute that was added above cέ. No punctuation is noted at the end of 8, whether in *PSO* or in *POxy*. All five adoneans of the previous poem in *PSO* end with a high stop, which corresponds with a sentence end. Only the stop at the end of line 8 of the *BP* seems to be wrong, but the scribe might easily be deceived since the verse ends with a complete sentence. There is also no high stop after line 4 ὀνέχηcθα in *PSO* (in *POxy.*, line 4 falls short before the papyrus edge), though the interrogative πᾶι that opens the next line suggests the start of a new sentence.

However, almost any conceivable proposal for filling the opening of line 9 would require an unaccented cε. Still, some accents and punctuation marks of *POxy.* 1231 fr. 16 should be reconsidered. These lectional signs, among them the accent on cέ, are written by second hand, with only a few exceptions, like the apostrophe of line 2]τ'τινι, which separates between double consonants, and the one of line 7 μ'οὐ, which marks an elision. Also by first hand is, possibly, the high dot which occurs in both papyri before line 6 γονω, a *diastole* for preventing reading αντι and γονω as a single compound word, as already noted by Obbink. The marks of line 11 are notable. The sign after] ˰αν', where a high dot is expected, is an apostrophe, and reversely the high dot of δ·ἐμ' is in place of an apostrophe.

Obviously, the corrector decided to add a high dot and an apostrophe on the already written text, but he put them in the wrong order. Further, the acute on the second *alpha* of line 5] ᾱλεμάτ[is erroneously struck through with a cancel stroke, since the ending in *PSO* presupposes an acute on the penult. Unless we should take μ' ἀλέματον as the correct reading and transfer the pity arousing adjective to the speaking poetess. We cannot explain the signs on lines 10 πάθη[and 12]νόιδα, both acutes with crosswise strokes combined with dots. There remains the high dot in 9 cέ·, which happens to be placed right under the acute. It is certainly preferable to take it as a punctuation mark and not as a cancel dot deleting the accent, unless both the acute and the high stop are a peculiar way to prevent reading c' ἐθέλω. In any case, the accent is added by second hand, possibly by a student, and it cannot be considered as a reliable witness of what Sappho meant to stress or not. Adding the accents to their textbook was a usual exercise for students, while a teacher corrected them deleting the wrong ones, apparently either by cancel strokes or cancel dots or both.[12]

9–15. The portion of the poem surviving only in *POxy.*: see fr. 26 V. for previous attempts. It is better to avoid supplementing the text with *e.g.* conjectures, though line 10 τοῦ]το πάθη[ν (Hunt) or τωὖ]το πάθη[ν or τωὖ]το πάθη[μα πάcχην are possible. The rest is too fragmented to yield any trustworthy piece of information. However, three details, though small and seemingly insignificant, may allow some faint glimmers of truth. First come lines 11f. ἔγω δ' ἔμ' αὔται / τοῦτο cύνοιδα, from Ap. Dysc. *GG* II/1 51.1 ff. and 80.10 ff., though, unlike *P. Oxy.*, both passages transmit ἔγων, not ἔγω. The verb with or without reflexive pronoun does not denote mere knowledge or even full knowledge, but rather knowledge of which the subject can bear witness, "I can testify, I can bear witness about this". A similar statement occurs in fr. 16.5 f. V. πάγχυ δ' εὔμαρες cύνετον πόηcαι / πάντι τοῦτ(ο), "It is easy to make this understood by everyone". There, it introduces the mythical *exemplum* of Helen. Can something similar occur here? The reflexive pronoun, ἔμ' αὔται, refers to personal knowledge about what the speaker plans to prove, not necessarily to personal experience. The second detail is the word]β[ρ]ότοιc in line 13, which, if correctly read, introduces us to a world of mortals/immortals, since the reference to mortals isn't accounted for without the involvement of the immortals. After all, reading ἀμ]β[ρ]ότοιc is equally possible. Finally, a third detail, extremely evasive, appears in line 11] ἄν, most likely]cἄν, which can suggest scores of different things, among them a third person plural aorist verb implying as subject some people, who possibly faced the same tribulation in the past. They must have been mentioned indefinitely for the first

---

12 See Turner, GMAW² 11, 19; Cribiore (2001), 140–142.

time in lines 7–9: οὐ πρόπαρ οἲ πέρηcαν | ὄττ' ὀνεέρξαι | – ‿ – × –] cε. Who these people are we do not know, but the sudden shift from a clearly personal theme to a generalized subject is interesting. In any case, the desperate condition of the papyrus does not allow any reliable conclusion.

A most interesting feature of the poem is the extreme familiarity that Sappho purports to enjoy with Kypris. We encountered the same familiarity in fr. 1 V., only that there the familiarity sprang from the goddess. Sappho is addressing the goddess with Κύπρι δέcποινα, "the earliest instance of a goddess being addressed" so and "an acknowledgment of Aphrodite's commanding power [...] over Sappho", as West (2014), 10, observes. It appears to be the form of address of an intimate handmaiden to her mistress. She starts with a displeased tone of excuse for being unjustly punished for violating the rules of Aphrodite and trying to be delivered from them. She continues with a complaint about partiality against herself and in favour of Aphrodite's son, Eros. She would be happy to satisfy Kypris' rules, but it is the goddess and her son who prevent her by making her erotic target behave coyly and pretend to be unresponsive to her advances. One has the impression that the painting of a shy girl (inscribed ΗΕ ΠΑΙΣ) that flees from Sappho yet coyly directs her gaze back toward her, in the calyx-crater of the Tithonos Painter,[13] is inspired from the present poem. We do not know whether the same tone continued till the end of the poem or not, but though the playful mood of fr. 1 V. seems to be absent here, a concealed air of jocularity is evident through the strong effort of the poetess to pose as a close though lower in rank partner of the goddess, jealous of her son's supremacy over herself.

Finally, the poem seems directly connected thematically with fr. 1 V. The parallels quoted below highlight the thematic affinity between the two poems more than any verbal proximity:

- fr. 1.3 μή μ' ἄcαιcι μηδ' ὀνίαιcι δάμνα ~ *KP* 1 πῶc κε δή τιc οὐ θαμέωc ἄcαιτο, 2 πάθε' ἐκδάμαccαι, 5 μ' ἀλεμάτωc δαΐcδηc, 6 με cίννεαι, 7 πόλλ' ἀπάμαι μ'.
- fr. 1.15, 16, 18 δηὖτε ~ *KP* 1 θαμέωc.
- fr. 1.15 ὄττι ... πέπονθα ~ *KP* 3 πάθε(α), 10 πάθην/πάθημα.
- fr. 1.17 κὤττι ... μάλιcτα θέλω ~ *KP* 3 κωὒ θέλοι μάλιcτα, 9 θέλω.
- fr. 1.23 αἰ δὲ μὴ φίλει, ταχέωc φιλήcει ~ *KP* 2 ὄττινα δὴ φιλήcαι.
- fr. 1.25 χαλέπαν δὲ λῦcον ἐκ μερίμναν ~ *KP* 6 εἰ μ' Ἔρω λῦc(αι).

---

13 Bochum, Ruhr-Universität, inv. no. S 508; see Yatromanolakis (2007), 88–105.

As we mentioned above, the difference is that, whereas in fr. 1 V. the poetess begs her patron goddess to help her in attracting the object of her desire, here she complains for not being allowed by the goddess to be freed from the bonds of Eros when the particular object repeatedly causes her distress by rejecting her love.

6 Sappho's Epithalamians

The Last Three Books

The epithalamian poems of Sappho constituted a separate book, references to which are found under this thematic title and not numerically as in the other books. D.H. *Rh.* 4.1 καὶ παρὰ Cαπφοῖ τῆc ἰδέαc ταύτηc παραδείγματα, ἐπιθαλάμιοι οὕτωc ἐπιγραφόμεναι ᾠδαί; Serv. *georg.* 1.31 *Sappho, quae in libro, qui inscribitur* Ἐπιθαλάμια, *ait* (seq. fr. 116); POxy. 2294.16–17 ἐπιγεγρα[|]λάμι͞α; D. H. *Comp.* 25.108 εἰ γὰρ τὸ Cαπφικόν τιc ἐπιθαλάμιον τουτί (seq. fr. 113). However, it cannot be excluded that in other sources there are references to the same book by number, so that the attempt to find the position of the book of Ἐπιθαλάμια in the numerical order of the Sapphic corpus may not be pointless.

Possibly, the answer can be found in POxy. 2294, which offers some information about the contents of one or two Sappho books, one of which is apparently entitled Ἐπιθαλάμια. In addition to other data, the papyrus offers a list of the first verses of the ten odes contained in a book of Sappho. Is it the book of Ἐπιθαλάμια or the book prior to it, as D.L. Page claimed?[1]

Primarily, as is well known, two absolutely reliable and completely independent sources assert that Sappho's books of songs were nine: (*a*) The epigram of Cicero's freedman Tullius Laurea, *AP* 7.17 (Τυλλίου Λαυρέα: Sappho addressing the passerby from her grave) 5–6

ἢν δέ με Μουcάων ἐτάcηιc χάριν, ὧν ἀφ' ἑκάcτηc
δαίμονοc ἄνθοc ἐμῆι θῆκα παρ' ἐννεάδι,

and (*b*) *Suda* (art. Cαπφώ) σ 107 ἔγραψε δὲ μελῶν λυρικῶν βιβλία θ'. The attempt of D. Yatromanolakis,[2] to disprove both data is unconvincing. Belonging to a highly cultured entourage, Laurea lived at a time when Sappho's complete work was widely circulating, highly favoured in Rome, and influencing leading poets like Horace and Catullus among many. Assumptions that Laurea was deceived by the ambiguity of the number θ' (first suggested by Lobel) or that he used a non-Alexandrian nine-book edition, whereas the Alexandrian one could have been of eight books, are made gratuitously, since there is not a single hint of an eight-book Sappho edition, Alexandrian or not. The fact that, among the numerous ref-

---

[1] (1955), 116–119.
[2] (1999).

erences to Sappho fragments, there is no reference to the Ninth book lacks evidential value, since there is also no reference to the Fourth book, and one cannot claim that the numbering jumped from three to five. To assume that Suda's Sappho article draws information from Laurea's epigram, which is cited in three lexical glosses, is absolutely impossible. Suda's biographical articles come from older biographical sources, principally Hesychios of Miletus (Ἰλλούστριος), and are not affected by the citations from epigrams that were later added to basic Synagoge glosses from the Anthology of Konstantinos Kephalas.³ It is also observed that the critical mark of asterisk is absent from the Sappho papyri, this absence indicating that the existing papyri do not come from the Alexandrian edition, but from editions of "collected poems". However, Hephaestion, 74.8, clearly notes that μάλιστα εἴωθεν ὁ ἀcτερίcκοc τίθεcθαι, ἐὰν ἑτερόμετρον ᾖ τὸ ᾆcμα τὸ ἑξῆc· ὃ καὶ μᾶλλον ἐπὶ τῶν ποιημάτων τῶν μονοcτροφικῶν γίνεται Caπφοῦc κτλ. So far as I can check, no Sappho papyrus survived presenting sequences of monostrophic heterometric poems, so that we might expect meeting an asterisk, and, if there occurred in small fragmentary papyri, the place where the asterisk should have stood is destroyed.⁴

Let us get back, however, to POxy. 2294. If we accept that the ten incipits belong to the book that is entitled Ἐπιθαλάμια, we shall have to face an obvious contradiction. The two epithalamians to which we have explicit references, frs. 113 and 116 referred to respectively by Dionysius of Halicarnassus and Servius, do not seem to come from any of the poems whose list of incipits is quoted in the papyrus. It is well known that Sappho wrote several songs related to weddings, songs included in more than one books. However, Servius refers to a particular book entitled Ἐπιθαλάμια, while Dionysius may not refer to a book title, but when he himself mentions in *Ars Rhetorica* (4.1) παρὰ Caπφοῖ [ ] ἐπιθαλάμιοι οὕτωc ἐπιγραφόμεναι ᾠδαί, it is highly unlikely that, when speaking in *De compositione verborum* (25.108) of Caπφικόν [ ] ἐπιθαλάμιον τουτί, he may mean another book.

Fr. 113 does not present serious critical or metrical problems, and seems certain that it is not the first verse of an ode:

---

3 Adler in *RE* art. Suidas, coll. 706–8, 713–4.
4 The case of the P.Colon. 21351+21376 is exceptional, since the last heterometric Orpheus poem, whether by Sappho or not, is written by a second careless and untrained hand after the last verses of the previous poem were omitted. The critical mark at the beginning of the poem is not an asterisk, but a certain ancora. In any case, the order of the poems in P.Colon. is different than in POxy. 1787, which may indicate a different edition; but why an eight-book one? See above '4. Sappho's Orpheus Song'.

οὐ γὰρ
ἀτέρα νῦν πάιc, ὦ γάμβρε, τεαύτα.

Fr. 116 is, however, very likely the opening of an ode, as was shown by Maas (ap. Diehl, *Anthologia Lyrica Graeca*¹, fasc. 5 p. 14):

χαῖρε, νύμφα, χαῖρε, τίμιε γάμβρε, πόλλα.

As for the metre, fr. 113 is very likely 3 io. Fr. 116, however, is not hipp || hipp ||, as noted *dubitanter* by Voigt who follows Snell in taking χαῖρε, νύμφα as the close of the previous verse, but rather cr x hipp ||, with the usual trochaic opening that we find in several complex Aeolic metres. Similar, in terms of wording and structure, are the openings of fr. 117 (†χαίροιc ἀ νύμφα†· χαιρέτω δ' ὁ γάμβροc⁵) and of the main song in Theocritus' dactylic Ἑλένηc ἐπιθαλάμιον (18.49 χαίροιc, ὦ νύμφα· χαίροιc, εὐπένθερε γάμβρε).

Yet, none of the ten incipits of POxy. 2294 (fr. 103) agrees metrically with either fr. 113 or 116. Thus, it seems that the problem is located at this specific papyrus.

The character of the papyrus is clearly described by Lobel (*The Oxyrhynchus Papyri* XXI): 'Bibliographical Details about a Book of Sappho'. Before proceeding to some different readings or proposals, it is useful to reproduce the original edition:

```
       ....
1                    ].ω[
2             ]cαν ἐν τῶι .[
3       ].δὲ (δέκα) κ(αὶ) ἑκάcτηc ὁ (πρῶτοc) [
4    ].εν τὸ γὰρ ἐννεπε[.]η προβ[
5    ].ατε τὰν εὔποδα νύμφαν [
6    ]τα παῖδα Κρονίδα τὰν ἰόκ[ολπ]ον [
7    ].c ὄργαν θεμένα τὰν ἰόκ[ολ]ποc α[
8    ]..ἄγναι Χάριτεc Πιερίδε[c τε] Μοῖ[cαι
9      ].[.ὄ]ππστ' ἀοιδαι φρέν[...]αν.[
10           ]cαιοιcα λιγύραν [ἀοί]δαν
11           γά]μβρον, ἄcαροι γὰρ ὑμαλικ[
12           ]cε φόβαιcι θεμένα λύρα.[
```

---

5 Several proposals have been put forward for reconciling the verse with Hephaestion's (*Ench.* 4.2 p. 13 C.) description as a catalectic iambic trimeter: χαίροιcα νύμφα ed. Iunt., Ursin., χαίροιcθα νύμφα Neue, χαίροιc cὺ νύμφα Yatromanolakis, ἀ νύμφα, χαίροιc LP. The transmitted text seems so impeccable, that I wonder whether an oversight on the part of Hephaestion can be excluded.

13   ]..η χρυcοπέδιλ<λ>[ο]c Αὔωc [
14   ]˙ cτίχ(οι) ρλ[ ]
15   ] μετὰ τὴν πρώτην [
16   ]φ έρονται ἐπιγεγρα[
17   ἐπιθα]λάμια
18   ] υβλίου καὶ βέλτ[[ε]]ιο[ν
19
20   ]ροπ .... [. .].ε.[

From a considerable scholarly literature I confine myself to referring only to Enzo Puglia, who offers a full overview of the status quaestionis, reproducing which would be redundant.⁶

1–3. Puglia rightly reads]cι in the opening of line 3. I do not dare supplement anything in lines 1–2, though it seems likely that they mark the end of the description of the previous book and the start of the present. ἐν τῶι *m* βυβλίωι (Puglia), with the number referring to the book of the incipits (4–13), cannot be excluded. Puglia actually believes that from line 18 onward there is reference to the next book of Sappho, and supplements there [*y* εἰcὶν αἱ ὠιδαὶ τοῦ *n*] βυβλίου καὶ βέλτ[[ε]]ιc[ται] | [εἰcὶν *z*, ὧν ὁ (πρῶτοc) ἐcτίν·], thus making the relics of line 20 belong to the first verse of the first ode of the next book. I would prefer, more simply, to devote the whole surviving papyrus to a bibliographical description of the book of the ten incipits. If 3 starts with εἰ]cὶ δὲ ῑ, even if the verb was different (διαφέρου]cι Puglia), the sentence should normally be complementary to the previous statement. For instance, in a similar bibliographical description: D. L. 2.122 ὅθεν cκυτικοὺc αὐτοῦ τοὺc διαλόγουc καλοῦcιν. εἰcὶ δὲ τρεῖc καὶ τριάκοντα ἐν ἑνὶ φερόμενοι βιβλίῳ. Here, e.g., 2–3]cαν ἐν τῶι ἑ[χομένωι | βυβλίωι· εἰ]cὶ δὲ (δέκα) κ(αὶ) ἑκάcτηc ὁ (πρῶτοc) [οὕτωc ἔχει·

4 (1).] ,εν τὸ γὰρ ἐννεπε[.]η προβ[

Before dealing with the verse, one or two reading improvements are necessary. Before the first Ε the joining tail of Μ is clear. More letters have joining tails, but it is only Μ that fits here. The gamma of γάρ is conspicuous, yet τὸ γάρ before a verb would be understandable in a grammatical text but would make no sense in a poem. An attempt to correct the gamma on the papyrus is visible. It is made by extending the horizontal to the left and somewhat upwards, since the space between Ο and Γ was narrow. The correction is now partly abraded, but it shows

---

6 (2008b).

that what the corrector intended was τότ' ἄρ'. For ἐννεπε[.]η, Gallavotti supplemented -πε [μ]ή or possibly -πε[τ'] ή and Treu -πε [δ]ή. However, none of the consonants supplemented fits whether the space or the shape of the relics. I read ἔννεπ' ἔον. The top part of the small O (see in the next word, πρΟβ[) is visible together with faint parts of the rest of the circle that can be discerned in an enlargement of the photo. N looks very much like H, but the oblique that ends almost horizontally at the middle of the right-hand vertical appears elsewhere too in this papyrus (2 εN, 4 ενNεπε), but is also not unusual in 2nd/3rd c. papyri. It is noteworthy that the right-hand foot of the vertical of H is always curved or has a short outward looking serif (e.g., 3 εκαcτHc) unlike the Ns. Also, the crossbar of H lies considerably higher.

Most scholars recognized the dactylic character of the verse. I believe it is a normal dactylic hexameter with feminine caesura. However, the three supplements by Gallavotti and Treu cited above do not allow any of the principal caesuras of the hexameter. With the emblematic imperative ἔννεπ(ε) the verse seems to open a poem introductory to a thematic book of odes invoking the Muse to report some outstanding past event/s (προβεβακ-; προβαίνω, 'be superior, surpass').

– ⏓] μέν τότ' ἄρ' ἔννεπ' ἔον προβ[εβακ ⏑⏑ – –

Still, I would prefer a slightly different approach. The mouthpiece of the Muse is the poet, so what Sappho is asking the Muse in indirect question is which event of the past she might juxtapose with what she plans to narrate in the poems to come. 'Which event can I sing as a mythical paradigm for the real-life event I am going to narrate?' What sort of events she is speaking about is evident from the content of some of the incipits (5 νύμφαν, 11 γά]μβρον): no doubt memorable weddings, mythical on the one side (e.g., Heracles and Hebe, Peleus and Thetis, Cadmus and Harmonia, Hector and Andromache), real-life ones on the other. We shall see how the two categories are divided in the poems to follow. Starting with another emblematic opening (Hes. Ἡοῖαι), I would propose, e.g.,

οἵων] μέν τότ' ἄρ', ἔννεπ', ἔον προβ[εβάκοτα λέκτρα,

with the invocation (Μοῦcα or Μοῖcα) opening the second line. 'Tell me, [o Muse, whose marriage] was more outstanding at that time'. If οἵων and λέκτρα are correct, they need not refer to many marriages. The plural λέκτρα means 'marriage', while οἵων may designate the couple. οἵων for οἵων, in indirect discourse from ἔννεπ(ε), actually foretells the trait of the couple in question: not human (where τίνων would be relevant) but divine beings. Given the shortness of the poems (see below on line 14), I would not expect in the first exceptionally dactylic poem a narrative account of any mythical marriage (as in Sa. 44), but rather further comments and explanations of the question. Actually, I would not even expect a poem longer than one or two distichs. We have here the typical quest of the most appropriate myth to serve as a paradigm for the main theme of the poem: a poetic mannerism we meet in several of Sappho's poems, but par excellence in Pindar, frequently expressed in priamel form. And the mere fact that a proemial poem introduces a mythical paradigm that will be narrated in one or more other poems links these poems more closely than what a common thematic title would require.

οἴων is the Lesbian of οἴων. The form ὄαν read in Sa. 7.5 (Hamm 27 § 55b1) is no more than a prosodical correption expressed in writing. Correption is very usual with οἶος both in the epic and in Attic poets. In Sappho, cf., e.g., P.Colon. 21351.i, 9 παί]ζοῖεν. As for ἔον used with plural neuter subjects, which was strongly disputed in the past (Hamm 163 § 248 b.1, A. Morpurgo-Davies, *Glotta* 42, 1964, 138–165, esp. 142 f., W. Blümel 186 § 200, esp. n. 213), it is now witnessed not only epigraphically, as before (*DGE* 644.12, Aeol. Aigai), but also from the Tithonus poem 5–6: γόνα δ' οὐ φέροιcι, | τὰ δή ποτα λαίψηρ' ἔον ὄρχηcθ' ἴcα νεβρίοιcιν. Still, I have a strong suspicion that, unlike the rest of the incipits, the first hexameter conformed to the epic dialect. If so, write οἴων and προβ[εβηκότα.

5 (2). ὑμνή]cατε τὰν εὔποδα νύμφαν [⏑ ⏑ – ⏑ – –

'Sing of the lovely-legged bride ['. Suitably supplemented by Snell (acc. Puglia). The sense allows also ἀεί]cατε or αἰνή]cατε, but the supplements of the two previous lines determine the left-hand margin, which fits precisely ὑμνή]cατε. Cf. Sa. 44.34 ὕμνην δ' Ἔκτορα κἈνδρομάχαν θεοεικέλοιc. The imperative is usually addressed to Sappho's pupil-friends, for whom attending or participating in marriage feasts was a typical activity (frs. 27, 30, 31, possibly 94). The metre is hipp^{2c}, and not gl^{2c} as Voigt notes alternatively. The verse was compared practically by every scholar with Sa. 103 B.2. It is advisable to quote the whole fragment, which is found in POxy. 2308 and which Lobel-Page published as *Incerti auctoris* 26:

```
      ]ρηον θαλάμω τωδεc[ ⏑ – ⏑ – –
      ]ιc εὔποδα νύμφαν ἀβ[ –
         ] ˌνυνδ[
         ]ν μοι·[
5           ]αc γε ˌ[.
```

At the end of 2, Snell proposed ἀβ[άκην, 'calm, gentle', a term not wholly laudatory, since it implies also taciturnity, incommunicativeness, reticence, naïveté. I believe it would match better the specific book of Sappho if we supplemented

]ιc εὔποδα νύμφᾶν Ἄβ[αν

In this way, the fragmentary phrase would come from the end of a ˌhipp²ᶜ verse. The short accusative ending of νύμφα is unique, but νύμφᾰ is well attested in both nominative and vocative, and it is a steady rule that substantives in -ᾰ keep the short in nom., voc., and acc. It is well known that the ending of νύμφα can be either short or long (-ᾰ or -η in Attic-Ionic), so that the last alpha in εὔποδα νύμφαν might be either long or short depending on the metrical position. The preceding verse, is most likely to be read ἄ]ρηον (Treu) θαλάμῳ τῷδε ϛ[. Possibly, from a negative statement or a rhetorical question: 'nothing nobler than this bridal chamber' – 'anything nobler than this bridal chamber?', i.e. the wedding of Heracles and Hebe. The expression recalls the hypothetically supplemented 4 (1) προβ[εβάκοτα λέκτρα. Hebe is mentioned in the incipits of lines 6 (3) and 7 (4), so that fr. 103 B may well come from any of the group's poems. The fact that the verse 103 B.2, if completed, would be shorter than the previous one, does not necessarily indicate a tristich strophe ˌhippˣᶜ || ˌhippˣᶜ || ˌhippˣ⁻¹ᶜ ||| like that noticed by Voigt in fr. 88 and doubtingly in 64a, 65, 73, and which M. Steinrück (*ZPE* 131, 2000, 11) diminished to ˌhippᶜ || ˌhippᶜ || ˌhipp |||. As far as we cannot know how 103 B.1 ended, the evidence remains unclear.

The rare epithet εὔπους is used in classical authors for animals, mainly horses and hounds. Only Callimachus (fr. 302) used it for Hecate and, much later, Nonnus frequently, mainly for the fleet-footed Horae. So, it is difficult to determine whether Hebe was described as 'lovely-footed' (= εὔcφυροc, καλλίcφυροc) or 'lovely-legged' or even 'swift-footed'.[7] But the employment of so rare an epithet whether for the real-life bride or for Hebe in fr. 103 B arouses suspicions that even the verse of line 5 (2) (ὑμνή]cατε τὰν εὔποδα νύμφᾶν [⏑ ⏑ – ⏑ – –) may refer to Hebe. It would be easy to supplement ἰόκολπον Ἄβαν, had not the same closing formula occurred in the next two incipits. Or, on the contrary, is the formulaic occurrence a reinforcing argument for supplementing identically? If so, ὑμνήcατε should not be an exhortation addressed by Sappho to her pupil-friends, but by the Muse to Sappho's maiden choir as an answer to the question

---

[7] In vase-paintings, Hebe, Zeus' cupbearer, is sometimes confused with Iris or Nike, being represented serving nectar to the gods while being winged and bearing winged sandals. In the latter case she can appear with short chlamys, showing her naked legs: Athenian red-figure amphora, c. 5th B.C., Munich Staatliche Antikensammlungen.

of the introductory poem 'What outstanding mythical marriage should I/we sing of?'

6 (3).]τα παῖδα Κρονίδα τὰν ἰόκ[ολπ]ον ['Άβαν

init. αἰ δή πο]τα suppl. Snell, φάμα πο]τὰ Puglia, ἔγω πο]τὰ Ferrari; finem suppl. Lobel

Puglia's proposal gives a satisfactory sense, given the parallels of Sa. 166 φαῖcι δή ποτα and the 'Tithonus poem' 9 καὶ γάρ ποτα Τίθωνον ἔφαντο, which introduce mythological exempla as here, but the opening is palaeographically problematic, as it contains two of the scribe's largest letters, Φ and Μ. To achieve an aligned left-hand margin, I propose, e.g., a different introduction to the myth:

"Ερωc ὄ]τα παῖδα Κρονίδα τὰν ἰόκ[ολπ]ον ['Άβαν.

παῖδα Κρονίδα can be either feminine, appositively connected with τὰν ἰόκολπον ῎Άβαν, since Hebe was a daughter of Zeus, 'When Eros (convinced) the daughter of Cronus' son, violet-bosomed Hebe, (to marry Heracles)', or can be masculine, periphrastically referring to Heracles, supplemented, e.g., γύναικ' ἀγάγεcθαι πέπιθεν. See the next item for the final selection. Be that as it may, it is practically certain that the reference is to the marriage between Heracles and Hebe. The relevance of the goddess of youth to epithalamians, a goddess whose marriage to Heracles was renowned, is self-evident. The metre is also ˬhipp^{2c}. Snell's ['Αφροδίταν would produce an unattested metre: ˬgl^{2c} ba.

7 (4).]˳c ὄργαν θεμένα τὰν ἰόκ[ολ]ποc α[

init. fort.]OC Voigt, ἐκ φρέν]οc Treu | fin. Α[ὔωc Puglia

The initial letter must be a short vowel, i.e., ε, ο, α, ι, υ. In spite of Voigt's remark and Treu's supplement, the bottom serif that is discerned cannot belong to Ο which obviously has no serifs, but neither to Ε, Υ, because their upper part should have been visible. It cannot belong to Α, whose connecting tail would normally touch the following letter (see 11 ΑCαροι). There remains only Ι, which in the script of our papyrus has a low rightward looking serif. I propose Δίοc πά]ιc for the necessary female subject:

Δίοc πά]ιc ὄργαν θεμένα, τὰν ἰόκ[ολ]ποc ῎Α[βα

The daughter of Zeus having planted an impulse, which violet-bosomed Hebe ...

ὄργα need not mean 'anger, wrath', but merely "natural impulse or propensity, hence temperament, disposition, mood" (LSJ). The impulse, presumably sexual impulse (cf. ὀργάω), was implanted by the daughter of Zeus in Hebe, the young cupbearer of the gods, also daughter of Zeus, and personification of youth, prior to her marriage to Heracles. The daughter of Zeus of the verse's opening is no doubt Aphrodite (Sa. 1.1 f. Ἀφρόδιτα, | παῖ Δίος) and θεμένα is middle transitive. The relative clause, continued in the next line, possibly specified that Hebe did not possess this impulse formerly: e.g. οὐκ ἐκτεάτιστο πρότερον. This interpretation explains also the previous incipit 6 (3). Sappho's myth assigns the couple's falling in love respectively to Eros as regards Heracles and to Aphrodite as regards Hebe. It seems that the successive poems 6 (3) and 7 (4) described separately their becoming enamoured of each other.

8 (5).   ] . . ἄγναι Χάριτες Πιερίδε[ς τε] Μοῖ[σαι

init. fort.]ΥΝ Voigt (δεῦτέ ν]υν sec. Lobel) | Πιερίδε[ς τε] Μοῖ[σαι vulg.

What I see in the beginning is the end of a top horizontal (Γ, Τ, occasionally Π) followed by the top of an uncertain leftward bending oblique, which most likely belongs to Υ, as Lobel read, and finally a triangular letter. Α is excluded since the following letter is alpha, and likewise Δ because the high projecting stroke of delta has normally a curved end. It is then necessarily a Λ. Between γυλ, πυλ, and τυλ, I choose the last, though all seem strange. Sappho, however, has used the feminine τύλα for 'cushion' (fr. 46). τύλ(α), neuter acc. pl., would be possible, but no neuter form is attested. The only way out I can think of is a synaloiphe of the type ἀθανάτᾱ Ἀφρόδιτα expressed in writing as ἀθανάτ'Ἀφρόδιτα. Here, it must be the dual τύλᾱ with ἄγναι. Charites are not only the divinities of joy and festivity, but also the attendants of Aphrodite and Hera, the two goddesses that are involved in the marriage event. So, it is not surprising to find them laying the two cushions or pillows[8] for the marrying couple: ἔθεντο] τύλ ἄγναι Χάριτες.

At the end of the line, Lobel read and supplemented τε] Μοῖ[σαι, a unanimously accepted reading. However, no Μ is visible, while ΙΔ is clearly seen before ΟΙ. Actually, the last Ι is found exactly at the edge of the papyrus, and so can belong to any letter with a left-hand vertical. I propose Πιερίδε[ς τ' ἄε]ιδον, with the temporal augment of the verb, as usually, omitted:

---

8 The dual seems to favour 'pillows'. Sa. 46 V. speaks clearly of 'cushion'. Phryn. *Ecl.* 145 Fischer τύλην, εἰ καὶ εὕροις που, cὺ κνέφαλον λέγε. The latter is used for both 'cushion' and 'pillow'.

ἔθεντο] τύλᾶγναι Χάριτες Πιέριδέ[ϲ τ' ἄε]ιδον .

The chaste Charites laid the two cushions (or pillows) while the Pierians sang.

Obviously, the beginning of the ceremonial consummation of the marriage of Heracles and Hebe is described.

Depending on the similarity with Sa. 128 (⊗ Δεῦτέ νυν ἄβραι Χάριτες καλλίκομοί τε Μοῖϲαι) and supplementing accordingly, Lobel proposed 3cho ba. Yet the metre is ˌhipp²ᶜ.

9 (6).] ˌ[ˌ ὅ]ππot' ἀοιδαι φρέν[. . .]αν ˌ[

'ἄοιδαι an ἀοίδαι ?' Lobel; ἄοιδαι ... [ἔμ]αν ἔθ[ελξαν Lasserre, acc. Puglia

At the end, the gap after φρέν[, which former editors measured as three letters wide, can accurately accommodate EM. Also, after ἔμ]αν, the right-hand low end of E and the left-hand curve of Θ are clearly visible, and so Lasserre's [ἔμ]αν ἔθ[ελξ- is verified.[9] Assuming that 5 (2) (ὑμνήϲατε τὰν εὔποδα νύμφαν) is spoken by the Muse, it is here, after 4 (1), that the real-life lyric 'I' reappears (φρέν' ἔμαν). It is naturally impossible that Sappho may have been charmed by the songs of the Muses of the previous poem. It must be a choir of girls, like those she used to set up and train for participating in marriage ceremonies (e.g., Sa. 27). χόροϲ παῖδ]ω[ν would fit the space, the whole supplement aligning with the left-hand margin, and even the trace before ὅ]ππot' would agree with the top end of the right-hand curve of ω. If so, ἀοίδαι (dat.) and ἔθ[ελξε would be preferable; cf. *Od.* 12.44 ἀλλά τε Ϲειρῆνεϲ λιγυρῆι θέλγουϲιν ἀοιδῆι. More options are no doubt possible, but the general sense does not change. E.g.,

χόροϲ παῖδ]ω[ν, ὅ]ππot' ἀοίδαι φρέν' [ἔμ]αν ἔθ[ελξε.

10 (7).]ϲ ἄϊοιϲα λιγύραν [ἀοί]δαν

'CAÎ errore, ut vid.' Voigt

Contrary to Voigt's suspicion, the large curve above CAÎ is not a circumflex but a hyphen, for averting reading]ϲα ἴοιϲα. The long ending -ϲα, which bothered Page, p. 118 n. 2, is hesitantly explained by Hamm, 20 § 26, as due to the ϝλ- that possibly follows. However, to the best of my knowledge, no etymologist has ever

---

9 (1989), 62–80.

proposed such an opening. Further, at Sa. 70.11 λίγηα does not lengthen the preceding]δε. A dual participle might be considered as a possibility, but the feminine gender excludes the marrying couple:

×–⏑⏑– –]ϲ ἀϊοίϲᾱ λιγύραν [ἀοί]δαν.

E.g., ἀ Νὺξ ἄμα κΑὔω]ϲ ἀϊοίϲᾱ κτλ. The combined mention of Night and Dawn (cf. Hes. *Th.* 748) both hearing the girls singing would imply an advanced time, later than what would be expected for the girls to sing, an issue discussed in detail in the next three incipits. However, so long a supplement is bound to be extremely uncertain.

11 (8).γά]μβρον ἄcαροι γὰρ ὑμαλικ[

Provisionally,

ὑμνήϲατε νῦν γά]μβρον· ἄcαροι γὰρ ὑμάλικ[εc ϝοί.

Now sing of the groom; for his own companions are disgusted.

Lobel notes: 'γ αρ: parum convenit ρ; est angulus in linea, litt. α caudam contingens, litt. δ similis, sed nequaquam sufficit spatium'. However, the angle is the bottom part of a P, which occasionally has a short vertical ending in a rightward bending serif; e.g., αcαPοι, the previous word.

The incipit seems to be in symmetrical correspondence with 5 (2) ὑμνή]ϲατε τὰν εὔποδα νύμφαν [. The songs, mentioned in 9–10 (6–7), which Sappho takes delight in hearing, must be songs praising the bride. Similar with the proposal printed here are the proposals of Lasserre and Puglia. The first finds that what the comrades are fed up with is the singing, the second, accepting Page's ὑμαλίκ[εccι, finds that it is the hymns (ὕμνοι) that are boring the comrades: αἴνητε, κόραι, γά]μβρον, ἄcαροι γὰρ ὑμαλίκ[εccι. All are possible, though I doubt that Sappho would describe the wedding songs as tedious or tiresome. What the groom's comrades are tired of can be just anything: eating, drinking, dancing, singing, but mainly the length of the celebration. It might be specified or not in the next verses. As for the nature of the songs that the groom's comrades sang in comparison to the epithalamians sung by the pupil-friends of Sappho, the issue shall be soon discussed.

I supplement the possessive (ϝοί) for highlighting the distinction between Sappho's pupil-friends who participated in the marriage feast by singing, and the friends of the groom (Sa. 30.7 coὶc ὑμάλικ[αc) who were supposed to praise him by singing, but are now satiated to the point of boredom. There is no problem with the lengthened ending of ὑμάλικες before ϝ; cf. Alc. 336 ἔκ ϝ' ἔλετο φρένας, 349 b.2 ἄτερ ϝέθεν.

In any case, what Sappho describes is a snapshot of a marriage celebration and, to judge from the condition the comrades are in, a temporally advanced episode. Further, since the song's aim is to praise the bridegroom, we can guess that the song was performed outside his house after the bride was taken into the marriage chamber. The songs that were supposed to be sung there by the friends of the bridegroom, belonged to the part of the ceremony that was called ἐπαύλια: Paus. att. ε 49 Erbse (ex Eust. IV 864–5 van der Valk), Photius lex. ε 1380 Theod. (= Su. ε 1990 Adler), al. A comparable scene appears in Sa. 30, where the singing duty is divided into two shifts. First sing the girls till late into the night. The speaker, i.e., Sappho, speaking on their behalf in her capacity as choir-master, complains to the groom that they cannot continue all night. So, she requests him to get up from the nuptial bed and go to his comrades, apparently for urging them to start their shift, so that the girls might get some sleep:

> νύκτ[...].[
> πάρθενοι δ[
> παννυχίσδοι[c]αι̣[
> cὰν ἀείδοις[ι]ν φ[ιλότατα καὶ νύμ-
> 5   φας ἰοκόλπω.
> ἀλλ' ἐγέρθεις ἠϊθ[έοις πρὸς ἔςλοις
> cτεῖχε cοὶς ὑμάλικ[ας, ὤς τι μάccον'
> ἤπερ ὄccον ἁ λιγύφω[νος ὄρνις
> ὔπνον [ἴ]δωμεν.

4 suppl. Wil.; an ὤς κε | cὰν ἀείδοιεν? Ts.   6 suppl. Voigt   7 suppl. Ts.   8 suppl. Lobel

Voigt's ἔςλοι is appropriate for the groom's friends ('faithful'; LSJ s.v. I 2), but is obviously used ironically, 'your fine comrades'. Apparently, the groom's ὑμάλικες in fr. 30 were ἄcαροι as here. If so, it is very unlikely that Sappho would now urge the girls' choir to take over the comrades' shift too. I would therefore rather opt for a different opening, namely:

ἐγέρρατε νῦν γά]μβρον· ἄcαροι γὰρ ὑμάλικ[ες ϝοί.

In any case, we should not think of formal double choir hymenaei, like Catullus 62, which have no place in this book of short epithalamia.

12 (9).   ]cε φόβαιcι<ν> θεμέγα λύρα̣ .[

λύραι γ[άρ Lasserre, λύραι [γάρ Puglia

Lasserre's reading is impossible. Puglia more cautiously stops at λύραι [. Obviously, both scholars punctuate after θεμένα. Only the low part of the supposed iota has survived, and it is noticeable that it lacks the rightward looking bottom serif that is typical of our scribe's iotas. It is the first vertical of nu that has normally no serif whatsoever. The rest of the nu falls in a completely abraded area, though some relics of the oblique, similar to the form of N discussed in 4 (1), survive. Unlike 7 (4) above, here θεμένα governs an object denoting a material thing, no doubt λύραν. In this case, τίθημι -θεμαι are regularly followed by a dative or a prepositional phrase or an adverb specifying where the θείc or θέμενοc placed the object. And, as it is unlikely that the female subject put the lyre upon someone's locks of hair, we should disjoin φόβαιcιν and θεμένα. Thus, since no prepositional phrase (and very few datives) can fit into the single last syllable, I propose the adverb που.

I do not enter the discussion whether ν ἐφελκυcτικόν can lengthen 'by position' the previous syllable in the Lesbians. Lobel refuses it, but Hamm 40 § 82d and Treu 170 ad Sa. 30.4 accept it. I do not know whether or not Sa. 30.4 càν ἀείδοιεν φ[ιλότατα, sc. πάρθενοι ... παννυχίcδοι[c]αι, is possible both palaeographically and syntactically, instead of the published ἀείδοιc[ι]ν φ[ιλότατα.[10] Here, however, the metrically necessary <ν> may well be added to the next word (-cι <ν>θεμένα), not only for solving the prosodical problem but also for specifying better the indefinite που.

As for]cε, it can belong to the main verb, either as present imperative or as a third person sing. aorist. I definitely prefer the first, with Sappho urging the girl to adorn her hair, but, as I was unable to find an imperative (of the type πράc]cε) that might be relevant with arranging or adorning one's locks, I resort to the third person sing. of a sigmatic aorist. E.g.:

x – cτέφανον δή]cε φόβαιcι <'ν>θεμένα λύραν [που.

Thus, what Sappho describes is the girl's actions after she ended singing; she laid aside the lyre somewhere in the house, and went outdoors to pick flowers and

---

10 Lobel, who publishes αειδοι ν, notes (*Ox. Pap.* XXI p. 123): 'I am not sure that there is not room for an ι between the doubtful letter and ν. -c[ι] would appear to suit the context better than -εν, but the available evidence is against crediting Sappho with ν ἐφελκυcτικόν in such employment (Cμ. xxxvii, lxxiii)'. However, the tiny relic of the doubtful letter agrees better with the tip at the middle of the scribe's occasionally angular ε than with the curved c. Syntactically, the context I would expect is 'we did not agree that the girls would sing your marriage staying awake all night', i.e., a final clause depending on a secondary tense, therefore expressed in optative + κε: ὠc κε | càν ἀείδοιεν φ[ιλότατα.

prepare a garland which she placed around her hair. The initial two syllables must be covered by the female subject, probably a personal name.

Now, fr. 81 V., which partly coincides with POxy. 1787 fr. 33, runs as follows:

]ἀπύθες.[
]χισταλ[
]εμπ[
cὺ δὲ ϲτεφάνοιϲ, ὦ Δίκα, π₁έρθεϲ₁θ' ἐράτοιϲ φόβαιϲιν
5   ὄρπακαϲ ἀνήτω ϲυν<α>₁ἐ₁ρρ₁αιϲ₁' ἀπάλαιϲι χέρϲιν·
εὐάνθεα γὰρ <θέα> μέλεται καὶ Χάριτεϲ μάκαιρα<ι>
μᾶλλον προτέρην, ἀϲτεφανώτοιϲι δ' ἀπυϲτρέφονται.

1 ἀπύθεϲθ[αι Hunt   **2** ὄττι τά]χιϲτα Diehl   **4** ἐράταιϲ Ath., -τοιϲ Fick coll. Hes. *Th.* 576–7 ϲτεφάνουϲ ... ἱμερτοὺϲ περέθηκε   **5** ἀννήτωι Ath., corr. Casaubonus | <α> add. Ahrens | ἀπαλλαγιϲη Ath., ἀπάλαιϲι Casaubonus   **6** εὐάνθεα γὰρ πέλεται Ath., εὐάνθεα γὰρ <θέα> μέλεται Ts. | μάκαιρα Ath., corr. Blomfield   **7** προτερην Ath., προτόρην Seidler (deb. προϲόρην Ahrens), προφέρην Lobel, προτέρην Ts. | ἀϲτεφανώτουϲ Ath., -τοιϲι Schweighäuser

6 <θέα>: Haplology is a common source of errors. | μέλομαι c. inf. in the sense 'care for' (= 'feel interest for, attach importance to'); LSJ s.v. μέλω B.II. | **7** The transmitted προτέρην of προτερέω/-ημι, 'take the lead, have the advantage', makes perfect sense. 'For the goddess cares, and so do the blessed Charites, that nicely flowery objects rather are in the lead, while they (the goddess and the Charites) turn away from the ungarlanded.'

If line 1 should be supplemented ἀπύθεϲθ[αι (Hunt), as is most likely, whether the infinitive functions as imperative, as possibly πέρθεϲθ(αι) does in line 4, or not, it is likely that one or more persons are advised to put away or lay aside something. Further, the poetess urges Dika to pick shoots of dill for making garlands and place them around her locks. Dika cannot be the bride, because it is inconceivable that the bride would receive instructions from Sappho. It is obvious that she is the leader of the choir that had been trained by the poetess, as choir-master, for participating in the marriage festivities. The mention of the liking for wreaths by 'the goddess' and the Charites clearly suggests a ceremony. 'The goddess' remains unnamed in the surviving text, but it is well known that the Charites belonged to Aphrodite's (and Hera's) entourage (*Od.* 8.364, 18.194).

A similar involvement of a girls choir sent by Sappho to a marriage ceremony also under another leader, apparently older than the rest of the group, appears in Sa. 27 from the First book.

Ἄτθι] – καὶ γὰρ δὴ cὺ πάιϲ ποτ[' ἦϲθα
5   εὐτ]ύκηϲ μέλπεϲθ' – ἄγι ταῦτα [παῖϲιν

> σὺ] ζάλεξαι, κἄμμ' ἀπὺ τῶδε κ[ῦδος
> ἄ]δρα χάριccαι·
> c]τείχομεν γὰρ ἐc γάμον· εὖ δ' ἐ[πίcτεαι
> κα]ὶ cὺ τοῦτ'· ἀλλ' ὄττι τάχιcτα [κῆcε
> 10 πα]ρ[θ]ένοιc ἄπ[π]εμπε· θέοι [δὲ τ' εὔνοι-
> άν κ]εν ἔχοιεν.[11]

Remarkable is also the claim of the poetess about the implication of the gods in the marriage celebration, both in Sa. 27.10–11 and in 81.6–7.

In any case, the juxtaposition of fr. 81 V. with the incipit of line 12 (9) discussed here is very useful. Primarily, it provides the two-syllabled name that is missing in the incipit:

Δίκα cτέφανον δῆ]cε φόβαιcι <'ν>θεμέγα λύραγ [που.

In 81 V. she was advised to lay aside something and plait garlands for placing them around her/their locks. She has done exactly these two actions in the incipit: she laid aside the lyre and bound the garland she prepared around her locks. However, the two cannot belong to the same poem, since line 12 (9), which describes a scene temporally subsequent, is the first of the poem (9). The only solution to the problem can be the acknowledgment of two successive poems narrating successive happenings. The immediately prior poem in the list of incipits, the one that starts with the girls being urged to rouse the bridegroom because his comrades would not sing, is not simply an epithalamion; it is a snatch of the narration of a marriage ceremony scene. It is noteworthy that both the incipit of 103.11 (8) and fr. 81 imply a stage where the girls' singing shift has ended. Fr. 81 possibly closes the poem (8), while 103.12 (9) starts by continuing the same scene as (8), only having passed to a somewhat later stage.

13 (10).] ̣ ̣η χρυcοπέδιλ<λ>[ο]c Αὔωc [

'] ̣ ̣: fort. litt. tres, ante H, litt. Δ sive Λ, ut vid.' Voigt

I read × – ⏑ ⏑ – – ⏑]νι δὴ χρυcοπέδιλ[λο]c Αὔωc. The top ends of the first three letters are clear enough, but supplementing is problematic. I venture, e.g.,

νῦν πότνι' ἔφαννε χθό]νι δὴ χρυcοπέδιλ[λο]c Αὔωc.

---

[11] See below '11. Sappho 27 V., Alcaeus 308 Lib., and the Homeric *Hymn to Hermes*'. The readings are reprinted here undotted. The initial name is given exempli gratia.

Cf. Hes. *Th.* 372 Ἠῶ θ', ἣ πάντεccιν ἐπιχθονίοιcι φαείνει. Puglia rightly notes that the length of the papyrus gap makes χρυcοπέδιλ[λο]c (not -πεδιλ<λ>[ο]c as L.-P., nor -πεδιλ[ο]c as Voigt) compulsory. The Aeolic spelling with λλ is extensively debated (Chantraine *DELG* s.v. πέδιλον).

The similarity with Sa. 123 ἀρτίωc μὲν ἀ χρυcοπέδιλοc Αὔωc has been observed. However, the metre of that fragment is different. It may be cr hipp, as noted *dubitanter* by Voigt, though more options are also possible. If fr. 123 is a first line, as suggested by Diehl, the golden-sandalled Dawn appears to open two poems of different books. Or, in other words, the events described in two poems start on a new day at sunrise.

What event might the sunrise mark in the last poem of a series of epithalamian songs that speak, wherever we can tell, of successive happenings in a marriage ceremony? The Scholia to Theocritus *Id.* 18 (Ἑλένηc ἐπιθαλάμιοc) offer some illuminating data: Arg. τῶν δὲ ἐπιθαλαμίων τινὰ μὲν ᾄδεται ἑcπέραc, ἃ λέγεται κατακοιμητικά, ἅτινα ἕωc μέcηc νυκτὸc ᾄδουcι· τινὰ δὲ ὄρθρια, ἃ καὶ προcαγορεύεται διεγερτικά. I propose that the verses that would follow after the mention of the golden-sandalled Dawn in its opening would refer to such 'daybreak' or 'rousing' songs from the girls choir, after they had stopped their 'lulling' songs and possibly had themselves 'a sleep slightly longer than the nightingale's' (Sa. 30.7-8). Their 'daybreak' songs mark the end of the ceremony.

To sum up with the incipits, we can safely deduce that, except for the first poem that was in dactylic hexameters, all other poems were written in ˎhipp^{2c}, a conclusion supported both by the proposed supplements and by the left-hand margin wherever the supplements could produce an alignment. Hephaestion, *Ench.* 11.5 p. 36 C., specifies about this metre that it is called Αἰολικόν, ὅτι Cαπφὼ πολλῷ αὐτῷ ἐχρήcατο. E. Puglia's restoration (pp. 6-7) also keeps the same metre. The poems of this metre appear in the papyri predominantly in distichs. It is extremely unlikely that some of the incipits here belonged to poems composed in tristich stanzas (ˎhipp^{xc} ‖ ˎhipp^{xc} ‖ ˎhipp^{x-1c} ‖‖); see above on 5 (2).

So far as the supplements can be trusted, the poems were not arranged in alphabetical order. This is only natural, since apart from the general thematic connection of the poems as epithalamians, there seem to exist even closer affinities between the successive poems: 4-5 (1-2) question to the Muse ~ answer of the Muse; 5-8 (2-5) marriage of Heracles and Hebe; 9-13 (6-10) real-life marriage; 6-7 (3-4) Heracles' falling in love ~ Hebe's falling in love; 8-9 (5-6) transition from the divine celebration to the real-life festivity (Muses' choir ~ girls' choir); 10-13 (7-10) late and last stage of the marriage celebration; 10 (7) the girls possibly sing late at night close to the dawn; 11 (8) the groom is raised from bed to urge his idle comrades to sing, while Dika, the choir-leader, is advised to lay the lyre down, end the singing, and go outdoors to pick flowers for plaiting garlands; 12 (9) Dika complies with the advice; 13 (10) last songs in the next morning. The prevailing impression is that we are not dealing with independent poems, but with excerpts of a longer description. The poems seem to belong to a cycle of short not fully autonomous poems divided in two sections, the first serving as mythical exemplum, the second as real-life description, with each section's poems placed in temporal order of the described event.

 14.] η̄ cτίχ(οι) ρ̄λ̄[ ]

H̄ is practically certain, since a considerable part of the letter's crossbar survives. Lasserre's] α̣ is impossible just like his supplement εἰc τὴν ᾠδῶν] α̣ cτίχ(οι) ρ̄λ̄[.]. Puglia reads [ᾠιδαὶ] ῑ. The numerical dash above is fairly longer than what an iota would require; see Ī in line 2. The fact that the dash is slightly off-centered is negligible; so is also the dash above Ā in line 2. However, regardless of the reading, after having stated that the odes (or in Puglia's approach, the distinguishing odes) are ten and after having quoted ten incipits, what would repeating for a third time 'odes ten' serve? Much like the colophon of the First book in P.Oxy. 1231 (fr. 30 V.), which reads

ΜΕΛΩΝ Α

ΧΗΗΗΔΔ

I would follow Page in reading

 μελῶν] η̄ cτίχ(οι) ρ̄λ̄[ ]

For reasons of balance in the written part of the line, possibly

 Cαπφοῦc μελῶν] η̄ cτίχ(οι) ρ̄λ̄[ ]

The number of verses that follows (between 130 and 139, or 138 if the dactylic poem was also in distichs) is surprisingly small. I would calculate an average of 14 verses (or 7 distichs) for the 9 melic poems and a number from 4 to 12 (or 2 to 6 distichs) for the initial dactylic one, granted that the initial poem was also in distichs, which is most likely. More combinations are, of course, possible. However, I would rule out the possibility that tristich strophes were included in the present book.

 15.] μετὰ τὴν πρώτην̣ [

'After the first', sc. ᾠδήν, posits a distinction between the first and the next nine poems and since we have seen that the most conspicuous difference between the first and the rest of the poems concerns the metre, I would again follow Page in supplementing something like ὁμοιόμετροι δὲ] μετὰ τὴν πρώτην [πᾶσαι.[12] Only for securing an approximate alignment with the left-hand margin, I would propose e.g.,

εἰσὶ δὲ ὁμοιόμετροι πᾶσαι] μετὰ τὴν πρώτην [ᾠδήν·

16.   ]φέρονται ἐπιγεγρα[

Most editions publish επιγεγρα[and supplement ἐπιγέγρα[πται, thus detaching by punctuation the word and what follows from the previous sentence. However, ἐπιγέγρα[πται is impossible, since the Α is clearly joined with the left-hand low tail of Μ. Cf.]λΑΜια in the next line. Then, ἐπιγεγραμ[μέν- is indispensable, with the predicative participle depending on φέρονται. So Lasserre: ἐπι]φέρονται ἐπιγεγραμ[μέναι. I believe that what we have here is the extremely common scholiastic formula φέρεται ἔν τισιν, used for noting MSS variants; similarly Snell, e.g., ἐν ἐνίοις. Also *exempli gratia*, I propose:

ἔν τισι δὲ τῶν ἀντιγράφων] φέρονται ἐπιγεγραμ[μέναι

17. Ε̱ΠΙΘΑ]ΛΑΜΙΑ̱

It is unknown whether, following ἐπιγεγραμ[μέναι, the author continued straight with the title or the title was preceded by οὕτως or another adverb. Since, however, it is unlikely that anything followed after ἐπιγεγραμμέναι in 16, it is reasonable to conclude that line 17 contained nothing more than the ornamented title. However, if 'Epithalamians' was the title of this short book of 10 odes with a total of 130–138/9 verses, what would be the title of the book that contained numerous nuptial odes of diverse metres not included in the Eighth book discussed in POxy. 2294? As we have seen, one of these nuptial odes is referred to as coming from a book named Ἐπιθαλάμια (fr. 116) and another is named ἐπιθαλάμιον (fr. 113) by an author who knows of a Sapphic book entitled Ἐπιθαλάμια (D. H. *Rh.* 4.1). The

---

[12] Yet Page (1955), p. 118 and n. 1, does not mention the metre of the first incipit, though he concerns himself about that of the others: ₐhipp^{2c}, as suggested by Lobel for line 5, or 3 cho ba? Voigt, does not find the metres homogeneous and, apart from the metres mentioned by Page, suggests also gl^{2c}. Ferrari (2007), 114 n. 2, proposes, alternatively to Page, that the author of the papyrus text noted that all the odes except the first were choriambic, a hypothesis that would allow a variety of Aeolic metres.

problem will be discussed later, but preliminarily I would somehow hesitantly propose for the title written in line 17: δεύτερα ἐπιθα]λάμια or, more simply, β̄ ἐπιθα]λάμια.

18.   ] ˳υβλίου· καὶ βέλτ[[ε]]ι˳ο̣[ν

'dubio procul]βυβλ-, quamquam prim(ae) litt(erae) vestigia parum in β quadrant: h(asta) v(erticalis) crassior, pes sinistrorsum ut vid. flexus' LP

The initial vertical stroke is no doubt an iota deleted by blacking out, and so appearing thicker than usual. Its foot seems to have both a rightward and a leftward bend, the impression of a leftward bend being given by the blackening, which is thicker at the bottom, possibly with a low crossing out. Apparently, the scribe started writing βιβλίου, but after writing the second letter he changed it to βυβλίου. In the last word, the second epsilon is deleted with a cancel dot, but it is uncertain what was written after βέλτ[[ε]]ι ˳ [. Two variants of orthography in the same line are corrected in two different ways: the first (βιβλίου > βυβλίου) by blacking and possibly crossing out, but the second (βέλτει ˳ [> βέλτι [) by cancel dot. This is due, I suppose, to the scribe's awareness that a cancel dot over the first iota of βιβλίου might be confused with the usual overdot of iota. All editors publish the common idiomatic phrase καὶ βέλτιο[ν, but Puglia prefers, as we noted above on 1–3, to refer to the odes of the next book by καὶ βέλτιc[ται, noting that 'il redattore segnalò che tutte le dieci odi migliori, tranne la prima, sono epitalami'. I cannot reject the proposal, though, speaking of odes, I would prefer κάλλιcται, not βέλτιcται. In any case, I suggest, e.g., ἑτέρωc πωc τοῦ προτέρου β][[ι]]υβλίου· καὶ βέλτ[[ε]]ιο[ν; or καὶ βέλτ[[ε]]ιο[ν οὕτωc. 'Somewhat differently from the previous book. And it is better (in this way).' Cf. Pl. *Plt.* 295d ἑτέρωc πωc τῶν εἰωθότων. Also, Aelius Dionysius Atticista ω 11 Erbse (concerning ὦ τάν) οἱ γὰρ Ἀττικοὶ τὴν πρώτην cυλλαβὴν περιcπῶcιν, τὴν δὲ δευτέραν βραχύνουcιν· καὶ βέλτιον. 'Second Epithalamians' is slightly different from plain 'Epithalamians' and better than 'Eighth book'.

18/9. Following 18 the editors note a line either unwritten or written with a short text which does not reach the left-hand edge of the surviving papyrus. As noted above, Puglia proposes a supplement for this short text: [εἰcὶν z, ὧν ὁ (πρῶτοc) ἐcτίν·], thus making the next line (the editors' 20) the incipit of the first ode of the next book. It is true that the line spacing between 18 and 19 is wider than elsewhere, but by no means could a written line be inserted there. The regular line spacing is c. 0.4 cm., here it is c. 0.6 cm., while a blank in-between line would require c. 1.0 cm. I believe the scribe somewhat widened his spacing here, because it was here, at line 19, that the discussion about the next book started.

19. The editors publish]ροπ ....[..] . ε .[, to the end of which Puglia rightly added an ω. Following Π, Lobel noticed a second O ('e.g.', though it is clear). Then, the top tips of a N are visible, and, finally a top horizontal shorter than Γ or Τ, possibly Ζ. Two tiny vertical cuts of the horizontal should not deceive us. After a 3-letter gap, we can see the end of the upper arc of C followed by ΕΩ:]ροπονζ[...]ςεω[. τρόπος ζητήςεως is a common philosophical term for 'method of inquiry', but here it may simply designate the mode of reference to the specific books of Sappho; whether, that is, one should refer to them solely by number or solely by thematic title (or variants of a thematic title) or by both.[13] It seems that the discussion of the new book started with a specification of the book's identity.

With so many uncertain, precarious, and hypothetical reconstructions, it is no doubt too hazardous to attempt a definitive edition of POxy. 2294, but a comprehensive picture of what was proposed here is certainly useful.

```
                          . . . .
1                     ] . ω[
2                     ]ςαν ἐν τῶι ἐ[χομένωι
3             βυβλίωι· εἰ]ςὶ δὲ ι̅ κ' ἑκάςτης ὁ α̅ [οὕτως ἔχει·
4  (1)        οἴων] μὲν τότ' ἄρ', ἔννεπ', ἔον προβ[εβάκοτα λέκτρα
5  (2)        ὑμνή]ςατε τὰν εὔποδα νύμφαν [ἰόκολπον Ἄβαν
6  (3)        Ἔρως ὅ]τα παῖδα Κρονίδα τὰν ἰόκ[ολπ]ον [Ἄβαν
7  (4)        Δίος πά]ις ὄργαν θεμένα, τὰν ἰόκ[ολ]πος Ἄ[βα
8  (5)        ἔθεντο] τύλᾱγναι Χάριτες Πιέριδέ[ς τ' ἄε]ιδον
9  (6)        χόρος παίδ]ω[ν ὅ]ππότ' ἀοίδαι φρέν[ ἔμ]αν ἔθ[ελξε
10 (7)        ἀ Νὺξ ἅμα κΑὔω]ς ἀϊοίςᾱ λιγύραν [ἀοί]δαν
11 (8)        ἐγέρρατε νῦν γά]μβρον· ἄςαροι γὰρ ὑμάλικ[ες ϝοί
12 (9)        Δίκα ςτέφανον δῆ]ςε φόβαιςι <'ν>θεμένα λύραν [που
13 (10)       νῦν πότνι' ἔφαννε χθό]νι, δὴ χρυςοπέδιλ[λο]ς Αὔως
14                     Σαπφοῦς μελῶν] η̅    ςτί(χοι) ρ̅λ̅[ ]
15            εἰςὶ δὲ ὁμοιόμετροι πᾶςαι] μετὰ τὴν πρώτην [ᾠδήν.
16            ἔν τιςι δὲ τῶν ἀντιγράφων] φέρονται ἐπιγεγραμ[μέναι
17                     β̅ ἐπιθα]λάμια,
18            ἑτέρως πως τοῦ προτέρου β][ι]υβλίου· καὶ βέλτ[ε]ιο[ν.

19                          τ]ρόπον ζ[ητή]ςεω[ς
                          . . . .
```

All this discussion leads the investigation about the order of Sappho's books to new paths. If our proposal that in some copies the Eighth book of Sappho was named 'Second Epithalamians' is accepted, then the plain 'Epithalamians' must

---

13 Cf. the heading of the Vienna Epigrams Papyrus (P.Vindob. G 40611), an analogous bibliographical papyrus, τὰ ἐπιζητούμενα τῶν ἐπιγραμμάτων ἐν τῆι α̅ βύβλωι.

reasonably be the Seventh. And there is actually fairly strong evidence to suggest that this hypothesis is true. The only reference to the Seventh book comes from Hephaestion, *Ench.* 10.5 p. 34 C., ἔcτι δὲ πυκνὸν καὶ τὸ τὴν δευτέραν μόνην ἀντιcπαcτικὴν ἔχον, ᾧ μέτρῳ ἔγραψεν ᾄcματα καὶ Cαπφὼ ἐπὶ † τῆc τοῦ ἑβδόμου (fr. 102)

  ⊗ γλύκηα μᾶτερ, οὔ τοι δύναμαι κρέκην τὸν ἴcτον
    πόθωι δάμειcα παῖδοc βραδίναν δι᾽ Ἀφροδίταν.

Bergk faced the daggered critical problem in Hephaestion's text (τῆc τοῦ A, τε τοῦ H, τοῦ C, τῆc P) by writing τελευτῆc *vel* τέλουc. Much easier is, I believe, Cαπφώ, <ὡc> ἐπὶ τῆc τοῦ ἑβδόμου, *sc.* ᾠδῆc. In any case, the fragment introduced with this phrase belongs to the Seventh book. The important thing, however, is that the fragment has the character traits of an epithalamian and, what is more, of a lowbrow popular one. 'Sweet mother, I can't weave the web, subdued by desire for a boy because of slender Aphrodite.' The speaker does not seem to be Kleïs nor does the 'sweet mother' seem to be Sappho, much less can the speaker be the young Sappho addressing her own mother. It is likelier that the characters involved, daughter, mother, and boy, remain anonymous. Hephaestion, in his regular practice, offers the first verses of the ode. There is no doubt that the response of the mother will come in the verses following, and will suggest marriage as the ultimate solution to the daughter's problem. Here is a Modern Greek folk song comparable, even in the degree of directness and naturalness:

 – Δεν μπορώ, μανούλα μ', δεν μπορώ
  αχ σύρε να φέρεις το γιατρό. ...
  Αγάπησα, μάνα μ', αγάπησα,
  πικρά η μαύρη το μετάνιωσα. ...
 – Σώπα, τσούπρα μ', και μην κλαις εσύ,
  θα φέρω το γιατρό ταχιά πρωί.
  Θα φέρω το γιατρό ταχιά πρωί,
  να σου γιάνει, κόρη μ', την πληγή.

 – I'm unwell, mommy, I'm unwell,
  oh, go and fetch the doctor. ...
  I fell in love, mom, I fell in love,
  I bitterly regret it, poor me. ...
 – Quiet down, my poppet, do not cry,
  I'll fetch the doctor tomorrow morn.
  I'll fetch the doctor tomorrow morn,
  To heal, my daughter, your hurt.

The implication is that the doctor the mother promises to fetch is the groom and the healing of the wound is the marriage. No loom weaving is mentioned in this modern song, but it is found in another marriage song. Yearning and desire prevent Sappho's girl from weaving at the loom, but in the modern song the same sentiments urge the girl on to finish weaving the web for the expected groom's dress:

> Πέτα, σαΐτα μου, γοργή
> με το χρυσό μετάξι,
> νά ρθει ο καλός μου τη Λαμπρή,
> να βρει χρυσά ν' αλλάξει. ...
> Τάκου τάκου ο αργαλειός μου,
> τάκου κι έρχεται ο καλός μου. ...
> Τάκου και σε λίγο φτάνει,
> για φιλί και για στεφάνι.
>
> Fly fast, my shuttle,
> with the golden silk,
> so that my sweetheart coming on Easter,
> will find golden clothes to change. ...
> Taku taku my loom,
> taku, here comes my sweetheart. ...
> Taku, and he's about to show up,
> for a kiss and a wedding crown.

Significantly, the songs of Sappho that have common traits with Modern Greek folk songs happen to be associated with marriage. And, more significantly, these songs happen to diverge from the Sapphic canon of personalized poetry, where the poet and the lyric 'I' are identified. Truly, one of the principal traits of Sapphic poetry is the viewpoint of the poetess who is always present in the poems speaking almost exclusively in first person about matters that concern herself. Although practically the whole of her surviving poetry consists of fragments, some times of tiny size or even of one word, we can safely claim, wherever we can tell, that all the poems of the First book (1–42) present this character, nearly all the Second book (43–52), with the exception of the long fragment 44, whose beginning, however, has not survived and it has been proposed that the surviving part is a mythical exemplum, as well as all the Third book (53–57). The same feature is observed in the fragments assigned with uncertainty to the Fourth book (58–91). There follow some fragments of an uncertain book, but still of the same first-person character. Fr. 103 transmits, as we have seen, the incipits of ten poems that constituted the Eighth book. Some of the incipits preserve explicit first-person traits, while the others would apparently show the same traits in the subsequent verses. Finally, the fragments after 118 also seem, as far as one can tell, to have the same characteristics. It is not the same with frs. 104–117B. They are all ἐπιθαλάμια, as was the term given to marriage songs, irrespective of the stage of the wedding ceremony they were supposed to be sung in. In all these fragments, whether transmitted as ἐπιθαλάμια or identified as such from their content, Sappho is absent. The speaking characters are the anonymous persons involved in the betrothal (bride, groom, parents, friends), but not the poet. The folk traits are highlighted by frequent similes, sometimes exaggerated: like Hesperus, like the sweet apple, like hyacinth, like a Lesbian singer, like a slender bough, like Ares. We also find figures of anaphora (fr. 104 φέρ-, φέρ-, φέρ-), direct talks (102 γλύκηα μᾶτερ κτλ., with the mother's response in the missing verses, 109 δώcομεν, ἦcι πατήρ), childish play-like exchanges (114 – παρθενία, παρθενία, ποῖ με λίποιc' ἀ<π>οίχηι; | – †οὐκέτι ἤξω πρὸc cέ, οὐκέτι ἤξω, 115 – τίωι c' ... ἐικάcδω; | – ὄρπακι βραδίνωι cε μάλιcτ' ἐικάcδω), easy and straightforward praises and wishes (108, 113, 116, 117). The metres are varied, but the dactylic hexameter prevails, with its sung form some times accentuated through interpolated meshymnia (111). Frequently, the metres seem deformed, as is usual with folk songs sung for long periods of time in popular events. Sometimes, however, the metres seem to deviate from the formal rules.[14] The parallel traits of these songs with Modern Greek folk marriage songs have been observed: Contiades-Tsitsoni (1990), esp. 110–132; Karabataki (1997) and (2010). Marriage poems (Hochzeitsgedichte) existed in other Sappho books too, since the marriage was one of her favourite subjects, but also, as noted above, attending or participating in marriage feasts was a usual activity of her pupil-friends (frs. 27, 30, 31, possibly 94). However, the marriage in these poems is no more than the occasion for Sappho to give voice to her personal concerns. If fr. 31 (φαίνεταί μοι κῆνοc κτλ.) were sung during the marriage celebration, whether in antiquity or nowadays, it might lead to unexpected consequences. The same folkish characteristics as those of the other Sapphic marriage songs are found in the two fragments mentioned as coming from the book named Ἐπιθαλάμια: in 113 the anonymous πάιc and γάμβροc are combined with an exaggerated comparison, while 116 is a simple and artless greeting in the form of an acclamation to the anonymous bride and groom; cf. Mod. Greek

---

14 E.g., in fr. 114, quoted above, prosody seems to allow hiatus in everyday phrases and brevis in longo in strong caesurae: 1 παρθενία, παρθενία, / ποῖ με λίποιc' ἀ<π>οίχηι; 2 οὐκέτι ἤξω προτὶ cέ / οὐκέτι, <νύμφα,> ἤξω.

Να ζήσει η νύφη κι ο γαμπρός κι οι συμπεθέροι όλοι.

And the metres of these fragments are quite different from that of POxy. 2294 (‿hipp²ᶜ ||), i.e., what we designated as Eighth book; 116 (incipit): cr × hipp ||, 113: 3 io || (vel sim.). It is then reasonable to conclude that all these folkish marriage songs of varied metres belong to the Seventh book.

As mentioned above, the feast in celebration of the wedding must have lasted till the next morning after the ceremony. As is natural in every popular feast, the celebrants entertained themselves eating and drinking, singing and dancing. Sappho's pupil-friends, who were trained in singing by their teacher and choir-master, participated in the celebration with their songs, no doubt accompanied by lyre played by a somewhat older girl, possibly the choir-leader. The songs, words and music, were composed by Sappho. However, the song themes had nothing to do with the usual Sapphic themes that issued from her own personal passions. Such songs, mostly sad and pathetic, would not interest either the wedding couple or the merrymakers. Therefore, the girls' songs were popular-like, with no names or other personal references, so that they could easily be repeated in every wedding. We have seen that the friends of the bridegroom were also supposed to sing, but we know nothing about their songs. It is very unlikely that they also sang songs by Sappho, most of which are distinctly girlish. They may have sung plain popular songs. And if their singing shift was, as it seems, late, after midnight, when they were already intoxicated and the couple was in bed, it seems probable that their songs were bawdy and ribald.

Though keeping the folkish character, Sappho's epithalamians express a sense of gentility and delicacy, something only to be expected in view of Sappho's personal style, but also as they were written for being sung by young girls. The only exception to the rule is believed to be fr. 110a, b about the θυρωρός, his huge feet and his gigantic sandals that needed ten shoemakers to make. The song is characterized as trivial and prosaic by Demetr. *Eloc.* 167: σκώπτει τὸν ἄγροικον νυμφίον καὶ τὸν θυρωρὸν τὸν ἐν τοῖς γάμοις εὐτελέστατα καὶ ἐν πεζοῖς ὀνόμασι μᾶλλον ἢ ἐν ποιητικοῖς, ὥστε αὐτῆς μᾶλλόν ἐστι τὰ ποιήματα ταῦτα διαλέγεσθαι ἢ ᾄδειν, οὐδ' ἂν ἁρμόσαι πρὸς τὸν χορὸν ἢ πρὸς τὴν λύραν, εἰ μή τις εἴη χορὸς διαλεκτικός. I do not think anyone would agree with Demetrius' general inference, but what remains of the song is by no means vulgar. It is rather a childish entertaining song that inflates the exaggerated similes we saw above to monumental dimensions just for fun, reminding of modern amusing folk songs or scout songs or grammar school ones.

In any case, the delicate epithalamians must have had their original sources in non-surviving folk songs. Yet, as we have seen, the corresponding modern folk songs can serve as the naive and sometimes rough sources of the sophisticated

Sapphic epithalamians. Take, for instance, fr. 105a, one of the most delicate poems of Sappho:

οἶον τὸ γλυκύμαλον ἐρεύθεται ἄκρωι ἐπ' ὔcδωι,
ἄκρον ἐπ' ἀκροτάτωι, λελάθοντο δὲ μαλοδρόπηεc·
οὐ μὰν ἐκλελάθοντ', ἀλλ' οὐκ ἐδύναντ' ἐπίκεcθαι.

The poem was much disputed and the meaning that prevailed was that the bride likened to a sweet-apple was grown-up, beyond the marriageable age.[15] During this happy occasion in the bride's life, Sappho could neither reprimand nor make fun of or console her. Instead, she invents a praise for the precious and exalted object that was unreachable for the petty suitors. However, the folk source need not be either so delicate or so compassionate. A modern Cretan folk song is very outspoken:

Το μήλο όσο κρέμεται εις τη γλυκομηλίτσα
ψύγεται γή μαραίνεται γή τα πουλιά το τρώνε,
γή πέφτει στο περίστρατο και τρών το οι διαβάτες.
Ετσά 'ναι δα κι η κοπελιά σαν γίνει του καιρού της ...

As long as the apple hangs down from the sweet-apple tree,
it freezes or it shrivels up or is eaten by the birds
or it falls on the side street and is eaten by the passersby.
Such is the girl after she's passed her bloom of age ...[16]

One could claim that the coarser versions were preserved in the songs of the ὑμάλικες and the more delicate ones in those of Sappho's girls, but this is unprovable.

Composing personalized songs for every new marriage and teaching them to the girls before the wedding, as was the case with, e.g., Pindar's epinician odes, would be extremely difficult, unless a special order, possibly against remuneration, provided for it. But no evidence for such instances exists. On the other hand, I cannot imagine that the participation of the girls in the wedding celebrations was not hired, the reward being given to Sappho. At the same time, the involvement of the girls in the celebration served also as part of their course of study in poetry, music (choir or solo singing, lyre playing) as well as in social and sexual maturation.

---

15 Davison (1968), 243–246.
16 Kopidakis (2003), 41; Karabataki (2010), 254–261, provides more versions of the Cretan song from other Greek areas and makes an excellent discussion of the question.

The sole reference to Sappho's Eighth book is in Phot. *Bibl.* 161.103a.35 ὁ δὲ δεύτεροc (sc. λόγοc ἐκλογῶν διαφόρων Cωπάτρου cοφιcτοῦ) ἔκ τε τῶν Cωτηρίδα Παμφίλης ἐπιτομῶν πρώτου λόγου καὶ καθεξῆc μέχρι τοῦ δεκάτου καὶ ἐκ τῶν Ἀρτέμωνοc τοῦ Μάγνητοc τῶν κατ' ἀρετὴν γυναιξὶ πεπραγματευμένων διηγημάτων, ἔτι δὲ καὶ ἐκ τῶν Διογένουc τοῦ κυνικοῦ ἀποφθεγμάτων, καὶ μὴν καὶ ἐξ ἄλλων διαφόρων, ἀλλά γε καὶ ἀπὸ ὀγδόου λόγου τῆc Cαπφοῦc· ἐν οἷc καὶ ἡ δευτέρα βίβλοc τῶν cυλλογῶν. Sopater the Sophist (Suda σ 848), is credited with epitomes of many works (ἐπιτομὰc πλείcτων) and possibly with a certain collection of extracts whether historical or of various stories (τινὲc δὲ καὶ τὴν ἐκλογὴν τῶν ἱcτοριῶν). Among these epitomes and extracts were included excerpts ἀπὸ ὀγδόου λόγου τῆc Cαπφοῦc. By no means can this piece of information indicate that the subject of Sappho's book was the same as that of the excerpts from another work, that was included in the vast collection: Artemon's of Magnesia "stories written for women for advising them to live in virtue".[17]

As regards the contents of the Eighth book, a book with unusual structure, if our observations prove to be true, I would very hesitantly propose that it represents one long epithalamian poem, possibly written on special order. It must have consisted of ten short songs each one sung by a different girl. Each girl's part seems to pick up the threads of the story from the previous song, this being the explanation for the repetitions. Still, the poems, though apparently laudatory, are, at the same time, descriptive of two marriages, one from the mythical world and one from real life. They do not seem to be songs written to be sung in the marriage festivity for entertaining the guests who could even accompany the singing girls, as was the case with the folkish songs of the proper epithalamia. It is likelier that they form a musical performance on the occasion of a marriage, an encomiastic and congratulatory show. Possibly, this was the case also with Sa. 44 of the Second book, the wedding of Hector and Andromache.

Now, if the Seventh book was occupied with the 'Epithalamians' and the Eighth book with the 'Second Epithalamians', what were the contents of the Ninth book, to which D. Page, arguing forcefully, had assigned the 'Epithalamians'? The verse read on the book-roll held by Sappho on the Attic red-figured hydria-calpis of the National Museum of Athens,[18]

---

17 This seems to be the meaning of τῶν κατ' ἀρετὴν γυναιξὶ πεπραγματευμένων διηγημάτων, and not "Stories of Virtuous Exploits of Women" or "Stories of Exploits of Virtuous Women", and certainly not a book title. See also Yatromanolakis (2007), 184 n. 23.
18 Inv. no. 1260, ARV^2 1060, *Paralipomena* 445.

ἠερίων ἐπέων ἄρχωμ' ἀγνῶν ϲτεν[άχουϲα,

is found right after the word θεοί, which indicates the opening of a new book, irrespective of whether the word comes from the hand of Sappho or not. The verse is a dactylic hexameter like the first verse of the 'Second Epithalamians', but it also contains like that an emblematic word that testifies to its being proemial: ἄρχωμ(αι). Further, it specifies the contents of the poems that will follow: gloomy, chaste (i.e., non-erotic), and plaintive. If one adds the conclusion drawn from the theme of the vase-painting, namely that the songs pertain to the impending death of the poetess, as well as that Ἔπεα πτερόεντα, 'Winged words', the title of the book-roll in the painting, alludes to the posthumous fame of the poetess, one can easily surmise that a book of such a terminal character can only be the last in the series. I believe that all this evidence overwhelmingly indicates that Sappho's Ninth book contains mournful songs, what I call Epithanatians.[19]

I have conjectured above that Sappho fr. 81 V. (from Ath. 15.674 c-e), which overlaps POxy. 1787 fr. 33, is very likely to be a part of the poem whose incipit is given in the fr. 103.11 (8) of POxy. 2294. If the latter belongs to the Eighth book, as I claim in this paper, then 1787 must transmit fragments of that book. As, however, 1787, a large papyrus consisting of numerous fragments, large and small, contains more poems that obviously do not belong to the Eighth book, since their surviving incipits do not appear in 2294, it follows that 1787 contained the Eighth and an adjacent book, either the Seventh or the Ninth. It could not be the Seventh, because its metres are entirely different, whereas the Eighth of 2294 and all the fragments of 1787 share the same metre ($\smile$hipp^{2c} |||). Clearly, they must belong to the last two books of Sappho, Eighth and Ninth. POxy. 1787 was assigned to the Fourth book by A.S. Hunt, on quite unsatisfactory grounds,[20] but the assignment was consolidated in all subsequent editions. Hunt put forward some metrical considerations together with the evidence provided by Hephaestion. It is, however, precisely this evidence that disproves Hunt's arguments.[21] Yet, both the actual metre and Hephaestion do not suggest specifically any other book. It is on the one hand the testimony of Sa. 81 V. and on the other the plaintive content of the major fragments of 1787 that lead us to the final Ninth book. Accordingly, the exclusively epithanatian poems included in PColon. 21351+21376, one of which (the 'Tithonus poem') overlaps POxy. 1787, need to belong to the Ninth book. As far as one can tell, the metre of the last two books is identical, i.e., distichs of

---

[19] See above '1. Sappho Illustrated: The Epithanatians'.
[20] The Oxyrhynchus Papyri XV, 1922, 26.
[21] See n. 19 above. Also, Hammerstaedt (2011).

₰hipp²ᶜ ||, with the notable exception of the first poems in both books which are dactylic hexameters. Hephaestion (*Poëm.* 1.2, p. 63 C.) describes the two-line strophes, actually couplets of metrically identical verses, referring to Sappho's Second and Third Books. If he had mentioned also the Fourth book, he would have verified Hunt's suggestion, but he has not. However, he does not mention either the Eighth or the Ninth book, though their principal poems are presented in the papyri in distichs. It seems that Hephaestion's habit of illustrating each metre by the first verses of books or odes must have impeded him from including the Eighth and Ninth books in his description of two-line strophes, since their first verses, being dactylic, were different than the rest. Concerning the Ninth book, the metrically heterogeneous Orpheus poem, that follows the Tithonus poem in PColon. 21351+21376, is still a mystery awaiting solution.[22]

Finally, I would very hesitantly like to submit a further hypothesis about the number of Sappho's last book, and so of the number of her books. I mentioned above that the word θεοί written on the book-roll held by Sappho on the Attic red-figured hydria-calpis of the National Museum of Athens, before the dactylic verse ἠερίων ἐπέων ἄρχωμ' ἀγνῶν cτεν[άχουcα, indicates the opening of a new book, irrespective of whether the word comes from the hand of Sappho or not. If it is so, we should expect the same word to be written before every book of Sappho's collection of poems. But what if the word was written especially for this particular book? Both hypotheses are unprovable, but all the proposals made so far refer to the first of them. If we consider θεοί to stand for the title of the particular book, the Ninth in my proposal, we should demonstrate that the book's subject refers especially to 'gods'. However, though we find references to gods in the surviving fragments of the book, the subject seems to be the impending death of the poetess and her concern about the survival of her poetic work. Can we consider θεοί to be a numerical indication of the particular book, with the initial θ designating 'Ninth'? I was unable to find an ancient parallel of titles in the order of the phonetic alphabet (like our Alpha, Bravo, Charlie, Delta, etc.) but with numerical value (α β γ δ ε ϝ ζ η θ). In several books of Sappho, it has been observed that the poems were arranged in the alphabetic order of the initial of the first verse, but it is questionable whether this is a feature of Sappho's Alexandrian edition or of a pre-Alexandrian one.

---

[22] See above '4 Sappho's (?) Orpheus Song'.

7 Sappho *Tithonus Poem*

Two Cruces (Lines 7 and 10)

Line 3 of P.Colon. 21351, i.e., verse 7 of Sappho's *Tithonus Poem*, though absolutely clear in the papyrus, is metrically defective:

†τὰ† στεναχίζω θαμέως. ἀλλὰ τί κεμ ποείην;

The imperfect opening has been variously emended, all of the conjectures being possible and some even attractive. I submit here one more proposal:

τά <γ' ὀν>στεναχίζω θαμέως. ἀλλὰ τί κεμ ποείην;

τά γ(ε) referring to what precedes, frequently expressing a causative sense, is all too common in the epic. For ὀνστεναχίζω cf. *Il.* 10.9 ἀνεστενάχιζ' Ἀγαμέμνων, and, in the late epic, Q.S. 2.634, 10.253, Nonn. *D.* 20.17, 24.192. ἀν-στεναχίζω is also supported by the obvious parallel in Anacreon, a poem bemoaning the poet's old age like the *Tithonus poem*: PMG 395.7

διὰ ταῦτ' ἀνασταλύζω | θαμά.

ἀνασταλύζω (or ἀσταλύζω/ἀστυλάζω) = 'burst into tears'. So far as the evidence goes, γε is not used by the Lesbian poets but in conjunction with personal pronoun (Sappho 95.7 V., as edited, is patently erroneous). Yet, on the one hand, this is not a dialectal prohibition, but a feature of poetic idiolect, which by no means can be considered compulsory; and, on the other, τά (acc.) may indeed be considered a third person personal pronoun.

However, after meticulously inspecting three different digital images of P.Colon. 21351, I discerned a faint supralinear ΓAN written in small calligraphical letters right above the missing syllable. Before the gamma, a curved downward stretching stroke seemed to connect the three letters with the beginning of στεναχίζω. I interpreted it as a correction for τά ˋγ' ἀνˊστεναχίζω, written in pale ink which grew even dimmer with the passage of time. Prof. J. Hammerstaedt and Dr. Robert Daniel, who obligingly consulted the original on my behalf, did not discover anything and concluded that what I saw was a mirage and no more. Be

---

I am grateful to Professors †M.L. West and J. Hammerstaedt and to Dr. R.W. Daniel for their helpful comments and constructive remarks.

that as it may, I was racked by doubt whether I was dealing with a mere discoloration formed in the process of the papyrus's retrieval from the cartonnage. On the other hand, I knew that the soft acid used in this process behaves differently on the written text depending on the chemical composition of the ink. Also, I was told by art conservators that details invisible to the human eye are frequently retrieved through photographs, preferably ultra-violet ones, something I had partly experienced when deciphering the Derveni papyrus. Therefore, I insisted on my initial visible impression, which was, after all, a linguistically and grammatically sound proposal. ἀν- for Aeolic ὀν- was no problem, since the papyrus seems to present the not yet standardized pre-Alexandrian Sappho text; cf., e.g., -ίζω for -ίσδω.

Fig. 1: The dim supralinear addition ΓAN (left) and the same image with ΓAN overwritten (right).

In line 10, following ΕΡΩΙ, a Δ is clearly visible. After that, the faint traces of the middle of a vertical are perceptible, apparently an iota, followed by at least two parallel horizontals, most likely an epsilon. The papyrus fragments, as seen in the Web photograph, have to be adjusted as to the size of the gap between them. The gap after what we described above must close considerably, so that the left-hand margin might be aligned with the first four lines. Then, the upper part of the left-hand oblique and, faintly, the foot of the right-hand oblique of a triangular letter (apparently a Λ) are visible, followed by a more or less clear A with a marked serif in its right-hand foot, a frequent feature of the scribe's hand. There follows the upper left-hand part of a round letter (Θ, as proposed by M.L. West) and, after a short gap that would accommodate the right-hand part of the round letter and the left-hand part of the following E, a clear EICANBAMEN. Two microscopic ink traces at the bottom of a tongue of 21351 must belong to the I and the E that follow after Δ.

If so, we can read ΕΡΩΙΔΙΕΛΑΘΕΙCΑΝΒΑΜΕΝ, and accordingly reconstruct ἔρωι διελάθεισαν βάμεν'. Lesb. διέλαμι (= Att.-Ion. διελαύνω) means 'pierce through, thrust through', and is used of persons or sharp weapons (spears, lances –

arrows too, I suppose) that pierce through hostile combatants or their shields. The whole couplet would run

καὶ γάρ π[ο]τα Τίθωνον ἔφαντο βροδόπαχυν Αὔων
ἔρωι δι̱ελάθεισαν βάμεν' εἰς ἔσχατα γᾶς φέροισα[ν.

For, as the tale has it, once rose-armed Dawn, pierced through by love, went to the world's ends carrying Tithonus.

Yet, a metrical problem seems to be created. Hamm (1957), 26 (§ 52 b), observes that when διά suffers elision, whether as simple preposition or in compounds, δι is retained. It is only when διά/δια- is before a consonant, that it changes to δι̱ά/δι̱α- and this to ζά/ζα-. This observation means that διά in δι-ελάθεισαν, being elided, cannot change to δι̱- > ζ-, and διε- must be disyllabic, thus making the reading metrically illegitimate. Hamm notes, however, on both sides of the rule, exceptions, which she justifies, as the case may be: "metrisch bequemere 'Hochform'", "aus euphonischen Gründen", "die Wortgrenze des Kompositums hatte sich im Sprachgefühl verschoben". Actually, varieties of all kinds are possible: inc. auct. 35.7 ζάεισαι = δι-άεισαι of δι-άημι,[1] coll. Hsch. ζ 12 ζαέντες· πνέοντες; Alc. 129.21 διελέξατο (⏑ ⏑ – ⏒), Sapph. *Tithonus Poem* 10 (the point at issue here) δι̱ελάθεισαν (⏑ ⏑ – –); Alc. 129.4 ζέθηκαν = δι-έθηκαν; Sapph. 134 ζαελεξάμαν (⏑ ⏑ – ⏑ –). The last example, considered *valde corruptum* by Wilamowitz and variously emended by other scholars, is now restored in the form transmitted by Hephaestion 12.4 p. 39 C., cod. A. The curious form instead of διελεξάμαν, is possibly used for stressing the reciprocal nature of the conversation with the goddess. So, δι̱ελάθεισαν instead of ζελάθεισαν must be added to the witnesses of the not yet standardized pre-Alexandrian Sappho text that we have seen above: ἀν- for ὀν-, -ίζω for -ίσδω. δι̱ελάθεισαν is followed by another prosodically unattested form, βάμεναι, possibly also unconventional.[2]

One may choose between a metaphorical δι̱ελάθεισαν combined with ἔρωι and a literal one combined with Ἔρωι. In the second case, the image would be an early precursor of the fifth century, both in literature and in art, Eros Archer.

---

[1] Voigt's incerti auctoris 35 belongs to the group of fragments from P.Oxy. 2299 that were attributed to 'Sappho or Alcaeus' by Lobel (*Ox. Pap.* XXI), to Alcaeus by Lobel-Page (252–282), to Sappho by Treu (173), to inc. auct. by Voigt (28–41), and to Alcaeus by Campbell (253–263). Irrespective of the authorship of the whole group, there can be no doubt that inc. auct. 35 V. belongs to Sappho (cf. 8 ὄρχησθ[' ἐρό]εσσ' Ἀβανθι). Its metre, hag[xc], is compatible with hag[2c], the metre of Sappho's Tithonus poem and of the one prior to that in the Cologne papyrus, as well as with the metre of the poems preceding and following the same poem in POxy. 1787 (fr. 58 V.).
[2] See Bettarini (2005).

Sappho 88.27 (now 88.30; M. Steinrück (2000), 10)]σθαι βελέω[ν, mentions arrows in an erotic context ('de Dianae telis cog. Treu' Voigt). Anacreon, *PMG* 413, speaks of a big axe or hammer: μεγάλωι δηὖτέ μ' Ἔρως ἔκοψεν ὥστε χαλκεὺς πελέκει. For early parallels of Aphrodite or Eros shooting with the bow, from Pindar to Euripides, see W.S. Barrett on Eur. *Hipp.* 530 ff.

8 Sappho 1.18–19 V.

τίνα δηὖτε πείθω
.].cάγην[ἐc cὰν φιλότατα;

(I) = POxy. 2288, (II) = Dionysii Halicarnassensis De compositione verborum 23, (III) = eiusdem epitome

18 -πείθω- (II) cod. P, πειθω (II) cod. F, πειθὼ vel -ῶ (III); πειθὼ Rapicius, Steph., al., acc. interpr. Portus p. 184, Seidler 158, Πείθων Ahr., πείθῳ (dat.) Meister p. 157, πείθω (verb.) Faber, Herm., Elem. 678   **19** .]..Ā́TH.[(I). ubi .] spat. ut vid. unius litt. non amplius;]Ψ sive]Φ, tum C ut vid., infra in lin. punctul. (signo interpunct. sim.); H ex EI ut vid. factum; N[possis; 'ἄψ c' ἄγην possis, quamquam hac lectione nec punctum post C explicatur neque accent. nec signi Ā́ ratio redditur' L(P) : -μαι cαγήνεccαν (μαι ex βαι corr.) (II) cod. P, και cαγήνεccαν (II) cod. F (qui μαινο- super. vers. om.), (III), unde μάψ Blomf., λαῖc Seidler 158, μαῖc Bgk. '35, 210, μαῖc' *Buecheler ap. Dl.[1] (cf. Theander l.c. 58ss.); pap. lect. disput. Gall. '53, 163[1], Page, Kamerb. '56, 97, Verdenius l.c. ad v. 17;   ἐc ϝὰν Edm. PCPhS 115, 1920, 2s., quod accipiend. esse vid. L, si initio ἄψ c' ἄγην recte se habet

I reproduce the extended app. cr. of E.-M. Voigt's edition for showing to what extent the two words closing line 18 and opening line 19 have occupied the classical scholars. First, an error in the app. cr. should be pointed out: concerning the reading of cod. P of D.H. *De comp. verb.* μαι cαγηνεccαν Voigt first notes '-μαι', as if it were the ending of a word in Dionysius, and between parentheses '(μαι ex βαι corr.)', whereas it is the opposite that is true. As Lobel notes meticulously (Lobel/Page 1955): 'μαι (μ delet. caud. in β corr.)', that is to say, the scribe of P having deleted the tail of μ corrected the letter into β. Cod. P is the famous 10th/11th c. Paris. 1741, which, among other treatises, contains Aristotle's *Rhetorics* and *Poetics*. It is true that what would remain after erasing the tail of μ, would be a *u*, i.e., the beta of the scribe of P, whereas his kappa is quite distinct. However, the erasure was not made by the original scribe but by a *recentior*, for whom the truncated μ (*u*) would not have the value of β but of κ. Therefore, his intention must have been to produce και, as is uniformly transmitted in the whole MSS tradition of *De comp. verb.* and its *Epitome*.

D.L. Page discusses extensively the problem of the two verses (1955, 9–10), but, being convinced about the reading ἄ]ψ c' ἄγην of the papyrus, which, however, he cannot explain, resorts to an emendation: ἂψ τάγην ἐc càν φιλότατα, '(whom am I to persuade) to be reappointed to your friendship (to rank among your friends again)?' Still, he admits that he cannot 'explain why both the papyrus-text and the quotation offer cαγην instead of ταγην'. One could add that 'to be reappointed' requires a passive (τάγηναι) not an active infinitive. No doubt an apostrophe was omitted by oversight (τάγην' ἐc càν φιλότατα), but the omission cost Page his inclusion in Voigt's app. cr. Problematic are also all the other scholarly interventions. I limit myself to the descriptions made by Page: unconvincing, artificial, unparalleled, fictitious, indefensible, and monstrous.

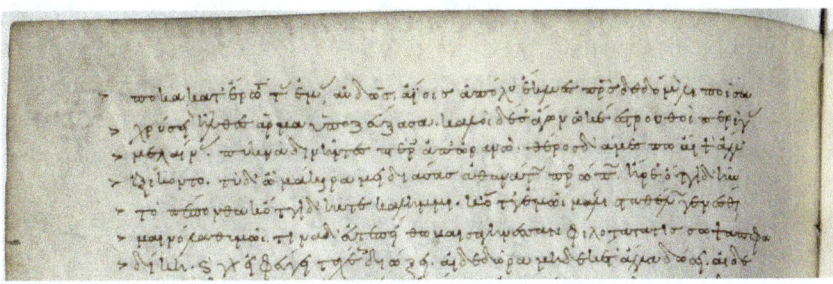

Fig. 1: Detail from cod. P of Dion. Halicarn. *De comp. verb.* 23. The correction of μαι cαγηνεccαν to καὶ cαγηνεccαν is visible in the penultimate line.

To begin with palaeography, what are the difficulties for extending the unanimous reading of Dionysius' quotation (the reading of cod. P included) to the papyrus as well? POxy. 2288 transmits incompletely the beginnings of the verses. In the opening of line 19 (.ˌ.cάγην$_ι$), there is space for two letters. However, high at the position of the letter prior to C, the top end of a vertical is clearly visible. In such a height the vertical could justify only Φ or Ψ, hence Lobel's proposal ἄψ, which proved very popular, though Lobel had himself expressed some, mainly palaeographic, reservations. He did not discuss the strange twist the plot would take with the reading ἄψ c' ἄγην ἐc cὰν φιλότατα. The interpretation 'to lead you back to your love' would be incoherent and unintelligible, thus leading to Edmonds's emendation ἐc Ϝὰν φιλότατα and to a story completely unattested in the rest of the poem, but also preposterous, if what we are dealing with is an older love affair which is now over, but Sappho is praying Aphrodite for help in becoming again accepted in her former lover's love. I believe that both readings, the papyrus, ..ϹΑΓΗΝ, and the quotation, ΚΑΙϹΑΓΗΝ(εccαν), can well conform to each other. What the papyrus scribe wrote was the result of the synaliphe of καί + ἐcάγην which is normally ΚΑϹΑΓΗΝ. Why ἐcάγην and not εἰcάγην? This must have been affected by the words immediately following: ἐc cὰν φιλότατα. Later on, a corrector intervenes. He is aware that in the Lesbian dialect ἐc precedes a consonant and εἰc a vowel: ἐc γάμον but εἰc Ὄλυμπον; also ἐcφερέτω but εἰcάιον. Accordingly, the synaliphe καὶ + εἰcάγην would produce ΚΑΙϹΑΓΗΝ. So, the corrector added an iota above the alpha: ΚΑ̇Ϲ. It is the end of the vertical which survived, and led to the famous ἄψ. The same corrector proceeded to other interventions too. They are the difficulties raised by Lobel against his own supplement ἄψ. When the papyrus scribe noticed that the whole phrase ΚΑΙϹΑΓΗΝΕϹϹΑΝΦΙΛΟΤΑΤΑ could be read καὶ cαγήνεccαν φιλότατα, as it was actually read by Dionysius' tradition and understood as 'and seductive love',[1] he placed a low dot between ΚΑἸϹ and ΑΓΗΝ, by way of hypodiastole, for indicating that the Ϲ belongs to the first component of the word and should not be read with what follows. Yet, as the risk of misreading still existed, he added both the breve sign and the acute upon ΚΑἸϹ.Ἄ́ΓΗΝ, the first to avert a confusion with some peculiar form of ἄγνυμι or of ἀγέομαι, the second with possible derivatives of cαγήνη.

Now, as regards the interpretation of the proposed unanimous reading of the papyrus and the quotation.

τίνα δηὖτε πείθω
κα,ὶ cάγην, ἐc càν φιλότατα;

After a string of Sappho's appeals teasingly (μειδιαίcαιc') listed by Aphrodite (ὄττι δηὖτε ... κὤττι δηὖτε ... κὤττι ...), the goddess ends with τίνα δηὖτε πείθω, 'whom am I to convince again', complemented with καὶ cάγην ἐc càν φιλότατα, the subject of the consecutive infinitive being the same as that of the principal verb; cf. Eur. *Or.* 946-7 μόλιc δ' ἔπειcε μὴ πετρούμενοc θανεῖν τλήμων Ὀρέcτηc (an undeservedly debated passage). The newly read καί has an intensive force that places emphasis on the consecutive infinitive: 'Whom am I to convince again so as even to lead that one into your love?' Speaking of the last and apparently most extreme of Sappho's requests, it seems reasonable to suspect a suggestive remark in Aphrodite's words: '... so as even to put that one into your bedroom'. However, Sappho's art succeeds in avoiding any hint of vulgarity and preserving a sense of decent playfulness by skilfully employing equivocal words: εἰcάγην, 'introduce ~ bring in as wife or lover', φιλότας, 'love, affection ~ sex', τίc, τίνα, used of both genders, the specific sex being revealed only in the last word of the goddess's speech (κωὐκ ἐθέλοιcα).

---

[1] By scribes unaware that the endings of adjectives in -ειc, -εccα are always preceded by a thematic vowel: -άειc -άεccα, -ήειc -ήεccα, -ίειc -ίεccα, -όειc -όεccα, -ύειc -ύεccα, -ώειc -ώεccα.

9 The Banquet of the Gods and the Picnic of the Girls

Observations on Sappho fr. 2 (with an Appendix on Ibycus *PMG* 286)

amicis papyrologis florentinis

1[a]   ..ανοθεν κατιου[c-|²
1   †δευρυμμεκρητεcιπ[.]ρ[   ]|³ .† ναῦον
        ἄγνον ὄππ[αι   ]|⁴ χάριεν μὲν ἄλσος
        μαλί[αν],|⁵ βῶμοι δ' ἔ<ν>ι θυμιάμε-
4   νοι [λι]|⁶βανώτω<ι>·
        ἐν δ' ὕδωρ ψῦχρο˳ν˳ |⁷ κελάδει δι' ὔσδων
        μαλίνων, |⁸ βρόδοισι δὲ παῖς ὁ χῶρος
        ἐσκί|⁹αστ', αἰθυσσομένων δὲ φύλλων |¹⁰
8   κῶμα †καταιριον·
        ἐν δὲ λείμων |¹¹ ἰππόβοτος τέθαλε
        †τωτ ... (.)ριν|¹²νοιcτ† ἄνθεσιν, αἰ <δ'> ἄηται
        μέλλι|¹³χα πν[έο]ισιν [
12   [   ]
        ἔνθα δὴ σὺ †cυ.αν†|¹⁴ ἔλοισα Κύπρι
        χρυσίαισιν ἐν κυ|¹⁵λίκεσσιν ἄβρως
        <ὀ>μ<με>μεί|¹⁶χμενον θαλίαισι |¹⁷ νέκταρ
16   οἰνοχόεισα

The famous Florence ostrakon containing Sappho's fr. 2, widely discussed since its first edition by Medea Norsa in *Annali della Reale Scuola normale superiore di Pisa* II 6 (1937) 8–15 (= *PSI* XIII 1300, which appeared in 1953, one year after Norsa's death), deserves further consideration. It may be difficult or impossible to solve all its numerous problems, both of reading and of interpretation, especially given the loss of nearly half of its text, but it might be worth attempting some new approaches. The ensuing remarks are easier to follow in parallel with Voigt's 1971 edition, whose rich apparatuses are extremely helpful. Her text, thoughtfully conservative, is reproduced above for reference purposes. For the same reason, the ostrakon line-numbers are added in superscript figures after the line-dividing upright. In the references made below, whenever there is question of palaeography

---

I am grateful to George Parássoglou for his palaeographic advice.

and reference to the ostrakon is necessary, its line-number is added in parentheses and smaller print after the poem line-number.

1ᵃ (1). ΟṚΡΑΝΟΘΕΝΚΑΤΙΟΥ[, the reading of Norsa, is certain, and even the first two letters can be published undotted. Giuliana Lanata, in her minute description of the letters, questions the two rhos, referring to the existing signs as peelings of the sherd.[1] This description is repeatedly mentioned in Lanata's paper, especially when there is a question of corrections of or tamperings with the original writing. It is, however, very common, both in papyri and in vase inscriptions, when the ink or the paint is peeled off, for whitish traces of the original writing to be left, sometimes even flaked spots on the surface. In any case, the traces of the two rhos seem to be ink. While the first rho is faint but certain, the second has lost most of its upright but is indubitably recognized from its low oblique serif characteristic of rhos; see on 5 (7).

With regard to this first line of the ostrakon, two principal suggestions have been made: (*a*) the words belong to the end of the preceding stanza of the present poem, (*b*) they supplement the omission of lines 11–12. Suggestion (*b*) would be better considered while discussing lines 11–12. (*a*) is the prevailing proposal. Al. Turyn's suggestion (1942, 308) καρἀνοθεν κατίοισα (κατίοισα iam Körte), implied that Cypris, who appears by name in the end of the poem, descended from the summit of a mountain before entering the temple or sacred precinct described in the verses following. Turyn did not specify the mountain, but others have either understood Olympus or, in combination with the alleged reference to Crete in line 1 (2), located it on that island. Treu in his 1952 edition, implying that the goddess descended from heaven, proposed

– ⏑ – ⨯] ὀρρἀνοθεν <⏑ – ⨯ >
<– > κατίοι[σα.

ὄρανος and ὤρανος appear on an equal footing in the Lesbians, but ὄρρανος is a theoretical construction.[2] And emending to ὠρανόθεν would presuppose a supplement and an emendation at the same time.[3] As made clear above, Turyn's καρἀνοθεν cannot be verified on the ostrakon. Yet, as it restores the metre and, partly, the sense expected, I would conjecture

---

1 Lanata (1960), esp. 70.
2 Hamm (1957), §36. Cf. Wackernagel (1916), 296 n. 1.
3 Mentioned hypothetically by Page (1955), 35 n. 2; accepted by Saake (1971), 85.

⏑ – ⏑ –] ὀρ<άνω κα>ράνο-
θεν κατίου[c-.

With the notion 'from heaven' dominant in his mind, the scribe must have made the leap from the first to the second PAN. Without backing it up with a relevant reading or supplement or testimony, Willy Theiler had already made the same proposal in an *exempli gratia* reconstruction of the first stanza:

<παῖ Διώνας Κυπρογένηα σέμνα,
παρκάλημμι σ' εἰς ἐράταν ἑόρταν,
ἔλθε δ' ὠκέως ὀράνω> | κ]αράνο-
θεν κατίοι[σα].⁴

Accordingly, translations like "von des Himmels Häuptern" or "von Himmelshöhen" are not uncommon.⁵

It has not, however, been noticed that the phrase οὐρανοῦ κάρηνα occurs in Synesius, *Hymn*. 9.55 ὑπὲρ οὐρανοῦ καρήνων. The author certainly had knowledge of Sappho's poems. Voigt, in the *Index fontium et testimoniorum* of her edition, has a single reference to Synesius: *Ep*. 3.21 (p. 639 H.) ὁ τοῦ θυρωροῦ πατήρ, ὡς ἂν εἴποι Σαπφώ (fr. 110). However, it is easy to identify, at least from *Hymn*. 9, a quasi cento religious poem in ionic dimeters and anacreontics, in addition to 55 ὑπὲρ οὐρανοῦ καρήνων, a number of manifest reminiscences of or references to Sappho's poems:

1 ἄγε μοι, λίγεια φόρμιγξ (cf. Sapph. 118.1 ἄγε μοι, δῖα χέλυ, as transmitted by Eust. 9.41; cf. Pl. *Phdr*. 237a; Hom. *Od*. 8.67),
3 μετὰ Λεσβίαν τε μολπάν,
6 f. νύμφαις ἀφροδίσιον γελώσαις (cf. Sapph. 31.5, speaking of a bride, καὶ γελαίσας ἱμέροεν),
20 ff. ὁ μὲν ἵππον εὖ διώκοι, ὁ δὲ ..., ὁ δὲ ..., ἐμὲ δὲ ... (cf. Sapph. 16,1 ff. οἱ μὲν ἱππήων στρότον, οἱ δὲ πέσδων, οἱ δὲ νάων ..., ἔγω δὲ ...),
28 ἀμαρύγμασιν προσώπων (cf. Sapph. 16.18 κἀμάρυχμα λάμπρον ἴδην προσώπω),
49 ἀμφί με ποτᾶται (cf. Sapph. 22.12 ἀμφιπόταται).

And I have no doubt that even more reminiscences of unknown Sapphic verses still lurk behind some other verses of the same hymn.

οὐρανοῦ κάρηνα does not occur in earlier poets, but, given the well-known confusion between Olympus and heaven, I believe it is absolutely legitimate. The

---

4 Theiler (1946) 22–24.
5 Schadewaldt (1950), 78 ff.; Fränkel (1962), 203 f.

confusion has been widely discussed in the ancient annotative literature in connection with epic passages such as *Il.* 5.749–751 and *Od.* 6.41–46. Perhaps the oldest discussion is in P. Derv. XII 3 ff.[6] κάρηνα is added to the discussion in Eust. 38.29 ff. on *Il.* 1.44 βῆ δὲ κατ' Οὐλύμποιο καρήνων; cf. also Eust. 27.30 ff. An interesting parallel in the Lesbians is Alc. 355 νιφόεντος ὠράνω, which, as already suggested, must be connected with *Il.* 18.616 Ὀλύμπου νιφόεντος.

On κατιου[c-| see the next entry.

1 (2–3). ΔΕΥΡΥΜΜΕΚΡΗΤΕ̣CΙΠ̣[.]Ρ̣[   ]|³.ΝΑΥΓΟΝ. This, or variations thereof, is how most scholars read the ostrakon, producing the verse δεῦρύ μ' ἐκ Κρήτας ἐπ[ὶ τόνδ]ε ναῦον or similar versions, as well as a great deal of conjectures about Crete or Cretans and Aphrodite's relationship with the island. The reading should, however, be reconsidered. The scribe initially wrote in line (2) ΔΕΥΡΥΜΜΕΙCΡΗΤΑ̣ΕCΠΡ[. Of the two mus, the first is written in strict majuscule, the second in a more cursive form, like the mus in line 3 (5) δεΜιθυΜι. What was read kappa (Κρητες or -ας) has its upright distanced from the crescent fork, almost identically with the certain kappa of 1ᵃ (1) Κατιου[or 8 (10) Καταγριον, though most other kappas in the ostrakon are written cursively. Schubart's reading was ΔΕΥΡΥΜΜΕΙ̣CΡΗΤΑ̣CΠ[.]Ρ̣[⁷; in response to which, Norsa made a meticulous description of the letter, categorically ruling out IC.[8] I would not be so certain. Schubart's reading is, to a great extent, correct. 10 (12) voIC is identical with the figures in question, and nobody would risk reading voK there. But what confirms IC in line 1 (2) is the bottom downward tail, like a cedilla, visible in Ç. This tail is distinctly used in some sigmas, e.g. 7 (8) κιÇκιαcτ, (9) αιθυÇÇομενων, 10 (12) -ριννοιÇ, but is never found in the fork of kappa. The letter following tau is most likely an alpha, as Schubart recognized. Schubart gives no interpretation of his ἐς ῥητας, neither does Siegmann who accepted his reading,[9] but West, who also accepted the reading, proposed ἐς βρήτας, "for the appointed days" (sc. of a festival).[10]

At some later stage, the text written in line 1 (2) was altered at three points. First, the second M was cancelled with an oblique stroke. Then, T was altered to Λ; the horizontal of tau was extended leftward and upward and its right-hand tip was, perhaps, erased. A curve was also added at the bottom of alpha together with a long mid horizontal changing the letter to theta, somewhat angular, but

---

6 See Kouremenos (2006) *ad loc.*, and add to his literature Funghi (1983), 11–19.
7 Schubart (1938), 297–306.
8 Norsa (1939), 11 f.
9 Siegmann (1941), 417–422.
10 West (1970), 307–330.

certainly a theta. Following epsilon, a faint but certain sigma is noticeable. The lambda and the theta produced after these interventions were, however, clumsy, and so, for certainty, (what passed unnoticed) all four letters following H were rewritten in small script underneath (λθες), now partly peeled off or rubbed out, but identifiable.[11] The resulting reading, ΔΕΥΡΥΜΕΙCΡΗΛΘΕC, allows of two different articulations: δεῦρύ μ' (μοι) εἴς ῥ' ἦλθες and δεῦρ' ὔμ' (ὔμοι = ὁμοῦ) εἴς ῥ' ἦλθες. Both are possible, preference between the two depending on the context, much of which is unfortunately lost. δεῦρυ was proposed by Pfeiffer, of course, in other combinations, and was accepted by many editors, on the evidence of Herodian II 933.9 L. παρὰ τοῖς Αἰολεῦσι καὶ δεῦρυ διὰ τοῦ υ; cf. *Epim. Hom.* δ 65, II 248.58 D.; Theognost. *Can.* ap. Cramer, *An. Ox.* II 161.5; 7 (= Hdn. I 506.19).[12] "Here you entered for me ..." would imply that Aphrodite has appeared to Sappho, possibly in response to a summoning from her. On the other hand, ὔμ', proposed by Schubart, also in a different combination, might indicate that Aphrodite entered together with some other beings, who, if also descended from heaven's summit, could only be the other gods. Now, in the last stanza of the ostrakon, it becomes clear that Aphrodite was not alone; she was in the company of some other beings, to whom she offered nectar in golden cups. There can be no doubt that Sappho refers to a banquet of the gods, who descended from heaven together with Aphrodite to participate in this occasion. Therefore, I believe that of the two articulations, δεῦρύ μ' and δεῦρ' ὔμ', the second is greatly preferable, the actions of descending and entering being extended to the other gods too.

I do not know what the elided vowel of δεῦρ' was: ο or υ. I refrain from belying the grammarians, but, though ὔ for ο is common in Lesbian, also in final position (ἀπύ), I am inclined to accept δεῦρ(ο), especially since both Lesbian poets, in spite of the fact that the two forms are metrically identical, seem to use elsewhere δεῦρο (Sapph. 127, Alc. 401 b).

For εἴς ῥ' cf. *Il.* 10.576 ἔς ῥ' ἀσαμίνθους βάντες (= *Od.* 4.48, 8.450, cf. *Od.* 17.87), *Od.* 10.361 ἔς ῥ' ἀσάμινθον ἔσασα, *Od.* 4.51 ἔς ῥα θρόνους ἕζοντο. With other prepositions *Od.* 3.468 ἔκ ῥ' ἀσαμίνθου βῆ, *Il.* 2.310 πρός ῥα πλατάνιστον ὄρουσεν, Orph. fr. 241 Bernabé (167b.7 Kern) ἐνὶ γαστέρι σύρρα πεφύκει. I would

---

[11] According to Lanata (1960), 71 n. 1, the trace of what I read lambda is a simple irregularity of the sherd.
[12] Pfeiffer (1937), 117–118.

publish ἔ{ι}ς ῥ' ἦλθες to comply with the Lesbian usage of ἐς before consonant and εἰς before vowel.[13]

The suggestions discussed so far make up the sentence ὀράνω καράνοθεν κατίοισα δεῦρ' ὔμ' ἔς ῥ' ἦλθες. The only word left undiscussed is Körte's proposal κατίοι[σα, which emends and supplements the ostrakon's κατιου[.[14] However, though ὔμ(οι), 'together', is associated with the group of gods who are mentioned at the end of the poem, here, at line 1, it remains pendent, since it is not said, at least in immediate vicinity, together with whom the goddess descended. Therefore, I wonder whether κατιου[might represent not a feminine nominative standing for Aphrodite (κατιοῦσα = κατίοισα), but a masculine dative plural standing for the gods (κατιοῦσιν). Just for the sake of illustration, I would supplement

σὺν θέοισιν ὦδ'] ὀρ<άνω κα>ράνο-
    θεν κατίου[σιν
δεῦρ' ὔμ' ἔ{ι}ς ῥ' ἦλθες ...

As for κατίουσιν, this is the first dative plural of an -οντ- participle to be found in the Lesbians, and so we cannot be sure what the product of the compensatory lengthening should have been: ου, as in Attic-Ionic, or οι, as in other dialects. In a cognate case, the nominative singular of the present participle of the non-thematic inflection, *διδοντς, Attic-Ionic διδούς, appears as δίδοις in Alc. 70.13. In consonant stems, Lesbian inscriptions present the longer dative form in -εσσι, but the poets also have a number of the shorter datives in -σι. The origin of the latter in Lesbian poetry is contested, but it seems likely that it is a borrowing, whether from Ionic or directly from the epic.[15] If so, it might be possible that the borrowing of the short ending was accompanied by the diphthong too: -ουσι and not -οισι. In any case, Körte's emendation and/or supplement are equally possible: κατίοι[σιν or κατίοι[σα.

At the edge of the ostrakon Π is clear, followed by the foot of an upright almost reaching the next line, no doubt a P. Norsa's reading was ΠΡ[, but Schubart and Lanata read Π[.]Ρ[, though the space between the two letters could hardly accomodate even an iota. πρός or προτί are quite likely. The Lesbians use πρός, but προτί might be borrowed from the epic. Conversely, Alc. 58.17 προτ' ἐνώπια for the epic πρὸς ἐνώπια.

---

[13] In any case, the two instances of εἰσέρχεσθαι in Sappho (111.5 εἰσέρχεται, 95.7 εἴσηλθ(ε)) are, I believe, corrupt.
[14] Körte (1939), 90–91.
[15] Bowie (1979), 119 ff.

ἔναυλον (masc.), proposed by Pfeiffer, is certain. (*a*) It obeys the regular syllable division observed throughout the ostrakon, whereas Lobel's τόνδ]|ε ναῦ{γ}ον is anomalous. (*b*) There is an unmistakable correction of the original Γ (.ναυΓον) to Λ on the ostrakon; to the vertical of Γ an oblique was added, which does not appear in the other two gammas of the ostrakon (2 (3) αΓνον, 8 (10) καταΓριον) and which deluded some early editors into believing they were dealing with a digamma. Norsa also noticed an attempt at cancelling the horizontal of Γ with an oblique stroke.[16] (*c*) With ἐπὶ τόνδε ναῦον, it would be absurd that the temple could contain a grove of apple-trees, a rose-garden, a brook, and a meadow with horses. The initial epsilon is hardly discernible, written in its two-piece form, usual in the ostrakon; e.g. (4) χαριΕνμΕν; see also below on 10 (11). ἔναυλος, ὁ, is used in Hes. *Th.* 129 and Eur. *Ba.* 122 for the countryside resorts of the gods, in Hesiod specifically θεᾶν χαρίεντας ἐναύλους Νυμφέων. Elsewhere, it is also used of countryside landscapes in a natural state, uncultivated and uninhabited; *H. Hom. Ven.* 74, 124, Eur. *H.F.* 371; metaph. Eur. *Hel.* 1107. For the Nymphs' fondness for virgin and unspoiled groves cf. Ibycus *PMG* 286, a poem possibly cognate with Sappho fr. 2, where, 3 f. a Παρθένων κᾶπος ἀκήρατος is described. It is not merely the use of a term as rare as ἔναυλος both by Hesiod and Sappho; it is also the use of χαρίεις for a natural object (2 χάριεν μὲν ἄλσος), which is perhaps limited to these two passages in Greek poetry; in prose, Plato, *Phdr.* 229b, 230b, uses it for the waters of Ilisos and for a Nymphaion spring. This is why I share the view that Sappho's ἔναυλος is, as in Hesiod and Plato, a Nymphaion.[17] It is there that the banquet of the gods took place, with the Nymphs participating as well. προτὶ θεᾶν ἔναυλον or a neutral προτὶ τόνδ' ἔναυλον (ἐπὶ τόνδε ναῦ{γ}ον Lobel) are equally possible. "Into the sacred precinct of the goddesses" or "into this sacred precinct". Verbs of motion are regularly constructed with πρός. Just as εἰσέρχεσθαι πρὸς Ἀγάθωνα means 'enter Agathon's house', εἰσέρχεσθαι πρὸς θεᾶν ἔναυλον should mean 'enter the resort of the goddesses'. In any case, the employment of εἰσέρχεσθαι presupposes a demarcated area, the precincts of a shrine or a temenos. Of course, the *locus amoenus* described in the next verses is not in heaven, otherwise Sappho would not be able to visit it.

---

[16] Norsa (1953), 49. Lanata (1960), 71 n. 9, denies the cancellation and sees only a small 'convessità' of the sherd. She may be right, because the traces seem to coincide with the tracks of the potter's wheel.

[17] Demetrius *Eloc.* 132 (Sapph. fr. 215) εἰσὶν δὲ αἱ μὲν ἐν τοῖς πράγμασι χάριτες, οἷον Νυμφαῖοι κῆποι, ὑμέναιοι, ἔρωτες, ὅλη ἡ Σαπφοῦς ποίησις.

2 (3). ὄππ[αι δή Lobel; not ὄππαι τοι (Page), since the ἔναυλος does not belong to Aphrodite. For δή with relative local adverbs see *GP* 219, and cf. below 13 ἔνθα δή. We shall discuss below the special function of these adverbs.

3 (4). A tiny but certain left-hand tip of a bottom horizontal at the edge of the ostrakon, at the height where the base horizontal of Δ, somewhat projecting leftward, would be expected (cf. 7 (9) Δὲ), points to Pfeiffer's μαλίδων or Μαλίδων. Supplements like μάλι[νον or μαλί[αν must be excluded. The reading is corroborated by Ibycus' *PMG* 286.1–2 Κυδωνίαι μαλίδες. Though a synonym of μαλία, μαλίς was possibly considered an affectionate diminutive, well matching χάριεν ἄλσος. Most editors prefer to supplement here μαλί[αν] and to choose at 6 (7) the reading of the quotations (see below on 5) μαλίνων, instead of μαλίαν (= μηλεῶν), which is the reading of the ostrakon. However, μαλίαν goes better with the new reading of 5 (7), i.e. ὔρχων μαλίαν; see *ad loc*. In any case, Pfeiffer's alternative proposal χάριεν μὲν ἄλσος Μαλίδων, i.e. 'a pleasant grove of the Malides, the Nymphs of apple-trees' is much preferable. Theocritus, *Id*. 13.45, names a single Nymph Μαλίς, though he includes her among water-nymphs: 13.43 ὕδατι δ' ἐν μέσσῳ Νύμφαι χορὸν ἀρτίζοντο. Yet, Sappho's precinct is also washed by a brook that babbles through rows of apple-trees: 5 f. ἐν δ' ὕδωρ ψῦχρον κελάδει δι' ὔρχων μαλίαν. Eustathius repeatedly refers to νύμφαι Μηλίδες, Μαλίδες or Μαλιάδες (*Il*. II 350.9, *Od*. I 385.16, II 325.46). Μαλιάδες also occur, together with other tree-nymphs, in the girls' game utterance ψίττα Μαλιάδες ψίττα Ῥοιαί ψίττα Μελίαι mentioned by Pollux 9.127.

3–4 (5). βῶμοι ΔΕΜΙΘΥΜΙΑΜΕΝΟΙ [λι]βανώτω: Out of several proposals, I waver between δ' ἔνι θυμιάμενοι (Pfeiffer, Vogliano) and δ' ἐπιθυμιάμενοι (Diehl).[18] I finally adopt the second, because ἐπί in ἐπιθυμιᾶν (see Voigt's apparatuses for parallels) seems to be more germane to βωμοί. The same applies to λιβανώτωι or λιβανώτω. Both are syntactically legitimate and equally documented. If I prefer the genitive, it is mainly because the image refers less to the action of people burning incense than to the altars emitting the odour of incense.

5 (6–7). The grave on 5 (6) ΨῪΧΡΟΝ, the only accent sign that occurs in the ostrakon, is not easy to explain. Normally, it should warn the reader that the word is to be stressed ψυχρόν and not, in the Lesbian manner, ψῦχρον. It is likelier, however, that this is no more than a further error of the ignorant scribe. It has often been asserted that the use of a potsherd for writing material combined with the careless handwriting and the corrupt text point to a schoolboy scribe. Others have objected that the handwriting, though careless, is professional, fluent, and

---

[18] Diehl (1942), 30 ff., 58 f.

practised, and they are, to a certain degree, right.[19] But the fact that the scribe committed an error in a sign especially employed in lyric texts, may indicate that, though skilled in handwriting, he was still an apprentice in studying dialectal poetry. His errors in the Lesbian dialect (βροτοιcοτε, πεc, καταγριον, χρυcεαιc) might possibly be explained otherwise. But the use, and, what is more, the erroneous use, of an accent must be connected with school practice. And this, combined with the use of the potsherd, as well as the kind of errors and the corrections made in the text, suggest a schoolboy, possibly senior. At what age were schoolboys taught dialectal poetry in Ptolemaic Egypt? On the other hand, if the writing of the ostrakon is assigned to the third century B.C., this would be the first accent to be met with in ancient documents, possibly contemporary with the introduction of the accent signs. But the date assigned to the ostrakon is not certain either. At least Norsa offers detailed arguments for dating it to the second century B.C., and I confidently share her views.[20] On the other hand, if, as I argue, haplography and homoioteleuton are responsible for the two extensive omissions of lines 1ᵃ (1) and 11–12 (13), then dictation, as a method of copying, becomes less likely, unless the omissions are imputed to the person dictating. Yet, see below on 10 (11–12).

The end of line 5 (7) has almost unanimously been read ΚΕΛΑΤΙΔΙΑΥΣΧΩΝ and restored, thanks to the quotations, as κελάδει δι' ὕσδων, i.e. δι' ὅζων. The verse, together with 7–8, was quoted by Hermogenes, *Id.* 2.4, 331.19 ff. Rabe: ὥσπερ ἡ Σαπφώ· 'ἀμφὶ δὲ ὕδωρ ψυχρὸν κελαδεῖ δι' ὕσδων μαλίνων' καὶ 'αἰθυσσομένων δὲ φύλλων κῶμα καταρρεῖ'. I omit the variants of Hermogenes' tradition, whether manuscripts or commentators of the rhetor. Lobel ineptly read ΥΣΔΩΝ also on the ostrakon ("fort. potius υcδων quam υcχων"), a reading which Page is inclined to accept. But, whether a reading or an emendation, the question is how a stream can flow and babble high through the branches – except on the awkward assumption that it flowed through broken and fallen branches. Page explains the sentence as "makes a sound which goes through, can be heard through, the branches" and offers some parallels which, however, do not speak of babbling through the branches. He also thinks of ὄσχων or ὠσχῶν (Hsch. ω 468 ὠσχοί· τὰ νέα κλήματα σὺν αὐτοῖς τοῖς βότρυσιν), but no vineyard or grapevine is mentioned in the description of the sacred grove. μῆλον and μηλέα may denote several fruits and fruit-trees beside apples and apple-trees, but certainly have nothing to do with grapes and vines.

---

19 Schubart (1938), 297, and Page (1955), 35, among others.
20 (1939) 12. See also below on 10 and 13; Schubart (1938) dates the script at the latest in the early first century B.C.

In any case, the ostrakon reads ΚΕΛΑΤΙΔΙΔΥΡΧΩΝ. P is clear, it has the peculiar serif-like oblique at the bottom of its upright that may also be discerned in other rhos (1ᵃ (1) ορΡανοθεν, 1 (2) εicΡη, 8 (10) καταγΡιον), its cant is not unusual (14 (14) χΡυcεαιc, (15) ακΡωc), only its upright is shorter than usual (1 (2) δευΡ is comparable). The reading points to κελάδει δι' ὕρχων μαλίαν, i.e. δι' ὄρχων μηλεῶν. ὄρχος, 'row of fruit-trees', makes perfect sense: "cold water babbles through rows of apple-trees". The variant δι' ὕσδων μαλίνων is at least as old as Hermogenes, but the ostrakon, apart from offering a more reasonable sense, is considerably older than the rhetor. The latter apparently quotes from memory; to ὕσδων μαλίνων for ὕρχων μαλίαν add also ἀμφί for ἐν and καταρρεῖ for κατάγρει; see below on line 8.

6 (8). BPOTOICOTE: The first T, which was written instead of Δ, is marked with one or two oblique strokes like the second M in 1 (2) υμΜ. This marking of an erroneous letter, without correcting it, attests, I believe, the presence of a teacher, and supports the view that the ostrakon is no more than a student's homework. Here too, Lanata (1960), 72 n. 4, negates the correction, observing two small peelings of the ostrakon's surface. These peelings, I believe, affirm my suspicion that the corrections were made with a sharpish instrument, apparently a metal stylus.

The peculiar form KICKIACTAI for ἐσκίασται has been assigned either to a misread ΑΙCΚ- (= ἐσκ-) in the scribe's model[21] or to his tendency to anticipate the next syllable.[22] A classroom error in forming the reduplication of a verb beginning with two consonants might also be considered; see below on 10 (11-12).

It appears that not the whole area (παῖς ὁ χῶρος) but only the area where the girls had their picnic was shadowed with rose canopies, artificial or natural one cannot know. Ibycus had no doubt read Sappho's poem, only substituting shady vines for shady rose canopies: *PMG* 286.4-6 αἵ τ' οἰνανθίδες | αὐξομέναι σκιεροῖσιν ὑπ' ἔρνεσιν | οἰναρέοις θαλέθοισιν.

7 (9). The forms recorded in Hesychius, θ 968 θύσσεται· τινάσσεται, 969 θυσσόμεναι· σειόμεναι, τινασσόμεναι, are not textual errors, but products of popular etymology, probably from compounds like διαιθύσσεσθαι, καταιθύσσεσθαι, παραιθύσσεσθαι, whose first components were mistaken for the prepositions διαί, καταί, παραί. If this is the case, Norsa's ἐσκίασται θυσσομένων might not be so utterly impossible.

---

21 Schubart (1938). Cf. 6 (8) πεc for παῖς.
22 Page (1955), 38. Cf. 3 (5) δεΜΙθυΜΙαμενοι, 10 (12) ΑΙαΑΙητΑΙ.

8 (10). The problems of the present verse have been accurately discussed by Risch,[23] and I have very little new to say. The ostrakon has neither ΚΑΤΙΡΡΟΝ, as read by Norsa, nor ΚΑΤΑΙΡΙΟΝ, as read by Schubart and Lanata, and published by Voigt, but ΚΑΤΑΓΡΙΟΝ, as read by Lobel/Page. The horizontal of Γ visibly starts from the top of the upright, but it does not cover its normal length as it stops at the obstacle of the tracks of the potter's wheel, where, however, it leaves a whitish trace. Lobel/Page are right that the scribe "κατάγρει ut vid. voluit", the dialect form, that is, of καθαιρεῖ, though Page, eventually, prefers καταίρει. Hermogenes, quoted above on 5, has καταρρεῖ. The reading of the rhetor and the emendation of Page are palaeographically close to κατάγρει, but are both dialectally erroneous (καταρρεῖ for the Aeolic καρρέει and καταίρει for the Aeolic καταέρρει). However, κῶμα κατάγρει presents no serious problems. Cf. Sapph. 149 ὅτα πάννυχος ἄσφι (= σφι) κατάγρει, with ὕπνος implied, Od. 9.372 κὰδ δέ μιν ὕπνος ᾕρει, and Hsch. κ 1039 κατάγρει· καθαιρεῖ· καταλαμβάνει.[24] In Erinna, SH 402.2 τὸ δὲ σκότος ὄσσε καταγρεῖ (Bergk: κατέρρει Stob.), it is not sleep but the underworld darkness that seizes the eyes of Baucis, Erinna's deceased friend. If κατέρρει, the reading of Erinna's transmission, were to be accepted here (already Sitzler in emending the Hermogenes quotation, before the publication of the ostrakon),[25] it would mean that, because of the surrounding odours and sounds, sleep either goes away ('abit, geht weg') or comes down (Lanata: 'vien giù, scende giù'). But what then of Erinna's verse? κατέρρει must needs be intransitive.[26] What would go away or come down? The eyes of Baucis or the underworld darkness? It is obvious that the soothing scent of incense and the fragrance of roses combined with the monotonous feeble sounds of the brook and the fluttering leaves had a relaxing and soporific effect on the visitors. The objection against κατάγρει is simply a matter of the absence of a direct object, which is present in the parallel sentences given above. Whom or what does deep sleep overtake? Now, when the direct object is τινά or πάντας in the usual sense 'anyone at all', it can be omitted (see LSJ⁹ s.v. τις A.II.15), thus making the verb absolute/intransitive. In the present case, the result would be 'steal, steal over' in the sense 'come upon, take possession gradually or imperceptibly'. Comparable is the synonymous καταλαμβάνω, which, apart from its regular transitive use, is also used intransitively; e.g., Thuc. 2.54 ἢν πόλεμος καταλάβηι. Theocr. Ep. 3.6 ὕπνου κῶμα καταγρόμενον, "the torpor of sleep that is overcoming" must

---

[23] Risch (1962), 197–201.
[24] With other feelings and the simple ἄγρημι, Sapph. 31.13–4, τρόμος δὲ παῖσαν ἄγρει.
[25] Sitzler, review of Lobel (1927), 993 ff.
[26] So Pfeiffer (1937), Vogliano (1937) Schubart (1938), al.

be a straight reminiscence from Sappho, only that the Hellenistic poet, feeling that the intransitive sense would be better expressed in the middle voice, ends up in producing an anomalous participle form for the regular καταγρήμ(μ)ενον in Aeolic, καταγρεόμενον or καταγρούμενον elsewhere.[27] The ostrakon's model might have had ΚΑΤΑΓΡΙ (cf. 5 (7) ΚΕΛΑΤΙ = κελάδει), which the ignorant scribe integrated as κατ' ἄγριον, to comply with κῶμα.[28]

κῶμα is used in archaic poetry for the magic sleep that is caused by the gods for a special purpose (Il. 14.359, Od. 18.201, Hes. Th. 798, Alcm. 7.2, Pind. P. 1.12). There is no reason, however, to believe that we are dealing here with such a miraculous interference.[29] The poetess describes the *locus amoenus* in accordance with her own present-time experience. Sappho and her companions are lulled towards sleep not by divine intervention, since no such special purpose is discernible, but by the physical stimuli described in the poem.[30] Thus, not "magic sleep steals over", but "sleep, as if magic, steals over".

10 (11–12). Reading, sense, and metre are very uncertain at the opening of the verse. On the ostrakon, following τεθαλε and before ριν|, Lanata read only ΤΩΤ...(.), while others read differently: Τ.ΤΙΥΠΦ Norsa, ΤΩΤΗΡΙ Schubart, ΤΩΤΙΤΟΝ Lobel/Page. The restorations proposed are also diverse: <π>ριν<ί>|νοις <ὑπ>' "under holm oak (flowers)" (Norsa), ἠρί{ν}|νοισ<ιν> "with spring (flowers)" (Vogliano), λωτ{ηρ}ί{ν}|νοισ<ιν> "with lotus (flowers)" (Schubart), [–] ἐράν|νοισ' "with lovely (flowers)" (Page), τιτυρίν|νοισ' "with reed (flowers)" (Gallavotti), and more. All seem attractive, but require extensive alterations. Vogliano's ἠρί{ν}|νοισ<ιν> seems particularly appropriate, given the formulaic phrase ἄνθεσιν εἰαρινοῖσιν in the epic: Il. 2.89, Cypr. fr. 4.2, Hes. Th. 279, Op. 75, cf. H. Hom. Cer. 401. The majority of the scholars who investigated the ostrakon read the first three letters as ΤΩΤ, which is admittedly the most plausible reading. For the rest, ΗΑ^ΙΡΙΝ|ΝΟΙϹ, is, I believe, the most reliable reading. The Η is similar to the same letter found in 13 (13) δΗϲυ, which is formed with a vertical followed by a mid zigzag stroke and no right-hand vertical, unlike the other two etas of the ostrakon (1 (2) Ηλθες, 10 (12) αιΗται), which are regularly formed with two parallel verticals and a mid crossbar. The zigzag stroke is joined to an alpha in the form of ∩, as is used in Ptolemaic documentary papyri of the mid-second century B.C.; see, e.g., Seider I 1, 13 (P. Merton 5; 149–135 B.C.) lines 10, 12, 13, 14, 16, 17; 14 (P.

---

27 Risch (1962) gives a plausible explanation of how the erroneous form was produced.
28 Page (1955), 37 f.
29 Page (1955), 37; Risch (1962), 198 f.; West (1966), 798.
30 West (1970), 317.

Amh. 35; 132 B.C.) line 12; see also below on line 13 (13). Between α and the following ριν, a high upright above the base line is visible. It does not look like an iota, which in the ostrakon always descends under the base line, but neither does it appear to be a later addition, such as a superscript iota, since it was written by the scribe along with the other letters.

It is obvious that the scribe intended ἠαρίννοισ', a form occurring in *H. Hom. Cer.* 401, Hippocr. *Vict.* vi, 68.10 L., and in some late inscriptions. I cannot explain either the mysterious τωτ or the upright after alpha. Admittedly, τέθαλε closes a period and no synapheia is needed with the opening of the next period (ἠαρίννοισ'), stylistically, however, the meeting would be smoother if a consonant intervened to cure the seeming hiatus. Such an intervention can be made with ϝ, which is indeed the initial of ἔαρ (Hsch. γ 224 γέαρ· ἔαρ, 544 γίαρ· ἔαρ, Lat. ver, al.) and could be misread as τ. Even so, however, either ωτ or τω – depending on which tau was misread – would remain unaccountable. It is believed that the digamma was in decline in the Lesbian poets, surviving only in specific environments: initially in the third person personal pronoun (ϝ(ε), ϝοι, ϝέθεν, ϝαύτῳ) and the possessive adjective (ϝόν, ϝοῖσι); before initial ρ represented by β (βραδίναν, βρόδα, βράκεα, al.), but also by ϝ (ϝρῆξις); between prefix and verbal stem unrepresented but preventing the vowels from contracting (ἐάνασσε, ἀπυείπην); intervocalically represented by υ (ἀυάδην, ἀυάτα, Ἄυως, al.); between vowel and ρ also represented by υ (εὔρηξε); elsewhere, it is dropped. I will not enter the discussion as to whether all this variety is a product of Alexandrian scholarship or not. I feel, however, that it is precisely this intermixture of retention, wane, and loss that could allow us here to reconstruct ϝηαρίννοισ'. The proposal of Schubart on how the erroneous κισκίασται was created implied that the ostrakon text is a product not of dictation but of visually copying a product of dictation: ἐσκίασται acoustically written αἰσκίασται; the latter visually copied κισκίασται (above on 6 (8)). This view might lead us to a similar thought. If the dictating person read ϝηαρίννοισ' by enunciating not the initial sound but the name of the unusual letter, i.e. ϝαῦ or ϝαϝ, pronounced vau or vav (Terent. Scaur. *GL* vii, 16.2, 17.5 Keil), the former scribe may have written ϝαϝηαριννοιϲ, which the ostrakon scribe, unfamiliar with the character, copied, trying to imitate the script of his model, as τωτηαριννοιϲ. Though I admit that the copying procedure I am proposing is too complicated, I prefer to pass ϝηαρίννοισ' into the text, without claiming that this would have stood in Sappho's Alexandrian edition.

The metrically necessary gemination of nu in ϝηαρίννοισ' must be attributed partly to 'expressive gemination', usual in personal names irrespective of dialect,[31] among which Ἤριννα, and partly to the gemination of the nasal between vowels, mostly at the point of composition with a prefix or a suffix, common in the Aeolic dialect.[32] The gemination here may prove the correctness of the suggestion that the adjective suffix in ἐαρινός is not -ινός but -νός, added to the case-form ἔαρι.

11–12 (13). ΠΝΕΟΙϹΙΝ Norsa, ΠΝ..ΙϹΙΝ Lanata. The epsilon is clear, the curve at the end of its long mid horizontal possibly standing for the omicron. There is a semicircle written over the iota; it may either be an omicron added by the corrector, who did not understand that the scribe had already scribbled it, or a sigma written by the scribe in advance, but immediately corrected to iota.

At the opening of this paper, after discussing suggestion (*a*) concerning line 1ᵃ (1), we decided to postpone the discussion of suggestion (*b*) to be dealt with here. This was Gallavotti's proposal, that the first line of the ostrakon was added by the scribe to supplement the omission of lines 11–12.[33] Actually, some letters in line 1ᵃ (1) are slightly thinner as if written with a sharper pen, giving the impression that they are smaller and that the interlinear space under the line is larger than in the rest of the ostrakon. Accurate measurement shows, however, that this is a false impression. At the end of a stanza, the scribe leaves a vacant space to indicate the division. Now, if κατίουσιν/-σα/-σαι/-σας is the end of a stanza, the space left vacant after it in the broken part of the ostrakon would have been larger than at the end of any other stanza. It is of course impossible to estimate the length of this broken, therefore unknown, part in line 1ᵃ (1). But even if it were equal with lines (2–5), whose length can be roughly calculated, it would be only natural for the scribe, when the end of the stanza was close to the edge of the ostrakon, to leave a somewhat larger blank space, rather than insert there only the first word of the next stanza, here δευρ. In any case, if Gallavotti's proposal was adopted, we might integrate the text combining Norsa's and Turyn's readings, e.g.: μέλλιχα πνέοισιν ὀρ<έων κα>ράνοθεν κατίοι[σαι, sc. the ἄηται. Homoioteleuton between πνέοισιν and κατίοισαι, to account for the omission, is not very likely but perhaps not impossible. κάτειμι (εἶμι) is used for winds: Thuc. 2.25, 2.84, 6.2. On the other hand, it is strange that the corrector would make a further omission when supplementing the omission. This is still worse in Gallavotti's own successive proposals (1941, 1947), which implied not only omissions but also errors to be emended and deleted

---

[31] For the Lesbian poets, Hamm (1957), §73.
[32] Hamm (1957), §77; Bowie (1979), 133.
[33] Gallavotti (1941), 175–202.

in the correction: <φόβαι δ' ἀπ'> ὀρράνω{θεν} κατίοι[σαι or <ἄυας> καράννοθεν κατιοί[σας. Further, one would expect that the winds that are described as coming down from the mountain tops would be rough and boisterous, not gently blowing breezes. But, most importantly, the poem cannot have started with δεῦρ' ὔμ' ἔ{ι}ς ρ' ἦλθες, without an invocation, with no hint as to what 'together' refers to. Thus, if it is necessary that one or more stanzas preceded line 1 (2–3), why not accept lines 1^(b-a) (1) as the end of these missing stanzas, especially since they cohere with the sense so germanely? If we adopt proposal (*a*), I would suggest for line 12 a dative plural (-οισιν/-αισιν), on the assumption that the omission after πνέοισιν is due to homoioteleuton and that the persons who experience what Sappho describes should be mentioned before the narration turns to the company of the immortals. Solely *exempli gratia*:

10   ϝηαρίν|νοισ' ἄνθεσιν, αἰ δ' ἄ{ι}ηται
      μέλλι|χα πνέοισιν <ἐν ἀδόναι ταὶς
12   παρθενίκαισιν>.

Though conjecturally proposed, cf. Hdt. 4.139 Σκύθησί ἐστι ἐν ἡδονῇ, Eur. *IT* 494 σοι τοῦτ' ἐν ἡδονῇ μαθεῖν, al. The dative plural of the feminine article, when used as an article and not a pronoun, is ταὶς not ταῖσι.

13 (13). Norsa read CTEM, which she supplemented στέμ[ματ', a widely accepted proposal. Lobel-Page rightly observed that the edge of the sherd was intact, and so nothing was written between CTEM and (14) EΛOICA. Page ends up with ... AN|EΛOICA and Lanata reads CY. AN|EΛOICA. I believe that CTAM is preferable to all these readings, with T written like a V, as frequently in this ostrakon and in numerous documentary papyri, and A in the form of ∩, as described above in line 10 (11). There follows a clear majuscule M. στάμ<νον> suggests itself. Given his record, it is unnecessary to ask why the scribe left the word unfinished. With στάμ<νον> | ἔλοισα, Κύπρι, ... ὠ<ι>νοχόαισας (see below), cf. Sapph. 141.3 Ἕρμαις δ' ἔλων ὄλπιν θέοισιν ᾠνοχόησε. Apparently, ὄλπις, πρόχοος (Diehl at 96.28), and στάμνος serve the same purpose in Sappho, that of wine jug or pitcher, possibly differing in size. If Cypris was to fill the cups of a number of gods, an ὄλπις might have proved insufficient. Yet, in Plato com. fr. 205 K.–A. (from Athen. ep. 11.783d) someone is filling a κύλιξ straight from a στάμνος: 1–2 λύσας δὲ ... στάμνον εὐώδους ποτοῦ | ἵησιν εὐθὺς κύλικος εἰς κοῖλον κύτος.[34]

---

34 λύσας δὲ ἀργὴν στάμνον Athen.; numerous suggestions are recorded in PCG; I would be astonished if nobody proposed μάργην, an adjective qualifying wine, used here of the stamnos by common hypallage.

14–15 (15–16). The letter before MMEIXMENON is difficult to make out, especially since the scribe, toward the end of the ostrakon, scribbles his text carelessly. I would prefer YMMEIXMENON to Lanata's ΑΜΜ- or Norsa's EMM-; Page denies all possible readings, AMM-, EMM-, OMM-, and YMM-. The ligature of CY in ακρωCYμμει| is identical with the CY in line 13 (13) (ἔνθα δὴ σύ). And of the two μ's the first is more squeezed than usual. Haplography is to blame both for the omission of one sigma in ακρως<c>υμ-, and of EM in -μ<εμ>ει-.[35] The ostrakon's <σ>υμμ<εμ>είχμενον agrees with Athenaeus' συνμεμιγμένον. The latter, however, in place of the ostrakon's ἄκρως, has ἁβροῖς. This has been emended either to ἄβρως (Bergk), going with οἰνοχόαισον or οἰνοχοοῦσα, 'pour / pouring gracefully', or to ἄβραισ᾽ (Schubart), going with θαλίαισι, 'graceful festivities'. Now, 'nectar mingled with festivities', graceful or not, may be a felicitous metaphor, fit for the style of, say, Pindar; cf., e.g., *Ol.* 7.7 ff., *Nem.* 3.76 ff. It is, however, completely alien to the plain and straightforward style of Sappho. Treu keeps Bergk's ἄβρως and translates "den zu frohem Feste bereiten Nektar", taking θαλίαισι as a dative of purpose or cause. συμμεμείχμενον might stand absolutely, 'prepared through mixing', like, e.g., συγκέρασον in Posidipp. 140.3 A.–B. Kappa and beta are being confused from the first century A.D. onward (u = B, K), in the age, that is, of Athenaeus, but the ostrakon is some two centuries older. Were it not for the fact that both witnesses have different readings (ἄκρως Ostr., ἁβροῖς Athen.), Treu's interpretation would be blameless. It would be possible, however, to keep the reading of the ostrakon: ἄκρως <σ>υμμ<εμ>είχμενον θαλίαισι νέκταρ, with συμμείγνυμαι in the sense 'be associated, combined': "nectar that is perfectly commingled with the festivities", in other words "the drink most appropriate for divine banquets". The kappa of ἄκρως, an angular variation of the cursive kappa, is certain (see 14 (14–15) ΚυλιΚεσσιν) and cannot be confused with beta.

The word needed at the end of line (16) is θαλίαισι. The ostrakon was read ΘΑΛΙΑΙΕCCΙΝ by Norsa and ΘΑΛΙΑΙΕCCΙ(Ν) by Lanata. The scribe, instead of writing his usual ligature for ΑΙ, apparently started writing a separate alpha which he then joined to the iota with a clumsy and intricate link-stroke. The last letters look like a wide ω, an impression which is, however, created by a circular abnormality in the shred's surface upon which a normal N was written. But the previous letter, where we expect an iota, is perhaps an imperfect E. I read very doubtfully ΘΑΛΙΑΙCΕΝ.

16 (17). The ostrakon has been read correctly by Gallavotti and Lanata ΩΝΟΧΟΑΙCΑ (others ΟΙΝΟ-), but it was not observed that, with the last Α

---

35 Siegmann (1941), 417–422, followed by Treu.

reaching the edge of the ostrakon, the scribe added a C above it, thus offering the form ᾠνοχόαισας. For AI some read EI, but see, e.g., 14 (14) χρυcεAIc. The question of whether the grammatical form is legitimate Lesbian or an Alexandrian hyperdialectism has already been discussed by scholars.³⁶ The fact that it represents a second person singular aorist which agrees with 1 ἦλθες cannot be disputed.

It is now obvious that the surviving portion of the poem consists of the account of an old event. "Together with the gods, who descended from the heaven's summits, you entered here into the sacred precinct of the goddesses, ... where you, o Cypris, took a pitcher and poured nectar into golden cups." In accordance with Athenaeus' ἐλθὲ ... οἰνοχοοῦσα, the last word of the ostrakon had been read either as imperative οἰνοχόαισον or as participle οἰνοχόεισα/-αισα. It is better, however, to reconsider Athenaeus' words. The argument discussed there is whether it is proper or not for the deipnosophistai to be engaged in "Dionysiac chats". The speaker, Plutarchos, addressing the other deipnosophistai, after providing arguments for his case from a number of quotations that praised drinking parties along with erotic activity, concludes (11.463e; the text as it appears in Athenaeus' cod. A): καὶ κατὰ τὴν καλὴν οὖν Σαπφὼ ἐλθὲ Κύπρι χρυσείαισιν ἐν κυλίκεσσιν ἀβροῖς συνμεμιγμένον θαλίαισι νέκταρ οἰνοχοοῦσα τούτοις τοῖς ἑταίροις ἐμοῖς τε καὶ σοῖς. And the speaker goes on now discussing a different subject: πρὸς οὓς (sc. ἑταίρους ἐμούς τε καὶ σούς) λεκτέον ὅτι τρόποι εἰσὶ πόσεων κατὰ πόλεις ἴδιοι. Obviously, Athenaeus adapts Sappho's verses to his own narrative. Both ἐλθέ, at the beginning of the quotation, and οἰνοχοοῦσα τούτοις τοῖς ἑταίροις ἐμοῖς τε καὶ σοῖς, at the end, are not only absent from the ostrakon text but also cannot be joined with it in any way. If we were to transfer the reasoning of Athenaeus' words to Sappho's verses, both the syntax and the image conveyed by the resulting sentence, i.e. ἐλθὲ ... ἐλοῦσα ... οἰνοχοοῦσα, would be, to say the least, awkward. As far as his last words are concerned, "these companions, mine and yours" – a much discussed portion of Athenaeus' text, which led to several 'restorations' of the first verse of a supposed next stanza –, he merely means the deipnosophistai, companions of the speaker and, as the argument requires, of Aphrodite. That Athenaeus' words paraphrase Sappho's verses has been contended since the 16th century: Voigt refers to the edition of prominent lyrical poetesses by F. Ursinus (Orsini), Antwerp 1568 (*non vidi*), and a long list of scholars thereafter. The view has, however, been contested at least since 1828 by G. Welcker in his review of Neue's 1827 Sappho edition (*non vidi*), but also lately.³⁷ That Athenaeus, by οἰνοχοοῦσα τούτοις τοῖς ἑταίροις ἐμοῖς τε

---

36 Chantraine (1950), 213; Page (1955), 23 f.; Hamm (1957), §49.
37 McEvilley (1972), 326.

καὶ σοῖς, means the deipnosophistai is clear. That the text he was adapting contained a corresponding group of companions of the goddess is, however, extremely likely. This group is, apparently, the gods taking part in the banquet. Could the words missing from the ostrakon belong to Sappho's address to Aphrodite in other parts of the poem? One cannot rule out the possibility that Sappho summons the goddess or that she refers to her female company as friends of herself and Aphrodite. But both the summoning and the reference cannot have been made in the part of the poem surviving in the ostrakon.

Though the plot of the existent text is placed in an indeterminate mythical past time, the local δεῦρ' and the second person addresses (ἦλθες, ὠινοχόαισας) place Sappho at the center of the plot, both locally and personally. The focal point around which the poem's story evolves is the sanctuary – probably a Nymphaion – as a local designation. This is why, apart from the detailed description of the site, so many local expressions recur in so short a text, especially at the opening of all stanzas: δεῦρ', ὄππαι δή, ἐν δ', ἐν δέ, ἔνθα δή. We may possibly be dealing here with a typical Sapphic device. Just as in fr. 96, an ordinary simile is imperceptibly transferred from its timeless occurrence to a present-day landscape depiction, here the background of a timeless mythical event is also imperceptibly transferred to a present-day landscape depiction. It is noticeable that this depiction, made exclusively with present or perfect tenses, is flanked on each side by the local relative adverbs ὄππαι δή and ἔνθα δή. The second of these maintains its demonstrative force, thus stressing the relationship of the antecedent present-day depiction with the mythical reference to the gods' presence: "It was here that you ...". The poetess is now in this place, and is addressing Aphrodite in second person, as she usually does. She is reminding the goddess of an old occasion, a banquet of the gods at the same sanctuary, in which Aphrodite participated as cupbearer. Sappho appears to have good knowledge of that banquet, we cannot say how. She is possibly exploiting a local legend with regard to the specific sanctuary. Or, more likely, she may have made the whole story up. Why does she remind the goddess of this old story? She is apparently employing the same pattern as in Sapph. 1 (ποικιλόθρον' ἀθανάτ'Ἀφρόδιτα). There, Aphrodite is summoned by Sappho to come and help her in a difficult amatory affair, just as she had descended from heaven in the past and had assisted her in a similar situation. And Sappho devotes five of the poem's seven stanzas to describing that incident from the past. The resemblance extends even to verbal similarities: Sapph. 1.7–12 πάτρος δὲ δόμον λίποισα χρύσιον ἦλθες ... ἀπ' ὠράνω αἴθερος, 2.1^b-1 ὀράνω καράνοθεν ... δεῦρ' ὔμ' ἔς ρ' ἦλθες.

There is, however, a significant difference. In Sapph. 1, both the old and the new episode are strictly personal, involving only one individual from the celestial and earthly worlds respectively. Here, in the old event, the goddess appears in a prominent role amid a company of gods. We should then expect that, in the present event too, a corresponding company of human beings is involved, with Sappho in a prominent role. A company of human beings with Sappho as their leader and spokeswoman inside a sanctuary, possibly of the Nymphs, can only be associated with an outdoor festivity, in that specific sanctuary, of the girls who attended Sappho. The analogy with the Nymphs is remarkable, since the girls were incipient νύμφαι and their diversion, like that of the Nymphs, consisted of singing and dancing, especially in the countryside[38]. West's 'picnic' is not at all out of place.[39] Cf., e.g., fr. 94, where, among the delights experienced by Sappho and her girls, the poetess mentions that "there was no sanctuary (ἶρον), no grove (ἄλσος), no dance ceremony (χ]όρος), from which we were absent". Then, the 'come' typical in cletic hymns is unavoidable, only that the antecedent is different. Not 'come to me as you came before' but 'come to this place as you came before'. It is from such a formulation that Athenaeus devised his ἐλθέ. And, as mentioned above, this summoning to the girls' festivity should not be found in the last ostrakon stanza, where Athenaeus places his own summoning, but doubtless in some other part of the poem. If, however, Aphrodite and the gods belong to the mythical past, whereas Sappho and the girls to the present-time occurrence, the Nymphs must belong to both. The precinct is their own, and their presence, though invisible, is taken for granted. So, my e.g. supplement of 11–12 ἐν ἀδόναι ταῖς παρθενίκαισιν may be applicable both to Sappho's maidens and to the Nymphs, all of whom enjoy the gently blowing breezes. Cf. Ibycus *PMG* 286.3 ἵνα Παρθένων κᾶπος ἀκήρατος, though no mortal maidens seem to be involved there.[40]

There has lately been some discussion regarding women's commensal habits in antiquity. J. Burton, speaking of Sappho's fr. 2, notes "the female camaraderie of this drinking occasion". And before Burton, Page had asserted that "the wine which Sappho and her companions drink is conceived of as being, or including, nectar poured by the hand of their invisible but unquestionably present patroness".[41] We should remember that we are not dealing with Cratinus' old drunkard

---

[38] Cf. Merkelbach (1957), 29 n. 2.
[39] (1970), 317; cf. Parker (1993), 346.
[40] It is pointless to question the identification of the Παρθένοι as Nymphs; Tortorelli (2004), 370–376 n. 28. νύμφαι are not only the newlywed brides, but also the marriageable maidens. Speaking of sacred gardens and groves that belong to female divine beings, it is impossible not to think of the deities that conventionally haunt such places.
[41] Burton (1998), 153 n. 54; Page (1955), 43; cf. also Parker (1993), 345.

women, but with little teenage girls on an outing. By no means were they supposed to drink alcohol. Furthermore, one should not expect that Sappho could ever conceive a desire, however poetic that might be, that her young girls would participate in a drinking party with the gods, would have Aphrodite for cupbearer, would drink from golden cups and, what is more, would be offered the forbidden nectar. Von der Mühll interprets nectar metaphorically for the gift of Aphrodite, i.e. love.[42] He adduces many parallels, all, however, from different sorts and styles of poetry, Hellenistic and Roman. Sappho's metaphors are simple and straightforward, and her detailed description of a banquet scene could not possibly be assigned a figurative interpretation. Naturally, the poetess may well aim at the capacity of the receivers of her poetry to expand and broaden their perceptive approaches, but that's another story. In any case, Von der Mühll hinges his arguments on the then current interpretation of Aphrodite participating in an earthly banquet. Also, Merkelbach strives at a poetic reconciliation of the two images: a real and earthly precinct of Aphrodite with a mythical garden of the Nymphs.[43] The new readings, however, confine the plot to an earthly Nymphaion, which has both a mythical past and a worldly present. The idea of a banquet of the gods has long since been set forth by Setti[44] and others, but the closing imperative, whether read as such (οἰνοχόαισον vel sim.) or transferred to Sappho from Athenaeus' words (ἐλθέ … οἰνοχοοῦσα), mixed the human entertainment with the divine banquet and reduced the role of Aphrodite to that of a waitress called to serve the mortal picnickers with nothing less than nectar.

Since the ostrakon starts in mid-verse and mid-sentence, the beginning of the poem is obviously missing. And since we cannot claim that the scribe, though demonstrably ignorant and careless, deliberately started copying half a text, the missing part must have been written either on another potsherd or, if such a hypothesis could be proved, on the back side of this one, having now been effaced by time. In the second case, the missing text must necessarily be the same size as the surviving one. And I suppose that in the first case too the lost sherd would be of a similar size to the surviving one. It is very likely then that the poem ended with ὠινοχόαισας, while some three or four stanzas must be missing from the beginning of the poem – the last one ending in ὀράνω καράνοθεν κατίουσιν. Eight stanzas in all is a reasonable total for a poem of Sappho's book 1. The opening must have contained the mention of the earthly festivity of Sappho's girls in a sacred precinct, most probably a Nymphaion, to which the poetess summons

---

42 Von der Mühll (1946), 24–25.
43 Merkelbach (1957), 25–29.
44 Setti (1943), 125–142.

Aphrodite. What she is summoning her for is, of course, only a matter of guesswork, but we can reasonably surmise that she is inviting her to watch the girls' singing and dancing, and possibly to offer them her blessing for their future amatory life. After this summoning, Sappho must remind Aphrodite of that old circumstance during which she descended from heaven and participated in the gods' banquet at the same sacred precinct. The poetess takes advantage of these verses of reminiscence to insert a three-stanza-long ekphrasis of the sanctuary.

Von der Mühll (1946), 25, closed his short note with an important remark: Ibycus PMG 286 might be a reminiscence of this or of a similar Sappho poem. H. Fränkel[45] and Merkelbach (1957), 26 ff., particularized the similarity with the Ibycus poem and collected the parallels which are indeed numerous and striking in such short fragments (16 and 13 verses). Adding my own suggestions, they are: S(appho) 1–2 πρ[οτὶ θέαν] ἔναυλον ἄγνον ~ Ib(ycus) 3-4 ἵνα Παρθένων κᾶπος ἀκήρατος, S. 2–3 ἄλσος Μαλίδ[ων] ~ Ib. 1–2 αἵ τε Κυδωνίαι μαλίδες; Παρθένων κᾶπος ἀκήρατος, S. 5-6 ἐν δ' ὕδωρ ψῦχρον κελάδει δι' ὕρχων μαλίαν ~ Ib. 2–3 μαλίδες ἀρδομέναι ῥοᾶν ἐκ ποταμῶν, S. 6–7 βρόδοισι δὲ παῖς ὁ χῶρος ἐσκίαστ' ~ Ib. 4–6 αἵ τ' οἰνανθίδες αὐξομέναι σκιεροῖσιν ὑπ' ἔρνεσιν, S. 9–10 τέθαλε ϝηαρίννοισ' ἄνθεσιν ~ Ib. 4–6 αἵ τ' οἰνανθίδες ... θαλέθοισιν, S. 10 ϝηαρίννοισ' ~ Ib. 1 ἦρι. But the strongest correspondence is the antithetical one. In Sappho, thanks to the surrounding conditions, 8 κῶμα κατάγρει, and, in this sleep-inducing environment, 10–11 αἰ ... ἄ{ι}ηται μέλλιχα πνέοισιν. In Ibycus, in spite of the identical surrounding conditions, 6–7 ἐμοὶ δ' ἔρος οὐδεμίαν κατάκοιτος ὥραν. There is no mention of sleep in the landscape depiction of Ibycus. Therefore, it is as if the antithesis responds not to the preceding image but to Sappho's verses: "(To others springtime and the accompanying delightful nature conditions may imply sleep; but not to me.) For me love is at no season at rest. (Instead of blowing like gentle breezes,) it blows like the violent Thracian north wind threatening to crush my heart." But neither is love mentioned in the surviving part of Sappho's poem. Yet, the ubiquitous presence of Cypris, as well as the inclusion of some of the poem's verses in an Athenaeus chapter that speaks of Dionysiac and erotic entertainment may suggest a poem where the love element, though partly suppressed, is not absent.

---

45 Fränkel (1955), 44.

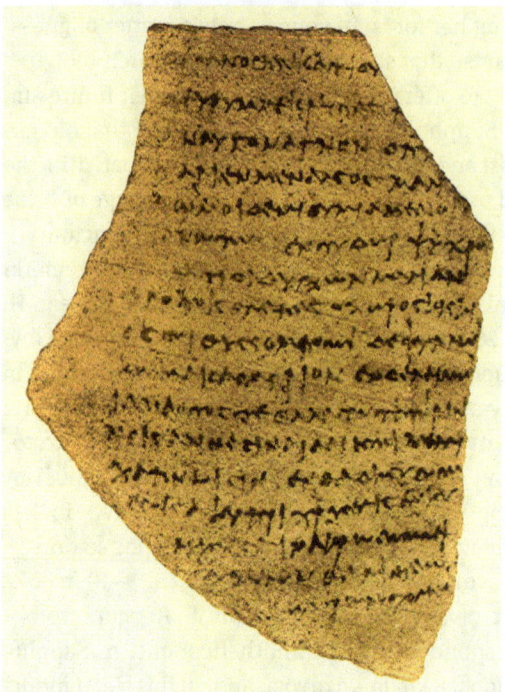

Fig. 1: The Florence ostrakon containing Sappho's fr. 2. From the first edition by Medea Norsa in *Annali della Reale Scuola normale superiore di Pisa* II 6 (1937) 8–15 (= *PSI* XIII 1300)

To conclude, here is the new text proposed for Sappho fr. 2:

1ᵇ   – ⏑ – ⋇ – |¹ ὀρ<άνω κα>ράνο-
1ᵃ   θεν κατίου[σιν |²
1   δεῦρ' ὔμ⟦μ⟧' ἔ{ι}ς ῥ' ἦλθες πρ[οτὶ θέαν |³ ἔναυλον
      ἄγνον, ὄππ[αι δὴ] |⁴ χάριεν μὲν ἄλσος
      Μαλίδ[ων], |⁵ βῶμοι δ' ἐπιθυμιάμε-
      νοι λ[ι]|⁶βανώτω·
5   ἐν δ' ὔδωρ ψῦχρον |⁷ κελάδει δι' ὔσχων
      μαλίαν, |⁸ βρόδοισι δὲ παῖς ὀ χῶρος
      ἐσκί|⁹αστ', αἰθυσσομένων δὲ φύλλων |¹⁰
        κῶμα κατάγρει·
      ἐν δὲ λείμων |¹¹ ἰππόβοτος τέθαλε
10   Ϝηαρίν|¹²νοισ' ἄνθεσιν, αἰ δ' ἄ{ι}ηται
      μέλλι|¹³χα πνέοισιν <⏑ – ⏑ – ×
        – ⏑ ⏑ -ισιν>.
      ἔνθα δὴ σὺ στάμ<νον> |¹⁴ ἔλοισα, Κύπρι,

χρυσίαισ<ιν> ἐν κυ|¹⁵λίκεσσιν ἄκρως
15   <σ>υμμ<εμ>εί|¹⁶χμενον θαλίαισι |¹⁷ νέκταρ
ὠ<ι>νοχόαισας.

The brief app. cr. that follows is not complete. It mainly documents the variants of the O(strakon) and the readings accepted in the present text.

1ᵇ ΟΡΡΑΝΟΘΕΝ **O**; <… ὀράνω> κ]αράνοθεν coniectura add. Theiler; καράνοθεν iam Turyn; ὀρ<άνω κα>ράνοθεν e Synesio Ts. (e.g., σὺν θέοισιν ὧδ'] ὀρ<άνω κα>ράνοθεν) || **1ᵃ** ΚΑΤΙΟΥ[**O**, κατίου[σιν vel κατίοι[σιν vel κατίοι[σα (hoc Körte, al.) Ts. || **1ᵇ⁻ᵃ** vid. etiam infra 11 || **1** ΔΕΥΡΥΜΜΕΙϹΡΗΤΑΕϹ **O**ᵃ·ᶜ·, ΔΕΥΡΥΜ[[Μ]]ΕΙϹΡΗΛΘΕϹ **O**ᵖ·ᶜ·; δεῦρ' ὕμ' ἔ{ι}ς ῥ' ἦλθες Ts. (δεῦρ' ὕμ' iam Schubart , δεῦρύ μ' Pfeiffer, Theander; εἰς iam Schubart, neg. Norsa); λθες litt. minusc. iteratum sub ἦλθες disp. Ts. | ΠΡ[**O**, sic Norsa, Π[.]Ρ[Schubart, Lanata, πρ[οτὶ Ts. | θέαν vel τόνδ' Ts. (hoc (τόνδε) Lobel-Page) | ΕΝΑΥΓΟΝ **O**ᵃ·ᶜ·, ΕΝΑΥΛΟΝ **O**ᵖ·ᶜ·, ἔναυλον Pfeiffer, τόνδ]|ε] ναῦ{γ}ον Lobel || **2** ὅππ[αι δὴ] Lobel, ὅππ[αι τοι] Page || **3** ΜΑΛΙΔ[**O**, μαλί[δων vel Μαλί[δων Pfeiffer, Μαλίδ[ων] Ts., μάλι[νον] Norsa, μαλί[αν Lobel | ΔΕΜΙΘΥΜΙΑΜΕΝΟΙ **O**, δ' ἐπιθυμ. Diehl, δ' ἔνι θυμ. Pfeiffer || **4** λ[ι]||βανώτω vel λ[ι]||βανώτω<ι> edd. || **5** ΕΝΤ **O**, ἐν δ' Norsa, ἀμφὶ δ(ὲ) Hermogenes | ΨΥΧΡΟΝ **O** | ΚΕΛΑΤΙ **O**, κελάδει Hermogenes (-δεῖ) | ΔΙΔΥΡΧΩΝ **O**, nec ΔΙΔΥϹΧΩΝ nec ΔΙΔΥϹΔΩΝ (hoc dub. Lobel-Page), δι' ὕρχων (= ὅρχων) Ts., δι' ὕσδων vel ὅσδων (= ὅζων) Hermogenes, edd. || **6** μαλίαν **O**, μαλίνων Hermogenes, edd. | ΒΡΟΤΟΙϹΟΤΕ **O** primo T deleto vel signato, βρόδοισι δὲ Norsa, Pfeiffer | ΠΕϹ **O** || **7** ΚΙϹΚΙΑϹΤΑΙΘ- **O**, ἐσκίασται (cum θυσσομένων e Hsch.) Norsa, ἐσκίαστ' (cum αἰθυσσομένων e Hermog.) Pfeiffer || **8** ΚΑΤΑΓΡΙΟΝ, nec ΚΑΤΑΙΡΙΟΝ nec ΚΑΤΙΡΡΟΝ, **O**, κατάγρει Bergk, καταρρεῖ Hermogenes || **10** ΤΩΤΗΑᴵΡΙΝ|ΝΟΙϹ sic **O**, ⲅηαρίννοισ' Ts., ({τωτ}ἠρί{ν}νοισ<ιν> Vogliano; alii alia) | ΑΙΑΑΙΗΤΑΙ **O**, αἰ δ' ἄηται Lobel-Page || **11** ΠΝΕΙϹΙΝ **O**ᵃ·ᶜ· (?), ΠΝΕΟΙϹΙΝ **O**ᵖ·ᶜ·; O vel C super primum I scriptum | finem strophae omissum scribam in marg. sup. (1ᵇ⁻ᵃ) posuisse prop. Gallavotti; quo accepto, πνέοισιν ὀρ<έων κα>ράνοθεν κατίοι[σαι dub. Ts.; si non, <⏑ – ⏑ – × | – ⏑ ⏑ -ισιν> per homoioteleuton (e.g., <ἐν ἀδόναι ταῖς | παρθενίκαισιν>) Ts. || **13** ϹΤΑΜ **O**, non ϹΤΕΜ vel alia, στάμ<νον> Ts., στέμ<ματ'> Norsa || **14** ΧΡΥϹΕΑΙϹ **O**, χρυσίαισ<ιν> ex Athen. (χρυσείαισιν) Neue | ΑΚΡΩϹ **O**, ἁβροῖς Athen., ἄβρως Bergk, ἄβραισ' Schubart || **15** ΥΜΜΕΙΧΜ **O**, συνμεμιγμ. Athen., <σ>υμμ<εμ>εί|χμ. (post ἄβρως) Siegmann | ΘΑΛΙΑΙϹΕΝ **O** (dub. Ts.), ΘΑΛΙΑΙΕϹϹΙΝ Norsa, ΘΑΛΙΑΙΕϹϹΙ(Ν) Lanata; θαλίαισι Athen. || **16** ΩΝΟΧΟΑΙϹΑ`Ϲ' **O**, ὠ<ι>νοχόαισας Ts.

(with the gods,) who descended from the summits of heaven,
you entered here together into this sacred precinct, where there is a pleasant grove of the Malides (apple-tree Nymphs), and altars smoking with incense;
therein cold water babbles through rows of apple-trees, and the whole place is shadowed with roses, and, as the leaves flutter, sleep steals over;
therein a meadow grazed by horses blooms with spring flowers, and the winds blow softly, (a delight for the maidens).
It was here that you, o Cypris, taking a pitcher poured into golden cups nectar perfectly commingled with the festivity.

Appendix

Ibycus *PMG* 286

Apropos of the suggestion that Ibycus *PMG* 286 is a reminiscence of Sappho fr. 2 and the collection of the similarities between the two texts, I have incidentally made an attempt, given below, at editing the Ibycus fragment, especially its second half which presents problems of metrical responsion. In any case, I have to admit that my use of the secondary literature was not that meticulous, so that the possibility that I may have appropriated other scholars' views cannot be excluded.[46]

Athen. XIII 601b (600f ὥς φησι Χαμαιλέων …) καὶ ὁ Ῥηγῖνος δὲ Ἴβυκος βοᾷ καὶ κέκραγεν·

	ἦρι μὲν αἵ τε Κυδωνίαι	dod^d ||
	μαλίδες ἀρδομέναι ῥοᾶν	dod^d ||
	ἐκ ποταμῶν, ἵνα Παρθένων	dod^d ||
	κᾶπος ἀκήρατος, αἵ τ' οἰνανθίδες	4da |
5	αὐξομέναι σκιεροῖσιν ὑπ' ἔρνεσιν	4da |
	οἰναρέοις θαλέθοισιν· ἐμοὶ δ' ἔρος	4da |
	οὐδεμίαν κατάκοιτος ὥραν.	ar^d |||
	<ἀλλ' ἅ>θ' ὑπὸ στεροπᾶς φλέγων	dod^d ||
	Θρᾳΐκιος Βορέας ἀείς,	dod^d ||
10	ἐὼν παρὰ Κύπριδος ἀζαλέος,	dod^d ||
	αἷς μανίαισιν ἐρυμνὸς ἀθαμβέσιν	4da |
	ἐγκρατέως πεδόθεν φλασσεῖ φρένας	4da |
	ἁμετέρας	4da …

Dialectica non notavi   **2** ῥοάν Athen. : corr. Musurus ǁ **4** οἰνανθίδος Athen. : corr. Musurus ǁ **7** κατάκητος Athen. : corr. Musurus ǁ **8** τε ὑπό Athen. : add. Mehlhorn (= <ἀλλ' ἅ>τε ὑπό) ǁ **9** θρηΐκοις Athen. : corr. Ursinus ǁ **9 sq.** ἀΐσσων Athen. : ἀείς, ἐὼν Ts. ǁ **10 sq.** ἀζαλέαις Athen. : ἀζαλέος, αἷς Ts. ǁ **11** ἐρεμνός Athen. : corr. Ts. ǁ **11 sq.** ἀθάμβησεν κραταιῶς Athen. : ἀθαμβέσιν ἐγκρατέως Ts. post ἀθαμβὴς ἐγκρατέως Schweighaeuser, Hermann ǁ **12** παιδ' ὅθεν Athen. : corr. Naeke ǀ φυλάσσει Athen. : φλασσεῖ Ts. post φλάσει Tortorelli et ἔφλασεν Hermann; σαλάσσει Mueller, τινάσσει Naeke, λαφύσσει West ǁ **12 sq.** ἥμετ. φρ. Athen. : transpos. Ts.

---

46 The relevant literature is profitably discussed by Tortorelli (2004), with whose proposals, however, I disagree (with the partial exception of 12 φλάσει; see below). He himself pinpoints the shortcomings of his proposed colometry in the dovetailing of the ibyceans (dod^d) and the disregard of word-end after the fourth foot of the dactylic tetrameters. Actually, this was the deficiency of practically every proposed restoration.

> In the spring, there where the undefiled garden of the Maidens is, flourish the Cydonian quinces, watered from flowing streams, as well as the grape-blossoms, growing under shady vine-branches. But for me love sleeps at no season. Nay, rather blowing like the Thracian north wind ablaze with the lightning flash, parching because of Cypris, strengthened by her undaunted frenzies, it will forcibly crush my heart from the roots.

ἀΐσσων, 'rushing', precisely because it seems to be extremely appropriate to the image described, precluded any emendation, so that it was thought that the metrical enjambement beyond the end of the ibycean was inevitable; and, if it was legitimate between lines 9–10, then why not in the verses following? ἀείς, 'blowing', present participle of ἄημι, is, however, equally appropriate, and ἐών in the opening of the next verse provides the copula. Palaeographically, the change from ΑΕΙϹΕΩΝ to ΑΕΙϹϹΩΝ and this taken as ἀΐσσων is easy. The same thing happens at the end of line 10. The wind or, metaphorically, love might well be rushing with parching frenzies, but the image would be much more reasonable if it were the wind/love itself that was parching and not its frenzies. Therefore, I separate the transmitted ἀζαλέαις μανίαισιν into ἀζαλέος, αἷς μανίαισιν. Again, palaeography is no obstacle: ΑΖΑΛΕ͂ΑΙϹ > ΑΖΑΛΕΑΙϹ. With both ἐὼν παρὰ Κύπριδος and αἷς μανίαισιν, the agency of Cypris, though not changing, is no doubt highlighted. I do not understand here ἐρεμνός, 'black, murky'. A λαῖλαψ may well be μέλαινα or ἐρεμνή. But here 'black' is the product of 'parching', and it would be awkward for the North wind to parch and blacken itself through the frenzies of Cypris. 'Black' should normally characterize the victim, not the agent as here. ἐρυμνός, 'strengthened, armed, strong', used whether of love or the wind, is absolutely to the point, especially when accompanied by the instrumental dative αἷς μανίαισιν ἀθαμβέσιν. Many interpret ἀθαμβής as 'shameless', but both its, admittedly limited, usage and its derivation speak for 'undaunted, fearless'. It can well qualify μανία. In Bacchylides 10.58 f., ἀθαμβής is applied to Ὕβρις, a notion relevant to μανία.[47] Athenaeus' φυλάσσει was strongly supported against West's λαφύσσει and other conjectures by Maria Grazia Bonanno, whose arguments depend on the parallel of ἔμπεδα φυλάσσειν *vel sim.*[48] No mat-

---

[47] E.g., Damon mus. fr. 9.7 ἀνελευθερίας καὶ ὕβρεως καὶ μανίας καὶ ἄλλης κακίας, Pl. *Plt.* 307b 10 ὑβριστικὰ καὶ μανικὰ λέγοντες, Arist. *Probl.* 953b 4 (on wine drinking) ἔτι δὲ μᾶλλον πινόμενος ὑβριστάς, ἔπειτα μανικούς, PCG fr. com. anon. 16.11–12 (on wine drinking) ἐὰν δ' ὑπερβάλῃς ὕβριν (sc. ποιεῖ)· | ἐὰν δ' ἴσον ἴσῳ προσφέρῃ, μανίαν ποιεῖ, Cerc. fr. 10 μανίας ὕβρεώς τε; alia plurima.
[48] West (1966), 154; Bonanno (1986–87), 13–18.

ter how close the affinity of ἔμπεδον and πεδόθεν is, 'to guard firmly' is absolutely relevant, but 'to guard from the bottom like boisterous wind' is rather incoherent. φλάσει was proposed by Tortorelli after (ἔ)φλασεν Hermann, but the dialect demands φλασεῖ and the metre φλασσεῖ, which is closer to Athenaeus' φυλάσσει than all proposals made so far. Cf. Theocr. 5.148 φλασσῶ τυ. Nothing need be said about the transposition of ἡμετέρας φρένας.

But the important thing is that these easy interventions, mainly to the endings of words, which, as always, suffered most from corruption, restore a normal metre, identical to the one of lines 1–7. It is obvious that we are dealing with two responding strophes. Whether these were then followed by an epode to form a strophic triad, as in Ibycus *PMG* 282, one cannot say.

10 The Danaans in Lesbos

(Sappho Fr. 17 V.)

Starting point of the present article[1] has been my stubborn attempt to decipher the fuzzy photograph of P. GC inv. 105 published on p. 8 of S. Burris-J. Fish-D. Obbink (2014) [henceforth BFO]. I remind that, concerning fr. 17 V., P. GC inv. 105 supplemented the data already known to us from PSI 123 and POxy. 1231 (+2289, 2166). The textual and interpretative contribution of the article may prove interesting. However, as I have admittedly perused only a portion of the relative literature, I must leave to other scholars interested any possible exploitation of my findings.

⊗   Πλάςιον δή μ[οι Δ]ανάοιϲ᾿ ἀ[γέcθ]ω,
     πότνι᾿ Ἥρα, cὰ χ[αρίε]ϲϲ᾿ ἑόρτᾳ,
     τὰν ἀράταν Ἀτρ[είδα]ι ̣πόηϲάν
4   τ᾿ οἰ βαϲίληεϲ,
     ἐκτελέϲϲαντεϲ μ[εγά]λοιϲ ἀέθλοιϲ
     πρῶτα μὲν πὲρ Ἤ[ραον], ἄψερον δ᾿ α[ὖ
     τυίδ᾿ ἀπορμάθεν[τεϲ·] ὄδον γὰρ εὔρη[ν
8   οὐκ ἐδύναντο,
     πρὶν cὲ καὶ Δί᾿ ἀντ[ίαον] πεδέ[[ϲ]]᾿λ᾿θην
     καὶ Θυώναϲ ἰμε[ρόεντα] παῖδα.
     νῦν δὲ κ[ἄμμεϲ, θέα Ζυ]γία, πόημεν
12   κὰτ τὸ πάλ[αιον
     ἄγνα καὶ κά[λλιϲτα· πόλυϲ γὰρ ὄ]χλοϲ
     παρθέν[ων τυίδ᾿ ἴκετο καὶ γ]υναίκων,
     ἄμφιϲ ο[ἴκηων πὲρ ἔραιϲ᾿ ἑκάϲτᾱ
16   ᾿μετρ᾿ ὀλ[όλυξαι,
     ἆϲ τιν[- × – ⏑ ⏑ – ⏑ – ⏓
     θ]έα̣, [ϲ]ὺ̣ν ἰλ[λάεντι νόωι ⏑ – ⏓
     ἔμμενα[ι × – ⏑ ⏑ – ⏑ – ⏓
20   ἦ]ρ ἀπίκε[ϲθαι.   ⊗

1 μ[οι Δ]ανάοιϲ᾿ Ts., μ[ελπο]μένοιϲ᾿ BFO, μ[οιϲο]πόλοιϲ Ferrari, Μ[ᾶτε]ρ̣ ἔκοιϲ᾿ Lidov | ἀ[γέϲθ]ω BFO, ἀ[ήϲθ]ω Ferrari, ἀ[νάξ]ω Lidov **2** cὰ χ[αρίε]ϲϲ᾿ post Wil. BFO, cὰ χ[άριϲ ἐ]ϲτ̣᾿ Ferrari, cὰ<ν> χ[άριν ἴ]ϲθ᾿ Lidov | ἑόρτᾳ leg. Ts., ἐόρτ[α] ̣[vel ἑόρτ[α]ν BFO, alt. malunt Ferrari, Lidov **3** αραταν PSI, ἐράταν PSI alt. man. add. ε et ˝ s.l. (contra metrum) | Ἀτρ[είδα]ι (dat. sing.) BFO, Ἀτρ[έϊδα]ι (nom.) Wil. **3–4** ποηϲαν/τόι PGC (τοι PSI, POxy),

---

1 I am grateful to Sotiris Tselikas for his valuable comments. For the construction of the app. crit. I am indebted to Obbink (2016), esp. 20–21.

πόηcάν / τ' οἰ, sc. τ(οι) οἰ Ts., πόηcαν / τοὶ (demonstr.) BFO, πόηcαν/τ' οἰ Neri, πόηcάν / τοι West, Ferrari, πόηcαν / τοὶ (pron. emph.) Nagy; an πόηcάν / coι emendandum Obbink? **6** Ἥ[ραον Ts., Ἴ[λιον Page (ι̣ .[Lobel in POxy. 2289), Εἴ̣[λιον BFO | δ' α[ὖ Ts., δὲ BFO **11** κ[ἄμμεc West, κ[αὶ BFO |]για disp. Ts., θέα̣ Ζυ]γία vel ὦ Ζυ]γία supplens,] ρα̣ BFO, ταῦτα π]έρα̣ West, κ[ύρι' ἀμμετ]έρα̣ Burris **12** πάλ[αιον Wil., πάλ̣[αι δὴ Neri **13** κά̣[λλιστα· πόλυc γὰρ ὄ]χλοc West, κά[λ' ὄργια ταῦτ', ὁ δ' ὄ]χλοc Ferrari, κά[λ'. εἶcι δὲ τυΐδ' ὅδ' ὄ]χλοc Neri **14** παρθέ[νων τυΐδ' ἵκετο καὶ γ]υναίκων West, παρθέ[νων τ' ἄμ' εὐχομέναν γ]υναίκων Neri **15–6** ἄμφιc ο̣[ἰκήων πὲρ ἔραιc' ἑκάcτᾱ/ μετρ' ὀλ̣[όλυξαι e.g. Ts., ἄμφι c[ὸν βῶμον δ' ὁcίωc θέλοιc' ἔμ/μετρ' ὀλ̣[ολύcδην West, μέτρ' ὀλ̣[ολύγαc Ferrari; an ἀμφὶ ϝὸ[ν γένοc (vel τέκοc) τε πόνηc' ἑκάcτᾱ Ts.? **17** ἆ̣c τιν[leg. Ts. **18** θ]έα̣, [c]ὺ̣ν ἰλ̣[λάεντι νόωι Ts. **20** ἦ̣]ρ Ts., ᾽Η]ρ' Milne

Close to me let the Danaans celebrate, lady Hera, your charming festival, which, prayed for by the Atreid, the kings performed for you,
first after they accomplished great games round Heraion, and later on in turn setting out over here; for they couldn't find their way back,
before coming to pray to you and to Zeus of suppliants and to Thyone's lovely son. And now, o Conjugal goddess, we too celebrate as in the past
chastely and most nobly; for a large throng of girls and women came here, each one separately wishing to cheer on exceedingly for their kin,
till some [ ] o goddess, with favourable mind [ ] to be [ ] spring to come.

1. πλάcιον ... Δ]ανάοιc(ι):]ανάοιc is quite clear in the photograph. Of the initial α only the foot of the right-hand oblique survives, which could also belong to λ. In the second letter, two parallel verticals linked with an oblique unequivocally suggest ν. Finally, the last trace, though somewhat faint, clearly indicates an α. πλάcιον is construed normally c. dative, just like the adjective and the verb (πλήcιοc, πληcιάζω).[2] The emergence of the Danaans, i.e. the Greeks who fought in Troy, provides strong clues for the factual interpretation of the poem. ἀ[γέcθ]ω is a most likely supplement (BFO) with Δ]ανάοιc(ι) as a dative of the agent. West stressed the fact that πλάcιον always means 'near' in a spatial sense.[3] The proximity, however, can be either real or fictional. Sappho, as the sequence of the poem shows, is present in Hera's precinct celebrating the festival, but imagines and represents, as if close by herself, the old scene of the Greek army returning from Troy and celebrating Hera's festival at the same place. This is a usual stratagem employed by Sappho in her poetry, as for instance in fr. 2 V., where, while being inside a Nymphaion, she is watching the gods descending from the sky and having a banquet at the same place (see above '9. The Banquet of the Gods and the Picnic of the Girls').

---

[2] Neri (2014), esp. 14.
[3] West (2014), esp. 4.

2. ἐόρτ[α] or ἐόρτ[αν] is pointlessly discussed. The left-hand part of the alpha is clearly visible, and possibly its low right-hand tip. No letter was written after it. The upper half of the line is abraded, but the low part is intact, and it shows plenty of space unwritten after the alpha. The supposed oblique of ν (quite distanced from α) seems to be a mere discoloration.

3–4. ἀράταν: In PSI 123, sscr. ε s. prim. α,˘′ s. alt. α, i.e. ἐράταν, contra metrum; 'prayed for' BFO, 'vowed' West, 'attractive, agreeable' Caciagli. If ἀράταν is taken as a verbal adjective in -τός, it can take a dative agent. Otherwise, it must be a descriptive adjective, as taken by Caciagli.[4] But what would the predicative ἀράταν ... πόησαν mean? Caciagli notes "Here ἀράταν possibly means 'attractive' or 'agreeable,' maybe in reference to Hera", which would, however, imply that the kings made a formerly unattractive (?) festival attractive to Hera. Ἀτρ[είδα]ι, dative of agent (BFO), seems to be the best option. The Atreid Menelaus (the only Atreid who was in Lesbos according to Nestor's narration at *Od.* 3.133 ff., since Agamemnon stayed in Ilion for placating Athena) 'prayed for' and the kings, standing for their armies, celebrated a festival in honour of Hera. An explanation is, however, necessary. ποιεῖν ἐορτήν does not mean 'to establish, to institute a festival', but 'to celebrate, to perform a festival', obviously one already existing. The same verb is used for offering regular sacrifices, not for originating new ones; LSJ s.v. ποιέω A. II 3. The verb for establishing a new festival (or sacrifices) is τίθημι; LSJ s.v. τίθημι A. VI, cf. III, V; e.g., Pind. *O.* 3.21 καὶ μεγάλων ἀέθλων ἁγνὰν κρίcιν καὶ πενταετηρίδ' ἁμᾶ θῆκε, Aesch. *Ag.* 845 κοινοὺc ἀγῶναc θέντεc, *Eum.* 484 θεcμόν, τὸν εἰc ἅπαντ' ἐγὼ θήcω χρόνον. Here, 3 τὰν πόηcαν refers to the performance of the festival in a particular year. At 11 πόημεν ἄγνα καὶ κάλλιcτα (int. object) refers to the regular year after year performance. As for the βαcίληεc, they were neither the Atreids, since one of the two was absent, nor the Lesbian Penthilids as has been proposed (Penthilus was a son of Orestes), since they postdate the events described, but the three Danaan kings present in Lesbos, i.e., Menelaus, Nestor and Diomedes. The first of them, possibly acting as commander-in-chief, 'prayed' to the goddess, i.e. to the priesthood of the precinct, for celebrating the festival. Instituting a new festival would justify ἀράταν as 'vowed for', but, since the festival already existed, 'prayed for' is necessary, being tantamount to 'on priestly permission'.

The accent on τόι in P. GC inv. 105, in contrast to τοι in PSI 123 and P.Oxy. 1231, does not seem to make it emphatic (Nagy). Such subtleties are very rarely expressed in writing, let alone recognized by the scribes. Possibly, it is an attempt to show that τοι is neither = coι nor = the particle τοι, nor = τ(ε) οἱ, nor

---

4 Caciagli (2016), esp. 430.

ποήcαν/τ(ο) οἱ. The scribe must have erroneously thought it was the epic article (or demonstrative pronoun), which would require the accent on τοί. I believe it is either τοι = coι or, more likely, τ(οι) οἱ = coι οἱ. Very hesitantly, I choose the latter.

5–6. ἐκτελέccαντεc μ[εγά]λοιc ἀέθλοιc πρῶτα μὲν πὲρ Ἥ[ραον. Not πὲρ Ἴ[λιον (Page) or πὲρ Εἴ[λιον (BFO). The letter following πὲρ was read ι̣[by Lobel (POxy. 2289), because of the horizontal that touches the vertical printed ι̣ at its low part: "litt. ι̣ parti inf. opposita est h.h. pars extrema sin." L-P. Actually, the horizontal meets the vertical at the latter's middle part, and must be read H. The height of the visible part of the vertical under the horizontal is equal to the same part of H in, e.g., Sa. 9.2 οὐκ ἐχH[from the same papyrus. The letter is quite dissimilar to the scribe's epsilon. Even when the epsilon's back is somehow straight, its bottom is curved. The use of ει for ῑ in the second century AD, when the papyrus was written, is widespread in prose texts and everyday documents, but the trend did not affect the archaic dialectal poetry texts. The only parallel adduced to the supposed Εἴλιον is from P. GC inv. 105, Kypris Poem, line 6 εἰμέρω<ι> for ἰμέρω<ι> as reconstructed by S. Burris in *ZPE* 201 (2017) 12–14. However, in K. Tsantsanoglou-S. Tselikas, 'P. Sapph. Obbink: the *Kypris Poem*', *Eikasmos* 28 (2017) 23–36, esp. 28 (here, above '5. P. Sapph. Obbink: the *Kypris Poem*'), we showed that the proper reading should be εἰ μ' Ἔρω with the exhorting interjection εἰ (LSJ s.v. εἰ A) combined with the middle imperative λῦ{ι}cαι: "Come now! Set me free from Eros". Here, the μεγάλοι ἄεθλοι were not the military labours around Ilium, but the great athletic contests the kings organized around the Heraion, apparently for recreation of the army.

6–7. ἄψερον δ' α[ὖ | τυίδ' ἀπορμάθεν[τεc. The letter after δ, in line 6, is clearly α, not ε. The expression denotes sequence of time, not necessarily repetition, also with αὖθιc or, more usually, αὖτε, sometimes δὴ αὖτε or δηὖτε. After performing the athletic games, the kings and their armies moved into the temenos of Hera for consulting the divine triad about the safest route for their return home. (ἀφ)ορμάομαι denotes departing for whatever destination, short or long: Sapph. fr. 44.23 V. ὄρμαται [- - -] ἐc Ἴλιον, the married couple from the outskirts of the city, where they are greeted by the citizens, to the palace; *Il.* 2.794 ναῦφιν ἀφορμηθεῖεν Ἀχαιοί, the Achaeans from their ships to the city wall.

11–12. κ[ἄμμεc, θέα Ζυ]γία, πόημεν | κὰτ τὸ πάλ[αιον. The letters before πόημεν are clearly]για. The alpha was recognized already by BFO, 22, but they described the letter(s) before it as "the topmost part of a curved letter […] Thus perhaps] ρ̣α πόημεν"; π]έ̣ρα̣ πόημεν (West). Ἥρα Ζυγία had been connected with Sappho already by R. Westphal (*Jahn's Jahrbücher für Philologie* 81, 690; cf. J. Maehly, *RhM* 21, 1886, 301), who described an ode-like passage of Himerius (*Or.*

9, 266 Colonna) containing the phrase ἀργυρόθρονον ζυγίαν Ἥραν as an imitation of Sappho; see Bergk, *PLG*[4] Sapph. fr. 133 ζυγίαν θέον ἀργυρόθρονον Ἥραν. Possibly, ἀργυρόθρονον ζυγίαν <⏑> Ἥραν, with a preposition filling the missing breve (δι', ἐς, πρός), would be metrically preferable. Here, ὦ Ζυ]γία seems to be two letters shorter than what would be necessary for filling the gap. If the wide μμ of κάμμες and the ω do not suffice, then θέα Ζυ]γία is the likeliest choice. Ζυγία, the Conjugal goddess, is a well documented epithet of Hera (Sch. Pind. *N.* 10.31 Ἥρα τελεία, Ζηνὸς εὐναία δάμαρ] ἔςτι γὰρ αὐτὴ Γαμηλία καὶ Ζυγία; Sch. Ar. *Lys.* 217 καὶ βοῶπις ἡ Ἥρα καὶ Ζυγία καὶ Γαμηλία; it is recorded literarily (A.R. 4.96, D.H. *Rh.* 2.2, Clem.Al. *Protr.* 2.36, Nonn. *D.* 32.57, Musae. 275, al.), epigraphically (*IGBulg.* II 667.2; *Inschr. v. Pergam.* 324.16, 576 B.5), and lexicographically (Hsch. ζ 189, al.). It clearly characterizes the festival as concerned with nubile girls. The celebration contemporary to Sappho is made κὰτ τὸ πάλαιον, in other words, the activities in which the females of Lesbos were engaged in the festival since its origins were ἄγνα καὶ κάλλιςτα.

13–14. West's κά[λλιςτα is strongly suggestive of Καλλιςτεῖα, the beauty contest held in Lesbos at the temenos of Hera, i.e., the Ἥ[ραον of l. 6. Sch. Hom. (D) 9.130 [Λεσβίδας, αἳ κάλλει ἐνίκων] Παρὰ Λεσβίοις ἀγὼν ἄγεται κάλλους γυναικῶν ἐν τῷ τῆς Ἥρας τεμένει, λεγόμενος Καλλιςτεῖα. Also, Thphr. fr. 564 FHS&G = Ath. 13.610a κρίςεις γυναικῶν ... ἑτέρωθι δὲ κάλλους ..., καθάπερ καὶ παρὰ Τενεδίοις καὶ Λεσβίοις; Hsch. π 4342 πυλαιίδεες· αἱ ἐν κάλλει κρινόμεναι τῶν γυναικῶν. The Hesychius term deserves some expounding. Scholars usually connect it with the otherwise unknown ὄρος Πύλαιον of Lesbos, mentioned but not localized by Strabo, 13.3.3 (see below). However, I very much doubt that a mountain could be the venue for a pan-Lesbian congregation with a variety of events. Nor could the Danaans make their great games round Heraion, if the precinct was on a mountain. Since πυλαιίδεες are αἱ ἐν κάλλει κρινόμεναι τῶν γυναικῶν, 'those of the women who are distinguished, picked out in beauty (εἶδος)', one may consider -ειδεῖς as the second part of the compound (εὐειδεῖς, δυςειδεῖς, θεοειδεῖς, ἀγλαοειδεῖς). As for πύλαι, among its numerous meanings, it is a general term for 'straits' (LSJ s.v. πύλη II 3: 'of narrow straits, by which one enters a broad sea' followed by examples about the Straits of Gibraltar, the Thracian Bosporus, the Euripus between Boeotia and Euboea). The word is synonymous with εὔριπος, one of the most famous εὔριποι being the one near the town of Pyrrha in Lesbos, ὁ Πυρραίων εὔριπος, which is none other than the strait leading from the Gulf of Kalloni to the Aegean Sea. Thus, the compound πυλαιειδεῖς (Lesb. πυλαείδεες), could possibly mean "The belles of Pylai", i.e., "The belles of the Pyrrhaean Strait". It is even possible that the ὄρος Πύλαιον of Strabo (though the author presents a local mythological aition for its naming) is the same as Theophrastus's (*HP* 3.9.5) Πυρραίων ὄρος τὸ πιτυῶδες, which is plausibly identified with the pinewooded heights of Τcαμλίκι (= Turk. çamlık, 'pinewoods'). It is interesting that the beauty contest of the goddesses that led to the Trojan war is named in Eur. *IA* 1307–8 κρίcιc καλλονᾶc (also, Herod. *Mim.* 1.35 θεαὶ κρι]θῆναι καλλονήν), while the area and the bay where, in the prevailing opinion, the Heraion was established, is named to the present day Καλλονή.[5]

By ἄγνα, Sappho is stressing the decent character of the festival. Concerning the appearance of the Lesbian girls in their beauty contest, Alcaeus describes them as ἐλκεcίπεπλοι (fr. 130b.13 μακάρων ἐc τέμ[ε]νοc θέων ... 17 f. ὄππαι Λ[εcβί]αδεc κριννόμεναι φύαν | πώλεντ' ἐλκεcίπεπλοι). Obviously, the Lesbians attached special importance to the festival's decorum, so that it should be concerned not only with beauty but also with decency. Further, κάλλιcτα may well be used in a moral sense, "beautiful, noble, honourable", LSJ s.v. καλόc, III. West's γάρ, which I strongly believe is correct, offers an explanation of ἄγνα καὶ κάλλιcτα, 'chaste and most noble', by describing the festival as a familial congregation. This is also, I think, the reason for using the epithet Ζυγία ('Conjugal') for Hera.

15–16. I have been greatly tormented by the letter following ἀμφι. In POxy. 1231, Hunt read c, Lobel c or θ. Yet, what I could see after ι, right before the cut, was the microscopic trace of a short left-hand vertical, which could belong to numerous letters (among them c). In P. GC inv. 105, the shape of the letter looked dissimilar from both c/θ or a vertical, but was strangely close to the numeral koppa (ϟ). Initially, assuming that the scribe confused the peculiar letters by writing ϟ instead of ϝ, I supplemented, e.g., ἀμφὶ ϝὸ[ν γένοc (vel τέκοc) τε πόνηc' ἑκάcτᾶ, even though ϝ appears twice in the surviving papyrus (fr. 3 col. ii. 12, 15 = Sa. 5.3, 6 V.). However, J. Hammerstaedt advised me that c is not impossible. Though I persist with my doubting, I was reconciled with the prevailing opinion. West's ἀμφὶ cὸ[ν βῶμον seems satisfactory, but does not add anything to the story described. I propose, e.g., ἄμφιc ... ἔραιc' ἑκάcτα, i.e., 'each one separately wishing' (LSJ s.v. ἀμφίc A. II 1), complemented by οἰκήων (*vel* οἰκήαc) πὲρ ... ὀλόλυξαι, 'to cheer on in favour of their kin'. It is only natural that among the throng of females each one would cheer on their relative/s.

---

[5] The place-name is old, witnessed in modern times at least since 1333 in connection with the conquest of Lesbos by the Genovese Domenico Cattaneo (Joann. VI Cantacuzeni *Historiae*, vol. 1, 478–479 Schopen); cf. also Piri Reis's Ottoman *Book of Navigation* (1520–26), where the gulf is named *Qalenye*.

If West's ἔμμετρ(α) was correct, the female spectators would be presented by Sappho as acclaiming either in a moderate manner or in metre. The first alternative would contradict Alc. fr. 130b.18–20 περὶ δὲ βρέμει | ἄχω θεσπεσία γυναίκων | ἴρα[ς ὀ]λολύγας ἐνιαυσίας | ς[υμ]φ[ώνω]ν ἀπὺ πόλλων. (See below '12. Alcaeus on the Lesbian Triad Festival'.) As for the second one, a reference to metrical, i.e., poetic, ὀλολυγή would be unheard of both pragmatically and linguistically. The ὀλολυγή (unless used metaphorically, which is not the case here) is a meaningless ululation practised by women in expression of joy and honour, even nowadays in Middle East populations. And the technical use of μέτρον for poetic 'metre' does not occur before Aristophanes. ἄμετρ(α) (int. object) would mean 'extremely, exceedingly' agreeing with Alcaeus' description. Were then both Lesbian poets so much impressed by the ululations, that they felt they were worthy of being immortalized? Or rather was ululating part of the procedure in the festival's rite? It seems likely that the winning girls were selected not by a committee of judges, but by public acclamation (βοῆι) and the judges' task was to determine which acclamation was the loudest, as was the case, for instance, in issuing public decrees in the Spartan assembly. Naturally, along with the contestants their female relatives thronged in the Heraion, each genos trying to surpass the others in ululating. Why was it only the women who were shouting? See at the close of this paper.

ἄμφις ο[ἰκήων πὲρ ἔραις' ἐκάστᾱ | 'μετρ' ὀλ[ολύξαι *exempli gratia*. LSJ s.v. ἀμφίς A.II.1; e.g., ἀμφὶς ἕκαστα εἴρεσθαι, 'to ask each by itself' (*Od*. 19.46). ἐκάστᾱ ἄμετρα > ἐκάστᾱ'μετρα in the typically Lesbian prodelision or synaloiphe because of the same vowel (Hamm § 80 a, h); cf. Alc. 129.19 ἤ'πειτα, Sapph. *KP* 5 πᾶι'μάλοισι, i.e., πᾶι ἀμάλοισι.[6]

17. " . . . . [" (BFO), but transcribed πα̣ς̣[. This line, whose upper part obviously comes after the paragraphos and what survives of 16, is joined with a small piece which is meant to provide the lower half of the line. However, the traces of letters in the two pieces are absolutely different and cannot fit together by any means. In their Palaeographical notes (13), BFO combine data from both pieces. If we disconnect them, we can read α̣ς̣τιν[in the upper half, which is in its proper place, but]παν[in the lower half, whose proper position cannot be determined. We do not even know whether the lower piece, which comprises also two more letters from a second line (]χω[?), is to be placed at the left-hand beginning or somewhere in the middle of the lines it comes from. The last two letters of 17 (ιν[) are clearly read. Then, ἆ̣ς τιν[, 'until some', can introduce the end of the celebration and the ululations: 'until they proclaim some girl winner'.

---

[6] See above '5. P. Sapph. Obbink: the *Kypris Poem*'.

18–19. Naturally, by removing the piece joined at the lower part of line 17, we are also annulling any trace of line 18 in P. GC inv. 105, being restricted only to the traces seen in POxy. 1231. Lobel questions about the traces: ͅ[ͅ] ͅνιλ or ͅ[ͅ. ͅ. ͅ] ͅνιλ? also "ante ν, fort. ω vel η". What I discern is, however, different: ͅ]εα[ͅ. ͅ]υνιλ[, possibly, θ]έᾳ, [c]ὺν ἰλ[λάεντι νόωι; cf. Alc. 129.9–10 V., addressing the three gods, ἄγιτ' εὔνοον θῦμον cκέθοντες. The infinitive of line 19 suggests an imperative or optative of a verb of will at the end of 18: e.g., θέληςον or θελήςαις.

20. Remarkable is the end, usually supplemented ῞Η]ρ', ἀπίκεcθαι (Milne), as a reprise of πότνι' ῞Ηρα in line 2. Four invocations in the vocative to the same goddess in a poem of twenty lines (2, 11, 18, 20), the last two close to each other, can be considered too much. However, another possibility can cancel the fourth vocative: ἦ]ρ ἀπίκεcθαι. The genitive of the contracted ἦρ = ἔαρ occurs in the Lesbians: ἦροc Sa. 136, Alc. 367.1; the nominative in Alcman 20.3; ἦρ is common in Thucydides, the Hippocratic Corpus and the medical literature; with ἀπίκεcθαι, cf. Longus, *Daphnis et Chloe* 4.8.3 ἀφίξεται τὸ ἦρ. Can Hera be invoked to be favourable in letting spring to come? One is given the impression that the similarity between ῞Ηρ(α) and ἦρ, assisted by the Lesbian psilosis, is not accidental.

Another possibility of interpretation may be offered by Alc. 130b.17 ff. V., the parallel description of the festival by Alcaeus, where I have made a painstaking papyrological inspection:

```
       ὄππαι Λ[εcβ]ίαδεc κριννόμεναι φύαν
18     πώλεντ' ἐλκεcίπεπλοι, περὶ δὲ βρέμει
       ἄχω θεcπεcία γυναίκων
20     ἴρα[c ὀ]λολύγαc ἐνιαυcίαc
       —
       c[υμ]φ[ώνω]ν ἀπὺ πόλλων· [[τ]]ὄτα δὴ θέοι
22     [θέαιναί] τε π[ι]φᾳ<ύ>cκοιcιν Ὀλ᾽ύ᾽μπιοι·
```

At 21, the high tip of φ and the position of the accent suggest c[υμ]φ[ώνω]ν, the word order being ἄχω θεcπεcία ἴραc ὀλολύγαc ἐνιαυcίαc περὶ βρέμει ἀπὺ πόλλων cυμφώνων γυναίκων, "the wondrous echo of the sacred yearly ululation roars around from many women shouting in unison"; cf. Ar. *Av.* 220–222 διὰ δ' ἀθανάτων cτομάτων χωρεῖ | ξύμφωνοc ὁμοῦ | θεία μακάρων ὀλολυγή. What follows ascribes the selection of the winners to the Olympian gods and goddesses: ὄτα δὴ θέοι | [θέαιναί] τε π[ι]φα<ύ>cκοιcιν Ὀλ᾽ύ᾽μπιοι·, "when the Olympian gods and goddesses give a sign …".

Let us return to Hera's festival. Hesychius' article (μ 932) μεcοcτροφώνιαι ἡμέραι· ἐν αἷc Λέcβιοι κοινὴν θυcίαν ἐπιτελοῦcιν has been plausibly associated by L. Robert with the festival in question. Robert made also the association of μεςο- with Messon (modern τὰ Μέςα), the location where, in his view, the precinct of Hera was situated and where the festival was performed: "je pense que c'étaient les jours où les Lesbiens séjournaient au sanctuaire de Messon pour y célébrer un sacrifice fédéral, solennel, à tout le moins une fois par an, et animaient le lieu par la panégyrie des Lesbiens venus de toutes les villes de l'île sur le bord de l'Euripe, dans la vallon de Messon".[7] Gr. Nagy interpreted μεcοcτροφώνιαι ἡμέραι as "days that turn at the middle" and noted that "there may be a connection between the semantics of *mesostrophoniai* and Messon".[8] St. Caciagli follows Robert: "The adjective '*mesostrophonios*' that names the days in which – according to Hesychius – the Lesbians perform a communal sacrifice (ἐν αἷc Λέcβιοι κοινὴν θυcίαν ἐπιτελοῦcιν) possibly hints at Messon: its meaning is perhaps 'when (the Lesbians) move on towards Messon'".[9]

However, the linguistic obstacles in this way of interpreting the adjective are too great to overcome. Firstly, it is not the Lesbians who 'move on towards' but the days. Secondly, they do not 'move on towards' but they 'turn or rotate towards'. Thirdly, they do not 'turn or rotate towards Messon' but 'towards the middle or the half'. 'Days that rotate' recall the popular image of turning or rotating time (περιτελλομένου ἔτεος, περιπλομένου ἐνιαυτοῦ, ἐνιαυτοῦ κύκλοc, ἐνιαύcιοc κύκλοc, τροχοί or τρόχοι, *al.*). Here, it is the days that rotate toward the middle, ἡμέρα being used in its round-the-clock sense, from midnight to midnight, so that their two parts, daylight and night, come to the middle. In other words, the days that were before shorter than the nights now rotate to reach the middle point and become equal to the nights.

The arrival of the days at the middle occurs at the vernal equinox (Gr. ἰcημερία),[10] a time of worldwide celebrations for welcoming spring (20 ἦ]ρ ἀπίκεcθαι), the season of nature resurrection and rebirth. It is in that time that the people of Lesbos assembled for offering a communal sacrifice. It cannot be precluded, of course, that in parallel to this astronomical meaning a folk etymological interpretation existed connecting the word with Messon, if this was the

---

7 (1960), esp. 303–304, (reprinted (1969), vol. 2, 801–831); the suggestion was already made by Robert in *RÉG* 38 (1925) 423 n. 5.
8 (2016), esp. 463–464 and n. 29.
9 (2016), 428 n. 21.
10 The automnal equinox as well, which, however, does not concern us here. It is strange that modern scholarship has fully disregarded Max Treu's opinion, who also approached the solution from an astronomical point of view; [4]1968 ([1]1952), 236. The only difference is that he took μέccον as referring to 'years' and not 'days' (μεcοcτροφώνιαι ἡμέραι), and so he concluded with summer or winter 'solstice', instead of 'equinox', when day and night are of equal length.

location of the common festival. No doubt a temple of the late 4th or early 3rd c. BC was discovered at Messon in 1885/86 excavations, and the hieron was mentioned inscriptionally (ἐν τῶ ἴρω τῶ ἐμ Μές[σω *IG* XI,4 1064, b.1, 45, 2nd c. BC), but date considerations prevent identification with the precinct of Hera spoken of by Sappho. Still, given that the folk etymology mechanism is alien to formal linguistics, further investigation may produce different conclusions.[11]

Alcaeus speaking of the festival in question and the same gods as Sappho refers to Hera: 129.6–7 V. σὲ δ' Αἰολήιαν κυδαλίμαν θέον | πάντων γενέθλαν. Many centuries later, inscriptions in Lesbos (Mytilene) and in Lesbian dialect (*IG* XII,2 208, 211, 212, 213, 214, *IGRom*. IV 1300) present Agrippina the Elder as having adopted the local title of Hera: θέα Αἴολις Καρπόφορος. The designation Καρπόφορος is substituted for Alcaeus' πάντων γενέθλα from the same context of fertility cult. The epithet is usually given to Demeter in the sense of 'fruit-bearing', of the fruits of the earth, but its use for Hera must refer to the goddess who protects or ensures childbearing to the celebrating marriageable girls. After all, the title Καρπόφορος was awarded to Agrippina by the Mytilenaeans in c. 18 AD, when she gave birth in Mytilene to her third daughter, Julia Livilla.[12] It is clearly the same notion as the Biblical καρπὸς κοιλίας (*fructus ventris*).

Concerning the location of the Heraion, the current certainty about Messon overshadowed an important piece of evidence referred to by M. Paraskevaidis, *RE* 47 (1963) art. Pyrrha, Nachtrag 1403–1420, esp. 1419. Alcaeus speaks of the Heraion as εὔδειλον τέμενος μέγα ξῦνον (129.2–3 V.) and μακάρων ἐς τέμενος θέων (130 b.13). An anonymous epigram (*AG* 9.189) begins with Ἔλθετε πρὸς τέμενος γλαυκώπιδος (sic MS; ταυρώπ- coni. Hecker) ἀγλαὸν Ἥρης. And, though τέμενος is a usual term for any precinct, it seems that the specific one was predominantly designated as τέμενος. This is confirmed by a late 3rd–early 4th c. AD cadastral inscription which mentions Τέμενος as part of a land property in the area (*IG* XII,2 79.6), but more specifically by a place-name still in use on the East shore of the gulf of Kalloni (in modern times noticed by Newton (1865), I 92 f.), and Τεμενίτης, a nearby hill, some 11 km. SW of Messon and 7,5 km. SW, as the crow flies, of the area where Pyrrha is located. The remains of a settlement were found there, and close by some sunken harbour constructions. Even prehistoric remains contemporary with Troy V are observed in the area. However, it would be presumptuous to claim that the modern place name determines the precise site of the Heraion. Literary evidence and archaeological survey are still incomplete and place names very often shift from their original location.

---

11 See below '13. The Location of the Lesbian Triad Temenos'.
12 Robert (1960).

The Hesychius article μεcοcτροφώνιαι speaks of ἡμέραι, not ἡμέρα. It is natural that Lesbians from all over the island, men leading cattle to be slaughtered in the sacrifice, women and girls, could not gather in the precinct of the gods on a single day. And the different events (sacrifices, beauty contest, music and dance exhibitions) should have lasted several days. Did one of these events belong to the participation of Sappho? Was this participation made with her group of pupils-friends? Even, was Sappho's celebration made with this particular prayer-song? Her first mention to this celebration, 1–2 μοι ... ἀγέcθω, πότνι᾽ Ἥρα, cὰ χαρίεcc᾽ ἑόρτα, speaks in first person singular. The second mention, 11–13 νῦν δὲ κἄμμεc ... πόημεν κὰτ τὸ πάλαιον ἄγνα καὶ κάλλιcτα, clearly refers to the Lesbian girls in general and not to Sappho's group. Since the poem looks like a sequel to the *Brothers Poem*, and in both poems there is no mention of pupils-friends, it is natural that both were written in Sappho's young age, before she had started her profession. This does not mean, of course, that she never celebrated at the Heraion with her pupils. In fr. 94 V., Sappho enumerates to a departing pupil the delights she enjoyed while she was in the group, and among them, 24–6 οὔτε τι | ἶρον ... | ἔπλετ᾽ ὄπποθεν ἄμμεc ἀπέcκομεν. Also, the anonymous epigram *AG* 9.189 mentioned above speaks of such a celebration of Sappho with a group of girls of Lesbos:

Ἔλθετε πρὸc τέμενοc γλαυκώπιδοc ἀγλαὸν Ἥρηc,
    Λεcβίδεc, ἁβρὰ ποδῶν βήμαθ᾽ ἑλιccόμεναι·
ἔνθα καλὸν cτήcαcθε θεῇ χορόν· ὔμμι δ᾽ ἀπάρξει
    Cαπφὼ χρυcείην χερcὶν ἔχουcα λύρην.
ὄλβιαι ὀρχηθμοῦ πολυγηθέοc· ἦ γλυκὺν ὕμνον
    εἰcαΐειν αὐτῆc δόξετε Καλλιόπηc.

Sappho connects her prayer to Hera with the story of the Greek army returning from the Trojan war and requesting Hera's assistance in showing them a safe way for sailing home. Then, the closing verse is possibly concluding a reference to the propitiation of wind, heavy sea and weather: 'Placate the elements (or Poseidon), so that spring comes'. ἦρ obviously marks the end of χειμών and the beginning of the Aegean sea's navigability. I cannot claim that Sappho's prayer lacks any personal objective and that she is just praying for her sailing compatriots. Maybe she has Charaxos, her brother, in mind and prays for him (Caciagli (2016)), just as she is doing in several other poems in the same papyrus (frs. 5, 9, *BP*), especially in the *Brothers Poem*, where Sappho is urging her mother to send her to the precinct of Hera in order to pray for Charaxos' safe return: 5 ff.

    ἀλλ᾽ ἄϊ θρύληcθα Χάραξον ἔλθην
6   νᾶϊ cὺν πλήαι. τὰ μὲν οἴομαι Ζεὺc

>   οἶδε cύμπαντέc τε θέοι· cὲ δ' οὐ χρῆ
> 8   ταῦτα νόηcθαι,
>   ἀλλὰ καὶ πέμπην ἔμε καὶ κέλεcθαι
> 10   πόλλα λίccεcθαι βαcίληαν Ἥραν
>   ἐξίκεcθαι τυίδε cάαν ἄγοντα
> 12   νᾶα Χάραξον
>   κἄμμ' ἐπεύρην ἀρτέμεαc.

It is true, however, that, if this was the main object of her prayer, very little is left for making it known; just the second part of line 19, though the mere mention of her brother's name might suffice. On the other hand, in a prayer that deals with specific events in the past history of a festival, it might seem improper to insert a request of narrow personal interest. After all, the spring and the navigable seas would anyway help Charaxos in his return voyage.

The formal symmetry by which the poem is exactly divided in two, the first ten verses devoted to the mythical past and the next ten to the present, is remarkable. In both parts the focus is on Hera's festival, and a hasty and concisely hinted at mention of Charaxos at the end of the poem would, I fear, spoil the symmetry, with the unexpected intervention of a new subject.

Though the general parallel is obvious: 'as you assisted the Danaan warriors at that time, help now the voyagers', still, the precise purpose for the Danaan intrusion into a prayer for calm seas escapes me. The mention of the Trojan incident in the beginning of the poem is presented as a specific legendary event. Its details differ, however, significantly from our only surviving source, *Od*. Book 3. In Sappho, the kings are inquiring the Lesbian triad about the safest route to be taken, but in the *Odyssey* they inquire one male god, no doubt Zeus. But apart from this, there is nothing in the *Odyssey* about athletic games outside the precinct of Hera, about the army moving into the temenos, or about celebrating a festival of the goddess. Do these facts come from a different source, whether of the Epic cycle (*Μικρὰ Ἰλιάc* or *Ἰλίου πέρcιc*) or a local legend? It is interesting that Lesches of Pyrrha, the city of Lesbos closest to the Heraion, was supposed to be the poet of *Ilias parva* (according to Paus. 10.25.5 of *Iliou Persis*), while Hellanicus of Mytilene has also rescued several legends concerning the fate of the Iliadic heroes after the sack of Troy. But, whatever the source, what is the point of emphasizing all these details about the intervention of the Danaans into the festival?

In absence of concrete evidence, we can possibly build some hypotheses depending on sporadic data. We do not know how the Danaans were received in Lesbos. But we should remember that, during the Trojan war, the Lesbians were enemies to the Achaeans.¹³ Lesbos belonged to the kingdom of Priam (*Il.* 24.544). Strabo, 13.3.3, with regard to the Lesbian implication in the war, refers to a legend of Lesbos: Λέϲβιοι δ' ὑπὸ Πυλαίῳ τετάχθαι λέγουϲι ϲφᾶϲ τῷ ὑπὸ τοῦ ποιητοῦ λεγομένῳ τῶν Πελαϲγῶν ἄρχοντι, ἀφ' οὗ καὶ τὸ παρ' αὐτοῖϲ ὄροϲ ἔτι Πύλαιον καλεῖϲθαι. Pylaeus and his brother Hippothous, sons of the Pelasgian Lethus, were in command of the Pelasgian allies of the Trojans who came from Phriconis Larissa, in the Asiatic coast opposite Lesbos; *Il.* 2.840–3 (cf. Dict. Cret. 2.35). According to Dictys Cretensis 3.14, they were both killed in the fighting, but Homer describes only Hippothous' killing; *Il.* 17.291–303. Odysseus and Diomedes are said to have killed Philomeleides, the king of Lesbos (*Il.* 4.342–4 = 17.133–5; Hellanicus of Lesbos *FGrHist* 4 F 150), while Achilles assaulted the island and carried numerous spoils which he shared with Agamemnon (see below).

We observe that the mention of the Danaans in Sappho's poem is linked with the strong claim about the decent character of Hera's festival and especially of the beauty contest of the girls of Lesbos. In spite of the difficulties in understanding the first stanzas, it seems extremely likely that the stay of the Danaans in Lesbos coincided with the 'charming' stage of the festival of Hera (cὰ χ[αρίε]ϲϲ' ἑόρτᾳ), i.e., the Kallisteia, this being the implied meaning of πλάϲιον: "Let me treat side by side the Danaans and your festival". If the Danaans anchored their ships in a harbour of the gulf of Kalloni, presumably Pyrrha (though not mentioned in Homer), the best haven in the direction of their destination in mainland Greece, it is natural that the men would encamp in a plain close to the harbour.¹⁴ And, as the poem implies, the camp was close to the Heraion. Then, we can only guess the results of the coexistence in the Heraion of an enemy army of tough and hardy men ten years sexually undernourished and a crowd of the prettiest nubile girls of Lesbos.¹⁵ The problem would be enhanced if the girls, no matter what Sappho claims, were accompanied by rumours of loose morals.

---

13 From a copious literature I pick out the old but clearly written article by Shields (1917/18), 670–681.
14 The numbers of the three kings' ships, according to the *Iliad*, added up to 230 (2.568: Diomedes eighty, 587: Menelaus sixty, 602: Nestor ninety); by no means a small contingent, even allowing for the possible losses.
15 The dates proposed by ancient commentators for the sack of Troy, depending on the astronomical interpretation of an *Ilias parva* verse ('it was midnight and the clear moon was rising'), are much later than the vernal equinox: Θαργηλιῶνοϲ ιβ' ἰϲταμένου or η' φθίνοντοϲ, Πανήμου or Ϲκιροφοριῶνοϲ η' φθίνοντοϲ, are dates in June/July. I doubt that we ought to trust these dates when interpreting legendary narratives, unless we surmise that the ἦ]ρ we are dealing with was the spring of the next year after the sack, if the Danaans delayed their departure for a few months in both Troy and Lesbos waiting for the sea to calm down.

There is one more reference to the festival and especially to the beauty contest that has not been discussed yet. At *Il*. 9.128–30 (cf. 9.270–72) Agamemnon is promising to offer Achilles seven Lesbian women for putting an end to his wrath:

δώcω δ' ἑπτὰ γυναῖκαc ἀμύμονα ἔργα ἰδυίαc
Λεcβίδαc, ἃc ὅτε Λέcβον ἐϋκτιμένην ἕλεν αὐτὸc
ἐξελόμην, αἳ κάλλει ἐνίκων φῦλα γυναικῶν.

It is concerning these verses that Sch. Hom. (D) 9.130 inform us that παρὰ Λεcβίοιc ἀγὼν ἄγεται κάλλουc γυναικῶν ἐν τῷ τῆc ῞Ηραc τεμένει, λεγόμενοc Καλλιcτεῖα. The passage must have given rise to offensive gossip against the women of Lesbos as to the services these women were supposed to offer Achilles or as to what the ἀμύμονα ἔργα they had knowledge of were. Jokes that were later voiced in Pherecrates' *Chiron*, fr. 159 K.–A., (A) δώcει δέ cοι γυναῖκαc ἑπτὰ Λεcβίδαc. | (B) καλόν γε δῶρον, ἔπτ' ἔχειν λαικαcτρίαc. Possibly, the *Iliad* passage was the birthplace of the widespread rumour in antiquity that Lesbians had invented and were practising *fellatio*.[16] Further, at *Il*. 9.664–665, Achilles sleeps in his hut, τῶι δ' ἄρα παρκατέλεκτο γυνή, τὴν Λεcβόθεν ἦγε, | Φόρβαντοc θυγάτηρ Διομήδη καλλιπάρηιοc. Wilamowitz very plausibly proposed (*Homerische Untersuchungen* 409) that Βριcηίc, the cause of Achilles' wrath in the *Iliad*, was no more than a girl from Βρίccα, the Lesbos village that kept its name unaltered since Homer (Βριcιά or Βρίcια or Βρίcα).[17]

In any case, the poem down to line 17 does not only exonerate from this scandalous gossip the Lesbian women, both those contemporary to Sappho and those contemporary to the Danaans (νῦν δὲ κ[άμμεc, θέα Ζυ]γία, πόημεν | κὰτ τὸ πάλ[αιον | ἄγνα καὶ κά[λλιcτα); it also exculpates the Danaans for entering the precinct and celebrating the festival. Their celebration was ἀράτα, 'prayed for' or, as I explained above, 'solicited by prayer, and so, on priestly permission'. Also, they did not enter the precinct before getting the permission, but performed their athletic games out of and around the Heraion (πρῶτα μὲν πὲρ ῞Η[ραον). They entered only when they realized that they would not find a safe way to return home unless they approach with prayers the Lesbian triad. Sappho is using the verb μετέρχομαι (πεδέλθην), LSJ s.v. IV 5, and not εὔχεcθαι πρόc or similar,

---

16 Sch. Ar. *Vesp*. 1346 a-d with quotations of Strattis frs. 41, 42, Theopompus com. fr. 36; cf. Ar. *Ran*. 1308, *Eccl*. 920. Also, numerous lexicographical articles: Ael. Dion. λ 6 (λεcβιάcαι), Phot. λ 207 (λεcβίcαι) = Su. λ 306, Hsch. λ 692 (λεcβιάζειν), λ 696 (λεcβίcαι), Suet. Περὶ βλαcφ. c. 13 p. 62 f. T.; further, Phot. c 258 (cιφνιάζειν καὶ λεcβιάζειν).
17 The village was greatly damaged by a recent (June 12, 2017) earthquake.

in order to justify the movement of the army into the precinct. Now, the truth behind the excuses that Sappho enumerates can only be hypothesized. L. Robert claims that, since the festival was federal, the temenos provided asylum to politically persecuted persons (like Alcaeus; Alc. fr. 130b V., though the poet is using an alias to avoid being identified).[18] Possibly, the same law provided that the beauty contest should be performed exclusively in the presence of women. Both Sappho and Alcaeus testify to the fact that no men, only women cheered on the contestants. The relics of the last two verses, 23–24, of Alc. 130b, after describing the women's ululations, can be read with difficulty:

[ο]ὐκ ἐπ' αὔδαις'
ἤι]εν κ[⏑ ⏑ – – ⏑ π]αρείϲιμεν.

Though an uncertain reading, it can give an account of the religious prohibition: "(A man) did not go in during the shouts [   ] to creep in". Apparently, men, among them Alcaeus, could listen from afar. In any case, the entrance of the male and enemy force of the Danaans into the precinct would be considered a violation of religious law. After all, inquiring the gods for the safe route to their homes could be accomplished in the presence of the three kings alone. The entrance of the whole body of troops must have had a different objective. Conceivably, a suspicion of a local legend of mass rape by the Danaans is hanging, cloaked in Sappho's elaborate pretexts. The mythological parallel of the rape of the Sabine women is significant. Not only is an enemy army involved, but also the background of the abduction and the rape is a federal religious festival attended by both rapers and victims. The festival was in honour of Neptunus, whose name was folk-etymologized from *nuptus*, *nuptiae*, 'marriage' (Varr. *L.L.* 5.72); cf. Ἥρα Ζυγία. Even more remarkable is, however, the literary attempt to exonerate the abominable incident by means of moralizing and rationalizing arguments, especially by Livy, but no doubt reflecting Roman legends and literary treatments. Be that as it may, it is better to stop here before crossing into the realm of wild guesswork.

---

18 (1960), 301–302. See below '14. Who was Onymacles the Athenian?'.

11 Sappho 27 V., Alcaeus 308 Lib., and the Homeric *Hymn to Hermes*

```
                        ]καιπ[
                     ].[.].[.]νος[
    3              ]σι·

           ...]. καὶ γὰρ δὴ σὺ πάις ποτ[
           ...]ικης μέλπεσθ' ἄγι ταῦτα[
           ..] ζάλεξαι, κἄμμ' ἀπὺ τωδεκ[
    7        ἄ]δρα χάρισσαι·

           σ]τείχομεν γὰρ ἐς γάμον· εὖ δε[
           κα]ὶ σὺ τοῦτ', ἀλλ' ὄττι τάχιστα[
           πα]ρ[θ]ένοις ἄπ[π]εμπε, θέοι[
    11        ]εν ἔχοιεν

           ] ὄδος μ[έ]γαν εἰς Ὄλ[υμπον
           ἄ]νθρωπ[       ]αίκ.[
```

Sappho fr. 27 V. is known to us through P.Oxy. 2166 (a) 5, now joined with P.Oxy. 1231 frs. 50–54 (in the Bodleian Library, MS Gr. class. c 76 (P), frame 2).

Voigt, app. cr. v. 4, notes that "a καὶ γάρ sententiam incipere magis placeret (in fine ποτ[' ἔσσα, cf. S. 121.2, vel ποτ[' ἦσθα), sed vetare vid.]CI· v. 3." Not exactly; because, a parenthetic sentence may well start with καὶ γάρ, preceded by any sentence term that the speaker needs to elucidate with the καὶ γάρ parenthesis. Lobel notes for line 5 (*The Oxyrhynchus Papyri* 21, p. 123): "Between θ and α ink which I cannot interpret either as stop or apostrophe." It must be a sign denoting something like our parenthesis or dash. It looks like a small mid-line 'c'. Actually, the indistinct character ( ].) at the beginning of line 4 need not be the relic of a letter, but, as the tiny traces indicate, of the same mid-line sign, denoting perhaps the opening of the parenthesis. Here, the just two syllables (–⏑) and the short space available before the parenthetic sentence (it measures no more than 3½ characters) combined with σύ, suggest a vocative. At line 5, what Lobel reads]ι is a long upright with its top cut at the edge of the papyrus. Apart from iota, it may well be an Y, which, in the scribe's handwriting, has a long upright and a very open, therefore short, fork placed high. I would then suggest for the stanza 4–7:

```
           Ἄτθι] — καὶ γὰρ δὴ σὺ πάις ποτ[' ἦσθα
    5      εὐτ]ύκης μέλπεσθ' — ἄγι ταῦτα [παῖσιν
           σὺ] ζάλεξαι, κἄμμ' ἀπὺ τῶδε κ[ῦδος
           ἄ]δρα χάρισσαι·
```

4 The reason for selecting Atthis from the number of Sappho's companions is, on the one hand, the size and the metrical form of her name's vocative (–⏑), and, on the other, the fact that she remained in the island of Lesbos, close to Sappho, after her coming of age; fr. 49 V. (ἠράμαν μὲν ἔγω σέθεν, Ἄτθι, πάλαι ποτά … σμίκρα μοι πάις ἔμμεν' ἐφαίνεο κἄχαρις) shows this clearly. On her singing excellence see 96.5 V. (σᾶι δὲ μάλιστ' ἔχαιρε μόλπαι), where the subject is Arignota, the missed friend, and σᾶι μόλπαι refers to Atthis.

5 εὐτυκής is parallel to εὔτυκος, 'ready, eager'. The form is attested only from Eusebius philos.[1] fr. 63, *FPG* 3.17 Mullach (ap. Stob. 2.9.6.12) εὐτυκέι πόνωι, 'with willing labour' (συνεχέι πόνωι *ap.* Mullach), but is also recorded in Hsch. ε 7256 εὐτυκές· εὐεργές, εὐχερές, εὐποίητον, ῥᾴδιον. It is also used in the same lexicon, in the definition of ε 7258 εὐτυκίσων· εὐτυκῆ ποιήσων. As for the meaning, Friis Johansen and Whittle discuss the matter in detail on Aesch. *Supp.* 959, claiming that εὔτυκος always connotes 'readiness'. Sometimes the readiness has to do with artistic display, as here: Pratinas *PMG* 709 = *TrGF* 4 F 4 Λάκων ὁ τέττιξ εὔτυκος ἐς χορόν, Bacch. 9.4–6 εὔτυκος … ὑμνεῖν. The adjective is occasionally constructed with infinitive: Bacch. *loc. cit.*, Aesch. *Supp.* 972–3 ἐπειπεῖν ψόγον … εὔτυκος.

6 Sappho, apparently in advanced age, assigns to Atthis the necessary preparation of the girls choir that was going to sing in a wedding: "you talk the matter over with the girls". 6 ἀπὺ τῶδε must not be temporal, "from now on", but must imply the source of Atthis' abundant favours (= ἀπὸ τοῦ μέλπεσθαι). It might then be followed by a noun in accusative as object of χάρισσαι, e.g., κῦδος or καύχᾱμ', or an infinitive, e.g. καύχασθ', since the singing merit of Atthis would demonstrate Sappho's excellence. Sappho is, elsewhere too, using the plural of the first person personal pronoun for herself; 24 (a).3 (?), 38 (?), 121.1, 147. All the proposed supplements form a perfectly aligned left-hand margin.

In the next stanza the supplement proposed by Snell in line 8 is suitable. The proposals for 9 and 10–11 are mine.

```
        σ]τείχομεν γὰρ ἐς γάμον· εὖ δ' ἐ[πίστεαι
        κα]ὶ σὺ τοῦτ'· ἀλλ' ὄττι τάχιστα [κῆσε
10      πα]ρ[θ]ένοις ἄπ[π]εμπε· θέοι [δέ τ' εὐνοι-
        άν κ]εν ἔχοιεν.
```

---

1 An otherwise unknown philosopher, whose surviving moralistic precepts, written in distinctly stressed artificial Ionic, are collected in Stobaeus and published by Mullach (*FPG* III 7–19) under the name of the 4th century CE Neoplatonist Eusebius Myndius.

8–9 εὖ δ' ἐ[πίστεαι | κα]ὶ σὺ τοῦτ': Parenthetic; cf. 26.11–12 ἔγω δ' ἔμ' ˌαὔται | τοῦτο σύˌνοιδα; 59.25 [ἴστε δὲ] τοῦτο (suppl. Di Benedetto); 88.13 (Steinrück) τοῦ[-⏑⏑--⏑⏑--] συνίηˌσθα καὖτα.

9–10 [κῆσε | πα]ρ[θ]ένοις ἄπ[π]εμπε: "Send the girls off there (i.e. where the wedding is taking place)".

10–11 "The gods then must have favour for you (τ' = τοι)." For εὔνοιαν ἔχειν τινί cf., e.g., Eur. *Med.* 345 εἰκὸς δέ σφιν εὔνοιάν σ' ἔχειν. The gods are naturally involved in the religious ceremony of the marriage, and will therefore treat favourably all those contributing in its successful performance. The optative + κεν denoting future possibility amounts to a vow that exhorts Atthis to take action.

12–13 I would supplement the verses as follows:

αἴπερ ἦς] ὄδος μ[έ]γαν εἰς Ὄλ[υμπον,
πάντες ἄ]νθρω[ποι βάμεν]αί κ' ἴ[σαν τάν.

See Voigt's ample apparatus for previous supplements. βά̓μεν]αί κ'ἴ̓[σαν τάν.]ΆΙ pap., "ΚΙ[, al., possis" Voigt. For βάμεναι cf. 'Tithonus poem' 10 and see Bettarini 2005; also, ἀμ-βατός, in a similar sense, Pind. *P.* 10.27 (ὁ χάλκεος οὐρανὸς οὔ ποτ' ἀμβατὸς αὐτῶι). εἶμι c. acc. cogn., ὁδὸν ἰέναι 'go a road', *Od.* 10.103. "If there were a road leading to grand Olympus, everybody would take it for going (there)". Apparently, we are dealing, from 12 on, with a new poem, as already suggested by Snell 1944, 287.

At line 6, though I have proposed alternative suggestions, I finally preferred supplementing κ[ῦδος. This is because this word was used in a parallel scene that occurs in the Homeric *Hymn to Hermes*, when the god honoured offers his musical invention, the lyre, to Apollo. Sappho addresses Atthis with the words: "You were always fond of singing. So, go and sing, and grant me abundant glory from this (your singing)". Hermes addresses Apollo with the words: "You heartily desire to play the lyre. So, play it and sing, and grant me glory (with your singing)." Sappho expects her renown among the people to be boosted through her songs sung by her pupil. Hermes expects his renown among the immortals to be boosted through his half-brother's songs sung by himself with lyre accompaniment: Sappho 27.5 κἄμμ' ἀπὺ τῶδε κ[ῦδος | ἄ]δρα χάρισσαι ~ *Hymn. Herm.* 477 σὺ δέ μοι, φίλε, κῦδος ὄπαζε.

Since the resemblance extends also to the praise of the musical ability of Atthis, on the one side, and of Apollo, on the other (εὐτύκης μέλπεσθαι ~ μέλπεο ... εὐμόλπει ... εὔκηλος ... φέρειν εἰς δαῖτα θάλειαν καὶ χορὸν ... καὶ ἐς ... κῶμον), I quote more verses from the Homeric Hymn:

475 ἀλλ' ἐπεὶ οὖν τοι θυμὸς ἐπιθύει κιθαρίζειν,
     μέλπεο καὶ κιθάριζε καὶ ἀγλαΐας ἀλέγυνε
     δέγμενος ἐξ ἐμέθεν· σὺ δέ μοι, φίλε, κῦδος ὄπαζε.
     εὐμόλπει μετὰ χερσὶν ἔχων λιγύφωνον ἑταίρην
     καλὰ καὶ εὖ κατὰ κόσμον ἐπιστάμενος ἀγορεύειν.
480 εὔκηλος μὲν ἔπειτα φέρειν εἰς δαῖτα θάλειαν
     καὶ χορὸν ἱμερόεντα καὶ ἐς φιλοκυδέα κῶμον,
     εὐφροσύνην νυκτός τε καὶ ἤματος.

I do not know whether the mention of granting glory (κῦδος ὄπαζε) "might be seen as a veiled request for a share in prophecy", as Richardson suspects, commentary *ad loc.*, but the connection he observes with Apollo's promise to Hermes at 458–462 is unquestionable.

     νῦν γάρ τοι κλέος ἔσται ἐν ἀθανάτοισι θεοῖσι
     σοί τ' αὐτῶι καὶ μητρί· τὸ δ' ἀτρεκέως ἀγορεύσω·
460 ναὶ μὰ τόδε κρανάϊνον ἀκόντιον ἦ μὲν ἐγώ σε
     κυδρὸν ἐν ἀθανάτοισι καὶ ὄλβιον ἡγεμονεύσω,
     δώσω τ' ἀγλαὰ δῶρα καὶ ἐς τέλος οὐκ ἀπατήσω.

Both promise and request are fitting parallels with Sappho's desire to achieve renown among the mortals for her poetry and music, especially when she realizes her approaching end and aspires to her posthumous reputation. Cf. P.Colon. 21351+21376.1–11, 'Tithonus poem', fr. 150 V., all probably constituting a 'cycle'; see above '2. Sappho on her Funeral Day'. That she was obsessed with this theme is clear from fr. 55 V. Also the poem starting at verse 12 of fr. 27 V., with the mention of the chimerical road to Olympus, is probably related with the same theme.

If the parallels are persuasive, as I believe they are, one should try to detect the direction of the dependence. That the Sapphic scene depends on the *Hymn* and not the other way around is, to my view, clear. In the *Hymn*, the symbolic recompense claimed by Hermes constitutes a necessary component of the myth. After all, if the conflict of the gods concerns the allotment of jurisdictions between them, what Hermes demands is the recognition of his part in the intellectual and spiritual domain that belonged by right to Apollo, actually the recognition of the essential role of cunning and craftiness in the artistic and poetic area. In the Sapphic scene, however, though the demand expresses a profound aspiration of the poetess, it is articulated as an everyday remark of a teacher expecting that her poetic superiority would be recognized through her pupils' singing merit. The remark might be expressed in many different ways or might be completely omitted without any serious repercussions. I very much doubt whether a hymnic poet might borrow from Sappho a commonplace remark for using it in the supporting skeleton of his myth.

The inevitable conclusion is that the Homeric *Hymn to Hermes* must be dated before Sappho's death. When this happened is unknown, but most scholars agree for a date not later than c. 560. Since, in the poem, Sappho seems to be aged, as she entrusts the singing task to her pupil of old and is satisfied with the renown she will earn from the girls' performance of her songs, the early sixth century would be a suited date for the composition of the Hymn. This date is between the late seventh century proposed by Allen, Halliday and Sikes[2] and the late sixth or the fifth century proposed by most modern scholars. The current dating assessments are summed up as follows: (*a*) M.L. West: "it is generally agreed on grounds of style and diction that [the *Hymn to Hermes*] must be the latest of the major Hymns. [...] to date our Hymn as early as 600 is implausible: it contains too many words and expressions that are not paralleled before the fifth century",[3] and (*b*) N. Richardson: "Various considerations [...] suggest, although they do not prove, a sixth-century date: the possible influence of the *Hymn to Apollo*, the allusion to the cult of the Twelve Gods at Olympia, the high estimation of a form of music which suggests comparison with personal lyric poetry, and the developed form of legal procedure and rhetorical technique. The untraditional language would also fit a date in this period. There does not seem to be any compelling reason to date the hymn later than *c.* 500 BC, as some scholars have done."[4] Richardson, evaluating vase-painting representations of several themes of the hymn together with cult considerations, though not conclusive, is especially convincing. Other criteria used so far for the dating were tenuous and, therefore, unreliable. The burlesque character of the Hymn, the invention of the seven-stringed lyre, the mention of places that supposedly did not exist at the poet's time, the riches of the Delphic oracle, the rhetoric technique of verisimilitude (εἰκός) in Hermes' argumentation, do not offer reliable evidence for a secure dating. On the other hand, vocabulary and diction in this hymn may well be different, and words and expressions may well be unparalleled, not because of a late date of composition, but precisely because of the hymn's different character, in the same way as vocabulary and diction are quite different between tragedies and satyr-play in a tetralogy necessarily written by the same poet at the same time. This character, however, does not seem to affect the general hymnic style. In Richardson's words (*ibid.*), "even when what is being portrayed is ludicrous the style is still elevated,

---

[2] Allen/Halliday/Sikes (1936), 275–276; in Allen and Sikes (1904), they had proposed the earlier part of the sixth century.
[3] West (2003), 14.
[4] Richardson (2010), 24.

and it is the combination of the comic and the dignified which gives this hymn its particular piquancy and charm".

Be that as it may, another non-'Homeric' Hymn to Hermes was already known, and this was by the second Lesbian, Alcaeus, fr. 308 Lib. Of its text no more than one Sapphic strophe survived, and this is the initial hymnic invocation to the god:

Χαῖρε Κυλλάνας ὁ μέδεις, σὲ γάρ μοι
θῦμος ὔμνην, τὸν κορύφαισ' ἐν αὔταις⁵
Μαῖα γέννατο Κρονίδαι μίγεισα
παμβασίληϊ.

The invocation also strongly recalls the opening of the Homeric *Hymn to Hermes*, as noted by Page 1955, 254–255: Alc. 1 Κυλλάνας ὁ μέδεις ~ Hom. 2 Κυλλήνης μεδέοντα, Alc. 1–2 σὲ γάρ μοι θῦμος ὔμνην ~ Hom. 1 Ἑρμῆν ὔμνει, Μοῦσα, Alc. 2–3 τὸν ... Μαῖα γέννατο ~ Hom. 3 ὃν τέκε Μαῖα, Alc. 3 Κρονίδαι μίγεισα ~ Hom. 4 Διὸς ἐν φιλότητι μιγεῖσα. It is true that all these resemblances are typical invocation formulas, but the fact that Alcaeus' first three verses are crammed with exactly the same specific formulas with which the Homeric Hymn opens, and not with any other of the numerous invocational epithets of Hermes, cannot be coincidental. It is significant that Bruchmann devotes 15 columns or 7,5 pages (104–111) to the epithets of Hermes that are transmitted in poetry.⁶ After all, the impression that we deal with "conventional formulas, which none needs to borrow from another", in the words of Page, is utterly deceptive. For instance, though the invocation of the god as 'son of Maia' is quite common, the relatival ὃν τέκε Μαῖα ...

---

5 κορυφᾶσι αὐγαῖς Choerob. in Heph. *Enchir.* 14.1 p. 252.15 ss. C., cod. K, -αῖσιν ἀγναῖς Choerob. cod. U; -αις ἐν αὔταις (vel ἄκραις) Meineke; -αισ' ἐν ἀγναῖς Hiller. I would rather propose κορύφαισιν αὔτας (sc. Κυλλάνας), with κορύφαισιν as dative of place and without the unorthodox short dative αὔταις (Liberman 1999, vol. II, 230). For αὐτός in Alcaeus used as 3rd person personal pronoun in possessive genitive, cf. 42.16 καὶ πόλις αὔτων. Further, I do not understand what 'on the very mountain-tops' might mean in this context. The corruption must have been old, since Philostratus, *Im.* 1.26.1 (τίκτεται μὲν ἐν κορυφαῖς τοῦ Ὀλύμπου κατ' αὐτὸ (Kays., αὐτοῦ codd.) ἄνω τὸ ἕδος τῶν θεῶν), seems to be rendering into prose Alcaeus' verses. The 'very mountain-tops' might mean something if they were connected with the 'very abode of the gods', i.e. the tops of Olympus. But the place of the god's birth in the standard myth was a cave on Arcadian Cyllene. The tops of Olympus were where the baby god was brought up by the Horae (fr. 308 c Lib.; cf. Philostr. *VA* 5.15, *Im.* 1.26.2), an account that, I fear, may have aggravated the confusion because of the equivocal sense of the verbs describing the task of the Horae: (*a*) κομίζονται ('bring to a place' ~ 'take care of') and (*b*) ὑποδέχονται ('receive into a place' ~ 'take in charge as nurses').

6 Bruchmann (1893), 104–111.

Διὸς ἐν φιλότητι μιγεῖσα ~ τὸν ... Μαῖα γέννατο Κρονίδαι μίγεισα appears only in these two instances. Also, though the god is commonly invoked as 'Cyllenian', the expression Κυλλήνης μεδέοντα ~ Κυλλάνας ὀ μέδεις reappears only in the 5th-6th century CE *Argonautica Orphica* 137, as Κυλλήνης μεδέων, in company with different epithets.[7]

As regards the contents of the two Hymns, it is only natural that the younger poet might add to or subtract from the subject-matter of the prior, as well as alter scenes,[8] expressions, and words. Influence, when speaking of highly personal poets, does not amount to duplicating. Finally, the direction of the dependence in Alcaeus is easy to determine. It is only to be expected that the material of an individual poet's short lyrical ode that hymns a god is derived from an authentic ritual hymn and not the other way around.[9] West admits that "Alcaeus very likely knew a 'Homeric' hymn on the subject", but declares: "Rather [the surviving Homeric *Hymn to Hermes*] is a later descendant of the hymn that Alcaeus knew".[10] The reasoning is admittedly possible, but after the involvement of Sappho in the dating problem combined with the cogent arguments analyzed by Richardson, it would seem that the Homeric *Hymn to Hermes* known to us may be dated in the early sixth century, and that both Lesbian poets could be familiar with it. Whether the text of the hymn the Lesbians knew was different from the text of the Alexandrian edition of the Homeric Hymns and to what extent, is impossible to answer, given the hymn's cultic nature and the adaptations it might be subjected to depending on the local festivals where it must have been performed.[11] Yet, even this plausible hypothesis cannot be viewed without reserve. On the one hand, direct and plain evidence is missing. On the other hand, religious texts are usually exposed to two diametrically opposite situations: they either experience adaptations freely according to the cultic circumstances or they stay dogmatically immutable – especially if, as is the case with the Homeric *Hymn to Hermes*, its personal character is intense. But this opens another story.

---

[7] I do not count, of course, the short Homeric *Hymn to Hermes* (18), which is no more than an identical replicate of several verses of the major *Hymn to Hermes* (4).
[8] The scene that describes how baby Hermes stole, in addition to Apollo's oxen, also his bow and quiver, is not contained in the Homeric Hymn (it is only implied as a possibility at 514–515), but must have been in Alcaeus' hymn: 308 *b* Lib.; Hor. *C.* 1.10.9 ff. (cf. Philostr. *Im.* 1.26.5; Schol. ABD ad *Hom. Il.* 15.256) with Porph. *ad v*. 9, p. 17 Hold., *fabula haec ... ab Alcaeo ficta*.
[9] P.Oxy. 2734 (*SLG* 264; 306C Lib.), a commentary on Alcaeus, shows that the 'Hymn to Hermes' is the second ode of the first book, preceded by a 'Hymn to Apollo' and followed by a 'Hymn to the Nymphs'.
[10] West (2002), 217; (2003), 14.
[11] Johnston (2002), 128–130.

12 Alcaeus on the Lesbian Triad Festival

The Lesbian poets, while versifying scenes of their personal lives, repeatedly referred to the Lesbian festival of Hera Aioleia, Zeus Antiaos, and Dionysus Omestes, what is now commonly abbreviated to 'Lesbian Triad'. The festival was celebrated at a famed in the Lesbian poets' time temenos. The poetic references to the festival and the temenos can perhaps help us in the quest of the location of the latter. In chronological order, the oldest reference must be in Sappho's youthful *Brothers Poem*, but much more comprehensively in fr. 17, which describes the fulfilment of the desire expressed in the previous poem. I have discussed both extensively above in '10. The Danaans in Lesbos (Sappho Fr. 17 V.)'. Here, I propose to discuss the Alcaeus references: fr. 129.1–12, 130a.16, 130b.13–24. However, since the specific references cannot be fully understood out of their context, I decided to make a full new edition of the three poems with a commentary on the new readings or interpretations. I have avoided a formal app. cr., because every new proposal is extensively discussed in the commentary.

129 V. (POxy. 2165 fr. 1 col. I 1–32; partim POxy. 2166 (c) 6)

(stropha Alcaica)

⊗ ὄχθοιcιν Ἀ]κράγα τόδε Λέcβιοι
    ἇ[ι] λάμπαc εὔδειλον τέμενοc μέγα
    ξῦνον κά[τε]ccαν, ἐν δὲ βώμοιc
4   ἀθανάτων μακάρων ζέθηκαν

    κἀπωνύμαccαν Ἀντίαον Δία
    cὲ δ' Αἰολήιαν [κ]υδαλίμαν θέον
    πάντων γενέθλαν, τὸν δὲ τέρτον
8   τόνδε κεμήλιον ὠνύμαcc[α]ν

    Ζόννυccον ὠμήcταν· ἄ[γι]τ' εὔνοον
    θῦμον cκέθοντεc ἀμμετέρα[c] ἄραc
    ἀκούcατ', ἐκ δὲ τῶν[δ]ε μόχθων
12   ἀργαλέαc τε φύγαc ῥ[ύεcθε.

    τὸν Ὕρραον δὲ πα[ῖδ]α πεδελθέτῳ
    κήνων Ἐ[ρίννυ]c ὤc ποτ' ἀπώμνυμεν
    τόμοντεc ἄcφι [μὴ προδ]ώcην
16   μηδάμα μηδένα τὼν ἑταίρων

ἀλλ' ἢ θάνοντες γᾶν ἐπιέμμενοι
κείσεσθ' ὐπ' ἄνδρων οἳ τότ' ἐπὶ κρᾷς ἦν
ἤπειτα κακκτάνοντες αὔτοις
20   δᾶμον ὐπὲξ ἀχέων ῥύεσθαι·

κῆν' ὦν ὀ φύσκων οὐ διελέξατο
πρὸς θῦμον, ἀλλὰ βραϊδίως πόσιν
ἔ]μβαις ἐπ' ὀρκίοισι δάπτει
24   τὰν πόλιν, ἄμμι δίδ[οι]ς π[ολ]{ε}ίταις·

οὐ κὰ`ν´ νόμον [π]όνοι̣[c ⏑ ⏑ – ⏑ ×
γλαύκας ἄτ' ἀ̣π̣ [π]αμφ[έγγεος ἀλίω
γεγραμ[μεν-
28   Μύρσιλ.[ο-

...].[
[   ]
[   ]
32   .]α̣τ[.]ρ̣π[⊗

By the banks of A]cragas the Lesbians set up this great communal precinct, conspicuous like a torch, and put in it altars of the blessed immortals, one for each,
and called Zeus by the name Antiaos (God of suppliants), you as Aeolian, glorious goddess, Genetrix of all, and the third, this one dressed in fawnskin, they named
Dionysus Raw-flesh-eater. Come on, with favourable spirit hear our prayer, and rescue us from these toils and the painful banishment.
As for the son of Hyrrhas, let their (i.e., of the killed comrades) Erinys pursue him, as we swore in the past sacrificing to them (i.e., to the three gods) never to [betr]ay any of our comrades,
or else to die and lie clothed in earth, (killed) by the men who at that time were at the head (of the state); or otherwise (i.e., if we abide by our oath), to kill them and rescue the people from pains.
Well, the pot-belly did not utter those words in earnest, but trod the oaths underfoot without restraints, and devours the city giving to us the citizens
unlawfully sufferings [   ] gleaming since lighted up from the all-sh[ining sun] painted [   ] Myrsilus [   ]
[   ] return from exile [   ].

The poem consists of an ἀρά, a prayer imprecation of revenge against Pittacus. The prayer is addressed to Hera (6 σέ), the principal goddess of the temenos (*Brothers Poem* 10 πόλλα λίσσεσθαι βασίληαν Ἥραν, 17.2 πότνι' ᾿Ηρα, σὰ χ[αρίε]σς' ἐόρτα, 17.4 πὲρ Ἥραον; anon. epigram *AG* 9.189 Ἔλθετε πρὸς τέμενος γλαυκώπιδος ἀγλαὸν Ἥρης), but straight away the poet turns to plural (9 ff. ἄγιτε, σκέθοντες, ἀκούσατε, ῥύεσθε) for the three gods who make up the 'Lesbian Triad', whom Alcaeus summons as witnesses. However, the main ἀρά is given from line 13 onward, when the addressee is the listener, since the poet refers to the same gods in 3rd person (15 ἄϲφι). By starting the imprecation with a description of the temenos and its surroundings combined with the demonstratives 1 τόδε and 8 τόνδε, Alcaeus indicates that he is now at the temenos itself. Also, since he mentions specifically the altars to each of the three gods right before the reference to the sacrifice that followed the oath of solidarity given by Alcaeus, Pittacus, and their companions in the past, and which Pittacus is now accused of having broken, it is likely that the oath and the sacrifice to the triad (15 τόμοντεϲ ἄϲφι) were performed right on these altars.

1.]κ̣ : End of a rightward sloping oblique joining the following P almost as a horizontal. The likeliest choice is A, but K is also possible, since the latter's lower prong sometimes raises its end to join the following letter almost horizontally (23 KI, 130b.2 KP, 12 KP). The fourth letter, which, according to Lobel, is dissimilar from any other letter in this pap. but could be intended for Ξ, is either T or Γ. The short underlining instead of a serif is a usual feature of the scribe which he applies to vertical letters (e.g., 1 λεϲβΙοΙ, 9 ζοΝΝυϲϲον, 12 Φυγ, 18 κεΙϲ, Τοτ, fr. 130 a.15 χεΝ, fr. 131.2 δαΙϲ). The leftward projection of the horizontal of Γ, which gives the impression of T, is also a feature of the scribe, apparent elsewhere too: fr. 130 b.6 κακΓ, 8 εΓ[, discussed by Page (1955), 204, on Alc. 130.23 (= 130b.8 V.). The letter is larger than the other gammas or taus in the pap., but so are all the letters of the first line. | 'supra tert. litt. atram(enti) vest(igium), sed non ut vid. PÁ' (Lobel); however, the tiny dot that touches the edge of the papyrus cut is the foot of a rightward ascending oblique; clearly an acute. | The Ā̀ ('accent. utique abnormis' Lobel) is the regular unaccented ending of a masculine ā-stem declension contracted genitive (Ἀίδα, Κρονίδα, Λατοΐδα); Hamm 31 §61.

I do not discuss proposals that presuppose the reading of ξ (Ἀράξηϲ, river of Armenia and Thessaly = Πηνειόϲ, compared by Lobel; perhaps river of Lesbos, proposed by Gallavotti; ὄχθαιϲ (acc.) παρ' Ἀ]ράξα, Collart; proper name, = Ἀγεϲιλαΐδαϲ?, from 130b.4, ἄνδρεϲ ποτ' ὦ]ραξα Diehl, too long; ὦ πότνι' ˚Η]ρα τᾶ<ι>, proposed also by Gallavotti, too short). However, the suggestion that a river is involved is very attractive. In accordance with my palaeographic observations and for reasons of space, I prefer, e.g., ὄχθοιϲιν (or ὄχθαιϲιν) Ἀ]κράγα; Herodian. *GG* III 1.53 Lentz = Steph. Byz. 62.18 Πολύβιοϲ δὲ (9.27.10 Büttner–Wobst) τὸν ποταμὸν καὶ τὴν πόλιν ἀπὸ τῆϲ χώραϲ ὠνομάϲθαι Ἀκράγηϲ διὰ τὸ εὔγεων, about the Sicilian city and river. ὄχθοϲ for ὄχθα in Sappho, 23.11, 95.12 f., πὰρ ὄχθαιϲ Alc. 325.4. Reading -ράτᾱ is unlikely, since the scribe's T is leftward bent. Parallel river-names are Εὐφράταϲ and Γαράταϲ, a river in Arcadia (Paus. 8.54.4). The trace before P cannot be φ, but it can be α.

Which river in Lesbos might be named Ἀκράγας, -ᾱ in the gen.? The river that flows less than ½ km from the north walls of Pyrrha, the city where Alcaeus lived during his second exile from Mytilene, is the one now officially called Βούβαρης. The name is a late regressive formation from "του βουβάρ' το ποτάμ'" = 'the river of the fish-pond' (from Lat. *vivarium*, 'fish-pond'; ψάρια βουβαρίcια, 'farmed fish'). A wide marshy area is formed at the river's mouth serving also as a fish-pond. However, Koldewey, in the end of the 19th century, knows the river by the name Καβουροπόταμος, 'crab-river'.[1] This name is still in use designating the main stream of the three tributaries that form the river. I shall elsewhere discuss the implication of the Lesbian river Ἀκράγας – Καβουροπόταμος – Βούβαρης in the location of Hera's precinct and Alcaeus' exile story; see below '13. The Location of the Lesbian Triad Temenos'.

2. α̣λ̣α̣μπαc: By enlarging and enhancing the image, one can discern at the opening of the line a slightly ascending base horizontal, compatible with the bottom stroke of A, then an uncertain angle as of Λ, followed by a left-hand bottom tip as of A. There follows a clear MΠ; then the left-hand part of the low angle of A, followed by a great part of the curve of C.

ΑΛΑΜΠΑC is not easily intelligible. However, the plural of the neuter relative pronoun has rarely the sense of 'as, like' (Nic. *Alex.* 215 βοάᾳ, ἅ τις ἐμπελάδην φώc), sometimes with the particle δή (Sem. 1.3 ἃ δὴ βοτά, Soph. *Aj.* 1043 ἃ δὴ κακοῦργοc); cf. ἅπερ, ἅτε. Schwyzer, II 647, explains it in the context of the omission of ὧν. Then, = ἃ λάμπας (ἔον) εὔδειλον, 'conspicuous like a torch'. On the other hand, more usual is the employment of ᾗ in this sense, dat. sg. fem. of the relat. pron. ὅc. Aesch. *Ch.* 558 ᾗ καὶ Λοξίας ἐφήμιcεν, Soph. *OC* 1603 ᾗ νομίζεται, Th. 8.71 ᾗ βούλονται. LSJ s.v. ᾗ adds "not in Hom., unless we read ᾗ θέμιc ἐcτί for ἣ θέμιc". The Lesbian equivalent would be ἆι, but no A<I> would be necessary, since our scribe often writes the AI with the iota stuck to the right-hand angle of alpha, with no extra space needed for the iota. Though the two choices are equivalent, I opt for the second for reasons of frequency: ἆ[ι] λάμπας εὔδειλον, 'conspicuous as a torch'.

No doubt, εὔδειλον does not necessarily imply an elevated place, but it does not imply either a non-elevated place. It certainly denotes a well illuminated place, and so visible from afar. 'As a torch' (= λαμπρόν) clearly indicates this meaning.

4. ἔθηκαν pap.; corr. in marg. ζέθηκαν = διέθηκαν, i.e. an altar for each god.

---

1 Koldewey (1890), 28.

5–9. Alcaeus lists the gods of the Lesbian Triad in the order of the Olympian hierarchy. Their epithets are found uniquely in Lesbos, and so the poet can claim that the naming was made by the Lesbians (κἀπωνύμαccαν – ὠνύμαccαν).

Zeus ἀντίαοc, 'besought with prayers' or 'protector of suppliants', is elsewhere known as Ἱκέcιοc. In a maritime island as Lesbos, the entreaties might well be intended for assistance to sailors. The tradition may go back to the Aeolian colonization of Lesbos by Makar(eus), son of Aeolus, lord of the winds, but primarily Aeolian. In *Od.* 3.173, the Achaean kings, who had moored in Lesbos, inquire for the sea route they should take for attaining a safe return (ἠιτέομεν δὲ θεὸν φῆναι τέραc) a male god, obviously Zeus, unless 'god, deity' in general is implied.

Sappho fr. 17 V. is describing the same incident but with the kings inquiring all three gods. In her poem, the god who is besought to bring the spring and to calm the seas is Hera. The epithets of the latter are given by Alcaeus as Αἰολήια and πάντων γενέθλα. The first of them highlights the traditional character of the goddess, her origins being traced back to the Aeolian colonization of Pelasgian Lesbos. The second describes her as fertility goddess, not so much with relation to the land productiveness as to the fecundity of women. I have discussed the matter above, in '10. The Danaans in Lesbos (Sappho fr. 17 V.)'.

ὠμηcτήc is a variant of ὠμάδιοc, also an epithet of Dionysus, because, according to Porphyry, *Abst.* 2.55, on human sacrifices, ἔθυον δὲ καὶ ἐν Χίῳ τῷ Ὠμαδίῳ Διονύcῳ ἄνθρωπον διαcπῶντεc, καὶ ἐν Τενέδῳ. Porphyry does not mention Lesbos, the island in-between Chios and Tenedos, but Alcaeus seems to extend the cult to his island too. The epithet appears again in a story repeatedly narrated by Plutarch (*Them.* 13, *Arist.* 9, *Pelop.* 21), about a human sacrifice to Dionysus Ὠμηcτήc ordered by Themistocles before the battle of Salamis on the advice of the mantis Euphrantides. We know nothing about this mantis, but Plutarch mentions Phaenias of Lesbos, the Peripatetic philosopher who came from Eressos, as his source. Hsch. μ 932 μεcοcτροφώνιαι ἡμέραι· ἐν αἷc Λέcβιοι κοινὴν θυcίαν ἐπιτελοῦcιν has been plausibly associated with the festival of the Lesbian Triad. Could Dionysus be presented in Lesbos so brutal? And could the 'common sacrifice' of Hesychius originally include such savage practices? Sappho (17.10) avoids naming the god, but describes him as Θυώναc ἰμε[ρόεντα] παῖδα. On the other hand, the tradition of the introduction of Dionysus to Lesbos also goes back to the Aeolian colonization and its leader Makar(eus), who is presented as priest of Dionysus and founder of the hieron of Βρηcαῖοc or Βρicαῖοc or Βρηcαγένηc Διόνυcοc; Androtion, *FGrHist* 324 F 56, *EGen* β 263 Lass.-Liv. Βρicαῖοc, Aelian. *VH* 13.2; *IG* XII, 2.478. The problem is that the hieron of Dionysus Βρicαῖοc is located at Βρίcα (mod. village Βρicιά or Βρίcια or Βρίcα), the southernmost site in the area, close to the entrance into the gulf of Kalloni or the Πυρραίων εὔριποc but outside it, an isolated and practically unreachable place in antiquity, completely inappropriate for pan-Lesbian congregations and festivals. Wilamowitz very plausibly proposed (*Homerische Untersuchungen* 409) that Βριcηίc, the cause of Achilles' wrath in the *Iliad*, is only a woman from Βρίccα.

The commentary of POxy. 3711 (fr. 306Ea Lib.) offers at least two different aitia for the epithet Ὠμηcτήc. After a greatly truncated part, where a story by Hellanicus of Lesbos combining Ὠμηcτήc and Cμινθεὺc Ἀπόλλων is mentioned, unfortunately incomprehensible, another aition by Myrsilus of Methymna is given. It seems that Lesbian scholars (Phaenias included) dealt with the legendary custom, expounding the local god's unusual epithet and discussing the inevitable suspicions of cruelty in his ritual. I print below a version of the text of lines ii 15–30 somewhat different than that of M.W. Haslam and the subsequent editors:

```
15      ἐπ' ἀτελείαι ποιοῦϲι [κατὰ τὸν Ἑλ-
        λάν{ε}ικον. ἑτέρῳ[c δὲ κατὰ τὸν
        Μυρ[cί]λον· ["ἔοι]κε ἐπὶ Μάκαρο[c ἱερέα
        Ὠ]μηcτὴν τοὔνομα [Λεcβίουc κε-
        λεῦcαι θύειν ὃ ἂν λη[φθῆ κάλλιc-
20      τον ἐκ τῶν πολε[μ]ί[ων]· τού-
        τουc οὖν εἰλ[η]φότας τ[οὺ]c ἐκ[λ]η-
        φθέντας ἀγ[αγ]εῖν παιδί[ον] καλὸν
        ἐκ τοῦ βαcιλικοῦ γένουc ὃν τῶι
        Διονύcωι θῦcαι τὸν Ὠμηc-
25      τὴν ἐπὶ τῆι ἱερω{ι}cύνηι τοῦ θε-
        οῦ. ἐντεῦθεν οὖν ὠμηcτὴν
        κεκλῆcθαι Διόνυcον. οἱ δὲ πολ-
        λοὶ διὰ τὰc μαινάδαc, αἳ ὠμὰ δι-
        αcπῶcι τῶ[ν] θηρίων τὰ εἰc χ[εῖ-
30      ραc αὐτῶν ἐλθ[ό]ντα."
```

The first aition ends clearly at the accusative Ἑλ]|λάνεικον (-οc Hasl.). [κατὰ τὸν Ἑλ|λάνεικον must conclude Hellanicus' suggestion about the purpose of the human sacrifice. Then, ἑτέρῳ[c (οὕ]τωc Hasl.) with Μυρ[cί]λον (-οc Hasl.) must introduce Myrsilus' explanation (therefore, δὲ κατὰ τὸν). What comes next seems to be [ἔοι]κε ἐπὶ Μάκαρο[c. The absence of a transitional particle (δέ, οὖν) shows that we have a verbatim quotation of Myrsilus. The scribe confirms this view by projecting the name Μυρ[cί]λον from the column margin like a lemma. As Myrsilus claims, "it seems that, at the time of Macar, a priest named Ὠμηcτήc urged the Lesbians (apparently, [Λεcβίουc]) to sacrifice to Dionysus the most beautiful of the spoils taken from the enemy. And they (τού]|τουc οὖν, not τοὺc οὖν, as

Hasl.), understanding (εἰλ[η]φότας, LSJ s.v. λαμβάνω I 9) by 'spoils' the captives (τ[οὺ]ϲ ἐκ[λ]η|φθέντας), carried off (ἀγ[αγ]εῖν) a pretty young child (most likely παιδί[ον], contrary to Haslam's view) of the royal family to Omestes for sacrificing to Dionysus as priestly services to the god (pap. τηϊἱερωιϲυνηι, not a correction from τῶι ἱερῶι, but a simple misspelling). This is how the god was named Omestes. However, the prevailing opinion is that the naming was due to the Maenads, who tear asunder the raw flesh of the beasts that came to their hands."

The two aetia end with an explanation of the purpose behind the human sacrifice: Hellanicus ἐπ' ἀτελείαι, Myrsilus ἐπὶ τῆι ἱερωϲύνηι τοῦ θεοῦ; cf. Xen. An. 3.5.18 ἐπὶ τούτοις ἐθύϲαντο, ὅπωϲ κτλ. The first, by combining Dionysus Omestes with Apollon Smintheus, the cause of the plague at the opening of *Ilias*, probably connects the sacrifice with propitiating the god with a view to gaining immunity (ἐπ' ἀτελείαι) from public disasters (?). The second, by ascribing the origin of the human sacrifice to a misunderstanding, probably implies that the custom is discontinued, limited to a priestly duty (ἐπὶ τῆι ἱερωϲύνηι τοῦ θεοῦ) that only keeps its original name. Also, who was the enemy and the king implied in Myrsilus' story? I suppose the Pelasgian inhabitants of Lesbos prior to the Aeolian colonization.

M.W. Haslam cogently compared the Salamis incident as described by Phaenias fr. 25 Wehrli (from Plut. *Them.* 13), where the παῖδεϲ slaughtered belonged to the royal family, children of the king's sister, but were also κάλλιϲτοι ἰδέϲθαι τὴν ὄψιν. I am, however, puzzled at the persistence on the selection of the κάλλιϲτοι (Myrsilus, Plutarch), if seen within the frame of a composite festival, a part of which was occupied with ritually selecting a καλλίϲτη παρθένοϲ, therefore called Καλλιϲτεῖα, and another with ritually 'sacrificing' a κάλλιϲτοϲ παῖϲ. The first part is related with Hera Ζυγία, as is obvious from Sappho's fr. 17, the second with Dionysus Ὠμήϲτηϲ. I cannot claim anything about the origins of the festival's parts, but I speculate about the second part that, given its Dionysiac character, at least in the historical ages, the whole ritual (selection of the κάλλιϲτοϲ παῖϲ and his sacrifice) would have turned to a masquerade ceremony, parallel to the pharmakos ritual in several places of Greece.

6. Though ἆι λάμπαϲ εὔδειλον might give the impression that the poet is gazing at the temenos from afar, 1 τόδε and 8 τόνδε show that he is already inside the temenos, close to the altars or, possibly, to effigies of the gods. However, this does not disprove that the temenos could be conspicuously seen from the place where Alcaeus had settled during his exile, i.e. Pyrrha.

7. τὸν δὲ τέρτον τόνδε κεμήλιον, 'and the third, this one dressed in fawnskin', confirms that the poet is looking at images of the gods. κεμάϲ, 'pricket, fawn', is a rare word for the young deer, the usual one being νεβρόϲ, and its hide (νεβρίc) is one of the typical accessories of Dionysus' image together with the ivy-wreath, the thyrsus, and less often the kothornos. *κεμηλόc does not survive, but some other adjectives with the common -ηλόc suffix (ὑψηλόc, χαμηλόc) form conglutinates with -ιοc: νοcηλόc, ἀπατηλόc > νοcήλιοc, ἀπατήλιοc.

11. τῶν[δ]ε μόχθων ἀργαλέαc τε φύγαc. More detailed description of the toils and his painful exile in fr. 130a–b.

15. ἄcφι: Following Á, I do not see 'a spot level with its top' (Lobel), but a clear left-hand arc of a curved letter. The next letter, of which the top of a tall upright has survived, can only be Φ, as proposed by Lobel. Therefore, I do not discuss ἄμφ[εν- = αὐχέν[(Lobel) or ἄμφ[αδον, ἄμφ[αδα (Diehl), ἄμφ[ω (Colonna), much less ἄργ[(Deubner, Kamerbeek). Of the fourth letter only a top spot has survived which can belong to numerous candidates. After a lacuna of c. 6 letters, there follows an acute upon a missing vowel or diphthong, then some uncertain top traces partly compatible with CHN. ἄcφι could fit the traces and the sense (see Sa. 149; cf. Alc. 313), though I cannot guess anything more than [. . . . . .] ´cην. Diehl's [– προδώ]cην, possibly [μὴ προδώ]cην, is satisfactory. I venture τόμοντεc ἄcφι [μὴ προδώ]cην, 'as we swore in the past on sacrifice to them (to the three gods) that we would never betray any comrade of ours'.

18. *Pace* Page, the letter following ΕΠΙΚ is neither E nor O, since it continues upwards above the crack, but the often short, backward bending P of our scribe. The next letter is the apex of Α topped by an acute. Then, traces of an upper left-hand arc topped by a downward curving horizontal: certainly C. The verse ends with a clear HN.

What the palaeographic account advocates is ἐπὶ κρὰc ἦν, i.e., ἐπὶ κεφαλήν, 'at the head (of the state)'. The gender of κράc is usually indeterminate, and its quantity is usually long. Schwyzer, *GG* I 583, δ, speaks of it as masculine or feminine and takes it as long. He does not speak about the possibility of a neuter κράc (Pind. fr. 8 τρία κρᾶτα, Soph. *OC* 473 ὧν (κρατήρων) κρᾶτ' ἔρεψον καὶ λαβάc), which would normally belong to the -ᾰc group of nouns (κέραc, τέραc, πέραc, κρέαc) with short quantity in nom., acc., voc.; Schwyzer, *GG* I 514 f. However, a prosodical confusion is observed even in these neuter nouns, which often have a long -α- in some grammatical cases. Another possibility would be to have an adverbial ἐπίκραc (cf. ἐπίκαρ, often printed ἐπὶ κάρ), though nothing would change meaningwise. Interesting is also the 3rd pl. of the imperfect of ἔμμι, which appears as ἦν, instead of the hapax recorded in a dactylic fragment (Sa. 142) ἦcαν. Hamm, § 248 b1, considers ἦcαν "nicht dialekteigen" and indicates that she would expect "die alte Form der 3. Pl. ἦεν (=ai. ásan)". On the other hand, ἦν as plural form occurs in Hes. *Th.* 321, 825, Soph. *Tr.* 520, and many more instances, where grammarians, both ancient and modern, waver between a dialect form and a syntactical peculiarity (cχῆμα Πινδαρικόν or Βοιώτιον); see West (1966), 84 and 255 (on v. 321).

19. ἤπειτα: Page is worried about the expression: "In Homer, ἢ ἔπειτα in the second half of a disjunction introduces the less desirable of the alternatives: 'let us do A; or, *then* (i.e. if we fail, and a further course of action is necessary), let us do B.'" This is, however, not a Homeric peculiarity, but the natural course of human thought. What Page finds in Alcaeus is that "ἢ ἔπειτα clearly introduces the *more* desirable of the alternatives, 'let us die fighting; or, alternatively, let us kill our enemies and rescue the people.'" However, what is described here is not a plan with two alternative outcomes, one more desirable than the other, but the alternative outcomes expected after a solemn oath; an ἀρά with a penalty inflicted on the perjurers or otherwise a success: "We swear not to betray our comrades, or else let us be killed by our enemies; or then (= or otherwise, i.e., if we abide by our oath), let us kill our enemies and rescue the people."

20. λύεcθαι is corrected to ῥύεcθαι (ρ supra λ). Though the sense is identical, the second is more frequent. Still, the repetition after 12 ῥ[ύεcθε, in exactly the same metrical position at the end of the stanza, is annoying.

21–22. Published as κήνων κτλ. Though the sense is clear, I am worried about the syntax. κήνων must refer to the content of the oath, διελέξατο to Pittacus' sharing in the utterance of the oath, πρὸc θῦμον to the manner the words were said, the latter clearly opposite to βραϊδίωc. However, a syntax of διαλέγομαι c. gen. is unheard of or, at least, not recorded. Therefore, I believe that Gallavotti's proposal ((1946), esp. 123) to read κῆν' ὦν, rather κῆν(α) than κῆν(ο), should be adopted. διαλέγομαι can be constructed with cognate accusative: e.g., Dem. 18.232 εἰ τουτὶ τὸ ῥῆμα, ἀλλὰ μὴ τουτὶ διελέχθην ἐγώ. As for ὦν = οὖν, this is the second time the particle has been recognised in the Lesbians, after Sa. 60.2 V.] θέλ' †ωνταπαίcαν (ΘΕΛΩ΄ΝΤΑΠΑΙCΑΝ PHal. 3 = POxy. 1787), i.e.] θέλ' ὦν τὰ παῖcαν, in spite of Voigt's hesitation. Ap. Dysc., *Conj.* 228.22, τὸν (sc. cύνδεcμον) ὦν, ὄντα καὶ Ἰωνικὸν καὶ Αἰολικὸν καὶ Δωρικόν. It is obvious that the scribe of POxy. 2165 by writing ΚΗΝΩΝ did not understand κῆν' ὦν, but thought he was repeating κήνων from line 14. In both Lesbian cases, ὦν is connective and inferential, belying Denniston's statement ((1950) 416) that this sort of οὖν/ὦν "is not firmly established before about the middle of the fifth century". "Well, the pot-belly did not utter those words in earnest, but, after trampling without restraints over the oaths, he devours the city, ...".

24–25. ἄμμι is certain, but the iota is written upon something unclear and so are the next letters: an unusual Δ followed by a peculiar ΟΙ (strangely read ΕΔ by Lobel), but also with an Ι written above the Ο. It is uncertain whether an acute above the area was written for stressing the original O or the corrected I. Hesitantly, I propose an original δόι̣[c corrected to δίδ̣[οι]ς̣. In the sequence, I agree with Gallavotti's πολίταιc, only reading π[ολ]είταιc'.

Naturally, πολίταιc' is appositively connected with ἄμμι. "he devours the city giving unlawfully sufferings to us the citizens ...".

26. Following γλαύκαc the editors print ἀ[.]..[.]..[, though some letters are more or less clear. After ἀ, a top horizontal can only belong to Τ (not Π), because of its proximity to the next Α. Then, another top horizontal, Π or Τ, a short lacuna, and a quite certain ΑΜΦ; of Φ only the very high tip of the upright is visible, but no other letter fits. γλαύκαc ἀταπ[.]αμφ[or γλαύκαc ἀτατ[.]αμφ[.

The fourth Α (ἀπ[or ἀτ[) is obligatorily long, whether naturally or 'by position', the latter being possible by means of a consonant that might fill the lacuna. The only possibility I was able to find is

γλαύκαc ἄτ̣' ἀ̣π̣ [π]αμφ[έγγεοc ἀλίω

(less likely αἴθεροc or ἄcτεροc). Cf. Sa. (?) *Orpheus Song* 7 πυριφέγγεοc ἀελ[ίω. For ἄλιοc instead of the more usual ἀέλιοc cf. Sa. 56.1 φάοc ἀλίω. For the typically Alcaic apocope of ἀπύ cf. Alc. 6.17 ἄπ πατέρω[ν, 371 ἄπ πατέρων μάθοc. Whether it was intentional to start the verse with five α-syllables in a row on stylistic purposes or not, I do not know.

Alcaeus must be recurring to his initial (line 2) theme of the temenos that was 'conspicuous like a torch or a beacon light'. What feminine object is gleaming (γλαύκαc) as it is lighted up from the all-shining sun and what it has to do with the situation described is not easy to specify. The fact that the adjective is elsewhere employed for Athena (Eur. *Heracl.* 754, Theoc. 28.1, an idyl written in Aeolic) prompted Diehl to propose γλαύκαc Ἀ[θανάαc. Gallavotti, more cogently, connected the adjective with Hera, as she is described in the anonymous epigram *AG* 9.189, which begins Ἔλθετε πρὸc τέμενοc γλαυκώπιδοc (ταυρ- coni. Hecker) ἀγλαὸν Ἥρηc. However, describing the goddess as 'gleaming', or even 'blue-eyed', 'grey-eyed', or 'with gleaming eyes', because of the all-shining sun, limits the image from an eternal spectacle to a temporary view. We saw above, with reference to 1 τόδε and 8 τόνδε, that the poet is inside the temenos, possibly close to effigies of the gods. 7–8 τὸν δὲ τέρτον τόνδε κεμήλιον, 'and the third, this one dressed in fawnskin', confirms that Alcaeus is looking at images of the gods. This must be the case here too. It is the effigy of Hera, the principal goddess of the sanctuary, that is gleaming bathed in sunshine. We do not know how the sentence started at the end of 25 and continued into 27, but it seems that Alcaeus repeats his supplication to Hera to avenge the murder of his comrades.

27. Lobel published γεγρά̣ [, noting 'Π possis nisi obstet accent. (de quo dubitationi locus)'. Actually, Π is impossible, because the surviving foot of the letter is curved unlike the straight upright of the left-hand stroke of Π. The letter is certainly a M. However, I agree that the acute is doubtful; actually, no acute is visible above A, in an area completely abraded.

The word then starts with γεγραμ[μεν-. Possibly genitive γεγραμμένας, if it is syntactically connected with γλαύκας. The participle confirms the conjecture that we are dealing with works of art, painted pinakes or reliefs or sculptures.

28. The last readable word of the stanza mentions Myrsilus, the tyrant that Alcaeus and Pittacus and, possibly, more conspirators swore to overthrow, but Pittacus betrayed them.

An extremely bold supplement, yet somehow elucidating the sense, might be, e.g.:

οὐ κἂν' νόμον [π]όνοι̣[ς. ἀτὰρ εἴκονι
γλαύκας ἄτ' ἀ̣π [π]αμφ[έγγεος ἀλίω
γεγραμ[μένας ἐπεύχομ' Ἥρας
Μύρσιλ[ον ἀμπλακίαν τίνεσθαι.

ἀμπλακίαν: gen. pl.

(giving to us, the citizens), unlawfully, sufferings. But to the image of the gleaming, as if painted from the all-shining sunlight, Hera, I pray to punish Myrsilus for his offences.

32. .]ατ[.]ρπ[is difficultly read. I conjecture κατέρπ-, not in the sense 'creep, steal down', but 'return from exile', as it is recorded in the inscription Syll.³ 306.54 (Delph. from Tegea, 324 BC) καθέρπουσι. Alcaeus seems to close his poem and his prayer to Hera with his ultimate wishes: the punishment of Myrsilus and Pittacus (the second in the illegible verses 29–31) and his return from exile.

130a V. = 130.1–15 LP (POxy. 2165 fr. 1 col. I 33–39 et fr. 2 col. I)

(metrum v. infra)

The poem has been published as the opening of Voigt's 130b, though both Lobel and Page (the second in a long introductory note, *S.&A.*, 200–201) discuss whether a verse is missing between 6 and 7, where there may be a gap before a detached piece of papyrus that contains only line 7, and a new poem starts at 16, or 17 if we add the missing line. Voigt did not accept the theory of the missing line and published the 15 verses under 130a as a separate poem of four 3-verse stanzas. Possibly, the verse omitted by Lobel ((1941), 2165) was not at the bottom of col. i, but at the worn out beginning of col. ii, right after line 2 of the column (then, 9 of the whole poem). Thus,]COMENAΠEΛOIC· would not belong to line 9, but to line 10. In either case, the poem has 16 verses, not 15, and obviously four 4-verse stanzas (see also below on 4). The first two verses are gl^c ||, the last two ˏgl^c ||. Only line 15 is ˏgl || instead of ˏgl^c ||, possibly through omission. The metre is cognate with that of 130b, the only difference being the third verse: 130a = ˏgl^c ||, 130b = hipp ||.

```
× × – ⏑ ⏑ – – ⏑ ⏑ – ⏑ –                               gl^c ||
× × – ⏑ ⏑ – – ⏑ ⏑ – ⏑ –                               gl^c ||
× – ⏑ ⏑ – – ⏑ ⏑ – ⏑ –                                ˏgl^c ||
× – ⏑ ⏑ – – ⏑ ⏑ – ⏑ –                                ˏgl^c |||
```

⊗ ἄχναςˌδημι κάκως· οὔτε γὰρ οἰ φίλοιˏ
 ἐπτάχ[οντες ⏑ – – ⏑ ⏑ – ⏑ –
 οὐδ' αὖτος ἄλητ[ον γάνυμαι τύ]κων·
4 κεῖλαι νέφ[εсίν τ' ἄρμοςα] καρδίαν·

 ν]αί, Λέρνˏ[αι κακοτάτων ⏑ ⏑ – ⏑] ˏεν
 .]π...᾿[
 θυγα[τρ ⏑ – – ⏑ ⏑ – ⏑ –
8 (col. ii) . .]ν[

 .] . υ[ ] . .
 . .] . [× – ⏑ ⏑ – – с]ˏομεν ἀˋμ'πέλοιс·
 ἐλύπ[ετ ⏑ – – ⏑ ⏑ –]αππέναιс
12 δι' ὕπν[ον ⏑ – – ⏑ са]οφρόνην

 ἄνη ˏ[– ⏑ ⏑ – – ⏑] ἔλει· πὰρ ὄ,
 περρέκβα [τε] πέρα κηὖθυ κατάс[[с]]ατο·
 αὖτον β[άλ]ε. <– – ⏑ ⏑ –> κάππέτων
16 ἔχ' ἔν[δυτ]α τεῖχος βαсιλήιον.   ⊗ τὸ τῆс Ἥραс

I feel wretchedly miserable. For neither my comrades, having cower[ed, ?come to my assistance], nor do I [take pleasure in pre]paring the meal by myself. And [I adapted] my mood to both heat and clo[uds];
verily, [we are falling] into an abyss of ills [ ] daugh[ter/s [ ]
 [we were dig]ging up vines. The man was in distress over those (fem. pl.) who were [con]sumed [with pains] [and together with] his drowsiness [he couldn't be sou]nd of mind, [so he suffered] a fat[al (accident) in the] swamp; by which he stepped out exceedingly and straightaway was greatly harmed. He [thr]ew himself. <Farewell, my friend,> and, having fallen off, be cl[oth]ed (interred) in the royal wall.

1–3. The first verse is integrated through the *Etymologicon genuinum* (A+B) α 1519 Lass.-Liv., but the relationship with the particular papyrus verse was reluctantly accepted by Lobel, till Gallavotti noticed that the quotation's οὔτε γὰρ οἰ φίλοι conforms well to the papyrus's 3 οὐδ' αὖτοc. 'I feel wretchedly miserable. For neither my comrades ... nor I ...'.

2. In Lesbian, the part. perf. act. is formed like the part. pres. act.; Hamm 92 §178. Therefore, the perf. act. part. of πτήccω, i.e., Att.-Ion. ἐπτηχότεc, is ἐπτάχοντεc in Lesbian. οὔτε γὰρ οἰ φίλοι ἐπτάχοντεc 'For neither my comrades, having cowered, [come to my assistance?], nor I ...'.

3. '... nor do I take pleasure in preparing my meal myself'. γάνυμαι is e.g. supplemented. Hyperbolically used for 'as I have been aristocratically raised, I am unaccustomed in living by myself'. Hsch. τ 1622 τύκω· ἑτοιμάζω. An aristocrat, living in exile abandoned by his comrades and obliged to change his way of life (130b.1-2), expectedly must have hired some local person for assistance in the agricultural tasks he was inexperienced with.

4. εἴλαι dat. 'I adapted my temperament to heat and clouds'. κᾳρδίαν: The upper oblique of Κ and the left-hand tip of Ἀ are visible. I do not know where Lobel's]ορδίαν came from. Under the last letter of the verse, the Ν of κᾳρδίαν, a baffling horizontal stroke is visible, similar to a paragraphos, but on the opposite side, not the beginning but the end of the verse.

5. Λέρνη κακῶν, 'an abyss of ills' (LSJ); a common proverbial phrase. κακοτάτων is e.g. supplemented. Possibly, περιπίπτομεν? The intense proverb is here accentuated with ν]αί, which sums up the previous unpleasant situations and heralds the description of the new mishap. A transitive κ]αί would be insipid after the previous verse that starts also with a transitive καί (κεῖλαι). It is noteworthy that from the second stanza onward the 1st person pl. is used (5]_ε_ν, 10 c]ςομεν ἀ'μ'πέλοιc), which can imply a transition from the poet's personal grievances to the misfortunes of a group, whether of comrades or of a family.

10. ὠρύc]cομεν ἀμπέλοιc? Alcaeus possibly refers to a man with whom he used to share his agricultural duties. Cf. 130b.2 ζώω μοῖραν ἔχων ἀγροϊωτίκαν. Were they together digging up vines when the accident described happened? If the Λέρνα κακοτάτων involved this man too, then the θύγατρεc of line 7 may have been this man's daughters.

11. To judge from the punctuation, here starts the description of the fatal accident, in which the man mentioned before was killed by falling into a swamp. The opening of the line is extremely uncertain. Possibly, ἐλύπ[ετ- – – ⏑ ⏑] ᾳππέναιc illustrates the unknown man's feeling of distress. The fem. acc. pl. participle no doubt represents the θύγα[τρεc of line 7, about whom the man was grieved.]ᾳππέναιc possibly indicates δεδ]αππέναιc. δάπτομαι, 'be consumed (by wretchedness?)'. It demonstrates some unhappy condition for the daughters, which affected the father. For the -ππ-, cf. Alc. 298.10 ἀπαππένα γενείω, where the schol. =

ἀφημμένη. On the peculiar phenomenon of progressive assimilation in Lesbian (πμ → ππ) see Blümel, §148, and Slings (1979). E.g., ἐλύπ[ετ' ὄδ' ἄλγεσσι δεδ]αππέναις, 'the man grieved about them (the girls) who were consumed with pains.'

12. At the beginning of the line, Lobel published ου̣ .̣ [, and noted "fort. ουπ[, sed neque π neque το[satisfacit". However, the papyrus shows a crystal clear iota with its usual bottom serif, but as the second letter. The first is almost completely abraded, but for a faint leftward bending upright. In spite of Lobel's doubts, the letter next to υ is a clear π. There follows an uncertain left-hand vertical. The group .ιυπ.[can well be supplemented δι' ὕπν[ον. Arist. *GA* 744b 6, speaking of the heavy eyelids, observes that ἂν ... βάρος γένηται περὶ τὴν κεφαλὴν δι' ὕπνον ἢ μέθην ἢ ἄλλο τι τῶν τοιούτων, οὐ δυνάμεθα τὰ βλέφαρα αἴρειν. Here, the unknown man was drowsy, possibly because he had stayed awake all night out of grief and distress about the condition of his daughters, something the poet must have described in the completely illegible lines 6–9. In any case, this drowsiness may have led him οὐ ... σαοφρόνην, to behave, that is, absent-mindedly or in confusion.

13-14. ἀνήκ[εστον/-στα, if this is the correct supplement, indicates a fatal event, which must be related with a marsh (] ἔλει). E.g., ἀνήκ[εστα πέπονθ' ὦν ἐν] ἔλει, 'in the marsh'. To clear up the sense of the composite period, an entirely *exempli gratia* supplement might be:

ἐλύπ[ετ' ὄδ' ἄλγεσσι δεδ]αππέναις,
δ]ι' ὕπν[ον ἄμ' οὐκ ἦχε σα]οφρόνην,
ἀνήκ[εστα πέπονθ' ὦν ἐν] ἔλει· πὰρ ὂ κτλ.

The man, in distress over the girls who were consumed with pains, and besides being drowsy, could not be clearheaded; so he suffered a fatal accident in the swamp.

ὦν = οὖν inferential. The unrecorded πάρο is understood by the editors as 'is present' or 'is possible', on the analogy of ἐνό employed ἀντὶ ῥήματος, according to *Epim. An. Ox.* 1, 176.12, and is even compared by etymologists to the Mycenaean *paro*. It can be simply πὰρ ὄ, with ὄ taken as a usual relative pronoun referring to a preceding neut. noun that indicates a location 'by which, beside which'. The acute accent on ΠΆΡ designates the form πάρ instead of the elided παρ'. The neut. noun that indicates a location must be ἔλος, 'marsh, backwater', which closes the preceding sentence: ἐν] ἔλει. In the papyrus, the pronoun is separated by comma-like diastolae (,Ο,). The first diastole is muddled as it is overlaid with the acute of -σσάτω in the next line. Cf. in the same pap., 129.21 κῆν' ὦν ὁ φύσγων, where Ο is also written between diastolae.

περρέκβα [τε] πέρᾱ: The phrase must have been misunderstood by the scribe as an imperative, possibly περρέκβατε, and so the final verb with which it is copulatively connected was altered from indicative aorist -cατο to third person imperative -cάτω: 'you (pl.) get out and let him ...'. The alteration was noticed already by Lobel ("τω ε το corr.") and must be associated with the other changes made through lectional signs in the stem of the verb. Yet, the two indicative aorists could perfectly join with each other (περρέκβα τε ... καὶ ... -cατο). The subject, as it seems from the last verse and the scholion that follows it, must have been close to a marsh by the walls of the temenos of Hera.

The subject stepped out exceedingly from the edge of the marsh. This must be the meaning of the exaggeration περρ- (= ὑπέρ) πέρα. A metaphorical sense is also possible: 'he went out of reasonable bounds'; cf. Eur. *Med.* 56 ἐc τοῦτ' ἐκβέβηκ' ἀλγηδόνοc. However, it is likelier that the incident described is an accident rather than a suicide.

What happened then to the subject is designated as great harm. The verb describing this sensation is ἀάω, usually intrans. in aor. medium, ἀαcάμην, ἀάcατο, *Il.* 9.537, 11.340, or contr. ἄcατο, *Il.* 19.95. With κατά, the notion of ἄcατο is strengthened, so 'he was severely harmed'. However, all editions give the reading as καταccάτω (τω ε το corr.), disregarding the papyrus reading which is ΚΑ̇ΤᾹC̣C̣ΑΤΩ ̇. This means that the second sigma was deleted by cancel dots and a longum sign was added upon the second alpha. As for the correction of the final vowel, it certainly exists, but the other way around: ω was corrected to ο, as is clear from the thicker ink that closes the left-hand half of ω to a circle. The initial erroneous reading was ΚΑ̇ΤᾺCCΆΤΩ, and this was corrected to ΚΑ̇ΤΆC̣C̣ΑΤΟ, i.e. κατἄcατο, which can hardly be anything else than the contracted middle aorist of καταάω. With κατά, cf. Hsch. κ 1537 κατέβαcκε· κατέβλαψεν, coll. α 31 ἀάcκει· βλάπτει, φθείρει.

κηῦθυ Gallavotti; 'deb. καῦθυ' Voigt. "Beside which (the marsh), he stepped out excessively and straightaway was severely damaged."

15–16. αὖτον β[άλ]ε. <χαῖρ', ὦ φίλε,> κἀππέτων

A combination of acute on the α and grave on the υ of the αυ diphthong, instead of the usual circumflex. αὖτον βάλε; LSJ A. III 1 "intr., *fall*, ἐγὼ δὲ .. τάχ' ἐν πέδῳ βαλῶ ... Aesch. *Ag.* 1172 (lyr.)". Noteworthy is the pithy phrase that describes the final outcome of the emotional event: αὖτον βάλε, 'he threw himself, he fell dead'. The verse is the only one that scans ˍgl‖, without the expected choriambic expansion. Therefore, I conjecture a − − ⏑ ⏑ omitted before the final participle. E.g., αὖτον β[άλ]ε. <χαῖρ', ὦ φίλε,> κἀππέτων. The conjecture accounts for the omission as a case of homoeoteleuton: βάΛΕ~φίΛΕ. ὦ μέΛΕ would also fit.

καππέτων is uniformly considered the aor. part. of καταπίπτω. However, καππέτων (= καταπεсών) would form a further asyndeton and a fully dislocated period. I believe we must read κἀππέτων (= καὶ ἀποπεсών), 'and having fallen off ...'. Lobel publishes ἐχέπ[; acc. Voigt; 'initium mirum : nescio an ἐχέτ[possis, unde ἐχέτ[ω tentaueris' Liberman. It was not noticed that between X and E a high dot was written, which can stand for an apostrophe (Turner, *GMAW* 11 n. 47). Then ἔχ(ε) must be an imperative connected with χαῖρ(ε) by the copulative κ(αί) of κἀππέτων. The letter after the second E has a top horizontal stroke slightly sloping. It cannot be Π, whose top horizontal is always absolutely straight. It could be T or Γ, but the likeliest candidate is N, whose oblique sometimes starts with a slight slope; cf. 129.14 ἀπώμNυμεN, 15 τόμοNτες, 20 δᾶμοN, 24 πόλιN. N also, unlike Π, is likelier to have the serif-like short underline under its first vertical, as is the case here. I wonder what the βαсιλήιον τεῖχος could be for the man after his death. I suspect something in the area of the common metaphor γᾶν ἐπιέμμενοι, 'dressed in earth' (Alc. 129.17), so I propose ἔχ' ἔνδυτα τεῖχος βαсιλήιον. ἔχω is commonly used of arms and clothes: LSJ s.v. ἔχω A II 3, ἔνδυτ' ἔχοντας Eur. *HF* 443, νεβρίδος ἔχων ἱερὸν ἐνδυτόν *Ba*. 138, εἷμα δ' ἔχ' ἀμφ' ὤμοιсι *Il*.18.538, τάδε εἵματ' ἔχω 17.24. Alcaeus closes the poem by bidding his companion farewell and emphasizing the burial close to the walls of a sacred precinct. The interpretation of the scholiast connects the 'royal' fortification with the Heraion (Ἥραον), the temenos of Hera, referred to in Alc. 129 and 130b, as well as in Sa. fr. 17 and the 'Brothers Poem'. In the last (Sa. 9a.6), as mentioned above, Sappho is urging her mother to send her to βαсίλnαν Ἥραν in order to pray for Charaxus' safe return. βαсίλεια or βαсιλίс is a panhellenic title of Hera used both literarily and inscriptionally, documentation of which would be redundant (Eitrem (1912), 'Beinamen im Kultus', col. 382–383).

The two locations mentioned in the poem can possibly be identified. Since the first understandable verses describe the conditions during Alcaeus' exile, the scene must be located in the area of Pyrrha. It is in the same area that we have to look for the Heraion, the τέμενος of Hera. Extended ruins of fortification walls are found in the area, defending the city, but possibly the temenos too. As for the marsh, the area has numerous wetlands; those closest to the coast are used as salt-pans, and all are nowadays popular bird-watching sites. Also the river that flows along the north walls of Pyrrha (Βούβαρης, Καβουροπόταμος, Ἀκράγας?) forms a wide (c. 150 acres) marsh at its mouth; see above on fr. 129.1 V. Was the wall of Hera's temenos in the vicinity?

The place name Τέμενος is recorded in the cadastral inscription *IG* XII,2 79.6 (285–305 AD), naturally not precisely located. In modern times (Newton (1865), I 92 f., and numerous references henceforth) the place name and the neighbouring hill Τεμενίτης are placed some 6–7 km as the crow flies to the SW of the site where archaeologists place Pyrrha. Can the place name have moved from its original location or has it spread over a wide area of the ancient Heraion's district?

130b V. = 130.16–39 LP (POxy. 2165 fr. 1 col. II 16–39)

metrum: x x — ⌣ ⌣ — — ⌣ ⌣ — ⌣ —   gl^c ||
         x x — ⌣ ⌣ — — ⌣ ⌣ — ⌣ —   gl^c ||
         x x — ⌣ ⌣ — ⌣ — —   hipp |
         x — ⌣ ⌣ — — ⌣ ⌣ — ⌣ —   ˌgl^c |||

λϛ′

⊗ Ἀγνώτ[ο]ις βιότοις [β]αῖς ὀ τάλαις ἔγω
  ζώω μοῖραν ἔχων ἀγροϊωτίκαν,
  ἰμέρρων ἀγόρας ἄκουσαι
4 καρυ[ζ]ομένας, ὦ (Ἀ)γεσιλαΐδα,

  καὶ β[ό]λλας· τὰ πάτηρ καὶ πάτερος πάτηρ
  καγγεγήρασ' ἔχοντες πεδὰ τωνδέων
  τὼν [ἀ]λλαλοκάκων πολ[[ε]]ίταν,
8   ἔγ[ωγ' ἀ]πὺ τούτων ἀπελήλαμαι

  φεύγων ἐςχατίαις· ὠς δ' Ὀνυμακλέης
  ὠθάναιος ἐοίκης' ἀλυκαιχμίαις
  φ[εύγων] τὸν [π]όλεμον· ςτάςιν γὰρ
12 πρὸς κρέ[ςςον]ας οὐκ ἄρμενον ὀννέλην·

  εἶ[ρ]πο[ν] δ' ὦν μακάρων ἐς τέμ[ε]νος θέων
  ἐς π[ρηῶνα μ]ε[λ]αίνας ἐπίβαις χθόνος·
  χλίδα[ι]ς δὴ ςυνόδοιςιν αὔταις'
16 οἴκημι κάκων ἔκτος ἔχων πόδας·

  ὄππαι Λ[εςβ]ίαδες κριννόμεναι φύαν
  πώλεντ' ἐλκεςίπεπλοι, περὶ δὲ βρέμει
  ἄ{λ}χω θεςπεςία γυναίκων
20 ἴρα[ς ὀ]λολύγας ἐνιαυςίας

  ς[υμ]φ[ώνω]ν ἀπὺ πόλλων· [[τ]]ὄτα δὴ θέοι
  [θέαιναί] τε π[ι]φα<ύ>ςκοιςιν Ὀλύμπιοι·
  [ο]ὐκ ἐπ' αὔδαις'
24 ἤι]εν κ[⌣ ⌣ — — ⌣]αρειςιμεν.   ⊗

Having passed through unfamiliar ways of living, I, poor wretch, pass my life having an agricultural lot, yearning to hear the assembly being summoned, o Agesilaidas,
and the council. What my father and my father's father have grown old with, among these citizens who harm each other, therefrom I have been driven away

fleeing to the middle of nowhere. And as Onymacles devoted to Athena (or 'the Athenian')
I settled, a runaway av[oiding] the war; because to prevail in a rebellion against more
pow[er]ful people is illogical.
So, I came to the precinct of the blessed gods having climbed on the pro[montory] of the
black earth, and actually revelling in the gatherings themselves, I dwell keeping my steps
out of trouble;
where L[esb]ian girls walk back and forth with trailing robes being judged for beauty, and
all around rings the divine sound of the sacred yearly shout of women,
from many (of them) sh[ou]t[ing in uni]son; when the Olympian gods and [goddesses] give
a sign; [ ] not [by] shouts [ ] to enter.

The typical coronis is missing, but a short oblique stroke stands in the margin marking the beginning of the new poem, possibly a mark for adding at some later time the coronis, a mark that went unnoticed. Two separate characters written at the left-hand end of the space between 130a and 130b were given several interpretations. Lobel read them as λι and considered them an interlinear gloss upon the first word of the poem ἀγνο-, i.e. λινο-, both interpreted as alternative namings of the shrub known as chaste-tree. Page actually followed this interpretation, only changing λίνοc to λύγοc, though avoiding to read the second character as υ. Diehl, followed by Gallavotti, read λει or λc, interpreting them either as λεί(πει), sc. cτίχοc, or λ(είπει) c(τίχοc), and connecting them with the question of whether a verse is missing from 130a or not. I read the two characters as numerals λϛ, i.e., λϝ, with the digamma written in the typical manner of the 1st–2nd century, i.e., close to a c with its upper curve horizontally extended. This means '36'. Whether 36 is the serial number of the poem (130b) in the book's edition or something else, I do not know. The number has been added after the poetic text was written, since the line spacing of the poems (130a and 130b) has not changed. It is impossible to check whether numbers were also written between the other poems in this papyrus. The left-hand margin, in the area of the first lines of 129, is entirely worn out. Some tiny traces hardly visible to the right of the coronides in the spaces between 129 and 130a as well as 130b and 131 (above the initial T of Tᾶc, not Γᾶc, as published) are completely uncertain.

1–2. ἀγνοιc ̣ ̣cβιότοιc ̣ ̣ιc: Lobel. Page describes the papyrus data for the ending of αγνοιc as follows: "The letter following αγνο looks like an iota with a horizontal line through its middle, but there is some further ink to the right of its apex and quite a long stroke at its foot inclining downwards from right to left." By enlarging the photograph we can see that the horizontal line runs through οι and stops at the back of c touching it. There is no doubt that the horizontal stroke is intended to delete these letters, but it is uncertain whether c is included to those deleted. Further, the iota was blackened as if the scribe first attempted to delete this letter. Two parallel horizontal strokes appear also above the omicron (possibly extended more to the right, but a lacuna obstructs reading). However, the upper parallel is delusive, because it is no more than the serif-like underline frequently written by our scribe under the left-hand vertical of N, here the N of the preceding line (εχ·έN). The second parallel may well be the left-hand end of an acute horizontally written, as frequently in this papyrus. Also, another horizontal stroke runs underneath, starting from the end of ν and linking ο and ι. I suppose that this low horizontal is a hyphen joining the ν with the letter following the deleted letters. The letter after c is a clear τ. | At the end of 2, ἀκρὸϊκὼτίκᾰν· pap.

δυϲβιότοιϲ Page, because "the noun βίοτοϲ is very seldom used in the plural number" (p. 202). In accordance with my papyrological observations, one can easily guess the intended correction of the scribe and write ἀγνώτ[ο]ιϲ βιότοιϲ. I cannot rule out ἀγνώcτ[ο]ιϲ, if the horizontal stroke did not intend to delete c as well, but the meaning is not affected. The correction ω should have been written above OIC, but the large lacuna there obstructs reading. As for the much talked ἄγνοϲ = λύγοϲ, 'chaste-tree', it is time to dispense with it.

The word following is [β]ᾳῖϲ. Even traces of the β are discernible in the faded area, very similar to the β of βαcιλήϊον in the previous line. Metaph. from βαίνω c. acc. loci (e.g., *Od*. 3.162 ἔβαν νέαϲ), in the sense 'Having gone through (having passed through) unfamiliar ways of living, I (now) pass my life having an agricultural lot', in either meaning of μοῖρα: 'the destiny of a rustic' or 'a plot of land'. The repeated changes in the way of living of the aristocrat Alcaeus accounts for the plural of βίοτοϲ. The same grievances are found in 130a.1–10, ἀχνάϲδημι κάκωϲ, also with the description of some of his miseries: 3 οὐδ' αὔτοϲ ἄλητον γάνυμαι τύκων; 4 κεῖλαι νέφεϲίν τ' ἄρμοϲα καρδίαν; 5 ναί, Λέρναι κακοτάτων περιπίπτομεν; 10 ὠρύϲϲομεν ἀμπέλοιϲ. In 129.11–12 he prays to the 'Lesbian Triad': ἐκ δὲ τῶνδε μόχθων ἀργαλέαϲ τε φύγαϲ ῥύεϲθε.

6. Lobel observed that the scribe wrote καὶ γεγήρᾰϲ᾽ which was later corrected to κακγεγήρᾰϲ᾽. This is why the new K was dissimilar to the kappas of the original scribe. Grammatically, καγγεγ- is preferable.

8. Page is wrong in disconnecting τά in line 5 from the civil rights mentioned in the previous lines (ἰμέρρων ἀγόραϲ ἄκουϲαι καρυζομέναϲ καὶ βόλλαϲ) and interpreting the sentence as referring to the fortune piled up by Alcaeus's forefathers, which he is not able to enjoy since he has fled to the middle of nowhere. There is no need of a strong stop at πολίταν, and Page's ἔγωγ(ε) is syntactically fitter than Gallavotti's ἔγω δ(έ). If Alcaeus was speaking here about his family fortune, he would not need to add πεδὰ τωνδέων τὼν ἀλλαλοκάκων πολ[[ε]]ίταν. It is with these citizens who desire to harm each other that Alcaeus' forefathers were in conflict in the assembly and the council.

9–10. φεύγων ἐϲχατίαιϲ(ι) said in exaggeration, 'in the middle of nowhere', though Alcaeus was living in Pyrrha, less than 30 km. from Mytilene. Strabon, 13.2.4, measures 80 stadia, from the surviving in his time προάϲτειον of Pyrrha to Mytilene, a much shorter distance. φεύγων and 129.12 φύγαϲ need not mean that he was officially sentenced to exile. The question of Alcaeus' banishment and his place of exile deserve a special treatment, and will therefore be separately discussed.[2]

11–12. πρὸϲ κρέ[ϲϲονα]ϲ is palaeographically possible. What Lobel saw as "litterae o ut vid. malae scriptae pars sup. sin." is actually an untidily written ε, with the upper curve very close to the mid stroke; cf., e.g., 6 Εχοντεϲ. The rest can be easily accomodated in the existing space, especially if the tiny pieces containing οϲ and κρε come closer to each other and both to the initial πρ, so providing for space of one more letter.

A long discussion took place on whether ϲτάϲιν ὀννέλην means 'to take up strife' or the opposite, 'to get rid of strife'. Parallel occurrences implied that in this context the active ἀνελεῖν means 'to get rid of', and that 'to take up', which seems to be expected here, was expressed only by the med. ἀνελέϲθαι. I am afraid, however, that the investigation has been moving in the wrong direction. One of the subdivisions of the 'take up' meaning concerns prevailing in agonistic activities, and here both act. and med. are equivalent. In the act.: *Il.* 23.736 ἀέθλια ἀνελόντεϲ, 551 ἀνελὼν ἄεθλον, Hdt. 5.102 ϲτεφανηφόρουϲ ἀγῶναϲ ἀναραιρηκότα, 6.36 Ὀλύμπια ἀναραιρηκώϲ. And in the med.: Hdt. 6.70 ἀνελόμενοϲ Ὀλυμπιάδα, 6.103 ἀνελέϲθαι Ὀλυμπιάδα, ἀν. τὴν νίκην. In Alcaeus ϲτάϲιϲ, 'strife, contest, sedition, row', takes the place of the athletic contest; and the verb has, naturally, the meaning 'win, prevail'. In other words, ϲτάϲιν πρὸϲ κρέϲϲοναϲ ὀννέλην means 'to win a rebellion against more powerful people'.

For the papyrus's unmetrical ἄμεινον, Latte offered, in my view, the best solution: ἄρμενον, med. aor. 2 part. of ἀραρίϲκω, coll. Theoc. 29.9 (πῶϲ ταῦτ' ἄρμενα;). οὐκ ἄρμενόν (ἐϲτι), referring to the preceding statement ('to win a rebellion against more powerful people'), means 'is unfit, is incoherent, is illogical'.

13. The upper and the low curve, as well as the mid horizontal of ε, are faintly visible before the clear ι. Then, uncertain traces, followed by an upper horizontal with a vertical slightly curving at its right-hand end like π. A vague circle like an omicron follows. The next letter is problematic, looking like a φ, because of a high mid vertical sloping to the left and almost touching the previous line. I prefer to leave it unsolved. What is next can be read δ'. Of the next letter only the end of a

---

[2] See below '14 Who was Onymacles the Athenian?'.

high vertical slightly curving to the left, while the last letter can more easily be recognized as ν.

εἶ[ρ]πο[ν] δ' ὧν is proposed very reluctantly, especially since one should expect ἦρπον: *an legendum* ἦλθον?

14. ἐc π[. The opening was read ἐοι[by Lobel, but a random vertical fibre was thought as closing the circle of a c, while traces of the horizontal and the two verticals of π are faintly visible. After the lacuna, Lobel notes "fort. με[λ]αίναc, sed confirmari non potest". I cannot discern any trace of μ.

Lobel is perhaps too cautious. [μ]ε[λ]αίναc ... χθόνοc can be considered certain. Alcaeus uses the same expression in 38.10, γαῖα μέλαινα is formulaic in Homer, and Sappho uses it, together with γᾶ μέλαινα, several times. The opening can well be filled with ἐc π[ρηῶνα, the form employed by Hesiod, *Sc.* 437, and numerous Hellenistic poets and considered by many etymologists as the original form of the common πρών. If correctly supplemented, the temenos must have been situated on an elevated (ἐπίβαιc) foreland or promontory.

15. Following χλί, the three strokes of the left-hand half of a Δ, are faintly seen, of the right-hand oblique only the upper free part, then a certain A can be discerned with its upper oblique cut off and the lower oblique cut short, then a short gap, the upper half of the curve of C, the left-hand tip of Δ, and, finally, the right-hand half of a clear H. All aggregate in ΧΛΙΔΑ[.]CΔH.

χλίδα[ι]c, pres. part. of χλίδαμι (= χλιδάω): χλίδα[ι]c δὴ cυνόδοιcι, 'and now revelling in these assemblies', 'lending myself some delicacies with these assemblies'. Alcaeus is declaring that he is fully satisfied with these gatherings which ensure him a peaceful way of life avoiding troubles, but literally avoiding τὰ κακά or τοὺc κακούc (κάκων ἔκτοc), in contrast to the Mytilene gatherings, whether ἀγόρα or βόλλα, where he had to deal with ἀλλαλόκακοι citizens. The scribe wrote ταύταιc, but the first τ is deleted and a μ is superscribed by a second hand. The usual transcription is μ' αὔταιc, which I am unable to interpret. χλίδαμι is an intransitive verb of emotion which regularly takes the dative (cυνόδοιcι). Where μ' (με? μοι?) should be attached to I cannot say. Can we postulate an unrecorded transitive usage in the sense 'entertain, τέρπω'? I find Page's proposal (p. 207 n. 1), that "it is worth considering whether the interlinear correction, μ, was not intended for ν, cυνόδοιcιν αὔταιc", very tempting. Then, αὔταιc would be tinted differently: 'and really revelling in the gatherings themselves', i.e., not with the specific delights of the festival, beautiful girls, songs, dances, but particularly with the gatherings as favoured substitutes for the political assemblies.

Hamm, § 233, discusses the short dative pl. -αιc, not excluding Gallavotti's proposal μ' αὔταιc' οἴκημι in synapheia with the fourth stanza verse. I believe the proposal is worth adopting, especially since it is corroborated by the metre, which connects a hypercatalectic glyconic with an acephalous expanded glyconic (3rd stanza verse: *hi*, 4th stanza verse: *tl*ᶜ), what West calls 'dovetailing'. This is why I decided to print the 4th stanza verse indented. See also 23.

16. I would rather take οἴκημι in parallel with 10 ἐοίκης(α) and explain it absolutely, 'I live at home', as if it were a compound οἴκοι ἦμαι, 'sit still, sit idle'; cf. Eur. fr. 10 τῷ κατ' οἴκους ἐκτὸς ἡμένῳ πόνων. The poet actually declares that he has fully abandoned the political strife, living away from troubles, and his only feast is attending the gathering itself, instead of his formerly longed for political assemblies.

17 ff. The description of the beauty contest is found also in Sa. 17, where my commentary is more comprehensive. Λεσβίαδες ... πώλεντ(αι), 'come habitually, frequent', does not particularly fit, since the coming of the Lesbian girls is specifically dated once every year. The verb rather implies the girls' walking back and forth during the beauty contest, what in hyperbole could be compared to a present-time parade down the catwalk, what truly accounts for Alcaeus' enjoyment and revelry (χλίδα). ἐλκεσίπεπλοι no doubt suggests the decency of the contest, which in different contexts might be dispraised as indecent. | I cannot explain the peculiar error 19 ἀλχώ for ἀχώ.

21. A slight trace might belong to the high arc of c. After a two-letter gap a very high tip of a vertical suggests φ. The next letter is accented with acute. After a new two-letter gap, a clear ν is visible. The final ν, for which Lobel was uncertain ('N vix satisfacit'), is absolutely clear, only it belongs to the group with the oblique slightly sloping, as discussed on 130a.15–16 concerning the ν of ἔν[δυτα]. Then, πόλλων was clearly written, but a thick oblique and then a thick vertical were scribbled upon the ω together with a high hyphen joining the last two letters. The only explanation I can give is that πόλλων was first corrected to πόλλαν, fem. gen. pl., but then the correction was deleted with the thick vertical. Next, τότα was initially written (πότα Lobel), but the first letter was deleted, and another hyphen was added joining the first two letters of ότα.

I venture ϲ[υμ]φ[ώνω]ν ἀπὺ πόλλων in the sense 'from many women shouting in unison'. The corrected 'when the gods ...' is preferable to the initial 'then the gods', which would turn the traditional belief to an occurrence experienced by Alcaeus. Lobel adopts the word before its correction, which, as he claims, was πότα, and so takes the high stop at the end of 22 as a question-mark.

22. A horizontal, most likely τ, meets the upper part of ε. Then, follows the left-hand half of a π. After a short gap, an uncertain high vertical like φ, followed by the right-hand oblique of α with an acute on its apex. Then, cκοιcιν, but the first ι extremely thick after correction (initially υ?). Next, ολμπιοι more or less certain, with an ύ added upon the λ. At the verse's end, -μπιοι /, a high stop (-πιοι·) as several times before.

π[ιφ]άϲκοιϲιν for πιφαύϲκοιϲιν, "freq. v.l. for πιφαύϲκω in Hom." (LSJ). The Olympian gods and goddesses give a sign of their preference for the winner of the contest, i.e., the most beautiful girl. The absolute use of πιφαύϲκω in the sense 'make signal, give a sign' is obvious in *Il.* 10.502 ῥοίζηϲεν δ' ἄρα πιφαύϲκων Διομήδεϊ δίῳ. Obviously, if the winning girl was selected by public acclamation (βοῆι), here the ἄχω θεϲπεϲία γυναίκων ἴραϲ ὀλολύγαϲ ἐνιαυϲίαϲ, as I am discussing at Sa. 17, a body of judges was necessary to conclude which girl drew the loudest acclamation. The most appropriate panel would be the priests of the three gods, the proclamation of the winner being thus assigned to the Olympian gods, not as objective assessment of the sound's loudness but as expression of the divine will.

23–24. Though numerous traces of ink are visible in 23, none is easily intelligible. Very reluctantly, I venture]υκεπ'αυδαιϲ. If αὔδαιϲ is correct, is it an accusative pl. or a short dative pl. or, possibly, an elided long dative pl. in synapheia with the fourth stanza verse, as discussed above in 15? In 24, the first visible letter is certainly ε, but at least one letter before it is missing. εἶ]εν is possible, but I would prefer ἦι]εν, followed not by α, as read by Lobel, which would not scan, but by κ or λ; "... they never used to come during the shouts". The subject must be the men, who, as it seems, were not allowed to enter the temenos during the beauty contest, in other words, over the shouts, apparently the most impressive event of the festival. ἐπ' αὔδαιϲ(ι) like ἐπὶ τῇ κύλικι. The poem, after a gap, closes with an uncertain]αρειϲιμεν (-μεϲ *ante correctionem*), possibly γ]ὰρ εἴϲιμεν or] ἄρ' εἴϲιμεν or π]αρείϲιμεν. Much likelier, however, than first pl. verb is, I believe, the infinitive: παρείϲιμεν, 'to go in'. 'For no men are allowed to go in'.

13 The Location of the Lesbian Triad Temenos

The temenos of the 'Lesbian triad', i.e., Hera Aiolēia, Zeus Antiaos, and Dionysus Ōmēstēs, has been almost unanimously situated at the locality of Messon (modern τὰ Μέcα), a region really placed at the middle of the island of Lesbos. The proposal was originally made by L. Robert on the basis of the Hesychius article (μ 932) μεcοcτροφώνιαι ἡμέραι· ἐν αἶc Λέcβιοι κοινὴν θυcίαν ἐπιτελοῦcιν. Robert plausibly associated the pan-Lesbian sacrifice with the festival at the temenos of Hera mentioned by Sappho (fr. 17, and *Brothers Poem* 9–12, the first partly and the second completely unknown to Robert) and Alcaeus (frr. 129, 130a, 130b), while the temenos was also mentioned in the anonymous epigram *AG* 9.189. Robert made also the association of μεcο- in the name of the festival (μεcοcτροφώνιαι ἡμέραι) with Messon, where, in his view, the sanctuary was situated and where the festival was performed: "je pense que c'étaient les jours où les Lesbiens séjournaient au sanctuaire de Messon pour y célébrer un sacrifice fédéral, solennel, à tout le moins une fois par an, et animaient le lieu par la panégyrie des Lesbiens venus de toutes les villes de l'île sur le bord de l'Euripe, dans la vallon de Messon".[1] Lately, Gr. Nagy interpreted μεcοcτροφώνιαι ἡμέραι as "days that turn at the middle" and noted that "there may be a connection between the semantics of *mesostrophoniai* and Messon".[2] St. Caciagli follows Robert: "The adjective '*mesostrophonios*' that names the days in which – according to Hesychius – the Lesbians perform a communal sacrifice (ἐν αἶc Λέcβιοι κοινὴν θυcίαν ἐπιτελοῦcιν) possibly hints at Messon: its meaning is perhaps 'when (the Lesbians) move on towards Messon'".[3]

However, the linguistic obstacles in this way of interpreting the adjective are too great to overcome. Firstly, it is not the Lesbians who 'move on towards' but the days. Secondly, they do not 'move on towards' but they 'turn or rotate towards'. Thirdly, they do not 'turn or rotate towards Messon' but 'towards the middle or the half'. 'Days that rotate' recall the popular image of turning or rotating time (περιτελλομένου ἔτεοc, περιπλομένου ἐνιαυτοῦ, ἐνιαυτοῦ κύκλοc, ἐνιαύcιοc κύκλοc, τροχοί or τρόχοι, *al.*). Here, it is the days that rotate toward the middle, ἡμέρα being used in its round-the-clock sense, from midnight to midnight, so that its two parts, daylight and night, come to the middle. In other

---

[1] Robert (1960), 303–304, (reprinted in (1969), vol. 2, 801–831); the suggestion was already made by Robert (1925) 423 n. 5. See also Treu ²1958 (¹1954), 237.
[2] Bierl/Lardinois (edd.) (2016), 449–492, esp. 463–464 and n. 29.
[3] (2016), 428 n. 21.

words, the days that were before shorter than the nights or the other way around now rotate to reach the middle point and become equal.

The arrival of the days at the middle occurs at the equinoxes (Gr. ἰcημερία), whether vernal or automnal, but we can be pretty sure that it is the vernal equinox that we should concern ourselves with. That particular time is marked by worldwide celebrations for welcoming spring, the season of nature resurrection and rebirth. Sappho, speaking of the festival in question, closes her prayer to Hera (fr. 17.20) with ἦ]ρ ἀπίκεcθαι, 'spring to come' – not, as supplemented by the editors, ῞Η]ρ', ἀπίκεcθαι, 'Hera, to come'; cf. Longus, *Daphnis et Chloe* 4.8.3 ἀφίξεται τὸ ἦρ. Lesbos, an island of agrarian as well as seafaring inhabitants, in addition to celebrating the vegetation revival, had a special interest in the coming of spring, since it marked the beginning of the Aegean sea's navigability. It is in that time that the people of Lesbos assembled for offering a communal sacrifice.[4]

A temple was really excavated in 1885/86 at Messon, while the hieron was also mentioned inscriptionally: ἐν τῶ ἴρω τῶ ἐμ Μέc[cω *IG* XI,4 1064, b, (32) 45, ca. 200–167 BC from Delos (*IG* XII Suppl. 136); cf. δικάcταιc εἰc Μέccον McCabe, *Miletos Inscriptions* 26, C, (70) 79, post 167 BC (*IG* XII Suppl. 139). Its construction was, however, dated to the first half of the fourth century BC by Koldewey, its excavator, still later by other archaeologists.[5] Finally, a coin of the Κοινὸν Λεcβίων with the bust of Commodus struck under cτρατηγόc Pomponius Septorianus, AD 180–182, shows on its reverse the façade of an octastyle temple, apparently the seat of the koinon, no doubt the Messon temple. Not even the god worshipped in the temple was immediately evident. According to H.G. Lolling, the epigraphist who collaborated with Koldewey, it might be Aphrodite. The inscriptions, however, though late, indicate that the Messon hieron was a pan-Lesbian centre, where disputes between the cities of the island were arbitrated by independent mediators. In any case, no straightforward evidence connected the place with the sanctuary of Hera, Zeus, and Dionysus, and even if it did, date considerations ruled out the possibility that it could be the temenos mentioned by Sap-

---

4 It is strange that modern scholarship has fully disregarded Max Treu's opinion, who also approached the solution from an astronomical point of view; (1968), 236. The only difference is that he took μέccον as referring to 'years' and not 'days' (μεcοcτροφώνιαι ἡμέραι), and so he concluded with summer or winter 'solstice', instead of 'equinox', when day and night are of equal length.

5 Kourtzellis (2012), section 8.2, records a wide range of proposed datings from the early fourth cent. to c. 175 BC. A short selection: Koldewey (1890), 58 (first half of the fourth cent.); Picard (1962), II, 43–69 (c. 280 BC); Kontis (1977), 355 §1861 (second half of the fourth cent. or the early third); Acheilara (2004), 37 (last decades of the fourth cent.).

pho and Alcaeus. Yet, most items of scholarly bibliography that I was able to consult identify the Messon temple with the temenos of the Lesbian Triad. Only J. Quinn proposed a location in Ἅγιος Φωκᾶς, one of the southernmost capes of Lesbos, out of the Kalloni Gulf and the Πυρραίων εὔριπος. An inscription at the place testifies a sanctuary of Διόνυσος Βρησαγένης.[6] Finally, Picard (note 5 above) questioned both Messa and Cape Phokas.

However, the late seventh (Sappho) and early sixth (Alcaeus) century poetic references to the specific sanctuary and festival can perhaps help in answering the question about the location.[7] I have made a painstaking examination of the papyri that contain the particular poems and discussed the textual problems, offering a somewhat different text in places.[8]

Starting with Alcaeus, I read the beginning of fr. 129 as follows:

```
      ὄχθοισιν Ἀ]κράγα τόδε Λέσβιοι
      ἆ[ι] λάμπας εὔδειλον τέμενος μέγα
      ξῦνον κά[τε]σσαν, ἐν δὲ βώμοις
4     ἀθανάτων μακάρων ζέθηκαν
      κἀπωνύμασσαν Ἀντίαον Δία
      σὲ δ' Αἰολήιαν [κ]υδαλίμαν θέον
      πάντων γενέθλαν, τὸν δὲ τέρτον
8     τόνδε κεμήλιον ὠνύμασσ[α]ν
      Ζόννυσσον ὠμήσταν·
```

By the banks of A]cragas the Lesbians set up this great communal sanctuary, conspicuous like a beacon, and set up in it altars of the blessed immortals, one for each, and gave Zeus the eponym Antiaos (god of suppliants), (named) you as Aeolian, glorious goddess, Genetrix of all, and the third, this one dressed in fawnskin, they named Dionysus Raw-flesh-eater.

If the opening gap is correctly supplemented ὄχθοισιν Ἀ]κράγα, then the sanctuary must have been contiguous to a river. ᾱ-stem (first declension) Ἀκράγης was the name of the river running by and giving the name to the Sicilian city of Acragas. In Lesbian the first declension genitive would be Ἀκράγᾱ. The supplement is not certain, but the proposal for a river-name has been made by other scholars as well (Lobel, Gallavotti, Collart), though with a different name

---

6 Quinn (1961).
7 The proposed rough dates of the poems depend on the age of the poets when they composed the specific poems: Sappho, very young, since she pleads with her mother to let her go to Hera's festival, Alcaeus, mature, since he lives in exile at Pyrrha.
8 See above '10. The Danaans in Lesbos (Sappho fr. 17 V.)' and '12. Alcaeus on the Lesbian Triad Festival', from where some observations were literally reproduced here.

(Ἀ]ράξα). Reading Ξ is, however, impossible. Though Τ is possible, the letter must be Γ with a short leftward projection of the horizontal, as it appears elsewhere too in the same papyrus: 130 b.6 κακΓεγηρας', 8 εΓ[; discussed by Page (1955), 204. In any case, whatever its name was, the river closest to Pyrrha, the city built at the north of the east coast of the Kalloni gulf, where Alcaeus lived in exile when he wrote this poem, is the one now called Βούβαρης.[9]

However, Koldewey, in the end of the 19th century, knows the river by the name Καβουροπόταμος, 'crab-river', a name still in use for the principal one of the streams forming the river. Can it be accidental that the Sicilian Ἀκράγης was also a crab-river? Not only were the freshwater crabs of Ἀκράγης famous, but the crab was also the symbol of the city of Acragas and it prominently featured on the city's coins, sometimes together with a shrimp. The etymology given

Fig. 1: Coin of Sicilian Acragas

by Polybius, 9.27.10 Büttner–Wobst, τὸν ποταμὸν καὶ τὴν πόλιν ἀπὸ τῆς χώρας ὠνομάσθαι Ἀκράγης διὰ τὸ εὔγεων, i.e. from ἄκρα γῆς, is unacceptable. I do not know whether ἀκραγ- can be linguistically associated with crab or, generally, crustaceans. It may be significant that κραγών,[10] a kind of shrimp, is mentioned by Aristotle, *HA* 525b 2, together with the ποτάμιοι καρκίνοι, the river crabs, in

---

9 Regressively formed from ψάρια βουβαρίcια, 'farmed fish', from Lat. *vivarium*, 'fish-pond'. In recent years the lagoon in the river's mouth was transformed by means of large concrete barriers into an artificial fish farm.

10 The fem. noun, recorded only from Aristotle and Hesychius, vacillates between κραγών and κραγγών. Aristotle's best tradition (Cᵃ, P) gives κραγόνες at *HA* 525b 2, but κραγγών after a few lines, at b 21 and b 29 (where a group of MSS give κράγγη). Hsch. κ 3904 κραγών· ἔνυδρον ζῷον. καὶ εἶδος καρίδος has been unnecessarily 'emended' to κραγγών and is thus published. In reverse, the next article in Hesychius, κ 3905 κραγγών· κίccα, has also been 'emended' to κραγών.

the passage where marine animal life is explored, given that a great part of the philosopher's study was made at the lagoon of Pyrrha, in other words, at the mouth of Καβουροπόταμος.[11] Can then ἀκράγᾱς (ποταμός), with ἀ- intensive,[12] denote '(river) with an abundance of crustaceans'? The river flows to the north of Pyrrha, less than ½ km from the city's walls. Since also the sanctuary was ἆ̣[ι] λάμπας εὔδειλον, 'conspicuous like a beacon', it must have been well visible from Pyrrha, therefore quite close to the city.

Alc. 130a combined with the note of a scholiast asserts that close to Alcaeus' residence, i.e., Pyrrha, was the wall of Hera's sanctuary (τεῖχος βασιλήιον; schol. τὸ τῆς Ἥρας) and, contiguous with it, a marshy tract of land or backwater (ἕλει), which seems to suggest closeness to a river mouth.

In Alc. 130b.13–14

εἴρπ[ο]ν̣ [δ]' ὧν̣ μακάρων ἐς τέμ[ε]νος θέων
ἐς π[ρηῶνα μ]ε̣[λ]α̣ίνας ἐπίβαις χθόνος κτλ.

So, I came to the sanctuary of the blessed gods having climbed up the p[romontory] of the black earth, etc.

Admittedly, π[ρηών, 'headland, promontory', is by no means certain, but at least ἐπίβαις asserts that the place was elevated.

Sa. 17 most probably names the sanctuary as Ἥραον, but does not help particularly in identifying its location. Legend or not, one or more large docks must be presupposed for the numerous Danaan ships returning from Troy to be moored, as well as a wide flat countryside close by for the army of the three kings to encamp and to conduct athletic games. The first presumption applies better in the area of Pyrrha, where several inlets and bays might provide safer mooring facilities than the wide and fully open gulf of Messon. The second presumption can apply both in the wide plain of Messon and the extended flat seaside areas to the south of Pyrrha.

Now, close to the walls of Pyrrha, and the banks of Kavouropotamos there is a small rocky promontory, some 500 m. long, and c. 350 m. at its largest width. It is called Γιαλοβούνι, i.e. 'seashore-hill'. We can be sure that a construction on this foreland would be clearly visible from Pyrrha, especially gleaming like a beacon when the sun lighted it. Yet, no traces of ancient ruins have been detected upon Gialovouni.

---

[11] Leroi (2014). Biologists are still discovering new species of shrimps in Lesbos. *Hippolyte sapphica* is such a new species. D'Udekem d'Acoz (1993).

[12] Cf. ἄβιος 'rich'; ἄβρομοι αὐίαχοι 'shouting, yelling'; ἄεδνον· πολύφερνον; ἄξυλος 'thick with trees'; ἀσπερχές 'unceasingly'; al.

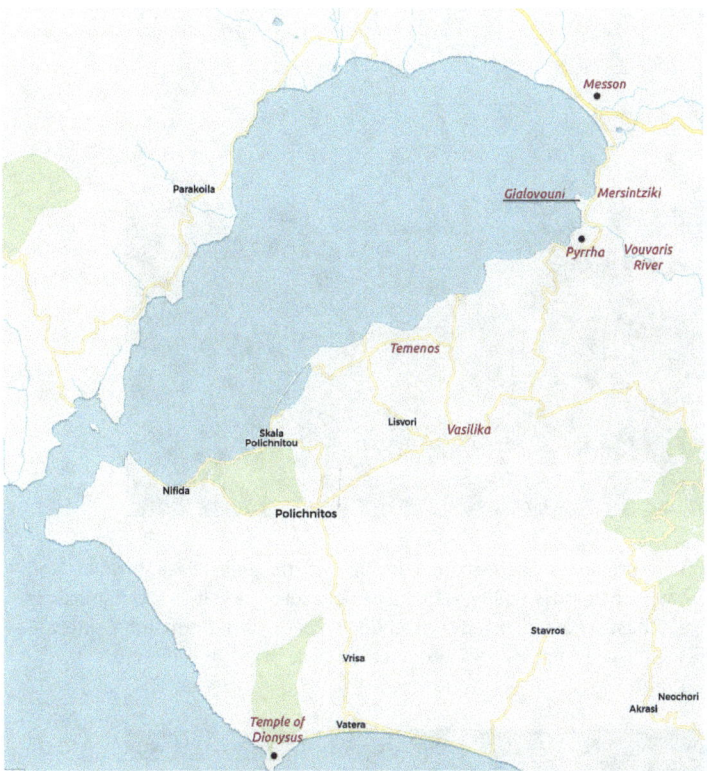

Fig. 2: The Πυρραίων εὔριπος or Gulf of Kalloni with the places mentioned in this article.

However, in the Google Earth images some clearly discernible traces speak for a destroyed temple at this area. Somewhat less than 200 m. from the base of the promontory, at a height of c. 50 m. in the southern side, i.e., the side visible from Pyrrha, a straight-line row of eight circular white spots, presumably remainders of column-bases, in equal distance between each other suggest a prostyle octastyle temple viewing to the northwest. (Coordinates: 39°09′57″ N, 26°17′07″ E). The length between the first and last spot is c. 24 m. – greater precision is impossible. In front of the columns there are distinct signs of the crepidoma. Nothing remains in the other sides of the construction, though the signs left beside the vegetation of trees and shrubs clearly suggest relics of straight-line masonry on the southwestern and the southeastern sides.

Fig. 3: The Γιαλοβούνι promontory as seen from the hill of Pyrrha. In-between, the mouth of Βούβαρης or Καβουροπόταμος is visible, with the modern concrete fish-farm constructions. The shore at the mouth must have changed since antiquity, because of the mouth's silting. Before and after the mouth, wide marshy areas extend even close to the modern road.

Fig. 4: Γιαλοβούνι in the Google Earth Images.

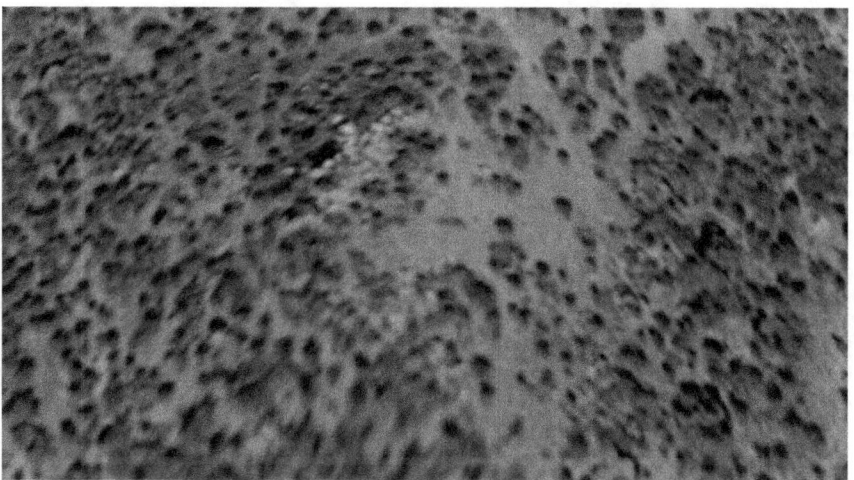

Fig. 5: Enlargement of the particular spot of the octastyle temple. Remarkable is the dark coloured parallelogram area in front of the columned façade, possibly a trench left after the entrance stairs were removed. Evident is also, among the trees and shrubs, the decolorized ground that outlines the area of the foundations of the destroyed temple.

Their margin is wider than the octastyle façade and longer than the expected dimensions of the temple stonework, as is normal with the temple crepidoma, which always extends beyond the margins of the building. The northeastern side of the rectangle is undetectable, but this may be due to the sunlight angle at the time the Google air-photograph was taken (June 3, 2016). There seem to be further traces of man-made constructions on the promontory, but nothing is certain. For instance, the base of the promontory seems to be walled all the way through: Alc. 130a.15 τεῖχος βαcιλήϊον; schol. τὸ τῆc Ἥραc. Can also the two semicircular structures to the north and west of the temple come from the altars mentioned by Alcaeus, 129.3–4 ἐν δὲ βώμοιc ἀθανάτων μακάρων ζέθηκαν?

Koldewey, speaking about the ruined church of S. Demetrius, somewhat beyond the southern walls of Pyrrha, mentions that relics of stylobate blocks and other shapeless pieces of volcanic rock (liparite) from the Messa temple were built in it.[13] The distance from the Messa temple is quite long (c. 4800 m. away as the crow flies, much longer by a land route), so Koldewey conjectures that the pieces were probably carried by boat. However, it would be immensely easier to carry the relics by land from the distinctly closer Gialovouni temple.

---

13 Koldewey (1890), 28.

I shall not discuss the problems posed by the references of Plinius and Strabo to the way Pyrrha was destroyed: Plinius, *N.H.* 2.206, *Pyrrham et Antissam circa Maeotim* (!) *pontus abstulit*; 5.139, *Pyrrha hausta est mari*; Strabo 13.2.4, ἡ δὲ Πύρρα κατέστραπται, τὸ δὲ προάστειον οἰκεῖται καὶ ἔχει λιμένα, ὅθεν εἰς Μιτυλήνην ὑπέρβασις σταδίων ὀγδοήκοντα. There has been an extended discussion for correcting, explaining, and reconciling the controversial references, which can possibly be definitely answered by the archaeological underwater survey projected at the area. But, whatever the answer might be, the agreement, on the one hand, between the two authors about the destruction of the city, and, on the other, the disappearance of the city's name from every literary or inscriptional source for more than one and a half centuries cannot be disputed. The likeliest surmise is a strong earthquake that demolished the city that was built on the solid rocky ground of the hill rising between the locality of Achladeri and the mouth of Vouvaris / Kavouropotamos, and whose ancient walls survived to a considerable range among extended ruins. After an indefinite period of time, Pyrrha or at least its suburban area must have healed its wounds and so it survived as an autonomous city, much before the time of Strabo and Pliny.

If the surmise about an earthquake is granted, the time this earthquake occurred is another question with no firm answer. No doubt, this was done some time within the wide margin between 334 and 167 BC, when, as mentioned above, references to the name of the city disappear from literary or inscriptional sources.[14] I do not know what evidence suggested the date of 231 BC put forward by M. Michaelides.[15] M. Paraskevaidis describes the suggestion as "ohne wissenschaftlichen Nachweis" and "unbegründete Hypothese".[16] I admit that the proposal I am making would require an earlier earthquake, possibly one closer to the turn of the century (± 300), but any hypothesis is unprovable.

What I am speculating is that the Messon temple was built, after the Gialovouni temple was destroyed together with Pyrrha, in order to be the venue for the pan-Lesbian festival that was compulsorily discontinued because of the demolition of the Gialovouni temple. The wide plain around it could offer facilities for thousands of visitors, unlike the narrow and rocky hill of Gialovouni, where the worshippers should have been accommodated in the flat seaside areas out of the promontory. The new location was not too far away, only some 3800 m. to the

---

14 Koldewey (1890), 28 f.
15 *Michaelides* (1909), I 43–44 (*non vidi*).
16 (1963), 1407. The seismologist G.A. Papadopoulos strongly criticizes the unauthorized date (2015), 24–28. Nevertheless, the ghost date of 231 BC is still repeated in numerous both erudite and non-scholarly publications whether as a fact or a possibility.

north, and so, if an extensive building project was undertaken, some intact shapeless pieces from the foundations and neutral blocks from the other stonework could be carried from the Gialovouni temple rubble to Messa for filling in parts of the masonry not visually exposed. The relics of foundations excavated by L. Acheilara and described as belonging to an archaic stage of the late classical (or early Hellenistic) temple may well have come from such a transference.[17] This presumption posits that the new temple, at least its superstructure, would be constructed with the same material as the previous one. Well, just a short distance, less than half km, to the east of Gialovouni an ancient quarry of rhyolite (liparite) has been identified, whose material is believed to have been used for the construction of the Messon temple. Actually, an unfinished column drum remains there undetached from the rock. However, another ancient liparite quarry, perhaps of the same vein as the Gialovouni one, is found much closer to the Messon temple, only 1780 m. to the south of it.[18] So, nothing precludes the same material being used much earlier in the adjacent to the quarry Gialovouni temple. This speculation adds, I believe, a further answer to the question posed by Kontis (1977), 356 §1868 f., why the humble liparite was preferred to marble in Messon.

Be that as it may, a most impressive evidence of the relationship between the two temples is the eight-column façade of both, a quite rare characteristic in ancient Greek temple architecture. A second impressive similarity is the width of the columned façade: c. 24 m. the Gialovouni temple, 23,78 m. the Messon temple. If the Gialovouni temple is of the prostyle type, it presents an unusual orientation: unlike the norm of Greek temples which are east-oriented (i.e., the direction in which the god of the cult statue is looking is the rising sun), here the temple is oriented to the northwest. As regards the Messon temple, the general assumption, already since the excavation of Koldewey is that it is east-oriented, an assumption that was materialized through Acheilara's restoration. Being completely unqualified for such a technical investigation and not an eye-witness, I am admittedly the least entitled person to raise objections. However, my feeling from the published air-photographs and architectural charts of the restored temple is that we are dealing with a northwest-oriented structure. If this impression could be confirmed, then the exceptional orientation of both temples might possibly point to the Thessalian Aeolis as the specific provenance of the Aeolian inhabitants of Lesbos together with the deity principally worshipped in the temenos, Hera Aiolēia. The Gialovouni temple is oriented c. 30° more to the north, but still to the

---

17 Acheilara (2004), 20, with photo.
18 Kontis (1977), 349 §1831; Acheilara (2004), map p. 53, positions 2 and 3; Kokkorou-Alevra *et al.* (2014), 19, position 26.

northwest. Possibly, the orientation was dictated by the uneven ground conditions on the rocky hill of Gialovouni, subsequently corrected in the smooth terrain of the Messon plain.

An interesting mention of Gialovouni comes from local folklore. Several narratives connect Βασιλικά, a village c. 8 km. in straight line from Gialovouni to the southwest, with a certain royal castle.[19] Some researchers identified the legendary castle with the Byzantine tower found at the site of Σκαμνιούδ' close to the seaside of the village Λισβόρι equally distanced from Gialovouni.[20] Others, however, linked it with the ruins on the hill of Pyrrha, which is in the immediate vicinity of Gialovouni.[21] This walled hill is considered to be the castle (Καστρί, Καστρέλλ') of the Byzantine Βασιλικά, the modern village being quite remote. Now, legend has it that an underground passage started from the castle, a tunnel so narrow that only a stooped man could enter it. It is said that only one man known to the elders of the village managed to pass it. The underground passage led to and ended in Gialovouni.

Though folk tradition links these legends with the Byzantine era and the imaginary passage with an escape route of an anonymous Byzantine king, I cannot help associating them with the mention in Alcaeus fr. 130a V. of a certain τεῖχος βαcιλήιον close to a marsh in his exile place, i.e., Pyrrha. The scholiast in the papyrus explains: τὸ τῆc Ἥραc, i.e., the wall of Hera's sanctuary. In Sappho's *Brothers Poem* 5–9 the young poetess pleads with her mother to send her to pray to βαcίληαν Ἥραν for her brother's safety. As we know from Sappho's fr. 17 V., we are dealing with the Ἡραῖον (Ἥραον), the temenos of Hera Aiolēia, where every year Lesbians from all over the island collected together for celebrating the coming of spring and where Lesbian girls gathered for competing in a beauty contest (Καλλιcτεῖα). The same custom *mutatis mutandis* lives on, since the inhabitants of Hagia Paraskevi, a town distanced at least 13 km. away, collect together every year in Mersintziki, a picturesque seaside location close to the base of the Gialovouni promontory, for celebrating May Day.[22] Apparently, the τεῖχος

---

19 Alvanos (2008).
20 Charitonidis (1960), 236 ff.
21 Moutzouris (1962), 51 ff.
22 The place name comes from Turkish *mersincik*, 'myrtle-grove', but it was changed by archaeologists to Messintziki, for connecting the site with the remote Messon by producing a hybrid toponym with the Turkish suffix -*cik*. Myrtle shrubs and trees (*myrtus communis*) grow in abundance in the specific area. In the map of the website lesvosgeopark.gr, the area is named Μυρσινιά. The site is right on the border with the pinewooded heights of Τσαμλίκι (= Turk. *çamlık*, pinewoods), i.e., Theophrastus' (*H. pl.* 3.9.5) Πυρραίων ὄροc τὸ πιτυῶδεc.

βαcιλήιον was the defensive wall of the temenos. Conclusively, tradition connects the Heraion (queenly) castle wall with the temple on the Gialovouni foreland.

By this entirely empirical observation, I wish to show firstly that the location of the sanctuary seen, visited, and described by Sappho and Alcaeus was on the Gialovouni promontory, and secondly that the Messa temple succeeded the Gialovouni one after the latter's destruction. We do not know when the temple was built inside the sanctuary, but when Alcaeus compares what he sees with a beacon, he must be seeing a temple. No doubt, relocation of a specific worship is questionable in Greek religious norm, but extraordinary circumstances, like a destructive earthquake, may have dictated it. If neither the temple nor the supporting city existed anymore, the situation might force such a relocation. The distance was short and the new site was still within the Pyrrhaean region. Also, the replication of some architectural characteristics (octastyle, c. 24 m. façade, possibly unusual orientation) perhaps with some of the old temple's materials, would mitigate the exceptional undertaking. Though, in the words of Alcaeus, "the Lesbians set up this great communal sanctuary", the old temenos was walled out of fear of enemy invasions. The new temple was constructed after the Macedonian state terminated inter-city wars, which accounts for the unwalled site of Messon.

I cannot prove that the relics on Gialovouni were of the archaic period, in other words that the temple seen by Alcaeus was the selfsame as the destroyed one, and that it had not experienced any changes or rebuildings during the centuries that elapsed till the earthquake. Another question that remains unanswered for me is the modern place name Τέμενοc still in use on the east shore of the gulf of Kalloni,[23] and Τεμενίτηc, a nearby hill, some 11 km. SW of Messon and 7.5 km. SW of Gialovouni, as the crow flies.[24] A late 3rd-early 4th c. AD cadastral inscription (IG XII,2 79.6) mentions χωρίον Λευκὴ Ἀκτὴ cὺν τεμένει as part of a land property in the area, indeterminately somewhere in the region. Answers can be given only through *in situ* archaeological investigation.[25]

---

[23] In modern times noticed by Newton (1865), I 92 f.
[24] Max Treu (¹1954), 237, though placing Τέμενοc to the SW of Pyrrha, still identifies it with the Messon sanctuary.
[25] My thanks are due to my colleagues G.M. Sifakis and M. Tiverios for substantial encouragement and advice; *in primis* to Dr. J. Kourtzellis, who gave me the benefit of his expert knowledge of Lesbos and its antiquities.

14 Who was Onymacles the Athenian?

(Alcaeus 130b V. = 130,16–39 LP)

⊗ Ἀγνώϲτ[ο]ιϲ βιότοιϲ [β]αῖϲ ὀ τάλαιϲ ἔγω
ζώω μοῖραν ἔχων ἀγροϊωτίκαν,
ἰμέρρων ἀγόραϲ ἄκουϲαι
4 καρυ[ζ]ομέναϲ, ὦ (Ἀ)γεϲιλαΐδα,

καὶ β[ό]λλαϲ· τὰ πάτηρ καὶ πάτεροϲ πάτηρ
καγγεγήραϲ' ἔχοντεϲ πεδὰ τωνδέων
τὼν [ἀ]λλαλοκάκων πολ[[ε]]ίταν,
8 ἔγ[ωγ' ἀ]πὺ τούτων ἀπελήλαμαι

φεύγων ἐϲχατίαιϲ· ὠϲ δ' Ὀνυμακλέηϲ
ὠθάναιοϲ ἐοίκηϲ' ἀλυκαιχμίαιϲ
φ⌊εύγων⌋ τὸν ⌊π⌋όλεμον· ϲτάϲιν γὰρ
12 πρὸϲ κρέ[ϲϲον]αϲ οὐκ ἄρμενον ὀννέλην·

Before proceeding with the interpretation of the first three stanzas of Alc. fr. 130b which concern the title question, it is useful to discuss a few textual or interpretative points that are necessary prerequisites for understanding the verses, which are read in POxy. 2165 fr. 1 col. II, lines 9–20 according to Lobel or, possibly, 10–21, according to my measurements. Understandably, I shall utilize the remarks I have already made in the full edition of the same poem, above '12. Alcaeus on the Lesbian Triad Festival'.

1 ΑΓΝΌΙϹΤ[.]ΙϹ pap. It is obvious that by deleting initially the iota (by blackening), then both omicron and iota (by striking through), then joining the nu with the sigma (by hyphenating), but keeping the acute above omicron, the corrector intended to substitute the ΟΙ with another accented vowel. The correct vowel must have been written in the intralinear area above the corrections, where, however, a large lacuna obstructs reading. ἀγνώϲτοιϲ, 'unfamiliar', obviously 'to me', suggests itself. | δυϲβιότοιϲ Page, because "the noun βίοτοϲ is very seldom used in the plural number". The plural is, however, inevitable, when one refers to more than one 'ways of living', whether because the subjects are many (Aesch. *Eu.* 960 νεανίδων ... ἀνδροτυχεῖϲ βιότουϲ), or because the ways of living or the 'livelihoods' are more than one, as here. It is the changes in the way of living of the aristocrat Alcaeus that accounts for the plural of βίοτοϲ. An oppositional reference to Alcaeus' integrity (ἄγνοϲ τοὶϲ βιότοιϲ, 'though I am moral in my life'), doesn't fit either the corrected letters or Alcaeus' character. As for the much talked about ἄγνοϲ = λύγοϲ, 'chaste-tree', it is time to dispense with it. |

The word following must be [β]αῖc. Even traces of the β are discernible in the faded area, very similar to the β of βιότοιc in the previous word. βαίνω c. acc. cogn. (e.g., Pi. fr. 191 ἔβαινε ... κέλευθον, Eur. *Ion* 96 τὰc Καcταλίαc ... βαίνετε δίναc, Theoc. 1.140 ἔβα ῥόον), is used metaphorically in the sense 'go through (pass through)'.

10 ὠθάναιοc: The reading was made possible only after M.W. Haslam published POxy. 3711 in *Ox. Pap.* LIII, 1986 (see below). Lobel/Page (1955) and Voigt (1971) publish ἔνθα[δ'] οἶοc.

12 πρὸc κρέ[ccova]c is palaeographically possible. What Lobel saw as "litterae o ut vid. malae scriptae pars sup. sin." is actually an untidily written ε, with the upper curve very close to the mid stroke, similar to, e.g., 6 Εχοντεc. The rest, though giving the impression that it is *longius spatio*, can be easily accomodated in the existing space, especially if the tiny pieces containing οc and κρε come closer to each other and both to the initial πρ, so providing for space of one more letter. | Parallel occurrences suggest that in this context the active (cτάcιν) ἀνελεῖν means 'to get rid of strife', and that 'to take up strife', which seems to be expected here, is expressed only by the med. ἀνελέcθαι. I am afraid, however, that the investigation has been moving in the wrong direction. One of the subdivisions of the 'take up' meaning concerns prevailing in agonistic activities, and in this case both act. and med. are equivalent. In the act.: *Il.* 23.736 ἀέθλια ἀνελόντεc, 551 ἀνελὼν ἄεθλον, Hdt. 5.102 cτεφανηφόρουc ἀγῶναc ἀναραιρηκότα, 6.36 Ὀλύμπια ἀναραιρηκώc. And in the med.: Hdt. 6.70 ἀνελόμενοc Ὀλυμπιάδα, 6.103 ἀνελέcθαι Ὀλυμπιάδα, ἀνελέcθαι τὴν νίκην. In Alcaeus, cτάcιc, 'strife, contest, sedition, row', takes the place of the athletic contest; and the verb has, naturally, the meaning 'win, prevail'. In other words, cτάcιν πρὸc κρέccοναc ὀννέλην means 'to win a rebellion against more powerful people'. | For the papyrus's unmetrical ἄμεινον, Latte offered, in my view, the best solution: ἄρμενον, med. aor. 2 part. of ἀραρίcκω, coll. Theoc. 29.9 (πῶc ταῦτ' ἄρμενα;), there too c. inf. Thus, οὐκ ἄρμενόν (ἐcτι), referring to the preceding statement ('to win a rebellion against more powerful people'), means 'is unfit, is incoherent, is illogical'.

> Having [g]one through unfam[il]iar ways of living, I, poor wretch, pass my life having an agricultural lot, yearning to hear the assembly being summoned, o Agesilaidas, and the council; what my father and my father's father have grown old with, among these citizens harmful to each other, therefrom I have been driven away fleeing to the middle of nowhere. And as Onymacles the Athenian I settled, a runaway avoiding the war; because to prevail in a rebellion against more [power]ful people is illogical.

The poem is addressed to an unknown Agesilaïdas, whether a personal name or a patronymic, apparently a friend and companion of Alcaeus. In the initial lines, the poet is deploring his repeated changes of livelihoods unfamiliar to him because of his aristocratic raising, till his present way of life, whereby he is obliged to earn his living by means of a μοῖρα ἀγροϊωτίκα, in either meaning of μοῖρα: 'the destiny of a rustic' or 'a plot of land'. Due to the intestine discord between the citizens, he is deprived of the right to participate in the civil and political life of his hometown, as well as to own and manage his paternal fortune. He has been excluded of these rights by living in exile 'in the middle of nowhere'.[1] Similar grievances are voiced also in 130a.1–10, ἀχνάcδημι κάκωc, also with the description of some of his miseries.[2] In 129.11–12 he requests that the 'Lesbian Triad' delivers him from these hardships and the painful exile: ἐκ δὲ τῶνδε μόχθων ἀργαλέαc τε φύγαc ῥύεcθε.

As the scholiast of Alc. 114 (PBerol. 9569) explains: κατὰ τὴν φυγὴν τὴν πρώτην, ὅτ' ἐπὶ Μύρcιλον κατακευαcάμενοι ἐπιβουλὴν οἱ περὶ τὸν Ἀλκαῖον καταφανέντες δέ, προφθάcαντες πρὶν ἢ δίκην ὑποcχεῖν ἔφυγον εἰc Πύρραν. It is clear that the synoptic scholion records what happened during the first exile (κατὰ τὴν φυγὴν τὴν πρώτην). Consequently, the plot against Myrsilus took place during the first φυγή, which naturally antedates the flight to Pyrrha. The latter was not a judicial exile, but an escape from Myrsilus' rule following the failure of the plot. In any case, it is clear that Alcaeus is now living in Pyrrha, some 30 km. from his hometown Mytilene.[3] Therefore, ἐcχατίαιc(ι), either 'on the outskirts' (of my hometown) or, referring to both exiles, 'in far-away places'.

The verses from ὠc δ' Ὀνυμακλέηc to τὸν πόλεμον recur in the form of lemma in the exegetical text of POxy. 3711 (*The Oxyrhynchus Papyri* LIII, 1986, ed. M.W. Haslam), fr. 306Ea col. II 31–36 Liberman:

```
31    ὠc δ' Ὀνυμακλέηc ὠθάναοc
      ἐοίκηc' ἀλυκαιχμίαιc φεύγων τ[ὸν
      π[όλ]εμον. Αἶνοc Θρ[ά]ικηc πόλιc ἐ[π'
34    Αἴνου τοῦ Γερωιέωc· ὤικηc[αν
      δὲ τὴν Αἶνον Ἀλωπεκον[νήcιοι·
36    ἠρη[μ]οῦντο δ' ὑπὸ Θραικῶ[ν . .] θε[
```

---

[1] Page (1955) disconnects τά in line 5 from the civil rights that Alcaeus longs for and interprets the passage as referring solely to the fortune piled up by his family, from which he is barred as he lives in exile. See p. 209: "[Alcaeus] broods over the loss of ancestral estates". However, it is clear that the ἀλλαλόκακοι πολῖται, 'the citizens who harm each other', deprived Alcaeus both of his civil rights and his wealth. In any case, Page's ἔγ[ωγ' is syntactically preferable to Gallavotti's ἔγ[ω δ'.

[2] See above '12. Alcaeus on the Lesbian Triad Festival'.

[3] Strabo, 13.2.4, measures 80 stadia, from the surviving in his time προάcτειον of Pyrrha to Mytilene, which is much less than the real distance. Possibly, 180 stadia?

31 δ' disp. Liberman   33 ἐ̣[π᾽ Ts. (LSJ s.v. ἐπί A.iii 2 'named after'); ἀ̣[πὸ Haslam ("though hardly suggested, is not excluded")   34 Γερωιέως perspicue legitur, Γερωιᾶ Haslam | ᾤικης[αν : κατῴικ[ιcαν Haslam   36 ἠρη[μ]οῦντο Ts., ᾐ[δι]κοῦντο Luppe | ἐπ]ιθέ[cεωc vel ἐπ]ιθέ[cεων vel ἐπ]ιθε[μένων?

We do not know how the text of POxy. 3711 would continue. Nevertheless, it has been noticed that since the lemma comes from a passage in Alcaeus' poem that specifies the conditions the poet has lived in during his banishment by using the aorist tense, ἐοίκης(α), it is distinctly possible that he refers to the place where he first dwelt as an exile, in contrast to his present situation for which he is using the present tense οἴκημι (line 16). On that account, since the exegesis starts with the mention of a city and its exact location, it is clear that this is the place where he first lived as an exile: "Aenus, a city of Thrace, named after Aenus, son of Geroeus." The exegesis goes on with the founding of Aenus by Alopekonnesians. It is clear, however, that the exegete's interest is restricted to Aenus only and he mentions the Alopekonnesians merely for introducing Aenus in a complete historical context. Further, if ἠρη[μ]οῦντο is correct, as I believe, Alopekonnesos did not exist at Alcaeus' time or rather its Greek population was totally evacuated. It seems that the evacuation (ἠρημοῦντο) of the city and the removal of the citizens to a new colony in Aenus was forced by the Thracian attacks.[4] Alopekonnesos was situated on the mid-northern coast of the Thracian Chersonese, and Aenus, just across the gulf, on the eastern side of the delta of Hebros. Aenus was populated by Aeolian Alopekonnesians who left their city and, after the establishment of the new colony, by colonists from Mytilene and Cyme, also Aeolians.[5]

Haslam refers to the mention of Aenus by Alcaeus in fr. 45, but finds "no link here with that". Also, he finds the Lesbians' clash with the Athenians over Sigeion in the Troad as the only Athenian activity in the region that might be associated with the Athenian Onymacles. Huxley (1987) added Ἐλαιοῦς, a Teian and Athenian colony on the tip of the Chersonese, whose oikistes, as Huxley claimed, was the Athenian Phrynon,[6] the same person who fought against and was killed by Pittacus over Sigeion, so that a previous implication of an Athenian from

---

[4] The city passed later into Athenian rule, but was again occupied by Thracian bandits and pirates; Dem. 23.166.
[5] Ephoros, FGrH 70 F 39, Αἶνος πόλις, ἣν Ἕλληνες τὰ πρῶτα Ἀλωπεκοννήςιοι κατῴκιcαν, ὕcτερον δ' ἐκ Μιτυλήνης ἐπηγάγοντο καὶ Κύμης ἐποίκους. Strabo 7a.1.52 πρὸς δὲ τῇ ἐκβολῇ τοῦ Ἕβρου διcτόμου ὄντος πόλις Αἶνος ἐν τῷ Μέλανι κόλπῳ κεῖται, κτίcμα Μιτυληναίων καὶ Κυμαίων, ἔτι δὲ πρότερον Ἀλωπεκοννηcίων.
[6] Though transmitted Φορβοων, which is usually emended to Φόρβας.

Elaious might be accounted for. However, in what way could this implication be compared with Alcaeus' situation, and why is Onymacles presented as Athenian and not Ἐλαιούςιος?

One of the best known topics in Alcaeus' biography is his involvement in the battle over Sigeion. Herodotus and Strabo describe how he gave up the battle throwing down his arms, which the Athenians seized and hung in front of the temple of Athena in Sigeion. Just like Archilochus (*IEG* fr. 5) or Anacreon (*PMG* 381b) or much later Horace (*carm*. 2.7), Alcaeus does not seem to be especially bothered for been accused of cowardice so far as he has saved his life; he rather appears to be amused at the idea that his arms are hung in front of Athena's temple. However, those in power in Mytilene (Melanchrus, Myrsilus?) could not be equally amused, especially if the offence of cowardice in battle came from an aristocrat whose family was noted for disruptive activity against the authorities. I do not think it would be too bold to claim that this offence won Alcaeus his first φυγή, his first flight, though no official indictment for desertion seems to have occurred. The place of this flight is unknown, but if the conjecture about ἐοίκηςα holds, it must be Aenus. The city was close to the Sigeion battlefield, avoiding the area of the Chersonese that was at risk of Thracian attacks. It was close to Mytilene: the c. 100 nautical miles needed a voyage of just 1 or 1½ day depending on the wind. It was populated by Aeolians, to a great extent Mytilenaeans, so that not only would Alcaeus feel living in a familiar environment, but would also be able to have contact, through voyagers, with his companions. He actually dispatches a message, no doubt in poetic form, to his companion Melanippus in Mytilene announcing his misfortune. This is the information given by Herodotus, 5.95 (Alc. fr. 401B b; test. 467): Ἀλκαῖος ὁ ποιητὴς ςυμβολῆς γενομένης καὶ νικώντων Ἀθηναίων αὐτὸς μὲν φεύγων ἐκφεύγει, τὰ δέ οἱ ὅπλα ἴςχουςι Ἀθηναῖοι καί ςφεα ἀνεκρέμαςαν πρὸς τὸ Ἀθήναιον τὸ ἐν Ϲιγείῳ. ταῦτα δὲ Ἀλκαῖος ἐν μέλει ποιήςας ἐπιτιθεῖ ἐς Μυτιλήνην ἐξαγγελλόμενος τὸ ἑωυτοῦ πάθος Μελανίππῳ ἀνδρὶ ἑταίρῳ. Strabo's information agrees, adding an Alcaeus distich to that effect, 13.11.38 (Alc. fr. 401B a; test. 468; metr. gl^d ia). The distich is problematically transmitted:[7] Ἀλκαῖός φηςιν ὁ ποιητὴς ἑαυτὸν ἔν τινι ἀγῶνι κακῶς φερόμενον τὰ ὅπλα ῥίψαντα φυγεῖν· λέγει δὲ πρός τινα κήρυκα, κελεύςας ἀγγεῖλαι τοῖς ἐν οἴκῳ·

> Ἄλκαος ςὸς ἄρ'· οἶ ἔντεα δ' οὐ τυχόντ' ἀλκτήριον
> ἐς Γλαυκώπιον ἶρον ὀνεκρέμαςςαν Ἄττικοι.

---

[7] For its restoration, I primarily depend on Strabo's cod. F (Vat. gr. 1329).

còc ἄροι Strab. F, explic. Ts., cóoc, cῶoc vel om. rell., cάoc {ἄροι} edd. | ἔντεα δ' Wesseling, ἐνθάδ' codd. | οὐ τυχόντ' Ts., οὐχυτον, οὐκυτόν, οὐκ αὐτόν codd. | ἀλκτήριον Casaubon, ἀληκτορίν codd.

Hey! This is your friend Alcaeus! But his arms, lacking a protection, the Attic men hung at the temple of Glaucopis.

The seemingly disjointed ἄρ' denotes the "surprise occasioned by enlightenment" (Denniston, *GP* 35) and is used in the sense of LSJ A.I 2 "to draw attention, *mark you!*". The same particle quite often closes short conversational sentences; Denniston, *GP* 41. Strict Lesbian prosodic rules should dictate a synecphonesis of οἶ ἔντεα as ὤντεα (Hamm 39 § 80), which would, however, be unintelligible to the common listener. For οἶ ἔντεα δ' ... ὀνεκρέμαccαν cf. Herodotus τὰ δέ οἱ ὅπλα ... ἀνεκρέμαcαν. The similarities indicate that Herodotus speaks of the same poem, but was further aware of the addressee. Also, cóc in the Strabo distich shows that there was only one recipient of the telegraphic epigram, and not generally οἱ ἐν οἴκῳ. For τυγχάνω c. acc. (usually but not necessarily plural) see LSJ s.v. B ii 2b and K.-G. i.350.

The poem that mentions Aenus (fr. 45) has a different metre and is more elaborate. Yet, it has some common structural features with other Alcaic poems of exile, those, however, written later in Pyrrha (frr. 129, 130b). They start with an acclaim of the site (fr. 45 Ἔβρε, κάλλιcτοc ποτάμων πὰρ Αἶνον | ἐξίηcθ' ἐc πορφυρίαν θάλαccαν κτλ. ~ fr. 129 ὄχθοιcιν Ἀ]κράγα τόδε Λέcβιοι | ἆ[ι] λάμπαc εὔδειλον τέμενοc μέγα κτλ.)[8] and continue praising a beautiful spectacle of the girls in the area (fr. 45 maidens applying with their tender hands the river's water as a balm over their beautiful thighs ~ fr. 130b maidens participating in the beauty contest).

Still, Ὀνυμακλῆc is unknown, and his part in the comparison with Alcaeus' situation is unexplained. Page (1955), 204, describes him as "a type of exile or hermit or lone-wolf". 'Exile' may be natural, but how can a 'hermit or lone-wolf' be compared with a man who describes himself as "yearning to hear the assembly and the council being summoned"? On the other hand, what business would an Athenian have in Aenus, a predominantly Aeolian and Lesbian city? It is noteworthy that it was in Aenus, i.e., after the Sigeion incident, that Alcaeus settled (ἐοίκηc') ὠc ... Ὀνυμακλέηc ὠθάναιοc. I suspect that Alcaeus did not settle 'like Onymacles', but 'as Onymacles', in other words, 'under the alias Onymacles'. It is the familiar adverbial use of ὠc in comparisons, 'as', Lat. *ut*. E.g., Aesch. *Pers.*

---

8 See the reconstruction of the first two verses of Alc. fr. 129 V. above, in '12. Alcaeus on the Lesbian Triad Festival'.

711 βίοτον εὐαίωνα Πέρςαιc ὡc θεὸc διήγαγεc (for Dareius), *Eu.* 296 θραcὺc ταγοῦχοc ὡc ἀνὴρ ἐπιcκοπεῖ (for Athena). Alcaeus may have produced the name in disguised self-worth over his aristocratic origin and his poetic excellence: 'a man of famous name'.

But what about the gentile adjective? Here, a strange prosodic anomaly is observed. The adjective appears in POxy. 2165 as ωθάνᾱιοc (the longum sign remained unobserved), but in 3711 as ωθαναοc (3711 rarely has lectional signs). In the Lesbian dialect, -ναοc is the proper form (*IG* XII,2.18; Hamm § 55), but the alpha in this case is, as a rule, short; cf., e.g., Ἄλκᾰοc, Μυτιληνάωι, Ὕρρᾱον. Inscriptionally, -αιοc occasionally occurs, influenced from the koine spelling, but not in poetic texts. Here the metre (gl^c) demands × × – ᴗ, which excludes ὠθάνᾰοc. The reading of POxy. 2165 ωθάνᾱιοc scans, but is not the ordinary Lesbian form. Unless a different adjective is posited. Ἀθανάα is confirmed basically through the Aeol. idyll Theoc. 28.1. In Alc. 298.9, 325.1 -να- falls in an anceps position. The unrecorded in Lesb. contracted Ἀθάνᾱ, whether from Ἀθανάα or straight from Ἀθαναία (Hamm § 64 d, θαᾶc[cει > θάccει, Παιάον' > Πάον'), should produce Ἀθάνᾱοc or even, with the pre-contracted form indicated in writing, Ἀθάνᾱιοc. Naturally, this would not mean 'Athenian' but 'of Athena', 'devoted to Athena', i.e., Att. Ἀθήναιοc, not Ἀθηναῖοc. Notably, though Alcaeus names the Athena temple at Sigeion Γλαυκώπιον, Herodotus, 5.95, names it Ἀθήναιον. Alcaeus has apparently invented a jocular alias counterpoising in playful self-abasement his great renown with his shameful conduct in the battle, reminiscent of the capture of his arms and their hanging up in front of the temple of Athena. No doubt, the alias "famous man devoted to Athena" is no more than a poetic wordplay, though, given the verb ἐοίκηc(α), it may have well worked as a real-life pseudonym. Possibly, some ignorant users might understand the gentile as 'Athenian'. However, I very much doubt that Alcaeus, while living in clearly Aeolian or Lesbian environment, would pose as citizen of Athens, the most hated city in Mytilene. Further, the employment of the name Ὀνυμακλέηc, and not the Attic Ὀνομακλῆc, is suggestive of Alcaeus' motives. For, though -κλέηc is a legitimate poetic form, Ὀνυμα-, irrespective of the word's prehistory, was distinctly Lesbian in Alcaeus' time.

The reading ἐοίκηcα λυκαιχμίαιc is strange. λυκαιχμίαιc can well mean 'a man fighting wolves', but the poet claims at the same time that he avoided fighting (φεύγων τὸν πόλεμον). Hsch. λ 1369 λυκαιχλίαc· ὁ λυκόβροτοc (*sic cod.*; -αιμίαc Latte; -βρωτοc Musurus), but λυκαιχμίαc· ὁ λυκόβρωτοc in the *Antistoecharium* of cod. Vat. gr. 23, a glossary based on Hesychius. If adopted in Alcaeus' passage, the interpretation 'eaten by wolves', even in the sense 'prey of wolves', would be immensely exaggerated, but, what is more important, the lemma λυκαιχμίας would be absurd, if the wolves were imagined to devour their prey with αἰχμαί, 'spears'.

ἀλυκαιχμίαις, 'fleeing from arms' (or 'having fled from arms'), would be a further designation of the disguised poet, also reminiscent of the Sigeion episode. The word was recognized in a palmary way by Antonietta Porro,[9] a reading which is corroborated by the habit of the scribe of the exegetical text of POxy. 3711 to separate the words: εοικης ἀλυκαιχμιαις. Porro's reading was discarded by G. Liberman.[10] S. Caciagli also disagreed and returned to the old articulation.[11] The fact that the distance between the words in POxy. 3711 is unequal, and there are cases with longer distance, does not disprove the specific *divisio verborum*. Also the absence of an apostrophe at ἐοίκης in the papyri has no evidentiary weight, because POxy. 3711 seldom and 2165 sporadically use lectional signs. The scribe of POxy. 2165 clearly did not understand the word, especially its second component, striving to make sense of it by writing αλὐκαὶμῖ᾽ᾶις. However, the initial ἀ- was certainly included in the word, since a c was added above the υ. Moreover, as the scribe feared that the c, linked as it was with the grave accent, would not be recognized, repeated it in smaller size between υ and κ. Apparently, the corrector (possibly *prima manus*) was worried about the precise form of the first component and tried to connect it with the more obvious ἀλύςκω or ἀλυςκάζω, which, however, does not scan. Even the reading λυκαιμίαις was adopted by some scholars, who took ἐοίκηςα λυκαιμίαις to mean 'I settled in the wolf-thickets' depending on the hapax of Hsch. α 1955 αἱμοί· δρυμοί. Αἰςχύλος Αἰτναίαις (fr. 9), even though the interpretation appears elsewhere as δρόμοι or δρόςοι. (Haemus Mons is not a copse or thicket.) The grammatical case of the noun was obviously taken as fem. dat. pl., which is also questionable, since the other similar instances in this poem are elided long datives, whether in midverse (9 φεύγων ἐςχατίαις᾽, ὡς) or at the end of the 3rd stanza verse in synapheia with the 4th verse (15 f. cυνόδοιcιν αὔταις᾽ | οἴκημι; 23 f. ἐπ᾽ αὔδαις᾽ | ἦι]εν, no doubt, uncertain). Page, more prudently, translates λυκαιμίαις as "a man among wolf-thickets" (LSJ Suppl., s.v. λυκαιμία, wrongly refers to Page). The confused lexicographical evidence shows that even the ancient grammarians were perplexed with the unusual word. But certainly, none would add a c to λυκαιμίαις, if he was speaking of wolves. However, on the whole it is the sense that matters. Declaring that one lived away from battles, because it is unfit to fight more powerful people

---

9 Porro (1989). A second article by Porro responded cogently to some opposed views (see Porro (1992) for complete citations).
10 Liberman (1999), vol. II, 215 n. 135.
11 Caciagli (2009).

in authority, yet lived fighting wolves or being fought by them or among wolf-thickets, is not very coherent or reasonable. It seems that the noun is a coinage by Alcaeus for avoiding the overcharged ῥίψαϲπιϲ: ἐοίκηϲ' ἀλυκαιχμίαιϲ φεύγων τὸν πόλεμον, "I settled as a runaway avoiding war". And it is no coincidence that there is an accumulation of esoteric wordplays, puns, and coinages (Ὀνυμακλέηϲ ὠθάναιοϲ, ἀλυκαιχμίαιϲ) in the same sentence that recalls the disgraceful past incident of the poet.

At Aesch. *Pers.* 1025 οὐ φυγαίχμαϲ, Triclinius comments οὐ φυγαιχμίαϲ] οὐ ῥίψαϲπιϲ, adding οὕτωϲ εὑρέθη ὁ ϲτίχοϲ ἔν τινι λίαν παλαιῷ βιβλίῳ, καὶ ἔχει πρὸϲ τὸ μέτρον ὀρθῶϲ· οἱ δὲ 'φυγαίχμαϲ' γράφοντεϲ ἀγνοοῦϲι τὰ μέτρα· ἴαμβοϲ γὰρ χρὴ εἶναι ὁλόκληροϲ.[12] The antistrophe belies Triclinius' certitude about the metre of the whole verse (Triclinius deletes the entire corresponding verse 1037), but the existence of the word, no matter if in the form φυγαίχμαϲ or φυγαιχμίαϲ and, mainly, in the meaning ῥίψαϲπιϲ is substantiated.

To recapitulate the different aspects of the conjecture, I would surmise that, after the unhappy incident in Sigeion, Alcaeus, being a ῥίψαϲπιϲ, or ἀλυκαιχμίαιϲ, as he coined it, did not return to Mytilene, but settled for some time in Aenus, whence he dispatched the distich of fr. 401 B to Melanippus in Mytilene announcing his misfortune. Later, still in Aenus, he must have written the poem of fr. 45, where he describes his pleasant experiences from the settlement. Subsequently, now in Lesbos, after an unsuccessful attempt against Myrsilus, he escaped to Pyrrha, whence he dispatched the poem of fr. 130b to Agesilaïdas, another colleague,[13] describing his adversities because of the changes in his life habits. At the same time, he assumed a nickname, Ὀνυμακλέηϲ ὁ Ἀθάναιοϲ, that served as an alias for the hiding out exile, but also humorously combined his aristocratic and poetic renown with his dishonourable performance at the Sigeion battle, when his thrown away armaments were hung by the Attic enemies in front of Athena's temple. He also describes a distraction from the depressing realities of his life by visiting the temenos of the Lesbian triad and attending the beauty contest of the Lesbian girls from afar. In the poem of fr. 129, possibly during the same visit to the temenos, he vindictively recollects that it was on the same altars of the Lesbian triad that the conspirators against Myrsilus had sworn, an oath which Pittacus, one of the swearers, had trampled all over and should therefore be punished as perjurer.

---

12 Massa Positano (²1963).
13 Unless Agesilaïdas is a patronymic, possibly of Melanippus himself.

Bibliography

Acheilara, L. (2004), ἐν τῶ ἴρω τῶ ἔμ Μέccω, Mytilene.
Acosta-Hughes, B. (2010), *Arion's Lyre: Archaic Lyric into Hellenistic Poetry*, Princeton.
Adler, A. (1931), art. Suidas, *RE*.
Alvanos, G. (2008), *Το χωριό μου Βασιλικά Λέσβου*, Athens.
Allen, T.W./Sikes, E.E. (1904), *The Homeric Hymns*, London.
Allen, T.W./Halliday, W.R./Sikes, E.E. (^{2}1936), *The Homeric Hymns*, Oxford.
Aly, W. (1920), art. Sappho, *RE*.
Bastianini, G./Casanova, A. (eds) (2007), *I papiri di Saffo e di Alceo. Atti del convegno internazionale di studi, Firenze, 8–9 giugno 2006* , in: Studi e Testi di Papirologia N.S. 9, Florence.
Barrett, W.S. (1964), *Euripides* Hippolytus, Oxford.
Beazley, J.D. (1928), *Greek Vases in Poland*, Oxford.
Beazley, J.D. (^{2}1963), *Attic Red-Figure Vase-Painters*, Oxford.
Beazley, J.D. (1971), *Paralipomena*, Oxford.
Bergk, Th. (^{4}1878–82), *Poetae Lyrici Graeci*, Lipsiae.
Bettarini, L. (2005), "Note linguistiche alla nuova Saffo", *ZPE* 154, 33–39.
Bettarini, L. (2008), "Saffo e l'aldilà in P.Köln 21351, 1–8", *ZPE* 165, 21–31.
Bierl, A. (2009), "Der neue Sappho-Papyrus aus Köln und Sapphos Erneuerung: Virtuelle Choralität, Eros, Tod, Orpheus und Musik", Center for Hellenic Studies (http://nrs.harvard.edu/urn-3:hlnc.essay:Bierl.Der_Neue_Sappho-Papyrus_aus_Koln.2009).
Bierl, A./Lardinois, A. (eds) (2016), *The Newest Sappho: P. Sapph. Obbink and P.GC inv. 105, frs. 1–4*, Leiden/Boston.
Blümel, W. (1982), *Die Aiolischen Dialekte*, Göttingen.
Bonanno, M.G. (1986–1987), "Ancora su Sapph. fr. 96, 15–17 V.", *Mus. Crit.* 21–22, 7–18.
Bowie, A.M. (1979), *The Poetic Dialect of Sappho and Alcaeus*, Cambridge.
Bruchmann, C.F.H. (1893), *Epitheta deorum, quae apud poetas Graecos leguntur*, supplement to Roscher, W.H. (1886–1937), *Ausführliches Lexikon der griechischen und römischen Mythologie*, Leipzig.
Buck, C.D. (1955), *The Greek Dialects*, Chicago.
Burris, S. (2017), "A New Join for Sappho's Kypris Poem", *ZPE* 201, 12–14.
Burris, S./Fish, J./Obbink, D. (2014), "New Fragments of Book 1 of Sappho", *ZPE* 189, 1–28.
Burton, J. (1998), "Women's Commensality in the Ancient Greek World", *G&R* 45, 143–165.
Caciagli, St. (2009), "Lupi e codardi nell'Heraion di Lesbo", *ZPE* 171, 216–220.
Caciagli, St. (2016), "Sappho fr. 17: Wishing Charaxos a Safe Trip?", in: Bierl/Lardinois, 424–48.
Chantraine, P. (1950), Review of C. Galavotti, *La lingua dei poeti eolici,* Bari/Naples 1948, *RPh* 24, 213.
Chantraine, P. (^{3}1958, 1953), *Grammaire homérique*, 2 vols., Paris.
Chantraine, P. (^{2}1961), *Morphologie historique du grec*, Paris.
Charitonidis, S. (1960), "Ἀρχαιότητες καὶ Μνημεῖα νήσων Αἰγαίου: Μυτιλήνη", Ἀρχ. Δελτ. 16, Χρονικά. 235–243.
Clayman, Dee (2011), "The New Sappho in a Hellenistic Poetry Book," *Classics @* Vol. 4: E. Greene/M. Skinner (eds) The Center for Hellenic Studies of Harvard University, online edition.

Cole, S.G. (1981), "Could Greek Women Read and Write?", in: H. Foley (ed.), *Reflections of Women in Antiquity*, New York, 219–221, 223.
Collignon, M. (1878), *Catalogue des vases peints du Musée national d'Athènes*, Paris.
Comparetti, D. (1886), *Museo Italiano di Antichità classica*, II, 41–80.
Contiades-Tsitsoni, E. (1990), *Hymenaios und Epithalamion: Das Hochzeitslied in der frühgriechischen Lyrik*, Stuttgart.
Cribiore, R. (2001), *Gymnastics of the Mind: Greek Education in Hellenistic and Roman Egypt*, Princeton.
Dakaris, S./Vokotopoulou, I./Christidis, A.Ph. (2013), *Τα χρηστήρια ελάσματα της Δωδώνης των ανασκαφών Δ. Ευαγγελίδη*, vols. 2, Athens.
Dale, Al. (2015), "The Green papyrus of Sappho (*P.GC* inv. 105) and the order of poems in the Alexandrian edition", *ZPE* 196, 17–30.
Davison, J.A. (1968), *From Archilochus to Pindar*, London.
Del Corso, L. (2004), "Scritture 'formali' e scritture 'informali' nei "volumina" da Al Hibah", *Aegyptus* 84, 33–100.
Denniston, J.D. (²1950), *The Greek Particles*, Oxford.
Di Benedetto, V. (2004), "Osservazioni sul nuovo papiro di Saffo", *ZPE* 149, 5–6.
Di Benedetto, V. (2005), "La nuova Saffo e dintorni", *ZPE* 153, 7–20.
Di Benedetto, V. (2006), "Il tetrastico di Saffo e tre postille", *ZPE* 155, 5–18.
D'Udekem d'Acoz, C. (1993), "Description d'une nouvelle crevette de l'île de Lesbos: *Hippolyte sapphica* sp. nov. (Crustacea, Decapoda, caridea, Hippolytidae)", *Belg. J. Zool.* 123 I, 55–65.
Dumont, A./Chaplain, J. (1881), *Les Céramiques de la Grèce propre. Vases peints et terres cuites*, Paris.
Edmonds, J.M. (1922), "Sappho's Book as Depicted on an Attic Vase", *CQ* 36, 1–14.
Edmonds, J.M. (1922), *Lyra Graeca*, London/Cambridge Ma.
Eitrem, S. (1912), art. Hera, *RE*.
Elytis, Od. (1984), *Σαπφώ* (Mod. Greek translation), Athens.
Esposito, E. (2005), *Il Fragmentum Grenfellianum (P.Dryton 50. Introduzione, testo critico, traduzione e commento)*, Bologna.
Fernández-Delgado, J.-A. (2015), "The New Sappho Papyrus of Cologne or the Eternal Youth of Poetry", *MH* 72, 130–141.
Ferrari, Fr. (2007), *Una mitra per Kleis. Saffo e il suo pubblico*, Pisa.
Ferrari, Fr. (2010), *Sappho's Gift. The Poet and her Community*, tr. B. Acosta-Hughes/L. Prauscello, Ann Arbor (originally *Una mitra per Kleis. Saffo e il suo pubblico*, Pisa)
Ferrari, Fr. (2014), "Saffo e i suoi fratelli e altri brani del primo libro", *ZPE* 192, 1–19.
Fränkel, H. (1955), *Wege und Formen frühgriechischen Denkens*, Munich.
Fränkel, H. (²1962), *Dichtung und Philosophie des frühen Griechentums*, Munich.
Friis Johansen, H./Whittle, E.W. (1980), *Aeschylus, The Suppliants*, Copenhagen.
Funghi, M.S. (1983), "P.Bruxell. Inv. E 7162 e P.Med. Inv.71.82. Due discussioni su 'Olimpo'", *PP* 38, 11–19.
Gallavotti, C. (1941), "L'ode saffica dell'ostracon fiorentino", *SIFC* 18, 175–202.
Gallavotti, C. (1946), "Postilla a nuovi carmi di Saffo e Alceo", *PP* 1, 119–125.
Gallavotti, C. (1947–1948), *Saffo e Alceo*, Napoli (²1956–57).
Gentili, B. (1966), "La veneranda Saffo", *QUCC* 2, 37–62.
Gronewald, M./Daniel, R.W. (2004), "Ein neur Sappho-Papyrus", *ZPE* 147, 1–8.
Gronewald, M./Daniel, R.W. (2005), "Lyrischer Text (Sappho-Papyrus)", *ZPE* 154, 7–12.

Gronewald, M./Daniel, R.W. (2007), *Kölner Papyri*, Band 11 (*Papyrologica Coloniensia* vol. VII/11), no. 429, pp. 1–11.
Gudeman, A. (1922), art. 'Kritische Zeichen', *RE*.
Haines, C.R. (1926), *Sappho. The Poems and Fragments*, London.
Hamm, E.-M. (1957), *Grammatik zu Sappho und Alkaios*, Berlin.
Hammerstaedt, J. (2011), "The Cologne Sappho: Its Discovery and Textual Constitution", *Classics @* Vol. 4: E.Greene/M. Skinner (eds) The Center for Hellenic Studies of Harvard University, online edition.
Hardie, A. (2005), "Sappho, the Muses and Life after Death", *ZPE* 154, 13–32.
Haslam, M.W. (1986), *The Oxyrhynchus Papyri*, Part LIII, London.
Heydemann, H. (1881), "Epigraphisches auf Griechischen Vasen", *RhM* 36, 465–472.
Hunt, A.S. (1922), *The Oxyrhynchus Papyri*, Part XV, London.
Huxley, G.L. (1987), "Onomakles and the Alopekonnesians", *JHS* 107, 187–188.
Immerwahr, H., Online Corpus of Attic Vase Inscriptions.
Immerwahr, H. (1964), "Book rolls on Attic vases", in: Ch. Henderson (ed.), *Classical, Mediaeval and Renaissance Studies in Honor of Berthold Louis Ullman*, 17–48, Rome.
Immerwahr, H. (1973), "More Book Rolls on Attic Vases," *Antike Kunst* 16, 143–147.
Johnston, S.I. (2002), "Myth, Festivals, and Poet: The Homeric Hymn to Hermes and Its Performative Context", *CPh* 97, 109–132.
Karabataki, K. (1997), *Σαπφικά επιθαλάμια: Απ. 104a, 104b, 105a, 105b V. Ποίηση εθιμική και προσωπική*. (Postgraduate essay), Florina.
Karabataki, K. (2010), *Σαπφώ και λαϊκή λογοτεχνία*. (Ph.D.), Thessaloniki.
Kokkorou-Alevra, G., et al. (2014), *Corpus Αρχαίων Λατομείων*, Athens.
Koldewey, R. (1890), *Die antiken Baureste der Insel Lesbos*, Berlin.
Kontis, I.D. (1977), *Ἡ Λέσβος καὶ ἡ Μικρασιατική της περιοχή*, Athens.
Kopidakis, M.Z. (2003), *Ἐν λόγῳ ἑλληνικῷ*, Athens.
Körte, A. (1939), "Literarische Texte mit Ausschluß der christlichen (Nr. 847–931)", *APF* 13, 78–132, esp. 90–91.
Kouremenos, Th./Parássoglou, G.M./Tsantsanoglou, K. (2006), *The Derveni Papyrus*, Florence.
Kourtzellis, I. (2012), *Παρελθόν και Εικόνα. Αναπαράσταση Αρχαιολογικών Χώρων και Μνημείων με Ψηφιακά Μέσα*, Mytilene.
Kretschmer, P. (1894), *Die griechischen Vaseninschriften ihrer Sprache nach untersucht*, Gütersloh.
Lanata, G. (1960), "L'ostracon fiorentino con versi di Saffo: note paleografiche ed esegetiche", *SIFC* 32, 64–90.
Lang, M. (1976), *Graffiti and Dipinti*, Princeton.
Lasserre, Fr. (1989), *Sappho. Une autre lecture*, Padova.
Leroi, A.M. (2014), *The Lagoon. How Aristotle Invented Science*, Bloomsbury Circus.
Liberman, G. (1999), *Alcée. Fragments*, 2 vol., Paris.
Lidov, J. (2011), "The Meter and Metrical Style of the New Poem", *Classics @* Vol. 4: E, Greene/M. Skinner, (eds) The Center for Hellenic Studies of Harvard University, online edition.
Livrea, E. (2007), "La vecchiaia su papiro: Saffo Simonide Callimaco Cercida" in: Bastianini, G./Casanova, A. (eds), *I papiri di Saffo e di Alceo*, Florence, 67–81.
Lobel, E. (1925), *Σαπφοῦς μέλη*, Oxford.
Lobel, E. (1927), *Ἀλκαίου μέλη*, Oxford.
Lobel, E. (1941), *The Oxyrhynchus Papyri*, Part XVIII, London.
Lobel, E. (1951), *The Oxyrhynchus Papyri*, Part XXI, London.

Lobel, E./Page, D.L. (1955), *Poetarum Lesbiorum Fragmenta*, Oxford.
Lundon, J. (2007), "Il nuovo testo lirico nel nuovo papiro di Saffo" in: Bastianini, G./Casanova, A. (eds), *I papiri di Saffo e di Alceo*, Florence, 149–166.
Luppe, W. (2004), "Überlegungen zur Gedicht-Anordnung im neuen Sappho-Papyrus", *ZPE* 149, 7–9.
McEvilley, Th. (1972), "Sappho, Fragment Two", *Phoenix* 26, 323–333.
McNamee, K. (1992), *Sigla and Select Marginalia in Greek Literary Papyri*, Bruxelles.
Magnani, M. (2005), "Note alla nuova Saffo", *Eikasmos* 16, 41–49.
Massa Positano, L. (^{2}1963), *Demetrii Triclinii in Aeschyli Persas scholia*, Naples.
Merkelbach, R. (1957), "Sappho und ihr Kreis", *Philologus* 101, 1–29.
Michaelides, M. (1909), *Λεσβιακαὶ Σελίδες*, Mytilene.
Morpurgo-Davies, A. (1964), "'Doric' features in the language of Hesiod", *Glotta* 42, 138–165.
Moutzouris, Io. (1962), " Μεσαιωνικά κάστρα της Λέσβου", *Δελτίον τῆς Ἑταιρείας Λεσβιακῶν Μελετῶν* 4, 50–68.
Nagy, G. (2016), "A Poetics of Sisterly Affect in the Brothers Song and in Other Songs of Sappho" in: Bierl/Lardinois, 449–492.
Neri, C. (2014), "Una festa auspicata? (Sapph. fr. 17 V. e P. GC. inv. 105 fr. 2 c. II rr. 9–28)", *Eikasmos* 25, 11–23.
Neri, C. (2017), "Afrodite violenta (Sapph. fr. 26 = 'Kypris Poem')", *Eikasmos* 28, 9–21.
Newton, C.T. (1865), *Travels & Discoveries in the Levant*, London.
Norsa, Medea (1937), "Dai papyri della Società Italiana: Versi di Saffo in un ostrakon del sec. ii a.C.", *Annali della Reale Scuola normale superiore di Pisa* II 6, 8–15 (= *PSI* XIII 1300, printed in 1953).
Norsa, M. (1939), *La scrittura letteraria greca dal sec. IV° a.C. all' VIII° d.C.*, Firenze.
Obbink, D. (2014), "Two New Poems by Sappho", *ZPE* 189, 32–49.
Obbink, D. (2015), "Provenance, Authenticity, and Text of the New Sappho Papyri", www.papyrology.ox.ac.uk/Fragments/SCS. Sappho.Obbink.paper.pdf.
Obbink, D. (2016), "The Newest Sappho: Text, Apparatus Criticus", in: Bierl/Lardinois, 13–33.
Page, D.L. (1962), *Poetae Melici Graeci*, Oxford.
Page, D.L. (1955), *Sappho and Alcaeus*, Oxford.
Papadopoulos, G.A. (2015), *Λέσβος-Χίος-Ψαρά. Οι σεισμοί και τα τσουνάμι από την Αρχαιότητα μέχρι σήμερα*, Athens.
Paraskevaidis, M. (1963), art. Pyrrha, *RE*, vol. 47, Nachtrag 1403–1420.
Parker, H.N. (1993), "Sappho Schoolmistress", *TAPhA* 123, 309–351.
Pfeiffer, R. (1937), "Vier Sappho-Strophen auf einem ptolemäischen Ostrakon", *Philologus* 92, 117–118.
Picard, Ch. (1962), "Où fut à Lesbos au VIIe siècle l'asyle temporaire du poète Alcée?", *Rev. arch.*, 2, 43–69.
Porro, Antonietta (1989), "Un commentario papiraceo ad Alceo e il fr. 130B Voigt", *Aev. ant.* 2, 215–222.
Porro, A. (1992), "A proposito di Alc. fr. 130 B Voigt", *QUCC* n.s. 41, 23–27.
Puglia, E. (2008a), "Appunti sul nuovo testo lirico di Colonia", *ZPE* 164, 11–18.
Puglia, E. (2008b), "P.Oxy. 2294 e la tradizione delle odi di Saffo", *ZPE* 166, 1–8.
Quinn, J. (1961), "Cape Phokas, Lesbos - Site of an Archaic Sanctuary for Zeus, Hera, and Dionysus?", *AJA* 65, 391–393.
Rawles, R. (2006), "Musical notes on the new anonymous lyric poem from Köln", *ZPE* 157, 8–13.
Richardson, N. (2010), *Three Homeric Hymns: to Apollo, Hermes, and Aphrodite*, Cambridge.

Risch, E. (1962), "Der göttliche Schlaf bei Sappho: Bemerkungen zum Ostrakon der Medea Norsa", *Mus. Helv.* 19, 197–201.
Robert, L. (1925), "Lesbiaca", *RÉG* 38, 423–426.
Robert, L. (1960), "Inscriptions de Lesbos", *RÉA* 62, 285–315.
Robert, L. (1969), *Opera Minora Selecta*, Amsterdam.
Saake, H. (1971), *Zur Kunst Sapphos*, Munich, Paderborn, Vienna.
Schadewaldt, W. (1950), *Sappho. Welt und Dichtung. Dasein in der Liebe*, Potsdam.
Schefold, K. (1943), *Die Bildnisse der antiken Dichter, Redner, und Denker*, Basel.
Shields, E.L. (1917/18), "Lesbos in the Trojan War", *CJ* 13, 670–681.
Schubart, W. (1938), "Bemerkungen zu Sappho", *Hermes* 73, 297–306.
Schwyzer, E. (1939–1968), *Griechische Grammatik*, 3 vol., München.
Seider, R. (1967–1990), *Paläographie der griechischen Papyri*, 3 vol. Stuttgart.
Setti, A. (1943), *SIFC* 19, 125–142.
Siegmann, E. (1941), "Anmerkungen zum Sappho-Ostrakon", *Hermes* 76, 417–422.
Sitzler, J. (1927), review of E. Lobel's Σαπφοῦς Μέλη, *PhW* 47 993.
Slings, S.R. (1979), "ΑΠΑΠΠΕΝΑ ΓΕΝΗΩ. Some Problems in Lesbian Grammar", *Mnemosyne* 32, 243–267.
Smyth, H.W. (^{2}1956), *Greek Grammar*, Cambridge, Ma.
Snell, B. (1944), "Miszellen: Zu den Fragmenten der griechischen Lyriker", *Philologus* 96, 281–292.
Snyder, Jane McIntosh (1997), "Sappho in Attic vase painting", in: *Naked Truths. Women, sexuality, and gender in classical art and archaeology*, A.O. Koloski-Ostrow/C.L. Lyons (eds) London/New York, 108–119.
Steinrück, M. (2000), "Neues zu Sappho", *ZPE* 131, 10–12.
Theiler, W./Von der Mühll, P. (1946), "Das Sapphogedicht auf der Scherbe", *Mus.Helv.* 3, 22–25.
Thesleff, H. (1965), *The Pythagorean texts of the Hellenistic period*, Åbo.
Threatte, L. (1980, 1996), *The Grammar of Attic Inscriptions*, 2 vol., Berlin/New York.
Tortorelli, W. (2004), "A Proposed Colometry of Ibycus 286", *CPh* 99, 370–376.
Treu, M. (^{1}1952), *Alkaios*, Munich.
Treu, M. (^{1}1954), *Sappho*, Munich.
Treu, M. (1968), art. Sappho, *RE*, Supplementband XI.
Tsantsanoglou, K. (2007), "Callimachus *Aetia* fr. 1.7–17, Once Again", *ZPE* 163, 27–36.
Tsantsanoglou, K. (2008), "The Banquet of the Gods and the Picnic of the Girls: Observations on Sappho fr. 2 V. (with an Appendix on Ibycus PMGF 286)", *Eikasmos* 19, 45–69.
Tsantsanoglou, K. (2009a), "Sappho, Tithonus Poem: Two Cruces (Lines 7 and 10)", *ZPE* 168, 1–2.
Tsantsanoglou, K. (2009b), "Sappho on her Funeral Day: P.Colon. 21351.1–8", *ZPE* 170, 1–7.
Tsantsanoglou, K. (2009c), "The λεπτότης of Aratus", *Trends in Classics* 1, 55–89.
Tsantsanoglou, K. (2011), "Sappho 27 V., Alcaeus 308 Lib., and the Homeric *Hymn* to Hermes", *Trends in Classics* 3, 245–253.
Tsantsanoglou, K. (2017), "Sappho Illustrated. The Epithanatians", *ZPE* 202, 1–18.
Tsantsanoglou, K. (2017a), "Sappho 1.18–19 V.", *ZPE* 201, 15–16.
Tsantsanoglou, K./Tselikas, S. (2017), "P. Sapph. Obbink: the *Kypris Poem*", *Eikasmos* 28, 23–36.
Tsantsanoglou, K. (2018), "Who was Onymacles the Athenian? (Alcaeus 130b V. = 130.16–39 LP)", *Trends in Classics* 10, 275–284.
Tsantsanoglou, K. (2019), "The Danaans in Lesbos (Sappho fr. 17 V.)", *Eikasmos* 30, 1–15.
Turner, E.G. (^{2}1987), *Greek Manuscripts of the Ancient World*, London.
Turyn, Al. (1942), "The Sapphic Ostrakon", *TAPhA* 73, 308–318.

Ursinus (Orsini), F. (1568), *Carmina novem illustrium feminarum ... et Lyricorum*. Antwerp.
Vogliano, A. (1937), *Papiri della R. Università di Milano*, vol. I, Milan.
Voigt, E.-M. (1971), *Sappho et Alcaeus. Fragmenta*, Amsterdam.
Wackernagel, J. (1916), *Sprachliche Untersuchungen zu Homer*, Göttingen.
Welcker, G. (1828), review of C.F. Neue's 1827 Sappho edition, *Jahrbücher für Philologie und Pädagogik* 6, 389.
West, M.L. (1966), *Hesiod* Theogony, Oxford.
West, M.L. (1966), "Conjectures on 46 Greek Poets", *Philologus* 110, 147–168.
West, M.L. (1970), "Burning Sappho", *Maia* 22, 307–330.
West, M.L. (1973), *Textual Criticism and Editorial Technique*, Stuttgart.
West, M.L. (1974), *Studies in Greek Elegy and Iambus*, Berlin/New York.
West, M.L. (1982), *Greek Metre*, Oxford.
West, M.L. (1992), *Ancient Greek Music*, Oxford.
West, M.L. (2002), "The view from Lesbos", in: M. Reichel/A. Rengakos (eds.), *Epea pteroenta: Beiträge zur Homerforschung. Festschrift für Wolfgang Kullmann zum 75. Geburtstag*, Stuttgart, 207–219.
West, M.L. (2003), *Homeric Hymns, Homeric Apocrypha, Lives of Homer*, Cambridge, Ma.
West, M.L. (2005), "The New Sappho", *ZPE* 151, 1–9.
West, M.L. (2014), "Nine Poems of Sappho", *ZPE* 191, 1–12.
Wilamowitz, U. v. (1884), *Homerische Untersuchungen*, Berlin.
Wilamowitz, U. v. (1913), *Sappho und Simonides*, Berlin.
Yatromanolakis, D. (1999), "Alexandrian Sappho revisited", *HSCP* 99, 179–195.
Yatromanolakis, D. (2001), "Visualizing Poetry: An Early Representation of Sappho", *Classical Philology* 96, 159–168.
Yatromanolakis, D. (2007), *Sappho in the Making. The Early Reception*, Washington, D.C.
Yatromanolakis, D. (2008), "P. Colon. inv. 21351+21376 fr. 1: Music, Cultural Politics, and Hellenistic Anthologies", *Ελληνικά* 58, 237–255.

www.ingramcontent.com/pod-product-compliance
Lightning Source LLC
Chambersburg PA
CBHW061938220426
43662CB00012B/1955